Basic Economics

Thirteenth Edition

Frank V. Mastrianna

Dean Emeritus, Slippery Rock University

Thomas J. Hailstones

THOMSON

SOUTH-WESTERN

Australia · Canada · Mexico · Singapore · Spain · United Kingdom · United States

THOMSON

SOUTH-WESTERN

Basic Economics, 13e
Frank V. Mastrianna & Thomas J. Hailstones

Vice President/Editorial Director:
Jack W. Calhoun

Vice President/Editor-in-Chief:
Michael P. Roche

Publisher of Economics:
Michael B. Mercier

Acquisitions Editor:
Michael Worls

Developmental Editor:
Sarah Curtis

Sr. Production Editor:
Elizabeth A. Shipp

Executive Marketing Manager:
Lisa L. Lysne

Media Developmental Editor:
Peggy Buskey

Media Production Editor:
Pam Wallace

Manufacturing Coordinator:
Sandee Milewski

Production House:
Pre-Press Company, Inc.

Design Project Manager:
Rik Moore

Internal and Cover Designer:
Lisa Albonetti

Cover Illustration:
Wonderfile Corporation

Printer:
Phoenix Color/Book Technology Park

Preface

Basic Economics, 13th edition, is designed for a one-term survey course in economics and is intended primarily for those students in liberal arts, business, and pre-professional programs who will take only one course in economics. The text has also been used successfully for teaching economics in management development and teacher education programs.

Approach of this Text

Throughout the many editions of *Basic Economics*, the author has responded to the many suggestions made by professors, students, and reviewers of the text. Most authors have a tendency to expand the amount of information contained in each chapter, as well as to add entirely new chapters with each successive edition. But this approach can result in a proliferation of text and chapters that cannot be adequately covered in the limited time frame of one semester.

Fortunately, reviewers continue to provide direction by indicating the appropriate size of a one-semester book and by identifying material that needs to be expanded, shortened, or even eliminated. Based on their feedback, no new chapters have been added in this edition. However, the order of several chapters has been altered to provide a more consistent flow of information in the introductory macroeconomics section.

Each chapter has been reviewed carefully and updated with information currently available at the time of publication. Throughout the text, careful attention has been paid to making the subject matter as readable as possible for an introductory class, and key concepts and terms are sharply defined to enhance their understanding. Learning objectives are included to fit the content and should be valuable in focusing student attention on important areas of emphasis. Figures, tables, and statistics have been updated and vocabulary simplified to a minimal use of economic jargon. International coverage has been updated throughout the text in the form of examples and insights where relevant.

Summaries of each chapter are included, as in the past. However, in this edition summaries are presented in bullet form and are now consistent in form with summaries included in the Student Study Guide. This edition also includes Internet addresses that can assist students seeking more in-depth information on specific issues. For the first time, an Economic Applications section is included at the end of the chapter. This section directs students to current economic news, debates, and data that can provide greater insights into the subject matter.

Organization

The first part of the book presents students with a focused introduction to the subject matter of economics. Chapters 1 and 2 include important economic concepts and definitions to give the student a clearer understanding of the nature and scope of economics. The problem of scarcity and why scarcity forces individuals and societies to make choices is presented in Chapter 2. The production possibilities curve, specialization and exchange, and comparative advantage are presented in support of the scarcity concept. Chapter 3, "The U.S. Economic System," gives an overview of the workings of the U.S. economy and the roles of government, business, and the consumer. Material in this chapter has been updated, and the material dealing with regulation, deregulation, and privatization has been expanded. Chapters 4 through 7 provide an introduction to microeconomic principles. Because most students using this book do not continue their formalized study of economics beyond this course, sophisticated analytical techniques, mathematical exercises, and complex theoretical treatments are not included in these chapters. Only those tools deemed useful to the understanding of policy issues are presented. After basic economic concepts such as demand, supply, elasticity, cost, production, and profit are developed, the student is presented with the opportunity to apply these tools under conditions of both perfect and imperfect competition. The relationship between production and cost is developed in Chapter 5. "Perfect Competition" is presented in Chapter 6, while new examples of recent federal antitrust action and a complete section on competition among consumers are included in Chapter 7, "Imperfect Competition."

"The Circular-Flow Model" is now the subject of Chapter 8 instead of being positioned as Chapter 4 as in previous editions. The chapter describes the circular flow of income in a modern economy. Extensive graphic presentations are included to provide a framework for understanding economic activity. In response to reviewers, several circular flow models have been dropped from the text to provide greater readability. In their place, applied sections describing the impact of September 11, current fiscal policy, and the Asian economic crisis have been included. Chapter 9, "Measuring Output and Income in the United States," develops national income accounting methods using Bureau of Economic Analysis statistics. This chapter has also been repositioned to provide linkage with the circular flow of income treatment presented in Chapter 8.

Chapter 10, "Money in the U.S. Economy," and Chapter 11, "The Federal Reserve and the Money Supply," have been updated and expanded. Chapter 10 includes information on the deregulation of the financial services industry and on the use of electronic banking in the United States. New sections on industry concentration and federal deposit insurance have been added. Chapter 12, "Macroeconomic Models and Analysis" compares and contrasts the classical theory of macroeconomic analysis with Keynesian economics and develops the modern model of aggregate demand and aggregate supply. The chapter concludes with a comparison of the Monetarist and New Classical schools of thought. Chapter 13, "Employment," explains the importance of job creation in the economy and analyzes employment and unemployment in the nation's labor force. An analysis of the employment effects of the minimum wage is also included. As in previous editions, the chapter presents a section dealing with future employment opportunities provided by the Bureau of Labor Statistics.

Chapter 14, "Income Distribution," is a relatively new chapter and has been included in the text in response to the urging of reviewers. The chapter describes the distribution of income in the United States, presents the Lorenz curve and Gini coefficient as measures of income inequality, analyzes the causes of income inequality, and examines the extent and nature of poverty and welfare. Welfare-to-work programs are discussed in terms of their success and future challenges.

Chapter 15, "Business Cycles," remains essentially the same as in the previous edition, with the addition of information on the completion of the recent business cycle. Chapter 16, "Macroeconomic Policies," explains how monetary and fiscal tools can be used to change the equilibrium level of output in the economy, and historical sections provide students with an evolutionary framework of various public policy approaches. Macroeconomic policies available during wartime are included for the first time. Chapter 17, "Taxation, Budgetary Policy, and the National Debt," covers major theories of taxation, the use of the federal budget as a countercyclical device, and problems resulting from the national debt.

As in previous editions, international trade and finance chapters comprise the final section of the book. Chapter 18, "International Trade and Aid," includes updated material on U.S. trade, the World Trade Organization, the North American Free Trade Agreement, and the continued growth of the European Union. Chapter 19, "The Balance of International Payments," explains the balance of payments account, exchange rate determination, the workings of the International Monetary Fund, and the changing global environment.

Pedagogical Features

The 13th edition of *Basic Economics* has been thoroughly revised to improve readability and student understanding. Numerous pedagogical features are included for this purpose.

- Each chapter begins with learning objectives that identify important topics covered within the chapter.

- Key terms are boldfaced to indicate their importance.

- Key terms and their definitions appear in the margins as well as in the glossary at the end of the book.
- Graphs have been simplified to improve clarity.
- Each chapter includes at least one Internet address whose site contains additional information on specific chapter topics.
- A guide to economic applications, found at each chapter's end, is new to this edition.
- Chapters conclude with a summary, a list of new terms, and review questions suitable for a classroom discussion.

Supplements

STUDY GUIDE

The *Study Guide* that accompanies the 13th edition of *Basic Economics* helps students learn and review concepts developed in the text and improve performance on examinations. Each chapter begins with a summary, followed by review questions, problems, and a reading with discussion questions. The review questions include matching (covering all key terms and definitions), multiple-choice, and true-false questions. The problems require numerical or graphical solutions where appropriate. The questions that follow the reading require written answers that help students gain new insights into material covered in the text chapter. Every question in the *Study Guide* is answered so that students can check the accuracy of their answers.

TEXT WEB SITE

The text Web site at http://mastrianna.swlearning.com provides teaching resources, learning resources, Internet application links, an interactive Ask-the-Author section, links to relevant economics sites, and many more features. Online Quizzes feature multiple-choice and true-false questions and answers with explanations, so that students can learn quickly whether or not their answers are correct.

ECONOMIC APPLICATIONS

This site includes South-Western's dynamic Web features: EconNews, EconDebate, and EconData Online. Organized by pertinent economic topics and searchable by topic or feature, these features are easy to integrate into the classroom. EconNews, EconDebate, and EconData all deepen students' understanding of theoretical concepts through hands-on exploration and analysis for the latest economic news stories, policy debates, and data. These features are updated on a regular basis. The Economic Applications Web site is complimentary to every new book buyer via an access card that is packaged with the books. Used book buyers can purchase access to the site at http://econapps.swlearning.com.

POWERPOINT™ PRESENTATION SLIDES

PowerPoint™ slides are available on the text Web site and may be downloaded for use by instructors as a lecture aid or by students as a study aid.

INSTRUCTOR'S MANUAL AND TEST BANK

The *Instructor's Manual and Test Bank* contains the purpose, learning objectives, new terms and definitions, a chapter outline and lecture notes, answers to the text end-of-chapter discussion questions, and suggested readings for each text chapter. It includes transparency masters of figures from the text and a test bank of more than 1,800 true-false, multiple-choice, and discussion questions arranged by text chapter. The *Instructor's Manual and Test Bank* is available with a password on the text's Web site.

TESTING SOFTWARE

A microcomputer version of the test bank, *ExamView*®, is available to adopters of *Basic Economics*. This program is an easy-to-use test creation software compatible with Microsoft Windows. Instructors can add or edit questions, instructions, and answers, and select questions by previewing them on the screen, choosing them randomly, or choosing them by number. Instructors can also create and administer quizzes online, whether over the Internet, a local area network (LAN), or a wide area network (WAN).

Acknowledgments

A revision of any textbook requires the combined efforts of many individuals, and the 13th edition of *Basic Economics* is no exception. I am grateful to all those who have given their time and talent to the development of this book, not only for this edition, but for the many that preceded it.

Numerous comments were received from professors and students who used earlier editions of *Basic Economics*. I thank not only those who assisted with the first 12 editions but also those who offered suggestions for improvement of the 13th: Ronald A. Siltzer, Spartanburg Technical College; Arthur M. Hendrick, Madison Area Technical College; Vicki D. Rostedt, University of Akron; Trisha L. Bezmen, Old Dominion University; Dennis Debrecht, Carroll College; Jon A. Hooks, Albion College; Kathy Parkison, Indiana University-Kokomo.

A great deal of credit is due the many people at South-Western/Thomson Learning who helped make this book a reality, particularly Sarah Curtis, who served as Developmental Editor of this edition. Sarah diligently assisted the author with her direction and guidance, while ensuring the delivery of the text in accordance with publication schedules. Her patience, energy, and sunny disposition were invaluable from beginning to end. Special thanks are owed to Libby Shipp, who, as Production Editor, was instrumental in publishing the book. A word of appreciation also goes out to Gordon Laws of Pre-Press Company, Inc. for his work in making the manuscript as error free as possible.

As in previous editions, a great deal of credit is owed to Barbara Porter, administrative assistant to the dean of the College of Business, Information, and Social Sciences at Slippery Rock University. In addition to undertaking the tasks of preparing and typing revisions to the text, study guide, instructor's manual, and test bank, Barbara painstakingly critiqued material for content accuracy as well as for consistency of thought. Because of her many excellent contributions to this book over its many editions, Barbara has become an integral partner in this publication endeavor.

Frank V. Mastrianna

Brief Contents

Contents

1

The Nature and Scope of Economics

After studying Chapter 1, you should be able to:

1. Define the term *economics* and explain its scope.
2. Explain the relationship of economics to other sciences.
3. Distinguish between economic theory and economic policy.
4. Explain the concept of utility.
5. Identify the four productive resources and name the payment each receives for its contribution.
6. Identify the characteristics of an economic good or service.
7. Distinguish between microeconomics and macroeconomics.

Every day the important role that economics plays in our lives becomes more apparent. Economics applies directly to how we earn our incomes and how we spend our money. Our decisions about what profession to enter, where to work, and where to live are based in large part on economic considerations. If we own a business, economic factors dictate whether we earn a profit and continue to operate or fail and go into bankruptcy. We are also affected indirectly by economics. Economic policies help determine the levels of output and employment in the United States, the amount of taxes we pay, the quantity of aid we give to developing nations, and the resources we devote to preserving our natural environment. Economic measures influence the prices we pay, the purchasing power of our dollars, the availability of goods and services, and our overall standard of living.

Economics Defined

Economics means different things to different people. To some it means thriftiness, budgeting for household purchases, or saving for an automobile. To others it means analyzing a multimillion-dollar income statement. To the president of the United

Economics
A social science that studies how people and institutions within a society make choices and how these choices determine the use of society's scarce resources.

States it may mean studying economic conditions, developing a federal budget, and proposing various economic measures to maximize total production, employment, and income for the nation. The widespread presence of economics offers a challenge in deciding where to begin the study of economics. A logical place to begin is with a definition because it serves as a point of departure for explaining, examining, and analyzing the various aspects of the science of economics. **Economics** studies how people and institutions within a society make choices and how these choices determine the use of society's scarce resources. Choices matter because resources are limited, whereas wants are unlimited.

Economics in Relation to Other Sciences

Science
An organized body of knowledge coordinated, arranged, and systematized according to general laws or principles.

A **science** is an organized body of knowledge that is coordinated, arranged, and systematized according to general laws or principles. Frequently, when we think of science, we think of natural sciences, such as physics, chemistry, and biology. However, there are also behavioral sciences, including philosophy, sociology, psychology, politics, and economics. More specifically, economics is classified as a *social science*—a study of the behavior and interactions of human beings, individually and in groups.

As a science, economics is related to other sciences. Some of its laws, such as the law of diminishing returns, are based on physical phenomena; hence, economics is related to physics. Because it operates within a nation, economics is related to the political structure of that nation and therefore to political science. Income determines standard of living, and a low standard leads to social problems. Thus, economics is related to sociology.

Because it deals with human behavior, economics shares this sphere of interest with psychology. For example, the reasons why individuals spend or save are psychological as well as economic. Economics is also related to philosophy. Economic acts are human acts, which constitute a proper subject for ethics, a branch of philosophy.

Economics, especially at an advanced level, is closely related to mathematics. Modern economic theory and analysis rely on statistics, econometrics, calculus, linear programming, and other mathematical tools, as well as on computer applications. In its relationships with various sciences, economics depends on logic, the science of correct thinking. The study of any subject must follow the rules of logic, whether reasoning from a particular instance to a general principle or from a general principle to a particular application.

Natural scientists often test a certain stimulus under a given set of conditions to see what the reaction will be. These experiments will be repeated to test the validity of a theory. In economics and other social sciences, where we deal with humans, the results may never match exactly because of differences in personality, environment, intelligence, and other factors. Unfortunately, the economist also cannot keep all other economic conditions constant. In fact, the economist has little, if any, control over them. And once the effects of a stimulus have been measured, the constants cannot be reconstructed exactly as they were before the stimulus was applied in order to test an alternative change.

Finally, we need to distinguish between economic theory and economic policy. **Economic theory** develops rules and principles of economics and is a guide for action under a given set of circumstances. **Economic policy** refers to what is actually done under a given set of circumstances. It would be fine if economic policy always followed economic theory. But economic problems or issues often have political, military, and/or social aspects. As a result, economic policy is commonly modified by political, military, and social policy. For example, economic theory may dictate that we should maintain or increase taxes, but during an election year economic policy may instead yield to political policy in the form of a tax cut to woo voters. In another example, reducing a federal budget deficit may require cutting government spending in such a way that social programs for the poor receive less funding.

ECONOMICS AND PRODUCTION

In economics we define **production** as the creation or addition of utility. **Utility** is the economist's term for usefulness—the ability of a good or service to satisfy a want. We produce whenever we make a product or render a service that is useful. Television sets, video games, and computers are examples of goods that are produced to satisfy our wants, whereas education, banking, and police protection are types of services that are useful. The sum of all the goods and services produced by an economy over a given time period is known as its **total product.**

ECONOMICS AND DISTRIBUTION

At first glance you may think that distribution refers to the physical distribution of goods and services from the producer to the consumer—that is, to marketing distribution. But we use **distribution** here to refer to the allocation of the total product among the productive resources. Monetarily, it refers to the distribution of money incomes among the owners of the productive resources.

Productive Resources

Before a person or business can engage in the production of goods or services, resources are necessary. **Productive resources** are all the natural, synthetic, and human inputs that are used in creating goods and services. Productive resources are conventionally divided into four broad categories: labor, land, capital, and enterprise.

Labor. Labor refers to the time and effort expended by human beings involved in the production process. Labor includes the physical and mental efforts of individuals and groups in producing services as well as in producing goods.

Economic Theory
Develops rules and principles of economics and is a guide for action under a given set of circumstances.

Economic Policy
What is actually done under a given set of circumstances.

Production
The creation or addition of utility.

Utility
The ability of a good or service to satisfy a want.

Total Product
The sum of all the goods and services produced by an economy over a given period of time.

Distribution
The allocation of the total product among the productive resources.

Productive Resources
Inputs or resources necessary before a person or business can engage in the production of goods or services; specifically, labor, land, capital, and enterprise.

Labor
The time and effort expended by human beings involved in the production process.

Land
All the resources of the land, sea, and air.

Land. As used in economics, **land** refers to much more than real estate. It includes all the resources of the land, sea, and air. Such natural resources as coal, oil, lumber, minerals, water, air, and rain qualify as land in this sense.

Capital
Goods used to produce other goods and services.

Capital. Goods produced may be consumed directly or used in production. **Capital** refers to goods used to produce other goods and services. For example, blast furnaces, CAT scanners, buildings, bulldozers, computers, trucks, and airplanes are considered capital. Although the term *capital* is often used as a synonym for money, economists reserve the term for real tangible assets used to produce other goods and services. *Investment* is the act of adding to the supply of capital—such as the creation of a new warehouse and distribution center.

Enterprise
The act of organizing and assuming the risk of a business venture.

Entrepreneur
A person who organizes and assumes the risk of a business venture.

Enterprise. **Enterprise** is the act of organizing and assuming the risks of a business venture. An **entrepreneur** is a person who fulfills this role. The entrepreneur, or enterpriser, combines the other productive resources—land, labor, and capital—to produce the final product. Today, renewed emphasis is being placed on the importance of the entrepreneur. Many colleges and universities offer special courses and conduct workshops on the subject. Many individuals have become entrepreneurs. Both in the United States and abroad—particularly in developing countries—there is a growing need for entrepreneurs who can put all the resources together successfully to promote business and economic development.

The Problem of Distribution

When goods or services are produced, how should the total product or its value be allocated among the resources used in its production? In a barter economy, individuals produce for their own needs. If there is any excess, they may trade it with their neighbors. Under a barter system, individuals generally use their own labor (or that of their family), their own land, their own tools, and their own enterprise to produce the goods they need. No question can arise about the ownership of the goods produced or about the share to which the individual is entitled.

In a complex market economy, however, the problem is more involved. An individual who wants to produce must still use the productive resources. But in combining resources, the entrepreneur may use the labor of one person, the land of another, and the capital of a third to produce a good or service that has a certain value. Now the big question arises: What share or payment should each resource receive for its contribution to the total product? In a market economy, payment for use of the productive resources—labor, land, capital, and enterprise—is made in the form of wages, rent, interest, and profits, respectively (see Figure 1–1). This pattern is called the *functional distribution of income*.

The problem of distribution or allocation is very much with us today. A labor union, for example, seeks a larger share of the total product when it requests a wage increase for its workers. Management seeks a larger profit (and thus a greater share of the total product) when it increases prices or reduces costs. Many

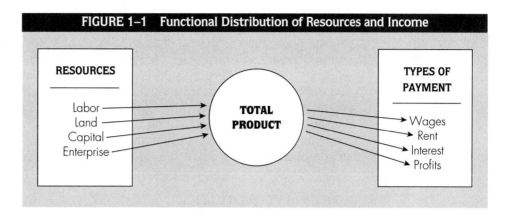

FIGURE 1–1   Functional Distribution of Resources and Income

RESOURCES — Labor, Land, Capital, Enterprise → TOTAL PRODUCT → TYPES OF PAYMENT — Wages, Rent, Interest, Profits

labor–management disputes arise from disagreements over this basic problem of allocation. Similarly, owners of capital may demand a higher rate of interest for the use of their assets and landholders may raise the rent. Here, too, the intention is to increase that resource's share of the total product. Clearly, it is impossible for every resource to increase its relative share of the total product. But each can have a larger absolute return by contributing to an increase in the size of the total product. Thus, increases in productivity from various sources provide a way to improve the return to all resources.

The U.S. Department of Commerce collects data that reveal how much of total output is allocated to each productive resource. Approximately 72 percent of the national income goes for wages, salaries, and benefits; about 2 percent for rental income; about 7 percent for interest; 9 percent for noncorporate business income; and the remaining 10 percent for corporate profit. However, this is not necessarily what the allocation should be. To establish any guidelines for a particular allocation, we would have to leave the realm of positive economics and delve into normative economics.

Positive economics is the scientific study of "what is" among economic relationships and concerns matters that are the result of investigations that are verifiable. For example, the relationship between higher wage rates and the supply of labor offered in the marketplace can be analyzed and verified. Positive economics is an area in which economists generally agree, but positive economics does not tell us what policies to pursue. Whenever economists go beyond scientific investigation to make value judgments as to "what ought to be" in economic matters, this is referred to as **normative economics.** Thus, to say that a greater share of national income should be received in the form of wages and salaries and less should be received in the form of corporate profit is a normative statement and is subject to widespread disagreement. Deciding on what ought to be is not just an economic function but a political one as well.

NET*Link*

For a virtual field trip to the Department of Commerce, set your browser to URL:

http://www.commerce.gov/

Positive Economics
The area of economics dealing with what is.

Normative Economics
The area of economics dealing with what ought to be.

ECONOMICS AND CONSUMPTION

Consumption
The use of a good or service.

Consumption refers to the use of a good or service. After getting up this morning, you may have consumed cereal or eggs for breakfast. If you drove to school or work, your car consumed gasoline. You do not have to absorb a good completely in order to consume it. Instead, you may consume it little by little, day by day, as you do with your car's tires, your home, or the soles of your shoes. Consumption may be the most important function in economics because it is the ultimate end of economic activity. Without consumption there would be little need for production and distribution.

GOODS AND SERVICES

Economic Good
An object or service that has utility, is scarce, and is transferable.

The last part of the definition of economics deals with economic goods and services that satisfy wants. **Economic goods** are goods and services that are useful, scarce, and transferable. Economic services are similar to material goods except they are intangible. To be an economic good, a good or service must have utility and satisfy a want. In other words, we consume economic goods to increase our enjoyment or satisfaction. But it is not the nature of the good or service that makes it useful; rather, it is the circumstances involved. Trash, for example, is not an economic good for a household, but it may become an economic good in other sectors of the economy as recycled materials.

Scarcity is another essential characteristic of an economic good. Scarcity means that there is not a sufficient amount available to meet everyone's wants, and as a result a price has to be paid to obtain the good or service. If a useful good or service exists in such abundance that anyone can readily obtain it without much effort, it is not scarce and does not have a monetary value. Consequently, it is not an economic good. Under normal circumstances you would not be willing to pay a price for air, but clean air in many places has become an economic good, for a price must be paid for its use. Generally, the greater the scarcity of an economic good, the greater its value or price.

If a good is useful and scarce but not transferable, it loses its value as an economic good. For example, the gold in seawater is not an economic good because the cost of extracting it is prohibitive. Certain minerals and metals known to be present in Antarctica are not economic goods at this time because there is as yet no way of extracting and transferring them to a place where they can be of use. Transferability and utility are what give an economic good its value.

Free Good
A good that lacks the element of scarcity and therefore has no price.

Public Good
An economic good to the supplier but a free good to the user.

There are three principal types of goods: economic goods, free goods, and public goods. We have already seen that an object that is useful, scarce, and transferable is classified as an economic good. A **free good** lacks the element of scarcity and therefore has no price. In this category we find air, sunshine, and, in some cases, water. A **public good** is an economic good to the supplier but a free good to the user. Public parks, libraries, and the interstate highway system are often classified as public goods. However, because these goods are provided by tax money (which the user ultimately pays), they are actually economic goods. This same classification can also be applied to services.

Economic goods are also classified according to their use. **Consumer goods** are goods directly used by individuals, households, and businesses. Items such as books, paper, electric energy, food, and clothing fit into this category. **Capital goods,** or producer goods, are economic goods used to produce other capital goods or consumer goods. Buildings, machinery, and equipment are durable capital goods. Inventories of raw materials used in the manufacturing process are non-durable capital goods.

WEALTH AND INCOME

Wealth may be defined as things of value owned at a particular time. Thus, it consists of a multitude of consumer and capital goods. The total wealth of the United States is estimated at $30 trillion. Some experts measure wealth by totaling only the physical assets of the individuals and firms in the economy. Others add to this total the property and assets of federal, state, and municipal governments. In counting resources, certain authorities want to include only those that have been extracted and are ready for use. Others want to include all resources, whether extracted or still in their original state.

What about the value of **human capital,** defined as the stock of labor talents and skills used to increase productivity? It would seem logical to include these forms of human capital in wealth because they are used to produce other goods and services. Many economists would like to see human capital included in the valuation of national wealth.

Should stocks, bonds, and mortgages be included in the count of wealth? The answer is no. Including them along with the physical assets they represent would result in double counting. Many people think of money as wealth, but this is incorrect. Money merely represents wealth or a command over goods and services. The more money an individual has, the greater the individual's command over goods and services. For this reason, although money is not wealth, wealth can be measured in terms of money.

People often confuse and misunderstand the concepts of wealth and income. Wealth is a stock concept; it is the total value of economic goods at any given time. Income is a flow concept; it is the value of total product—the goods and services produced over a period of time (usually a year).

Total income is derived from the production of goods and services because the owners of the resources are paid in dollars for their contribution to production. Thus, the incomes received are equivalent to the total value of goods and services produced. If we were to take a picture of the economy on the first day of a certain year, we might observe that the total wealth amounted to $30 trillion. If we then counted the value of the goods and services produced during that year, we might calculate a total of over $11 trillion. This would be the total income. Does this mean that the total wealth at the end of the year has increased by the total amount

---

Consumer Goods
Economic goods that are directly utilized by the consuming public.

Capital Goods
Economic goods used to produce other capital goods or consumer goods.

Human Capital
The stock of labor talents and skills used to increase productivity.

Total Income
The total value of the goods and services produced over a period of time (usually a year).

of production during that year? The answer is no because not all income or production is added to wealth. In fact, most of the income is consumed as it is produced. Only the portion that is not consumed is added to wealth.

There is frequently a correlation between wealth and income. Usually, the greater a nation's wealth, the higher its total income will be because the more resources at its disposal, the greater its productive capacity becomes. In turn, the greater a nation's total product or income, the higher its standard of living. Consequently, a nation should not consume everything it produces but should channel a portion of its output into capital and technological development. This will increase production and improve the standard of living for the future.

The definition of economics is evidently very broad. It encompasses all our business activity and much of our social activity. Furthermore, such special fields as production, finance, marketing, transportation, and labor are components of the study of economics. Economics arises in connection with the individual, the family, the firm, the industry, and the nation as a whole. It pervades our entire society and affects our daily lives.

Microeconomics and Macroeconomics

Microeconomics
Deals with the economic problems of the individual, the firm, and the industry.

Macroeconomics
Deals with the aggregates of economics, including total production, total employment, and general price level.

The study of economics can be divided into two broad areas: microeconomics and macroeconomics. **Microeconomics** deals with the economic problems of the individual, the firm, and the industry. It inquires into what motivates the individual to spend or to save. It applies the principle of supply and demand, investigates how the price for a product is determined, studies how individuals decide where to work, and assesses similar factors. **Macroeconomics** deals with the aggregates of economics, including total production, total employment, and general price level. It analyzes the problems of the economy as a whole rather than those of the individual, the firm, or the industry. Macroeconomics suggests ways and means of obtaining a high level of employment. It formulates ideas on monetary and fiscal policy that are designed to stabilize the economy. Finally, macroeconomics is concerned with the effects of interest rates and taxes on the economy.

Economics Is a Science of Choices

Because resources are scarce, individuals and society must choose how best to use them. Normally, there are many alternatives to consider in making economic decisions or choices. Making prudent choices requires determining and analyzing alternatives. But even after analyzing the alternatives, individuals and groups may be faced with many problems that have no clear-cut, definitive answers. There are many gray areas in economics. Often there is no way to determine who is right or wrong in such controversies. Much depends on the judgment of the individual or group involved. Prudence entails selecting the best means for the end intended, so a *prudential judgment* is based largely on the knowledge and experience of those who make it.

Therefore, the economist or policymaker has to make a judgment as to the best means of attaining the desired objective. This is especially true at the governmental or public policy level. Full employment, for example, is a widely accepted objective for the economy. If the economy is not at full employment, several policies can be used to attain full employment. Some economists may urge that the government increase spending as a means of stimulating the economy. Others may assert that it is better to reduce taxes. Both are pursuing the same end of stimulating the economy and reducing unemployment, but they disagree about the best way to accomplish this end.

An example of such a disagreement on an economic policy issue surfaced in 2001. With the economy in the throes of a recession, Congress and the president agreed that a fiscal stimulus package was needed to support the Federal Reserve in its efforts to stimulate economic recovery. The problem, however, was that the president and many members of the Congress had different views on how best to accomplish this goal. The president sought to stimulate the economy primarily by cutting corporate taxes and by accelerating previously enacted tax reductions for individuals, along with a capital gains tax cut. Congress, on the other hand, preferred to stimulate the economy by increasing government spending, primarily by extending unemployment benefits and by rebating taxes to lower-income individuals. As the debate continued, others proposed that the government do nothing insofar as the need for such action had long passed. Finally, in the spring of 2002, Congress and President Bush passed an economic stimulus package. The new tax law did not adjust individual tax rates, but did provide increased unemployment benefits and a variety of increased tax breaks for businesses, including greater depreciation allowances for investment expenditures. Differing opinions such as these among policymakers are confusing to the average citizen. By the time you finish your study of economics, you should be better able to understand and reconcile such differences.

Summary

- Economics is a social science that studies how people and institutions within a society make choices and how these choices determine the use of society's resources. Choices matter because resources are limited, whereas wants are unlimited.

- Economics is related to other sciences, including physics, psychology, sociology, political science, and philosophy. It also makes use of mathematics and logical processes.

- Economic theory deals with the rules and principles to be used under a given set of economic conditions. Economic policy deals with what is actually done under such conditions. Differences between the two frequently occur because economic policy is often mandated by political, social, and military policy.

- Economics focuses on the production, distribution, and consumption of goods and services. Production is a process that creates or adds utility. Distribution refers to the allocation of the total product or income among the four productive resources: labor, land, capital, and enterprise. For their contribution to the total product, productive resources are reimbursed in the form of wages, rent, interest, and profits.

- Consumption, the use of a good or service, is the ultimate end of all economic activity. An economic good is one that is a tangible item that has utility, is scarce, and is transferable. An activity that is useful, scarce, transferable, and tangible is an economic service.

- Goods can be classified as free goods that are not scarce and have no price or as economic goods. A public good is a good that appears to be free to the user but is actually paid for through taxes. Economic goods may be divided into two groups: consumer goods and capital goods.

- Wealth is a stock concept; it is the value of a total collection of economic goods at a specific time. Income is a flow concept and is equivalent to the value of total product—goods and services produced over a given period of time.

- The study of economics is divided into two broad areas: microeconomics and macroeconomics. Microeconomics deals with the actions of the individual, the firm, and the industry. Macroeconomics deals with aggregates such as total production, total employment, and total income. Economics is the study of choices. Making prudent choices about economic decisions requires determining and analyzing alternatives.

New Terms and Concepts

Economics	Labor	Free good
Science	Land	Public good
Economic theory	Capital	Consumer goods
Economic policy	Enterprise	Capital goods
Production	Entrepreneur	Human capital
Utility	Positive economics	Total income
Total product	Normative economics	Microeconomics
Distribution	Consumption	Macroeconomics
Productive resources	Economic good	

Discussion Questions

1. Will economics ever develop into an exact science? Why or why not?

2. In what ways does production involve more than the manufacture and fabrication of goods?

3. What are the four basic productive resources, and what form of compensation does each receive for its contribution to production?

4. Is it true that the more important a good or service is in our everyday lives, the higher the price we must pay to acquire it? Explain your answer and give examples.

5. Identify recent instances showing that distribution is a continuing problem in our economy.

6. Name some goods that were at one time considered free goods but are now economic goods.

7. How can the wealth of our nation be increased?

8. Should an estimate of the value of human capital be included in the measurement of our wealth? If so, how might it be measured?

9. What is the relationship between economic theory and economic policy?

10. Why do differences of opinion among economists on matters of economic policy occur so frequently?

Economic Applications

EconNews

Go to http://econapps.swlearning.com and click on the EconNews icon. Here, you will find a wealth of information and current news about economics. Look under the Economic Fundamentals heading to start learning the basics of economics.

1

CHAPTER REVIEW

2

Scarcity and Choice

After studying Chapter 2, you should be able to:

1. Understand why scarcity forces individuals and societies to make choices.

2. Explain the relationship between scarcity and choice using the production possibilities curve.

3. Discuss how increased productivity can help offset a shortage of resources.

4. Explain the process of specialization and exchange.

5. Differentiate between absolute advantage and comparative advantage and illustrate the importance of comparative advantage in production decisions.

Human wants are unlimited. No matter how many goods and services we obtain, there is generally something else we would like to have. For the individual or family, income available to obtain goods and services is usually limited. For an economy, however, the limitation is the productive resources available to produce the desired goods and services. As we learned in Chapter 1, economics is the process of allocating scarce resources in an attempt to satisfy unlimited wants, whether those of individuals, the domestic economy, or total world resources.

Scarcity and Choice

Scarcity and choice lie at the heart of economics. If all goods were free goods, there would be no need to economize. With free goods, we could have an unlimited quantity of all goods and services at no cost. But, unfortunately, we live in a world of economic goods, which implies that we must choose among restricting alternatives that are costly. Productive resources, time, and income are limited, and we must make hundreds of choices each day among the numerous alternatives available.

On a personal level, with limited income and unlimited wants, most of us must make decisions as to how to spend our money in order to maximize our satisfaction. Because each purchase may preclude the buying of others, consciously or subconsciously we form a subjective scale of preference for goods and services and purchase accordingly. For example, with limited financial resources, choices have to be made as to whether to buy a new car or repair the old one, what DVD player to buy, and where and whether to attend summer school, travel, or work full time to meet college expenses. These choices involve the allocation of our financial resources, but even nonfinancial decisions are economic ones. Choices such as what breakfast foods to eat in the morning, what clothes to wear on a given day, what professors to choose for certain classes, or whether to play tennis or study on a Saturday afternoon are economic ones, because costs and benefits are entailed in each alternative and to choose one is to do without the other.

Scarcity also drives businesses to make choices among alternatives. Decisions must be made concerning what products to produce, where to locate, how many people to employ, what equipment to acquire, what export markets to pursue, and what wages and salaries to pay. The choices of businesses are restricted by competition, government regulations, production costs, technology, and numerous other constraints.

On a national level, policymakers must also make important economic decisions that reflect costly alternatives. For example, unanticipated spending for the emergency relief of victims of hurricanes and floods may result in fewer expenditures on health care or highway construction. Reducing the national debt by raising taxes may diminish investment and savings. Downsizing the military to help balance the federal budget may result in higher unemployment, lower national income, and a decline in national security. Enacting free-trade agreements that seek to benefit the economy in the long run may have severe consequences for specific industries, regions, and workers in the short run.

The trade-offs encountered in the process of selecting among various alternatives are inherent to everyday living. They are also the focal point of economics. The basic function of any economic system is to provide the framework for choice. There must be some way of deciding what and how much to produce, how to produce it, and how to distribute the resulting goods and services to the people in the economy.

NATIONS MUST MAKE CHOICES

We must make choices not only individually but also nationally. No country has all the resources necessary to satisfy the wants of its people. It must therefore use the available productive resources to produce the maximum amount of goods and services. The total output and the standard of living of any nation depend on the extent and use of the nation's labor, land, capital, and enterprise.

Labor. Generally, the larger the population of a given nation is, the greater that nation's total output of goods and services. Total output is also influenced, however, by the educational level of the population, the size of the labor force, the skill and mobility of workers, and the psychological attitude of the people.

Land. Land (including natural resources) is an essential resource. The greater the amount of such resources at the disposal of a nation, the greater that nation's productive potential will be. Land consists of land area, raw materials, sources of energy, and atmospheric conditions. The fertility of the soil affects the total output of crops. A nation with ample forests, coal, petroleum, iron ore, and other materials has an economic advantage over a nation that lacks these resources. Rivers, lakes, and coastal waters are important not only as means of transportation and for the development of power but also as possible sources of food and minerals. Heat, water, steam, electricity, wind power, and even nuclear energy are derived or developed from the use of land, raw materials, and atmospheric conditions.

Capital. The amount of capital and technological development in a country has an important bearing on total output. People can produce more with the assistance of machinery, better technical processes, and human capital than they can through manual labor alone. The improvement in the standard of living in most countries over the past few decades has resulted from a more skilled workforce and better machinery and equipment. Widespread use of computers and communications equipment, new and more powerful machines, new chemical mixtures that create new products, new ways to process raw materials that make them less costly, and other technical developments all tend to increase the output of goods and services and to improve their quality.

Enterprise. Although people can use their labor, land, and even capital to produce goods and services, greater productivity can be obtained by properly combining these resources. Therefore, knowing how to use resources efficiently is important. Entrepreneurs with foresight and organizational ability are required; so is a proper framework or economic system within which to operate. In this regard, the nature and types of businesses, the monetary system, the capital structure of various industries, and the extent of government regulation all influence the entrepreneurial activities within a nation. Consequently, they also affect the total output and the standard of living.

PRODUCTION POSSIBILITIES CURVE

Even at full employment of all productive resources, scarcity exists, because we cannot produce all that society wants. Therefore, producers must choose what and how much of each item to produce. This relationship between scarcity and choice is often demonstrated with an economic model called the *production possibilities model*. The production possibilities model illustrates the concepts of scarcity, choice, and opportunity costs. Scarcity forces us to choose among alternatives, and each alternative selected entails opportunity costs.

*Production
Possibilities Curve*
A graphical view of the
alternative combinations
of different goods and services a society can pro-
duce given its available
resources and technology.

The **production possibilities curve** shows the alternative combinations of different goods and services that a society can produce given its available resources and technology. If we assume full employment of labor and capacity and the ability to interchange productive resources for different purposes, the production possibilities curve for houses and food will be as shown in Figure 2–1. This curve shows that at the extremes either 15,000 houses (shown at point *A*) or 5 million pounds of food (shown at point *F*) can be produced. The production possibilities curve illustrates the need to make choices. As we move in either direction along the curve, we choose among alternative combinations of houses and food. For any combination chosen, other possibilities must be sacrificed. For example, at point *D* in Figure 2–1 the combination of 9,000 houses and 3 million pounds of food can be produced, given existing resources and technology. If we move from point *D* to point *E* on the production possibilities curve, a reduction in housing is required to expand food supply. The sacrifice or cost of producing 4 million pounds of food at point *E* would be 3,000 houses because housing construction would have to be reduced from 9,000 units to 6,000 units in order to expand food production by 1

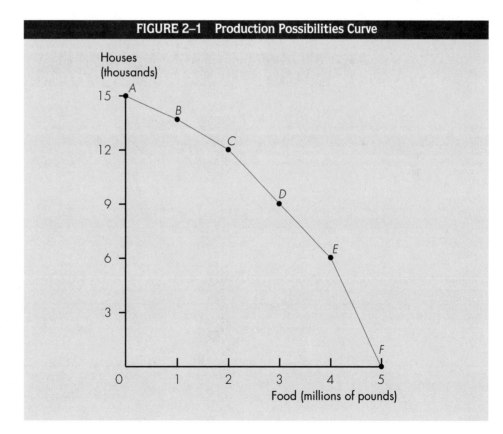

FIGURE 2–1   Production Possibilities Curve

Opportunity Cost
The value of the next best alternative that must be sacrificed when a choice is made.

million pounds. No matter where we move along the production possibilities curve, a trade-off between houses and food is evident. This trade-off is known in economics as opportunity cost. **Opportunity cost** is defined as the value of the next-best alternative that must be sacrificed when a choice is made.

Referring back to Figure 2–1, note that the production possibilities curve is not a straight line but is curved outward. This implies that the resources used in housing construction and food production are not equally suited for producing both outputs. As we move from point *A* to point *F*, the figures indicate that more and more houses have to be sacrificed to increase food output by 1 million pounds, because to produce more food we must use resources that are better suited for housing construction and switch them to food production. When moving from point *D* to point *E*, Figure 2–1 shows that 3,000 houses have to be sacrificed; but moving from point *E* to point *F* entails an even greater loss in the number of houses. The opportunity cost to increase food output by 1 million pounds is now the sacrifice of 6,000 houses. As more food is produced, the opportunity cost in terms of lost houses will continue to increase. It is the increasing opportunity costs that determine the shape of the production possibilities curve.

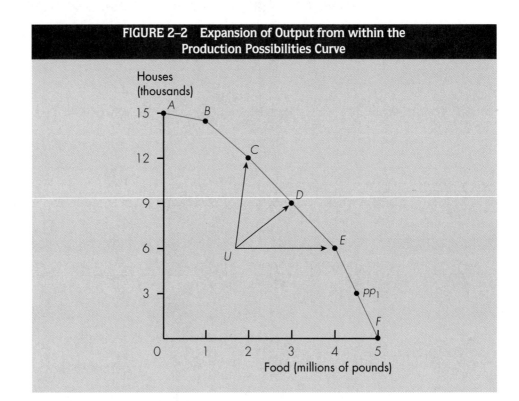

FIGURE 2–2   Expansion of Output from within the Production Possibilities Curve

Houses (thousands)

Food (millions of pounds)

A nation may not, however, be producing to full capacity, as shown by point *U* in Figure 2–2. This could result from idle resources during a recession or from less than maximum efficiency in the use of resources in a full-employment economy. As Figure 2–2 indicates, total output can be increased and better choices (for example, *C*, *D*, or *E*) can be made by employing idle resources and/or by maximizing the economic efficiency of these resources.

The production possibilities curve can be used to show the effects of economic growth on a nation's economy. **Economic growth** is defined as the increase in an economy's total output of goods and services. The sources of economic growth are many and may include the addition of labor and capital, new technology, invention, innovation, the discovery of resources, and improvements in productivity brought about by a better-educated and more highly skilled labor force. As a country experiences economic growth, it can enjoy an increase in both capital and consumer goods without trading off one for the other. For example, in Figure 2–3 assume that an increase in the size and quality of the labor force and greater use of technology increase productivity throughout the economy. This has the effect of shifting the

Economic Growth
An increase in an economy's total output of goods and services.

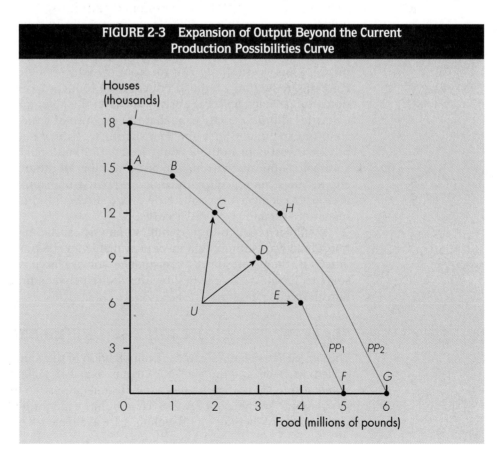

FIGURE 2-3   Expansion of Output Beyond the Current Production Possibilities Curve

production possibilities curve to the right. The new production possibilities curve is pp_2. Previously, the only way the economy would experience an increase in either food production or the stock of housing was to increase one at the expense of the other. But because of economic growth, the economy can now produce both more houses and more food. In Figure 2–3, if the economy were producing 3 million pounds of food and 9,000 houses at point D, it can now produce 12,000 houses and 3.5 million tons of food at point H. Once the economy is on the new production possibilities curve, the trade-off begins again.

In a developed country such as the United States, choices as to whether to produce more of one good or more of another are carried out in the marketplace with little or no disruption in the economy. In the case of developing nations, however, these choices can have more serious consequences. Poorer countries are less able to devote their scarce resources to the formation of technology and capital, for to do so means the forgoing of basic consumer goods necessary for survival. For this country to enjoy the benefits of economic growth, it will have to invest in such things as highways, power plants, and communication technology. But to create future economic growth by investing in capital goods industries such as these, it will have to curtail the consumption of foodstuffs. If the developing country does somehow succeed in creating new capital, it will increase its capacity to produce a greater number of goods and services in the future. Thus, in the long run the country will be better off. But in the short run, this reduction in the production of food can result in disease, starvation, and perhaps political uprisings. Given this dilemma, how can developing countries afford to create capital at the expense of basic consumption? Possible solutions include grants and loans from wealthier nations, as well as direct private investment in these countries by multinational companies. Assuming a favorable political environment, and a number of other positive conditions, the engines for economic growth could originate from sources outside the country. If efforts to achieve economic growth are successful, the country will move to a higher production possibilities curve.

A similar production possibilities analysis can be made for an individual or household by assuming that income available for the purchase of goods and services is the limited resource. As a student, you are faced with time as a limited resource, thus your curve may show the choice between time devoted to study and time devoted to leisure.

SCARCITY AND CHOICE IN THE UNITED STATES

The United States has an excellent combination of the four resources. First, it has a skilled, versatile, and mobile labor force of over 143 million out of a total population of about 287 million. As in most industrial nations, 45 to 55 percent of the total population is in the labor force. Second, it has a plentiful supply of land and natural resources. Therefore, raw materials are available for producing an abundance of goods and services. Third, the United States has the greatest amount of capital in the world. Much of this capital is highly complex and costly.

Today, machines and processes permit better use of brainpower. For example, how long would it take you to do your accounting or math assignments without a calculator? A computer used by one of our large jet aircraft manufacturers can complete in one minute or less the calculations it would take a mathematician years to perform on a desk calculator. The larger the amount of machinery and equipment at the disposal of the worker, the greater the productivity will be. Capital, as well as technological development, is responsible for much of our productivity.

The fourth resource that the United States and other modern industrial countries have is entrepreneurial skill—the technique and the ability to get goods and services produced. We have developed a large body of managerial techniques, and we place considerable emphasis on training young people for positions in business. For example, nowhere else in the world are business schools at the university level as common as in the United States. In recent years, however, a number of nations in Europe, Asia, and South America have established graduate schools of business patterned after some of the outstanding U.S. schools.

The United States today has one of the highest per capita outputs (and the highest total output) of goods and services among the major countries of the world. In 2002, total output was approximately $11 trillion worth of goods and services, over 3 times the output of Japan, which was second in the world. In 2002, over $36,000 in goods and services per person were produced in the U.S. economy. For decades the United States has been the world leader in output and income. In recent years, however, other industrial nations have been approaching the U.S. level of per capita output. Output per capita in Switzerland is 86 percent of the U.S. level; Germany, 80 percent; Canada, 76 percent; Japan, 75 percent; and the United Kingdom, 68 percent.[1]

The problems of scarcity that face people in the United States—choosing whether to use resources to construct highways or to build new homes, whether to buy a home entertainment system or to take a vacation, whether to go to college or to enter military service—are much more pleasant to deal with than those that many developing nations face. Often the decision in those nations involves determining which crop will have the greatest yield in order to alleviate hunger. But the United States and other industrial nations must start paying more attention to choices. With the rapid depletion of resources, environmental concerns, and the food shortages that have occurred throughout the world, productive resources must be used more effectively to maximize output and satisfy as many wants as possible.

1   Central Intelligence Agency, *World Fact Book: 2002* (Washington, D.C.: U.S. Government Printing Office, 2002).

Problems of Scarcity

Unfortunately, some areas of the world lack the proper ratio of land, labor, and capital required for high-level production. In fact, we are fortunate to live in a country that has all the requisites for a large output and a high standard of living. This is brought home by the fact that one-fifth of the world's population lives at the level of bare subsistence. Because one or more of the essential resources is lacking in these places, productivity is insufficient to provide the people with the basics for a comfortable living.

NATURE AND SCOPE OF PROBLEMS

Millions of people suffer from economic privation. For example, the People's Republic of China, with 1.3 billion people, is said to have ample natural resources. But it lacks sufficient capital needed to develop an adequate transportation system and the buildings, machinery, and equipment needed to process raw materials into finished products. What is produced for domestic consumption must be shared by an exceptionally large number of people. Thus, the annual per capita output or income is only the equivalent of 4,300 U.S. dollars per person. India and Pakistan are in a similar situation, with a combined population of over 1 billion people, only moderate resources, and a shortage of capital.

Some areas are short of capital and technology, others lack natural resources, and some have a shortage of skilled labor. Japan must allocate resources very wisely to produce enough to support 127 million people from the output of a land area that is about the size of Montana. Imagine what would happen if one-half of the people of the United States were crowded into the state of Montana and told to feed and clothe themselves from the resources of that area alone.

A SOLUTION: INCREASED PRODUCTIVITY

Frequently, when a country finds itself lacking the labor and/or land necessary for a high level of output, it can overcome the deficiency by increasing human capital. Japan, for example, has offset its lack of natural resources with an exceptionally high degree of industrial efficiency. This permits Japan to import raw materials, process them into finished goods, and sell them in domestic and foreign markets at a profit. A shortage of resources or labor may be overcome by the discovery of new resources, the development of new and better techniques, and the use of better machinery to produce greater yields from existing resources. There are thousands of examples of ways in which productivity has been increased. Using synthetic fibers in place of real fibers, plastics in place of metals, computers as a substitute for human labor, and lasers in place of old-fashioned surgical tools has increased productivity. In the future we will see more extensive use of geothermal and solar energy, commercial processing of seawater to extract valuable minerals, and new and better machines to do things we now consider highly improbable. All such de-

NET*Link*

Want a better understanding of the Japanese economy? Take a virtual field trip to Japan's Ministry of Finance. Set your browser to URL:

http://www.jinjapan.org

velopments will ease the problem of scarcity by obtaining more output from existing resources.

AID TO DEVELOPING NATIONS

Many nations, however, do not have the natural resources, skilled labor force, or capital to improve their standard of living. Furthermore, many of these developing nations produce at subsistence level and are unable to forgo current consumption in order to invest in additional capital. Approximately one-third of the world's countries have an annual per capita output of $2,000 or less. This compares with annual per capita outputs of over $36,000 in the United States and $20,000 or more in most developed nations. Many developing nations—especially those whose productivity is increasing at a slower rate than their population—need outside help. To alleviate hunger, poverty, and sickness, they need short-term aid in the form of food, clothing, and medical assistance. To solve their basic economic problem, however, they need long-term aid in the form of technical assistance and capital.

Specialization and Exchange

Specialization
The process of limiting the scope of an economic unit's productive efforts instead of trying to produce everything it needs.

Exchange
The process of trading surplus quantities of specialized products to others for other goods or services.

Productivity determines output, output determines income, and income determines a society's standard of living. Therefore, each individual or nation should try to increase productivity. One way of doing this is through specialization and exchange.

Specialization occurs when an economic unit (an individual, a firm, a geographic area, or a nation) limits the scope of its productive efforts instead of trying to produce everything it needs. In this way the economic unit can become very proficient at producing a few goods or services. **Exchange** is the process of trading surplus quantities of the specialized products to others for other goods or services. Overall, society can produce more through such cooperation than individuals can by each producing some of everything.

In the U.S. economy, individuals, firms, geographic areas, and the nation as a whole specialize. Individuals usually concentrate on a particular occupation or profession. Most firms produce a limited range and number of items. Many parts of the United States concentrate on the production of certain products—cotton in the South, cattle in the Southwest, autos in the Midwest, and electronics in the Silicon Valley of California. Internationally, Brazil concentrates on coffee, Argentina on beef, Cuba on sugar, and Britain on industrial products. An economy using specialization and exchange yields higher individual and total incomes than does an economy characterized by self-sufficiency. Specialization gives individuals the opportunity to become expert in a particular skill. As a result, total output is greater than it would be if each person tried to produce all the goods and services he or she desired.

The U.S. economy uses specialization and exchange extensively, limited only by the size of the market. Obviously, it is not profitable to engage in this process if sales of the items produced are insufficient to give the producer a decent profit or if the maker cannot produce enough to become more efficient than nonspecialists. Thus, we must look at the size of the market. If it is large enough, specialization and exchange make economic sense. The size of the market is determined not only by population size but also by its income or purchasing power. People cannot buy goods and services unless they have the money to do so. The size of the market is also affected by the economy's transportation system. The better and cheaper the transportation, the greater is the number of people who can be reached.

Absolute and Comparative Advantage

An individual, a firm, a region, or a country may develop an area of specialization naturally, but frequently choices must be made to determine what to produce for exchange or trade.

Absolute Advantage
The ability to produce a good or service using fewer resources than other producers use.

Producers should concentrate on the activity in which they have an absolute advantage. An **absolute advantage** is the ability to produce a good or service using fewer resources than other producers use. In the United States this situation occurs when one region of a country is more suited than another for producing certain products. Florida can grow oranges using fewer resources than Iowa, where heated greenhouses would be necessary. Iowa has vast, flat acreage and can produce corn much more efficiently than could Florida. Thus, Florida specializes in oranges while Iowa concentrates on corn, and the products are exchanged through the marketplace.

When each of two parties has an absolute advantage over the other in producing a particular good or service, it is easy for both to decide their areas of specialization. But what happens when one party can produce both goods or services more efficiently than a second party? Should the party with the absolute advantage produce both products for itself? Although this party has the advantage in producing either good, it should specialize in producing the good in which it has a compara-

Comparative Advantage
The ability to produce a good or service at a lower opportunity cost than other producers face.

tive advantage. **Comparative advantage** is the ability to produce a good or service at a lower opportunity cost than other producers face. This means letting the other party produce the good in which it has the lower opportunity cost. Total output will be greater, and exchange will allow both parties to have both goods.

Suppose a woman can make $50 per hour as a marketing consultant. Part of her work includes preparing reports for her clients. Suppose that, in addition to being a first-class consultant, she is more efficient at word processing than anyone she might hire to key the reports. Thus she might be able to key in one hour what it takes an assistant two hours to do. As a result, she reasons that, instead of hiring an assistant to do the work, she should do it herself. Is she right to do her own keying as well as consulting? If she does her own keying, she still must take an hour each day from her consulting to do so. The opportunity cost of keying is the $50 she could have earned consulting. The opportunity cost of consulting is the $20 she must pay an assistant to key the reports. So if she hires an assistant, she can devote her full time to consulting. Her gross earnings will be $50 greater per day. After paying the assistant $20 for two hours work, she will still have additional net income of $30 per day. Thus, the marketing consultant is better off specializing full time in the service for which she has the greater comparative advantage.

COMPARATIVE ADVANTAGE BETWEEN NATIONS

This same principle of comparative advantage applies to firms, areas, or nations. Disregarding other factors, such as exchange rates and transportation costs, let us compare two hypothetical countries: Shetland and North Mocha. Suppose that each of the two countries has 5 resource units (a resource unit is equal to a certain combination of labor, land, capital, and enterprise). Initially, each country devotes 3 units to producing cotton and the remaining 2 units to producing wheat. From these units, Shetland produces 30 bales of cotton and 60 bushels of wheat, while North Mocha produces 15 bales of cotton and 40 bushels of wheat. Shetland is therefore more proficient than North Mocha at producing both cotton and wheat, as summarized in Table 2–1. Table 2–1 shows that, overall, 10 resource units are being used to produce 45 bales of cotton and 100 bushels of wheat. Furthermore, Shetland has an absolute advantage over North Mocha in producing both wheat and cotton.

   Now the problem is to decide whether Shetland should produce both cotton and wheat and let North Mocha shift for itself, or whether Shetland should specialize in one of the two products. To satisfy the law of comparative advantage, Shetland would produce the good for which it has the greater comparative advantage. In our example, this good is cotton. Shetland has a 2 to 1 advantage over North Mocha in the production of this item, while it has only a 3 to 2 advantage over North Mocha in the production of wheat. If Shetland devoted all its resource units to cotton, it would produce 50 bales. If North Mocha channeled all its resource units into wheat, it could produce a total of 100 bushels of wheat. Thus, the new schedule of output would be as shown in Table 2–2.

   The two countries combined have the same output of wheat and a total gain of 5 bales of cotton. Of the total output, who gets what? That depends on the

TABLE 2–1 Production of Shetland and North Mocha Before Specialization

Country	COTTON Resource Units	Bales	WHEAT Resource Units	Bushels
Shetland	3	30	2	60
North Mocha	3	15	2	40
Total	6	45	4	100

	COTTON		WHEAT	
TABLE 2–2 Production of Shetland and North Mocha After Specialization				
Country	Resource Units	Bales	Resource Units	Bushels
Shetland	5	50	0	—
North Mocha	0	—	5	100
Total	5	50	5	100

exchange between the two countries, but it should work out favorably for both. To regain its former ratio of wheat to cotton, North Mocha would want 15 bales of cotton—the amount it gave up in order to specialize—in exchange for 60 bushels of wheat. On the other hand, Shetland could afford to give 20 bales of cotton—the amount it obtained through specialization—in exchange for the 60 bushels of wheat it originally produced.

The exchange rate of wheat to cotton will be set by bargaining between the two countries. The final settlement will depend on many economic circumstances. If the countries are of equal economic strength, they might split the difference and set the exchange ratio at 17.5 bales of cotton for 60 bushels of wheat. Trading on this basis assumes that Shetland exports 17.5 bales of cotton, fixing the total it uses domestically at 32.5 bales. As a result, each country has 2.5 more bales of cotton than it had when it produced both wheat and cotton.

In exchange for the cotton, North Mocha sends Shetland 60 bushels of wheat. The amount of wheat remaining in North Mocha is therefore 40 bushels—the same amount it had under the first plan. Likewise, Shetland has 60 bushels of wheat—also the same amount it had before any specialization and exchange took place. The final position of the two countries after specialization and exchange shows a total gain of 5 bales of cotton: 2.5 for Shetland and 2.5 for North Mocha. Both have the same amount of wheat they formerly produced (see Table 2–3). In this simple example, both nations benefited by using the principle of comparative advantage. In actual trade, however, many additional, complex factors, such as shipping costs and exchange rates, must be considered.

COMPARATIVE ADVANTAGE IN PRACTICE

Much can be gained by putting the principle of comparative advantage into practice. Individuals use it when they choose one occupation or profession over another. Large firms increase their profits in the same manner. For example, large auto producers can make most of the parts needed for manufacturing cars. Nevertheless, they buy most of these parts from independent suppliers and devote most of their time, money, and effort to actual assembly of the autos. In fact, you may

TABLE 2–3	Gains Resulting from Specialization	
Country	Cotton (Bales)	Wheat (Bushels)
Shetland	32.5	60
North Mocha	17.5	40
Total	50.0	100

have seen advertisements showing how many parts large auto firms buy from suppliers around the United States. Other companies build stores, sell them to a second party, and then lease them back. This permits them to put their money and time into their retail businesses instead of into property ownership.

Specialization and exchange can increase productivity and improve the standard of living, but a region or nation must be careful not to overspecialize. An economy made up of specialists without anyone to direct its overall activity may not be able to reach its maximum potential. Military considerations are another factor limiting the use of the principle of comparative advantage. Even though it may be more costly to produce certain goods domestically, it may be wiser in the long run to do so if those products are essential to military output. When war breaks out, a country may be cut off from its source of supply.

Furthermore, undue dependence on one or a few products by a region or a nation can lead to severe economic problems if the demand for those products fluctuates or collapses. For example, Michigan is vulnerable to business recessions because of its heavy concentration on auto production. When auto sales fall off to any considerable degree, widespread layoffs in Michigan occur. Likewise, the demand for coffee has a major influence on business activity in Brazil. Also, weather, including rainfall, is always a concern for agricultural areas. It is economically wise to specialize, but not excessively. Some diversification in production is beneficial.

Summary

- Economizing is the process of applying scarce resources in an attempt to satisfy unlimited wants. Both individuals and nations must economize.

- Economizing involves the relationship between scarcity and choice. The relationship can be demonstrated through the use of a production possibilities curve. Opportunity cost is the value of forgone alternatives when choices are made. Total production is affected by the composition and age structure of the population and by the size, skill, and mobility of the labor force. Production ability also depends on the natural resources of a nation, including land, space, raw materials, energy sources, and weather, as well as capital and technological development.

- Total production can be enhanced by the use of specialization and exchange. In specialization, an economic unit limits the scope of its production efforts, enabling the unit to become proficient at producing a few goods or services. In exchange, surplus quantities of specialized products are traded to others for other goods or services.

- The basic economic problem of less-developed countries is that they lack the resources, skilled labor force, or capital to improve their standards of living. Such countries need both short-term aid (food, clothing, and medical help) and long-term aid in the form of technical assistance and capital.

- Specialization and exchange operate in conjunction with the principle of comparative advantage. If two or more parties have an absolute advantage over each other, the parties can easily determine their areas of specialization. But if one of the parties can produce two products or services more efficiently than the other parties, that party should specialize in producing the commodity in which they have the greater comparative advantage. However, all parties should be aware of the limitations to comparative advantage.

- A problem of comparative advantage can be worked out by comparing hypothetical parties, say, in the auto industry, or considering an individual, say a consultant, who has to determine which service provides the greater comparative advantage.

New Terms and Concepts

Production possibilities curve
Opportunity cost
Economic growth
Specialization

Exchange
Absolute advantage
Comparative advantage

Discussion Questions

1. To what extent do you engage in the process of economizing in your everyday activities?

2. Will an increase in the population of a given nation necessarily result in a decrease in the standard of living? Why or why not?

3. How will increased use of nuclear energy or other new sources of power affect the problem of scarcity?

4. How could nations that have an abundance of resources most effectively share them with nations that have inadequate resources?

5. What is meant by the following statement: "Goods and services are scarce because productive resources are scarce"?

6. If productive resources in the United States doubled in the next five years, would the problem of scarcity be eliminated?

7. In reference to the production possibilities curve, how might a nation increase its total output if it is already fully employing its resources?

8. Distinguish between absolute advantage and comparative advantage.

9. Indicate some ways in which you or your friends practice the law of comparative advantage.

10. Should a nation try to become as economically independent as possible? Why or why not?

Economic Applications

EconDebate
Find the EconDebate link at http://econapps.swlearning.com and click on "Scarcity, Choice, and Opportunity Cost" under the Economic Fundamentals heading. This link includes many debates that illustrate the role of scarcity and choice in real-world economic situations.

2

CHAPTER REVIEW

3

The U.S. Economic System

After studying Chapter 3, you should be able to:

1. Understand the roles of profit and competition in a market economy.

2. Explain how prices ration output, allocate resources, and help determine incomes in a market economy.

3. Differentiate among the four types of business organization.

4. Discuss the role of competition in the U.S. economy.

5. List and explain the major goals of the U.S. economy.

6. Summarize the differences among traditional, market, and command economic systems.

In the previous chapter, the production possibilities model depicted the type of choices that are necessary as long as there are limited productive resources and unlimited wants. The production possibilities curve, however, says nothing about how these choices are made. Scarcity dictates that decisions must be made about what to produce, how to produce, and what methods to adopt in allocating goods and services. These questions apply to any economic system, but they are not always answered in the same way.

What goods and services to produce and in what quantities? Many millions of goods are produced for the market each year and thousands disappear each year. Why is it that certain toys, cars, clothing of certain styles, and works of performing artists are no longer available for purchase? Conversely, what factors account for the millions of newer products on the market in use today, such as cell phones, digital cameras, personal computers, and DVDs?

How are goods and services produced? This question concerns the use of productive resources. Ideally, all resources in the economy should be put to productive use, and all resources should be used as efficiently as possible. Efficiency involves using the most efficient combination of resources in the production process. The type and number of resources employed in any industry will depend on their relative prices and availability. In many developing countries, labor is plentiful and capital scarce, whereas in developed countries the opposite is true. Hence, farming in poorer countries is labor-intensive and crops are planted and harvested by hand. In contrast, in the United States and Canada it is more efficient to substitute capital for labor in farming. Agriculture in these countries is highly mechanized, with a minimum use of labor. In determining how to produce, each area is guided by the cost and availability of resources.

Who gets what is produced? This question concerns how output and income is distributed among all members of society. Income and wealth do matter, for individuals and families with greater financial resources consume more goods and services than those with fewer financial means. This issue always raises the question of a distribution of income that is fair and equitable, but what constitutes fairness is vague and controversial. What might be best for one group isn't likely to be best for another. To say that one pattern of income distribution is better or worse than another involves normative judgments regarding equity and efficiency. If income inequality is deemed too unacceptable by society, government may need to intercede to create greater equality. Failure to respond can bring about social unrest leading to political and economic turmoil.

The three basic economic questions involve many normative and positive issues. How these questions are answered depends on the economic system in place. Keeping these decisions in mind, we now will examine the fundamental principles and policies adopted by the U.S. economy.

Market Economy

Market Economy
An economy in which the decisions about what to produce, how much to produce, and how to allocate goods and services are made primarily by individuals and firms in the economy.

Financial Capital
Money that can be used to purchase capital goods.

Profit
The incentive for obtaining and using resources to produce goods and services that consumers will buy; also, the excess of revenue over all costs of production.

In a **market economy,** decisions about what to produce, how much to produce, and how to allocate goods and services are made primarily by individuals and firms in the economy. In a command economy, on the other hand, a considerable degree of government direction and control of production and distribution exists.

Under the U.S. market system, land and capital goods are owned and used mainly by individuals and firms rather than by government agencies. The capital may be in the form of equipment and buildings, or it may be **financial capital—** money that can be used to purchase capital goods. The institution of private property is essential to a market system. This means not only that individuals have the right to own, use, and sell land, equipment, and buildings but that they also have the right to own the results of their productivity. Thus, when farmers use their labor and capital to grow cotton on their land, the cotton becomes their property and they can dispose of it as they see fit. Similarly, a firm that produces shoes has ownership of the shoes and can sell them as it desires. After compensating the owners of the other resources that contributed to the production of the shoes, the firm is entitled to what is left of the total revenue. **Profit** is the incentive for obtaining and using resources to produce goods and services that consumers will buy.

THE ROLE OF PROFIT IN A MARKET ECONOMY

Under the market system, individuals may offer their services to someone in exchange for wages, or they may let someone use their land in exchange for rent, or they may lend their money to someone in exchange for an interest payment. Alternatively, instead of selling productive services to someone else, a person can combine several resources to produce goods and sell them at a profit. But to operate a business, a person must produce goods or services that people want and must offer them at a price they are willing to pay. The farmers who grow cotton and sell it at a profit benefit not only themselves but also society by supplying a basic good that is needed or desired. Likewise, the shoe producer satisfies people's wants for shoes, in addition to making a profit. If the cotton grower and the shoe producer use the labor, land, and capital of others, they provide jobs and income for other members of the community too. Thus, in a model situation, the producer—by using resources to make a profit—increases the well-being of other people. For the producer to be successful, consumer demand must be satisfied. But in some situations the producer suffers a loss or exploits consumers by supplying an inferior product or by underpaying for the resources used.

In a market economic system, the ultimate use of labor and other resources and the allocation of goods and services are determined primarily by consumer demand. Individuals express their demand through the prices they are willing to pay for goods and services. Usually, the stronger the demand is (other things being equal), the higher the price that consumers will pay for a particular good or service. From these payments, businesses obtain the revenue they need to purchase the labor, land, and capital necessary for producing more goods and services. The opportunity to make profits is an incentive for businesses to produce these goods and services.

If the demand for a particular good or service is strong enough, the good or service will be produced. Sometimes, however, such a large demand for total goods and services exists that we lack sufficient land, labor, and capital to produce them all. What then is produced? Once again, in a model system, the consumers decide. The firms and industries that experience the strongest demand for products will have the revenue necessary to attract relatively scarce productive agents away from other uses. If consumer demand for a particular good is weak, however, and the price offered is so low that it does not yield a profit, few, if any, resources will be devoted to its production.

THE ROLE OF COMPETITION IN A MARKET ECONOMY

Competition
Rivalry among individuals and firms for sales to consumers; the natural regulator that makes the free market system work.

The market economy, relying as it does on private property and the profit motive, depends on **competition** to make the system function. Competition is rivalry among firms and individuals for sales to consumers; it is the natural regulator that makes the free market system work. Businesses compete for shares of the consumer's dollar. In the markets for productive resources, firms compete for scarce resources. In a command economy, on the other hand, output quotas are assigned to firms by a political leader or a planning committee. Resources are directed to various industries by similar means. But when allocation decisions are decentralized, as in a market economy, competition regulates the volume of output and the allocation of resources.

If competition is effective, the economy functions efficiently without an overseer. Through competition, consumers are protected from shoddy products and exorbitant prices. The prospect that rival firms will offer a better product at the same price or a comparable product at a lower price forces each firm to maintain quality and restrict price increases. Resource owners and workers are protected against exploitation by the opportunity for the alternative employment that competing firms make available. The opportunity to sell labor or resources to the highest bidder gives them economic leverage and prevents any one firm from keeping resources in its own employment at depressed prices. In this way, effective competition limits the power of businesses and keeps any one firm from dominating the market. Each firm is free to pursue its own profit without worrying about the overall allocation of resources and products in the economy. Yet the impersonal force of competition ensures the flow of resources toward the most efficient firms because these firms can afford to offer the highest prices for their use.

Of course, competition is not always effective, and it is seldom perfect. Sometimes firms may be able to exclude others from the industry and thereby exercise substantial control over price, industry output, and employment conditions. When this happens, the government must restore competitive conditions. But it does not do so by taking control of the industry or assuming ownership of the firms. Instead, the central political authority imposes legal sanctions against restraint of competition or other abuses committed in the name of competition.

The guiding principle of a market economy is that privately owned firms should produce the goods and services consumers want in the quantities they wish to buy. In this regard, competition is relied on as a mechanism for regulating trade. Only in areas where competition cannot work effectively—such as to provide police and fire protection—does the government step in to influence or control production. Otherwise, the government is expected to create and enforce laws ensuring that private enterprise and conditions of competition will prevail.

THE ROLE OF PRICES IN A MARKET ECONOMY

Although consumer demand chiefly determines what and how much is produced, the decisions are by no means made unilaterally by consumers. Supply also influences the price of goods and services and the ultimate determination of what and how much is produced. If a shortage arises in the supply of particular resources, consumers may have to pay a higher price than they would like in order to obtain a particular good or service. In such a case, they must decide whether to pay the price or do without the product. Thus, price is a rationing mechanism for deciding which consumers will receive the particular good or service.

Prices Allocate Resources

In determining what and how much to produce, the market economy works in a democratic manner based on dollar votes. Other things being equal, the use of land, labor, and capital is determined by the total number of dollars spent on particular goods and services. Thus, the more dollars an individual or group accumulates, the greater is the potential influence over what is to be produced. Although this is a democratic process according to dollar votes, it is not necessarily democratic as to personal preferences.

Because those with the most dollars have the most votes, imbalances may develop. If certain individuals or groups acquire an excessive number of dollars, the economy in general and other individuals in particular may suffer. For example, hoarding large numbers of dollars, rather than spending or investing them, could depress business activity and result in unemployment for workers and lower profits for business. Even when all available dollars are being spent, an economy might be so out of balance that, for example, numerous palatial homes, high-priced cars, and yachts are produced, while the larger community is deprived of much-needed low-cost housing. In other words, expenditures for luxury goods by one portion of society may crowd out funding for basic necessities for another part.

Prices Help Determine Incomes

Individuals not only determine what and how much is produced in the market economy but also determine in part the incomes paid to the various resources as wages, rent, interest, and profits. Revenue from the sale of goods and services provides businesses with money for obtaining the labor, land, and capital needed to produce the goods demanded. The payments to the owners of these resources allow them to purchase a certain portion of the goods and services the economy produces. Many things, including the productivity of resources, their supply, government regulations, labor unions, and other institutional forces, have a direct bearing on how much income is paid to each of the various resources. However, the ultimate source of income payments to resources is the revenue from consumer purchases.

In a market system, each resource is paid according to its economic contribution toward the good or service being produced. That contribution is measured by the price the firm is willing to pay for it, which in turn is determined by consumer demand. Thus, the strong demand for automobiles is one reason why U.S. autoworkers have historically been among the highest-paid workers in the world. The income a resource receives is also affected by its productivity and scarcity. If the supply of a particular type of skilled labor is limited, qualified workers will be able to command higher payment for their services than will unskilled workers. For example, superstar athletes and entertainers have special talents that permit them to command especially high compensation. But ultimately the fans at the sports arena or rock concert and, indirectly, TV audiences provide the revenue to pay the high compensation.

Business Organization in the U.S. Economy

The process by which we determine the allocation of resources, the flow of income, and the final distribution of goods and services in the United States is aided by our business firms. In a market economy, production to satisfy consumer demand usually is undertaken by privately owned firms. Starting a business involves risks, but the incentive of profit induces hundreds of thousands of individuals annually to try to become successful entrepreneurs. Some knowledge of the organization of various types of businesses will help you understand the operation of the U.S. economic system better.

There are over 23 million firms in the United States, not counting about 2 million farms. Most of these firms have fewer than 4 employees. Fewer than 1 percent have more than 500 employees. More firms fall into the sector of services than into any other nonagricultural category; most of these are sole proprietorships. Wholesale and retail firms, along with financial institutions, including insurance and real estate, are the most numerous forms of nonagricultural businesses.

FORMS OF BUSINESS ORGANIZATION

The four legal forms of business organization in the United States are sole proprietorships, partnerships, corporations, and cooperatives. Each form has certain advantages and disadvantages.

Sole Proprietorships

Sole Proprietorship
A business owned and run by a single person.

Sole proprietorship, or one-person ownership of a firm, was the earliest form of business firm. At present, there are over 19 million individually owned businesses and farms. In a sole proprietorship, one individual owns and directs the business. This person risks his or her personal property in the business. If the enterprise is successful, the individual receives all the profit; but if it fails, the person suffers all the losses.

Ease of entry is one major advantage of the sole proprietorship. Practically anyone who can accumulate a small amount of savings or borrow some money can go into business. Another advantage is the flexibility of management in a single proprietorship. The proprietor can make decisions without having to obtain the approval of a board of directors or to convince other owners of the firm.

One of the biggest disadvantages of the sole proprietorship is the lack of legal distinction between the business and the owner. If the business fails, creditors may take personal assets (such as the owner's house) through court action, as well as the assets of the business, to satisfy debts. Another disadvantage is the difficulty of raising sufficient funds for a large-scale operation. It is also hard to sustain the continuity of the business over an extended period of time because the death of an owner automatically terminates the proprietorship. The business can, however, continue under a new owner.

Partnerships

Partnership
A business owned by two
or more persons.

A **partnership,** as defined by the Uniform Partnership Act, is an association of two
or more persons to carry on as co-owners of a business for profit. The partnership
is usually found in small businesses requiring a limited amount of capital that can
be contributed by the partners. It is also found in professional practices, such as law
and accounting. At present, fewer than 1.8 million active partnerships are operating in the United States.

A partnership can usually raise more funds to operate the business than can a
sole proprietorship because it can obtain funds from each partner. Another advantage is the specialization of effort that it permits. Responsibility for various functions of the business can be divided among the different partners.

On the other hand, the partnership has most of the disadvantages of the proprietorship, plus a few of its own. Its continuity is uncertain because the withdrawal or
death of a partner legally dissolves the partnership. (However, the business may be
reorganized by the remaining or new partners.) In many respects, the action of any
one partner can be legally binding on the partnership. Thus, poor decisions or unsound commitments made by any one partner bind all the partners. Furthermore,
because a partnership, like a sole proprietorship, is not a separate legal entity, the
partners are personally responsible for the firm's debts. This means that the personal
assets of the partners may be seized if necessary to satisfy partnership debts. In addition, each partner is individually liable for all debts of the partnership incurred while
that partner is a member of the firm.

Corporations

In the *Dartmouth College* case (decided in 1819) regarding corporate liability, Chief
Justice of the Supreme Court John Marshall described a corporation as an artificial
being, invisible, intangible, and existing only in contemplation of law. Thus, a **corporation** is a separate legal entity, apart from its owners or shareholders, that functions as a business enterprise. It is a legal person in itself. Contracts can be made in
the name of the corporation, it can own real estate and other assets, and it can sue
and be sued.

Corporation
A separate legal entity,
apart from its owners or
shareholders, that func-
tions as a business.

The corporation has several advantages over other forms of business enterprise. It has continuity of life because ownership in the form of shares of stock can
be transferred without the corporation's being dissolved. Through the sale of stock,
it can raise large sums of money. And unlike a sole proprietorship or partnership,
the corporate owners have limited liability; they can lose only what they have invested in the business. Furthermore, owners can pledge their stock as collateral for
personal or business loans, whereas partners cannot easily pledge their interest in
their business for such loans. The owners elect a board of directors, which in turn
selects the management personnel to operate the business, so inefficient managers
can be removed by directors. Additional funds for expansion of the business can be
obtained by issuing more stock or by floating bond issues.

The corporation has certain disadvantages, however. It must pay its own income taxes, and the stockholders must also pay income taxes on the dividends

they receive out of corporate income. No such double taxation exists on sole proprietorship or partnership income. The state charges a fee for incorporating a business, and it often levies an annual franchise tax. A corporation can engage only in the business for which it is authorized. Before entering into other businesses, it must have its charter amended by the state. Numerous reports must be filed annually in the state where the firm is incorporated, as well as in other states where the corporation does business.

One salient feature of the corporate form of business is that ownership can be spread over a large segment of the population. Any individual can be a part owner simply by purchasing a few shares of stock. Most stocks sell for less than $100, so it is relatively easy to become a stockholder. In fact, more than 50 percent of all families (individually or through pension plans) own stock in the 5 million corporations in the United States.

Cooperatives

Cooperative
A business owned by the people who use it or buy from it.

A **cooperative** is a business owned by the people who use it or buy from it. A cooperative may be incorporated and pay dividends to its stockholders. But unlike in a corporation, each shareholder has only one vote in managerial affairs, regardless of the amount of stock that person holds. A major difference between cooperatives and other forms of business organization is the distribution of net income. In a cooperative, after a nominal dividend has been paid to shareholders, any net income is distributed among the customers of the cooperative on a pro rata basis according to the amount of their respective purchases from the cooperative.

Although the consumer cooperative has been in existence in the United States for more than 100 years, it has not achieved national significance. A major reason for its lack of success is that large chain stores and discount stores, operating on a low-markup, large-volume basis, offer goods at prices that are difficult for the cooperative to match. Nevertheless, consumer cooperatives are a significant economic force in many European countries.

In the United States, marketing cooperatives are most prevalent in agriculture. These are associations through which producers jointly sell their products under an umbrella name, such as Sunkist for oranges. Over 5,000 cooperatives in the United States market farm commodities and provide farm supplies. In addition some 11,000 credit unions exist, through which members can save and borrow money.

Competition in the U.S. Economy

In a market economy, production and distribution are governed by a multitude of independent decisions made by individuals and businesses. Buyers express their demand for particular goods and services through their dollar votes. Some buyers with more dollars will outbid others to obtain the particular goods or services they desire.

Producers in a market economy seek the business of individual buyers by underpricing other firms, by putting out a better product, or by giving better service. Competition among producers restricts any firm from charging an excessive price. Competition among consumers for products helps each company receive a reasonable price for its product. Competition among firms often leads to more and better products for consumers at lower prices. Competition is also responsible for new products, new techniques, and improved services. Thus, competition acts as the market regulator of the economic system.

Competition also implies freedom—that is, freedom to enter or to go out of business. It provides the opportunity to make a profit, but it does not insure against losses. Under competition, people are free to decide how they want to use their labor and whether they want to work for themselves or for someone else. The right to choose the type of work they desire is limited only by their qualifications. Landowners are free to use their land or to rent it to others, and owners of capital are free to use their capital or to loan it to others in return for interest. Entrepreneurs are free to combine the labor, land, and capital of others, if they pay the owners of these resources for their use.

In a market economy, workers compete against each other for jobs, and they frequently change jobs. Firms compete against each other for sales. New firms continually come into existence, and old firms go out of business. New ideas, new products, and new services constantly appear on the market, each competing for the consumer's dollar. In a market system, the consumer is sovereign. The consumer approves or disapproves of products by deciding to buy or not to buy them.

The degree of competition that exists in one economy compared with another varies greatly. Even within a particular economy, the amount of competition varies among different industries. Furthermore, markets do not fit the model of pure competition described in textbooks. Various qualifications, restrictions, and regulations are imposed—voluntarily or involuntarily—on individuals and firms in a market economy. Monopolies and oligopolies, as we shall see in later chapters, exert pressure on prices and output. Labor unions modify the free operation of labor and wage markets, while governments regulate many industries directly or indirectly.

GOVERNMENT-REGULATED MARKETS

Frequently, a market for a good or service may be more orderly and may serve the consuming public better if the firms involved are regulated to some degree by a government agency. Public utilities have traditionally fallen into this category. In the past, it has been in society's best interest to grant one firm a monopoly to supply water, gas, electricity, telephone service, transportation, or some other service for the entire community than to permit free competition in these fields. In exchange for the *franchise* that gives a firm a monopoly, the public service commission of the state or community maintains regulatory powers over the firm, to ensure that it charges reasonable prices and provides adequate service. However, with widespread changes in technology, several long-standing natural monopolies, such as the telephone and electric utility industries, have been deregulated. As a result, many companies find themselves facing intense competition.

Numerous industries in the United States are regulated in one form or another. For example, agricultural markets in the United States are regulated in large part by the U.S. Department of Agriculture. Airlines are regulated for safety by the Federal Aviation Administration. The sale of stocks and bonds and the operation of the banking industry are closely regulated by the Securities and Exchange Commission and the Federal Reserve. At the local level, the number of taxicabs operating in cities is controlled by local governments, and state governments control the number of establishments that can serve alcoholic beverages.

In addition to regulating certain markets, the government occasionally enters a business directly, as in the delivery of first-class mail. At other times, the government enters a business indirectly. For example, the government plans and funds multipurpose water projects that provide electricity, flood control, and irrigation.

MIXED ECONOMY

Mixed Economy
An economy that contains a mixture of perfect and imperfect competition and of regulated and unregulated industries.

In the United States, the determination of what to produce, how much to produce, how much to charge for finished products, and what compensation to offer to the resources is generally based on the free decisions of individuals and firms. Nonetheless, the U.S. economy is a **mixed economy,** which is an economy that contains a mixture of perfect and imperfect competition and of regulated and unregulated industries. Thus, even though the market economy is characterized by competition and freedom, the competition is not perfect and the freedom is not unqualified. For example, some decisions regarding output—such as the building of roads, schools, and municipal buildings—are made by federal, state, and local governments. Likewise, the use of labor in and outside the armed services is determined in part by military authorities.

Regulated public utilities operate alongside unregulated industries; monopolies coexist with highly competitive firms; giant corporations compete with small sole proprietorships; the government regulates some private industries and not others; and government operations occasionally compete with the private sector. Because the U.S. economy sustains many types of competition and includes both free and regulated markets, we are justified in referring to it as mixed.

The Changing Role of Government in the U.S. Economy

The concept of a mixed economy brings into focus an important question: What should the role of the government be in the economy? Should it be active or passive? Should it regulate or not regulate? Should it engage directly in business or refrain from doing so? Should it encourage business activity or not? Historically, the role of the government in the U.S. economy has been one of nonintervention, but over the long run the tendency has been toward increased government involvement.

ECONOMIC LIBERALISM

Economic liberalism was the prevailing economic philosophy in much of the nineteenth and early twentieth centuries, and the U.S. economy developed within its framework. **Economic liberalism** promoted freedom of action for the individual and the firm through the doctrines of free trade, self-interest, private property, laissez-faire, and competition.

According to this philosophy, individuals were free to seek their own occupations, to enter any business, and to act as they saw fit to improve their economic welfare. Economic society was held together by mutual exchanges founded on the division of labor and prompted by self-interest. Self-interest was thus the motivating force of the economy. For example, to increase personal economic welfare, an individual might decide to produce goods and sell them for a profit. But, in so doing, that individual automatically benefited the community as well—by purchasing raw materials, providing employment, and supplying goods or services. Workers seeking to increase their wages could do so by increasing productivity. This, too, benefited the employer and the community in general. According to Adam Smith (often called the father of economics), the individual, in seeking personal gain, was led by an invisible hand to promote the welfare of the whole community.

Under economic liberalism, individuals were free to engage in the trade, occupation, or business they desired. Workers were free to move from one job to another and to enter into or exit from any industry. Workers were free to work or not to work, and businesses were free to produce or not to produce.

Competition was the regulator of the economy under economic liberalism. Businesses competed with one another for consumer trade by developing new and better products and by selling existing products at lower prices. Free entry into the market ensured ample competition, and prices were determined by the free forces of supply and demand. Competitive forces determined not only the prices of goods and services but also wage rates.

Because a beneficial self-interest was the motivating and driving force of the economy and because competition was to serve as the regulator of the economy, a policy of **laissez-faire** (or no government intervention) prevailed. According to this policy, the government kept its hands off the economic activities of individuals and businesses. Its economic role was strictly to protect private property, to enforce contracts, and to act as an umpire in economic disputes.

In theory, economic liberalism was a sound philosophy, and the U.S. economy prospered under it. But it was not without its weaknesses. The most pronounced weaknesses were its dependence on the beneficial effects of self-interest and its undue reliance on competition to regulate the economy and promote the general

Economic Liberalism
An economic philosophy that promoted freedom of action for the individual and the firm through the doctrines of free trade, self-interest, private property, laissez-faire, and competition.

Laissez-Faire
A policy of no government intervention in the economic activities of individuals and businesses.

welfare. Unfortunately, self-interest in many cases translated into greed and abuse of economic liberty. At the same time, competition proved to be an inadequate guarantor of the free market.

Certain individuals and firms began interfering with the economic freedom of others. In the name of economic liberalism and under the guise of competition, large firms began exploiting small firms. Markets were controlled and consumers exploited. Competition for work pushed wages down, and the market wage employers paid was often less than the subsistence level. In stressing the individual aspect of private property, economic liberalism too often ignored the social aspect of economics.

GOVERNMENT INTERVENTION

Government intervention was and is necessary to remedy the inequities that developed under economic liberalism. Many of our railroad and subsequent interstate commerce regulations were designed to restrain the harmful actions of carriers. The antitrust laws are necessary to prevent the undermining of competition by monopolies and cartels. Labor laws are essential to protect the rights of workers. Public utility regulation is needed to prevent consumer exploitation; food and drug laws are designed to protect the health of citizens; antipollution measures are established to preserve the environment; and safety regulations are enforced to protect workers from injury.

In addition, the government has increasingly used socioeconomic legislation designed to promote the common good. The Social Security Act, for example, provides aid to survivors of workers, pensions and medical care for the aged, and compensation for the seriously disabled. Another part of that act set up a system of unemployment compensation. Fair employment practices acts help prevent discrimination with respect to job opportunities. Consumer product safety laws keep hazardous products off the market.

Today, virtually no area of importance in the U.S. economy is unaffected by legislation. There is little doubt that the amount of government regulation, restriction, and intervention in the economy is substantial. Certainly, we no longer have free markets to the extent advocated by nineteenth-century economic liberalism. Although much of the government intervention in the economy is necessary to correct abuses or to promote the general welfare, some of it may be unnecessary. Sometimes it is difficult to determine whether government action is needed.

DEREGULATION AND PRIVATIZATION

In an attempt to let market incentives play a greater role in determining the production of goods and services, the U.S. government began removing government regulations from several industries in the 1970s. The drive to deregulate these industries stemmed from growing evidence that society would be better served if competition prevailed. Under the umbrella of various federal agencies, regulated industries had little incentive to lower costs, reduce prices, or maximize service.

During the 1970s, the Civil Aeronautics Board, the federal agency that regulated airfares and service, was slowly phased out. As a result, airlines are free to set fares and provide service according to conditions in the marketplace. With the deregulation of the railroad and trucking industries shortly thereafter, the Interstate Commerce Commission was eliminated. These legislative actions created a transportation industry that is more flexible and more efficient in meeting the needs of customers. In the banking and finance area, the Securities and Exchange Commission eliminated regulatory control over brokerage fees charged by stockbrokers, an act that allows for greater competition among brokerage firms. With the passage of the Depository Institutions Deregulation and Monetary Control Act of 1980, interest-rate ceilings on deposits were removed. Continued deregulation permitted savings and loan institutions to offer many financial services similar to those of commercial banks. Legislation in 1999 eliminated restrictions on interstate branch banking in the United States.

One of the most significant acts of deregulation occurred in the telecommunications industry with the breakup of the American Telephone and Telegraph Company in 1982. Under the decree, AT&T was required to divest itself of its 22 local telephone companies, which were then formed into seven independent companies known as "Baby Bells." Consumers of long-distance telephone service now can select any supplier they wish.

Deregulation is not without its costs. As witnessed in the airline and banking industries, many firms that thrived in a regulated environment failed in a competitive one. Job reductions have occurred with increased frequency as companies strive to lower costs. For example, AT&T eliminated 40,000 positions in 1996, 5,000 in 2001, and another 5,000 in 2002. In some previously regulated industries, even those who continue to be employed are earning less. Also, some consumers who previously benefited from subsidized prices are now paying higher prices that more accurately reflect cost of service. Overall, however, deregulation has provided customers more choices and at prices lower than would be the case under regulation.

Along with deregulation, governments everywhere have been engaging in the privatization of economic services. **Privatization** refers to the shifting of government economic functions or services to the private sector of the economy. Privatization may occur in several ways. Perhaps the most dramatic form of privatization occurs when a government sells a company it owns to the private sector, an act often described as "denationalization." Denationalization usually takes place through auctions or widespread public stock offerings. Since the early 1990s, a number of countries have sold off government-owned assets. The Netherlands divested itself of some 30 percent of its postal and communications monopoly, Poland sold off over 400 state-owned enterprises, and the Czech Republic denationalized approximately 2,000 companies. During the same period, France sold off ownership in Air France, its national airline, while Great Britain privatized Heathrow and Gatwick airports in London as well as a number of railway lines and transportation systems.

NET*Link*

How did deregulation affect the telecommunications industry? Examine the AT&T, MCI, and Verizon home pages. What do they have in common? Are the services they are offering different? Set your browser to URL:

http://www.att.com
http://www.mci.com
http://www.verizon.com

Privatization
The shifting or returning of government economic functions or services to the private sector of the economy.

In the United States, large-scale divestitures by the federal government occur less frequently because it owns a much smaller share of the economy than governments elsewhere. Because of this, privatization activity in the United States is more prevalent at the state and local government levels than at the federal level. Privatization at these levels usually involves competitive bidding by private contractors or the direct sale of assets. State governments have privatized a number of services, including utilities, data processing, prison management, child foster care, and even worker compensation insurance. At the local level, practically all assets or services that a local government owns or provides have been privatized somewhere in the United States. That includes garbage collection, fire protection, certain elements of police protection, park maintenance, sewage treatment, parking garage management, computer operations, street lighting, snow removal, hospitals, jails, tree trimming, and even cemeteries. One of the more emotionally charged areas of privatization at the local level involves public education. Baltimore, New York, Milwaukee, Chicago, and Philadelphia are among a growing number of cities that have turned over public schools to private contractors.

Privatization may also involve subsidizing individuals to enable them to buy goods and services from the private sector. A case in point is the federal food stamp program. Rather than own and operate farms and soup kitchens, the federal government issues food stamps to low-income families that can be used to purchase food from private stores.

The underlying rationale for privatization is that private enterprise can provide certain goods and services more efficiently and less expensively than the government. In developing nations, additional goals include expanding their private enterprise sectors, attracting foreign capital to stimulate economic growth, and generating much-needed government revenues. South American countries, in particular, have benefited financially from the sale of assets. For example, Brazil received over $103 billion over the ten-year period ending in 2001 from the sale of assets to private investors, and Argentina earned $15 billion in 1999 from its privatizing activities. Latin American and Caribbean countries account for 77 percent of the revenues generated by developing countries from privatization. Most of the revenues are derived from the sale of telecommunication and electric energy companies. However, privatization is also growing rapidly in Asia. In 2002, China announced it was seeking to raise in excess of $10 billion by privatizing government-owned assets. Although privatization is taking place throughout the world, very little is taking place in Africa and the Middle East.

In the United States, privatization is entering a new phase aimed at important and highly controversial programs. One such program at the federal level is Social Security. Various studies are now calling for replacing the present system with one based on forced savings. According to most such plans, individuals would choose a fund manager who would then invest their funds in individual retirement accounts. Those opposed to privatizing Social Security consider such plans radical and financially perilous for future retirees. However, the movement is gaining momentum, for other countries throughout the world either have some form of a privatized system in place or are contemplating implementing one. Australia, for one, completed the implementation of its program in 2002. Under the Australian plan, employees can contribute up to 9 percent of wages into a private fund of their choice. The Australian system was enacted with goals similar to those sought by proponents in the United States—namely, to provide more retirement income for future retirees, to increase national savings, and to reduce long-term pressures on the national budget. Chile has had a privatized social security program in place since 1980. Another potential target for privatization is the U.S. Postal Service. It has long been criticized for alleged inefficiencies and waste, and some proponents of privatization are calling for the sale of the entire operation to private enterprise, while others seek to break up the Postal Service into regional private companies, as occurred with the breakup of AT&T.

Goals for the U.S. Economy

A number of goals for the U.S. economy have been established by private and government agencies. Originally, these goals did not constitute hard-and-fast objectives that had to be accomplished; rather, they suggested targets for the economy to aim toward. More recently, however, most of these goals have been incorporated into statutory law. There are five primary economic goals: (1) full employment, (2) stable prices, (3) economic growth, (4) a balanced budget, and (5) equilibrium in the international balance of payments. These goals are supplemented by numerous other goals, such as preservation of the environment, elimination of poverty, equal employment opportunity, and improvement in the quality of life.

FULL EMPLOYMENT

Full employment describes the condition in which 95 to 96 percent of the U.S. civilian labor force is employed. This allows for 4 to 5 percent frictional unemployment. In part, frictional unemployment involves instances where individual workers quit, get fired, are in transit from one part of the country to another, or are temporarily laid off. Consequently, we can always expect some slack, or unemployment, in the labor force. Nonetheless, for all practical purposes, we consider ourselves at full employment when unemployment is 5 percent or less.

STABLE PRICES

Stable prices prevail when the Consumer Price Index, which measures changes in the cost of living for a typical family, moves 2 percent or less in either direction in a year's time. Changes of more than this amount can have substantial effects on the purchasing power of families and on the value of the dollar. In fact, the Full Employment and Balanced Growth Act of 1978 requires a movement toward a zero rate of inflation.

ECONOMIC GROWTH

The economy requires a healthy rate of economic growth. Total output must grow if we are to absorb the millions of new workers who enter the labor force annually and those who are displaced each year as a result of technological change. If we produced the same level of output each year, instead of increasing, the economy would have fewer jobs, growing unemployment, and a decline in the per capita income of the nation. To maintain or increase the existing standard of living and to prevent unemployment from rising, we must increase real gross domestic product continuously.

Higher rates of employment and substantial per capita output gains seem to occur when the real economic growth rate exceeds 3 percent. Recent experience indicates that with a real growth rate of less than 2.5 percent, the U.S. economy suffers from higher unemployment and limited gains in per capita output and income. For example, unemployment in April, 2000 was 3.8 percent of the labor force. But by late 2002, unemployment exceeded 5.8 percent of the labor force. Why did this happen? Simply because the real output of goods and services declined in 2001. New entrants into the labor force (plus many of those displaced by technological change and a slow-growth economy) could not be absorbed, so unemployment rose. Instead of rising in 2001, the real GDP actually fell for much of the year. Even though economic growth resumed in late 2001, and continued throughout 2002, growth rates were insufficient to reduce the level of unemployment.

BALANCED BUDGET

Although a balanced budget has been a long-standing goal of the U.S. economy, it has been a difficult goal to meet. Prior to fiscal year 1998, the United States experienced budget deficits in all but one year since 1960. Deficits in the annual budget reached an all-time high in fiscal year 1992 when the federal government spent $290 billion more than it received in revenue. These deficits were caused by wars, recessions, discretionary government spending, and rapidly expanding entitlement programs. A general consensus exists that over the long run the federal government, like the household and the private business firm, should be fiscally responsible by keeping expenditures in line with revenues. Chronic deficits in the federal budget can bring about numerous long-term problems for the U.S. economy, both at home and abroad.

The federal government experienced a budget surplus of $69 billion in fiscal year 1998, the first such surplus since 1969. Budget surpluses continued during the next three fiscal years, due to the continued expansion of the U.S. economy. However, this string of budget surpluses came to an end in FY2002. The economic recession, which began in March, 2001, the September 11 attack on the United States, and the war against terrorism produced deficits once again in the federal budget.

BALANCE-OF-PAYMENTS EQUILIBRIUM

Economies throughout the world have become more and more interdependent. For this reason, events abroad can have a pronounced effect on the U.S. economy, and vice versa. This leads to the fifth major economic goal: equilibrium in the international balance of payments. If the value of U.S. exports equals the value of U.S. imports, the inflow and outgo of currencies will be in balance; as a result, the international value of the U.S. dollar will remain stable.

After decades of having a surplus balance of payments, the United States has experienced chronic balance of payments deficits since 1982. At the same time, wide fluctuations have occurred in the international value of the U.S. dollar. During the 1980s, Americans bought record amounts of foreign-made goods. In addition, U.S. businesses purchased a larger percentage of raw materials (such as oil and steel) and manufactured components from abroad than ever before. The 1990s brought a significant increase in U.S. exports, but even larger increases in imports, a trend that continues today. Thus, large balance of payments deficits persist.

It is evident that some U.S. economic goals have been legislated and quantified. We will discuss these goals further as we progress through this book. Incidentally, other major industrial nations have similar goals and even coordinate their economic policies to achieve their objectives.

Other Economic Systems

Traditional Economy
An economy based on self-sufficiency, with barter as the form of trade.

Economies are often said to fall into three basic categories: (1) traditional economies, (2) market economies, and (3) command economies. A **traditional economy** is one based on self-sufficiency, with barter as the form of trade. The traditional economy answers the three basic questions as it always has for generations. What is produced is what members of the family have always produced. If a father is a hunter, a fisherman, a farmer, or a cobbler, then it is customary for his son to follow in his footsteps. Regardless of the specialized roles individuals play, production techniques will be the same as they have been for generations. As for the question of distribution, the harvest and the spoils of the hunt are distributed among the community as they always have been; the goods and services produced by cobblers, tanners, carpenters, and other tradesmen are exchanged as barter. Traditional economies are found in rural, nondeveloped countries. Some parts of Asia, Africa, South America, and the Middle East have traditional economies. In the United States, the Pennsylvania Dutch and Amish communities are patterned after traditional economies.

A *market economy* is what we have been describing throughout this chapter. Leading examples are the economies of the United States, Canada, and Switzerland. In market economies, decision making is exercised primarily by individuals and firms. Not all people (including some critics in the United States) are sold on the advantages of the market economy. Many feel that its disadvantages—such as recurring recessions, unemployment and poverty, occasionally wasteful use of resources, and unequal distribution of property and income—offset some of its advantages. As a result, some governments may prefer a more centralized economy.

Command Economy
An economy in which a central authority makes most of the economic decisions regarding production, distribution, and consumption.

In contrast to a market economy, a **command economy** is one in which a central authority makes most of the economic decisions regarding production, distribution, and consumption. Command economies are usually led by dictators or central planning boards and are centrally controlled to achieve certain objectives. In some cases, these objectives may be ideological. In other instances, the goal may be military power or a luxurious lifestyle for the controlling elite.

Communism, fascism, and socialism are three types of command economies. *Communism* embraces government ownership of land and capital and government regulation of distribution. Under pure communism, the government would hold and use all assets for the benefit of a classless society; private property would be nonexistent. As with the purely capitalistic system, pure communism is not practiced by any nation in the world today, although the command economy of Cuba is close to it.

There are, however, a large number of command economies operating within the framework of socialism. *Socialism* involves strict government regulation of production and distribution and is advocated as a way to promote equality and economic development. Socialist countries include authoritarian economies such as existed in Eastern Europe and the former Soviet Union, as well as the democratic socialist states of several Scandinavian countries. Sweden and Denmark are two examples of countries that have mixed capitalism with extensive social welfare benefits.

The third type of command economy is *fascism*, a system that combines monopoly capitalism, private property, and a strong, dictatorial central government. In essence, fascism is an authoritarian state imposed on a capitalist system. Spain, Portugal, Germany, and Italy are examples of countries that have had fascist economic systems during the twentieth century.

In the 1990s, several of the world's command economies moved toward political democracy and market economies. The drive for economic reform toppled communist regimes in Czechoslovakia, Poland, Romania, Hungary, East Germany, and, of course, the former Soviet Union. The movement toward market-driven economies continues in many parts of the world. Although still largely a command-type economic system, China is initiating a number of market-oriented reforms and is opening up the economy to the outside world.

Summary

- The three basic economic questions that pertain to every economic system are what to produce, how to produce, and who gets what is produced.

- Consumer demand determines the allocation and use of land, labor, and capital in a market economy. Profit serves as the incentive for entrepreneurs to combine productive resources to produce goods and services. Prices serve as a rationing device in distributing goods and services, allocating productive resources, and helping determine incomes.

- There are four dominant forms of business organization in the United States: the sole proprietorship, the partnership, the corporation, and the cooperative. Most firms are sole proprietorships, but each type of business structure has its own advantages and disadvantages.

- Competition is the regulator of the market system. Although competition dominates the U.S. economy, some markets are regulated to achieve some desired goal. Because the United States has a complex mixture of competition, regulated and unregulated markets, and private and government businesses, it is said to have a mixed economy.

- The U.S. economy developed within the framework of economic liberalism. The main tenets of this philosophy were free trade, self-interest, private property, laissez-faire, and competition. Undue emphasis on self-interest, however, led to abuses and inequities, and competition proved to be an inadequate regulator. To correct these inequities, government intervention was required. As a result, the United States has moved a considerable distance away from the laissez-faire aspect of economic liberalism.

- Recent years have seen extensive deregulation and privatization of government assets and services, not only in the United States but also in many parts of the world. At some state and local levels of government, services such as data processing, prison management, garbage collection, snow removal, tree trimming, sewage treatment, fire protection, and public education have been privatized. At the federal level, Social Security is under discussion for possible privatization.

- The five generally accepted primary goals for the U.S. economy are full employment, stable prices, economic growth, a balanced budget, and equilibrium in the balance of payments. These are supplemented by numerous secondary goals.

- Three basic types of economic systems can be found throughout the world: traditional, market, and command economies. In recent years, more and more command economies have been moving toward market economies.

New Terms and Concepts

Market economy
Financial capital
Profit
Competition
Sole proprietorship
Partnership
Corporation

Cooperative
Mixed economy
Economic liberalism
Laissez-faire
Privatization
Traditional economy
Command economy

Discussion Questions

1. Discuss the importance of private property to the operation of a market economy.

2. How does consumer demand influence the determination of individual income?

3. How does the price system serve as a rationing mechanism?

4. What is the role of profit in a market economy?

5. Distinguish between a market economy and a command economy.

6. What are some advantages of the corporate form of business?

7. Briefly describe the philosophy of economic liberalism.

8. Describe a situation in which a high degree of competition may not be beneficial to consumers and to the economy in general.

9. How can an economy be a mixture of a market system and a command system? Can you give an example of such an economy?

10. Why are some nations moving away from a command economy toward more of a market economy?

Economic Applications

EconData

Look for and click on the EconData link at http://econapps.swlearning.com. Find the World Economy heading and click on "Comparative Economics Systems." Now that you have learned about the U.S. economy, this site will provide you with information about other economic systems.

3

CHAPTER REVIEW

4

Price: The Role of Demand and Supply

After studying Chapter 4, you should be able to:

1. Define *demand* and distinguish between a change in demand and a change in the quantity demanded.

2. Define *supply* and understand why a supply curve slopes upward to the right.

3. Explain what happens when a price is above or below the market price set by demand and supply.

4. Demonstrate what happens to price and quantity sold in response to changes in demand and supply.

5. Determine the possible results of price ceilings and price floors.

6. Explain the importance of elasticity and the concepts of elastic demand, inelastic demand, and unit elastic demand.

7. Understand the nature of cross elasticity, income elasticity, and the elasticity of supply.

In a market system, the interaction of supply and demand is relied on to determine prices. Consumers express their demand through the prices they are willing to pay for various products. Firms seeking profit cater to consumer demand by offering goods and services at various prices. Consequently, a market is established in which the final price of a good or service is determined on the basis of costs to the producer and utility to the buyer.

The Market Mechanism

Changes in either demand or supply bring about adjustments in the amount of goods sold or price changes, or both. If consumers throughout the nation, for example, begin buying more lawn mowers, retail outlets must order inventory replacements and additional mowers from wholesalers. Wholesalers, in turn, order more mowers from manufacturers, who begin producing more mowers. Depending on the available supply and the cost of resources, these additional mowers may be supplied at the same price or at a different price. At any rate, consumer demand is made known to the producers through the market structure. At other times, suppliers try to anticipate the demands of consumers and supply the goods before there is a strong expression of demand. The system does not work perfectly; at times gluts and shortages occur, and prices fluctuate. But considering the billions of items produced and sold each year, the market system does an excellent job of satisfying consumer demand.

Demand

When analyzing the influence of demand in the marketplace, it is important to recognize that the amount consumers will purchase is determined by a number of factors. The single most important of these factors is price.

LAW OF DEMAND

Law of Demand
The quantity of a good or service purchased is inversely related to the price, all other things being equal.

The critical relationship between the price of a good or service and the quantity demanded is expressed by the law of demand. The **law of demand** states that the quantity of a good or service purchased is inversely related to the price, all other things being equal. Thus, a lower price for a product increases the quantity demanded of that product, whereas a higher price decreases the quantity demanded of that product. The law of demand does not tell us how much quantity demanded is affected as a result of a change in price. It merely indicates an inverse relationship. As we shall see, it is the law of demand that accounts for the negative slope of the demand curve.

QUANTITY DEMANDED VERSUS DEMAND

Demand
A schedule of the total quantities of a good or service that purchasers will buy at different prices at a given time.

Individual Demand
The quantity of a good or service that an individual or firm stands ready to buy at various prices at a given time.

Market Demand
The sum of the individual demands in the marketplace.

To further clarify the law of demand, economists differentiate between the quantity demanded and demand. *Quantity demanded* refers to the quantities of a good or service that people will purchase at a specific price over a given period of time. **Demand** is a schedule of the total quantities that people will purchase at different prices at a given time. Demand implies something more than need or desire. An individual must also possess purchasing power if the need is to be satisfied. You may have a strong desire for a new Porsche, but unless you have the cash or credit to pay for it, your desire will have no influence on the market. **Individual demand,** then, refers to the quantity of a good or service that an individual or firm stands ready to buy at various prices. In other words, individual demand implies a desire backed up by purchasing power. **Market demand** is the sum of the individual demands in the marketplace.

DEMAND SCHEDULE AND DEMAND CURVE

Having established that the quantity demanded of a product varies inversely with its price, we can construct a hypothetical demand schedule. A **demand schedule** is a table showing the various quantities of a good or service that will be demanded at various prices. An accurate schedule of this kind for a specific good or service is difficult to construct because it requires knowing precisely how many units people would actually buy at various prices. Table 4–1 contains a hypothetical market demand schedule for computer time on the Internet during a particular month. Price per hour is presented in the first column, and the amount of time demanded per month at various hourly rates can be seen in columns 2–4. Notice that more time will be purchased at lower prices than at higher prices.

Figure 4–1 graphically represents the relationship between price and the amount of time demanded. The vertical axis indicates the price per hour, and the horizontal axis shows the number of hours demanded. To locate on Figure 4–1 the point for the demand for 5.1 million hours at $1.25 per hour, draw a horizontal line to the right from $1.25 and a vertical line upward from 5.1 million hours.

When all points have been located in this way, they suggest a curve that slopes downward to the right. If the changes in price and quantity were infinitely small, the resulting set of points of intersection would really form a continuous demand curve. A **demand curve** indicates the number of units of a good or service that consumers will buy at various prices at a given time. In effect, a demand curve is a graphic representation of a demand schedule. The demand curve can be either a straight or a curved line, it may have a slight or a steep slope, it may be continuous or discontinuous, and it may be smooth or jagged. These features depend on the nature of the demand for the particular product and the amount of information available to use in plotting the demand schedule. Consequently, there are all kinds and shapes of demand curves.

TABLE 4–1 Millions of Internet Hours That Will Be Demanded			
Price/Hour	D	D_1	D_2
$1.50	2.0	3.0	1.0
1.45	2.3	3.4	1.3
1.40	2.8	4.3	1.6
1.35	3.5	4.8	2.1
1.30	4.2	5.6	2.7
1.25	5.1	6.6	3.4
1.20	6.1	7.7	4.4
1.15	7.3	9.0	5.4
1.10	8.5	10.4	6.7
1.05	10.0	12.0	8.0

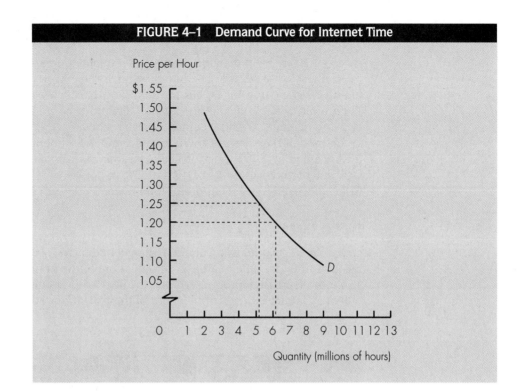

FIGURE 4–1 Demand Curve for Internet Time

CHANGES IN DEMAND

We have seen that on a typical demand curve more will be demanded at a lower price. Notice on the demand curve in Figure 4–1 that at a price of $1.25, a little more than 5 million hours of computer time would be demanded, but at a price of $1.20, more than 6 million hours of computer time would be demanded. Does this mean that if a price of $1.20 is charged instead of $1.25 there is an increase in demand? Absolutely not. Remember that we defined *demand* as a schedule of amounts that would be purchased at various prices at a given time. Even though changing the price from $1.25 to $1.20 results in a greater quantity demanded, this is not a change in demand. Nothing has happened to the demand schedule. We have simply moved to a lower price, and the quantity demanded has increased. This movement along the demand curve represents a **change in the quantity demanded,** and it occurs because the price of the product has changed.

Change in the Quantity Demanded
Movement along the demand curve that occurs because the price of the product has changed.

How does this differ from a change in demand? A **change in demand** is a shift in the entire demand curve because of changes in factors other than price. These factors were held constant when moving along a given demand curve to determine changes in the quantity demanded in response to changes in price. But if these factors are allowed to vary, demand will change. Thus, in Table 4–1, D_1 is a schedule showing an increase in demand from the schedule for D. When plotted, the

Change in Demand
A change in the amounts of the product that would be purchased at the same given prices; a shift of the entire demand curve.

demand curve for D_1 lies to the right of that for D, as shown in Figure 4–2. For example, it indicates that at a price of $1.25, the sum of 6.6 million hours will be pur-
chased. A decrease in demand means that a smaller quantity will be bought at each
price. In Table 4–1, D_2 is a schedule showing a decrease in demand from the schedule for D. The curve for D_2 lies to the left of that for D, as shown in Figure 4–2.
Thus, an increase in demand shifts the demand curve to the right, whereas a decrease in demand shifts the demand curve to the left.

Although they are not the only determinants of demand, the following four
factors are generally thought to be most important in addition to price: income,
taste and preferences, future expectations, and prices of related goods and services.
None, however, is more important than price.

DETERMINANTS OF DEMAND

Changes in income can bring about a change in demand. When people earn higher
incomes, they are able to afford not only more of the same goods and services but
also more expensive products they previously could not afford. For example, not
only may families increase the length of their vacations but they may also head to

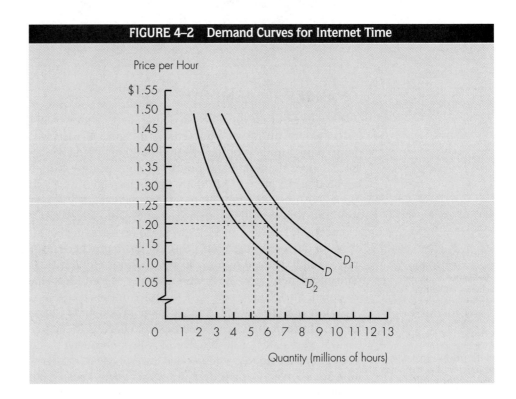

FIGURE 4–2   Demand Curves for Internet Time

Price per Hour

Quantity (millions of hours)

different destinations. A ten-day cruise in the Caribbean may replace a one-week camping trip in a nearby state park. Higher incomes may also result in family members eating out more often, but reduce the number of meals purchased at fast-food restaurants.

A shift in demand can also be brought about by a change in *taste and preferences.* A popular fashion item, such as cargo pants, may be out of style after one season, leaving retailers with unexpected excess inventories. In the automobile industry, the recent popularity of sport utility vehicles reflects a change in consumer preference for trucks. Despite higher prices, the sales of Explorers, Blazers, and Grand Cherokees have increased significantly, causing their demand curves to shift to the right.

Demand can increase or decrease as a result of *consumer expectations.* For example, if consumers believe that their incomes will rise in the near future, they are more inclined to buy more-expensive items today. Credit card and installment debt reflect consumer intentions to make monthly payments out of future income. On the other hand, if consumers are worried about losing their jobs, they are likely to postpone purchases of expensive items. Consumers can also cause a shift in demand if they anticipate a shortage of particular products—witness the shortage of many items in supermarkets immediately prior to the onset of snowstorms or hurricanes. A change in demand can occur if consumers believe price changes are forthcoming. Consumers will speed up purchases if prices are expected to rise and postpone purchases if prices are expected to fall.

The demand for one product may be affected by a change in the price of another. Some goods are *substitutes* for each other, and others are *complements.* Pepsi-Cola and Coca-Cola are highly substitutable products for many people. Thus, the demand for Pepsi may fall markedly with a sharp drop in the price of Coke. In the travel industry, complementary relationships exist among airlines, hotels, and rental car agencies. Thus, if the major airlines raise airfares substantially, the demand for rental cars at airports is likely to fall.

Supply
The total quantities of a good or service that sellers stand ready to sell at different prices at a given time.

Supply

Individual Supply
Quantities offered for sale at various prices at a given time by an individual seller.

Market Supply
Sum of the individual supply schedules in the marketplace.

Turning from our focus on the demand or buyers' side of the market, we can now direct our attention to the supply or sellers' side. **Supply** refers to the total quantities of a good or service that sellers stand ready to offer for sale at various prices at a given time. Supply does not refer to a single specific amount, but rather to a series of quantities. Instead, the specific amount that a seller would be willing to offer for sale at a particular price is referred to as the *quantity supplied.* The distinction between individual supply and market supply is similar to that which exists for demand. **Individual supply** is the quantities offered for sale at various prices at a given time by an individual seller, whereas **market supply** is the sum of the individual supply schedules in the marketplace.

SUPPLY SCHEDULE

As in the case of a demand schedule, it is useful for purposes of analysis to construct a supply schedule. The **supply schedule** is a table showing the various quantities that sellers will offer at various prices at a given time. Table 4–2 presents a hypothetical supply schedule for computer time on the Internet. A **supply curve** is a graphic representation of a supply schedule. It is a line showing the number of units of a good or service that will be offered for sale at different prices at a given time. The same method used to plot the demand curve for computer time can be used to plot the supply curve. This curve is labeled S in Figure 4–3. The **law of supply** states that the quantity offered by sellers of a good or service is directly related to price, all things being equal. Thus, the supply curve slopes upward from left to right, indicating that sellers are willing to offer more at a higher price than at a lower price. It must be noted that the law of supply is not a universal law, for there are exceptions. But the law holds true in nearly all cases. Whenever a supply curve is drawn, remember that everything else that might affect the quantities offered for sale is being held constant except for the price of the product.

CHANGES IN SUPPLY

As with demand, when price changes and a greater or lesser amount is offered for sale, there is no change in supply. Rather, there is movement along a given supply curve because the price of the product has changed. This constitutes a **change in the quantity supplied.** For a **change in supply** to occur, there must be a shift in the entire supply curve, indicating a change in the amount offered for sale at the same price. An increase in supply means that a larger amount is offered at the same price; a decrease in supply means that a smaller amount is offered (see Table 4–2). The supply curve for S_1, showing an increase in supply, lies to the right of that for S. The curve for S_2, showing a decrease in supply, lies to the left of that for S (see

TABLE 4–2 Millions of Internet Hours That Will Be Offered			
Price/Hour	S	S_1	S_2
$1.50	10.0	11.1	9.0
1.45	9.6	10.8	8.4
1.40	9.2	10.4	7.8
1.35	8.5	9.8	7.2
1.30	7.8	9.1	6.3
1.25	6.9	8.4	5.3
1.20	5.9	7.3	4.3
1.15	4.8	6.4	3.0
1.10	3.6	5.3	1.6

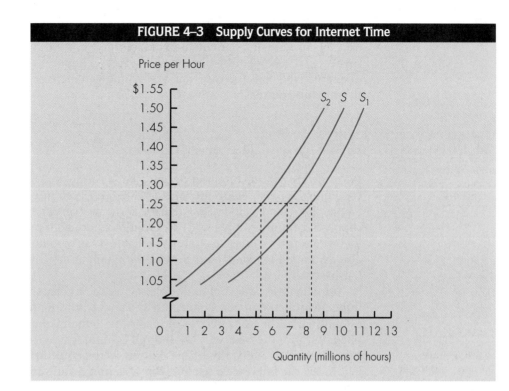

FIGURE 4–3 Supply Curves for Internet Time

Figure 4–3). Since price cannot cause a shift in the supply curve, other factors must be responsible. Possible causes include changes in the cost of production, changes in technology, expectations of future prices, and the prices of related products.

DETERMINANTS OF SUPPLY

Because the production of goods and services entails the use of productive resources, *changes in the cost of these resources* can result in a change in supply. If, for example, the cost of bricks increases sharply, the price of building brick homes will rise appreciably, and the supply of brick homes will decrease. *Technology* can also affect supply, for with improvements in technology products can be produced at a lower cost. This results in an increase in supply. An obvious example is agriculture. Sophisticated farm machinery, powerful fertilizers, and scientific applications to increase crop yields have lowered the cost of production and increased the supply of farm products. *Expectations of future prices* can determine supply. The supply of computer scientists graduating from college in the year 2008 will be influenced by the salaries expected in the field by college students selecting academic career programs in 2004. Finally, the supply of a product can be determined by the *prices of related products*. If a supplier has the opportunity of using productive resources for more than one purpose, the relative market prices may determine supply. If the price of corn is rising and the individual farmer has the choice of planting corn or soybeans, the supply of soybeans will decrease. Supply will decrease when prices of alternative goods increase, and the supply will increase when prices of alternative products decrease.

How Demand and Supply Determine Price

With the growth in computer usage, a large number of Internet services provide consumers with access to the World Wide Web. Assume, in our hypothetical example, that on a given day the demand for computer time on the Internet and the supply of computer time on the Internet in a particular market are given in the *D* and *S* columns of Tables 4–1 and 4–2. Table 4–3 reproduces these schedules. It is also assumed that consumers purchase time on an hourly basis, rather than on a flat-fee basis.

At what price will computer time sell on the Internet? The price will be determined by the interaction of demand and supply. More precisely, the price will be established at the point where the quantity demanded equals the quantity supplied. Because the market is cleared (all computer time supplied is purchased) at this price and quantity, this price is known as the **equilibrium price.**

Equilibrium Price
The price at which the quantity demanded equals the quantity supplied.

To see the interactive relationship of demand and supply, consider the superimposed demand and supply curves for the *D* and *S* schedules in Figure 4–4. These curves intersect at a point that indicates a price of $1.21 and a quantity of 6 million hours. What is the significance of this? It simply means that at a price of $1.21, 6 million hours of computer time will be offered for sale and an equal amount will be bought.

TABLE 4–3 Demand and Supply Schedules for Internet Time (Millions of Hours)		
Price/Hour	Demand	Supply
$1.50	2.0	10.0
1.45	2.3	9.6
1.40	2.8	9.2
1.35	3.5	8.5
1.30	4.2	7.8
1.25	5.1	6.9
1.20	6.1	5.9
1.15	7.3	4.8
1.10	8.5	3.6
1.05	10.0	2.0

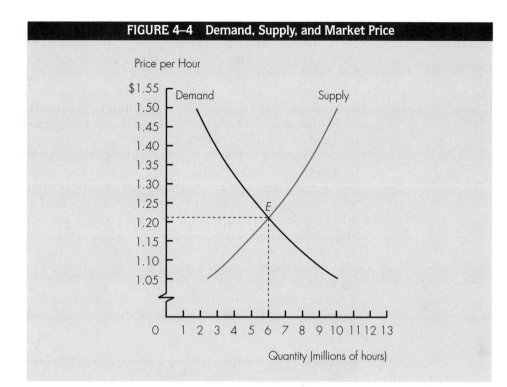

FIGURE 4–4   Demand, Supply, and Market Price

Price per Hour

Demand / Supply / E / Quantity (millions of hours)

Under these conditions of demand and supply, if the price were anything other than $1.21, the quantity of computer time that consumers would be willing to buy and the amount of computer time offered for sale would be out of balance. In such a situation, forces of the market would come into play to adjust the price to $1.21 (the equilibrium level). At a price of $1.25, for instance, the quantity of time that sellers would be willing to supply would exceed by approximately 2 million hours the quantity demanded by consumers. Consequently, not all the computer time would be sold. But notice that some sellers are willing to sell their time at lower prices of $1.24, $1.23, and so forth. Rather than hold onto their time off the market, they will offer to sell at the lower prices. As the price is lowered, certain consumers come forward who would not pay $1.25 for computer time but will pay $1.24, $1.23, or less. Therefore, as the market conditions push the price of computer time downward, the number of sellers decreases and the number of consumers increases until the amount of computer time offered for sale and the quantity purchased come into balance at the equilibrium price of $1.21.

On the other hand, if a price of $1.15 existed, the market would again be out of equilibrium. At that price the quantity demanded would exceed the quantity supplied by more than 2 million hours, and some potential consumers would have to go without. But some consumers are willing to pay more than $1.15 for an hour of computer time. Rather than do without, they will offer higher prices of $1.17, $1.19, and upward. As they bid the price upward, a twofold action takes place in the market. The higher prices deter some consumers from making purchases and induce more sellers to offer their services for sale. The resulting increase in the amount offered for sale and decrease in the amount purchased finally bring supply and demand into balance at the equilibrium price of $1.21. In a free market, no other price can prevail, because at any other price either a surplus or a shortage of the good would exist in the short run, as shown in Figure 4–5.

For the price to remain at other than the market price established by the free forces of supply and demand, the market has to be rigged or the forces of supply and demand changed. This is exactly what happens when the government sets a price for certain agricultural products that is higher than the market price or establishes a ceiling price that is lower than the market price during wartime. Business firms charged with price fixing are often guilty of collusion with other firms in an effort to interfere with free market forces. Similarly, the Organization of Petroleum Exporting Countries (OPEC) tries to limit the output of oil in order to raise its market price.

Under free market conditions, the number of possible relationships between demand and supply is practically infinite. For instance, demand may increase while

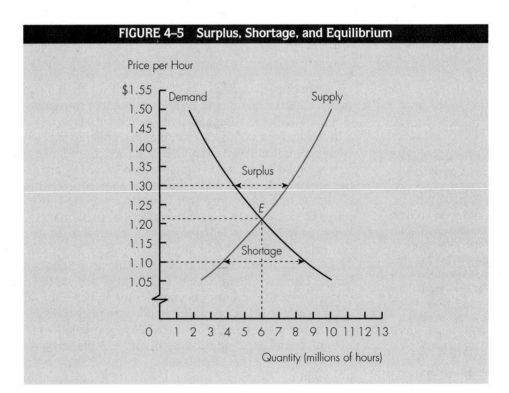

FIGURE 4–5   Surplus, Shortage, and Equilibrium

supply remains constant, or vice versa. Or demand may increase while supply decreases, or vice versa. Or both demand and supply may increase, with one increasing more rapidly than the other.

In any case, however, we can rely on this simple principle: In any new relationship between demand and supply, an increase in demand relative to supply
will result in a higher price, and any decrease in demand relative to supply will result in a lower price. On the other hand, an increase in supply will lower the price,
and a decrease in supply will raise the price, other things remaining unchanged
(see Figure 4–6). Based on these principles, it is easy to visualize why world oil
prices rise sharply when OPEC successfully imposes a petroleum export embargo.
The decreased supply of oil, coupled with increasing demand, can lead to substantially higher world oil prices.

Price Ceilings and Price Floors

We have seen in the previous discussion that as long as the impersonal forces of
supply and demand are allowed to operate freely, an equilibrium position will result that will clear the market. In other words, there will be no surpluses or shortages resulting from market forces. But what happens if there are price controls that
restrict market adjustments? Price controls can take the form of price ceilings or
price floors.

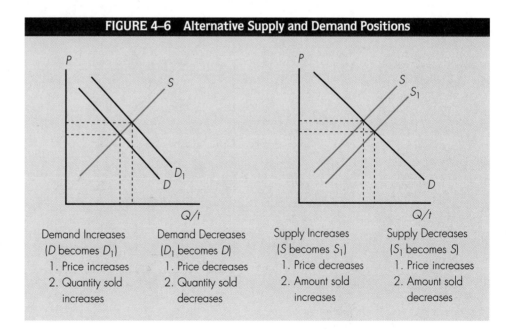

FIGURE 4–6   Alternative Supply and Demand Positions

Demand Increases (D becomes D_1)	Demand Decreases (D_1 becomes D)	Supply Increases (S becomes S_1)	Supply Decreases (S_1 becomes S)
1. Price increases	1. Price decreases	1. Price decreases	1. Price increases
2. Quantity sold increases	2. Quantity sold decreases	2. Amount sold increases	2. Amount sold decreases

Price Ceiling
A government-mandated maximum price that can be changed for a good or service.

A **price ceiling** is a government-mandated maximum price that can be charged for a good or service. At one time or another, the federal government has implemented price ceilings on gasoline, interest rates, and interstate shipments of natural gas. Local governments, including New York City, have enacted price ceilings in the form of rent controls on apartment dwellings.

The effects of price ceilings on the rents of apartment housing can be seen in Figure 4–7. At a monthly rental cost of $700, supply and demand are in equilibrium at 30,000 housing units. However, if local housing authorities enact rent controls that prohibit rents from rising above $500 per month, there will be a shortage of housing units. At that price, the quantity demanded of rental units increases, in accordance with the law of demand, to 40,000 units. At the same time, the amount of units offered to renters decreases to 18,000 units, following the law of supply. Figure 4–7 shows that as a result of price controls in the form of a price ceiling, the housing market is short a total of 22,000 units at the price of $500 per month. If the price ceiling were above the equilibrium price of $700 per month, the price ceiling would have no effect on the market. The purpose of rent control is to make housing more affordable to a greater number of lower-income families. However, as can be seen in this analysis, rent controls serve to reduce housing opportunities to those families they are intended to accommodate.

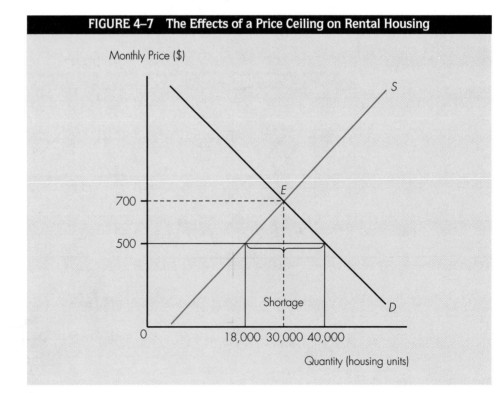

FIGURE 4–7   The Effects of a Price Ceiling on Rental Housing

Price Floor
A government-mandated minimum price that can be changed for a good or service.

If a government authority establishes a minimum price that can be charged for a good or service, this is known as a **price floor.** Two well-known examples of price floors are the federal minimum wage and agricultural price supports. In the case of agriculture, price floors seek to support farm incomes by mandating minimum prices for a number of farm products. Hypothetical supply and demand curves are shown in Figure 4–8. The market-clearing equilibrium price is $2.00 per bushel. At that price 100,000 bushels will be offered for sale and will be purchased in the market.

If the federal government sets a minimum price below which the price of a bushel of wheat cannot fall, a surplus of wheat can result. In Figure 4–8, the government-regulated price of $3.00 is above the market clearing price of $2.00. At this price, farmers are willing to offer 115,000 bushels for sale. But at the higher price, buyers are willing to purchase only 75,000 bushels. The result of the price floor on wheat is a surplus of 40,000 bushels. Agricultural price floors in the United States have resulted in huge surpluses of a number of crops. Because the federal government induces farmers to produce more than consumers are willing to buy at that price, the government must buy and store surplus crops at the public's expense. Note, however, that if the minimum price is below the equilibrium price of $2.00 per bushel the price floor has no effect in the market.

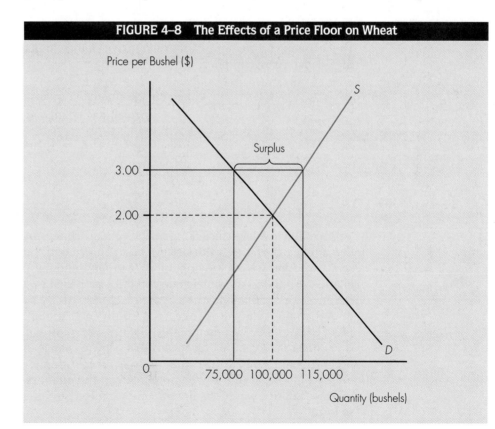

FIGURE 4–8   The Effects of a Price Floor on Wheat

Price Elasticity of Demand

Sellers are often faced with the problem of determining a price at which to offer goods for sale. It is true that a greater amount can be sold at lower prices. But will the greater revenue from the larger sales offset the reduced revenue from the lower price? Fortunately, there is a way to measure the change in relationship between price and amount sold. **Price elasticity of demand** is a measure of the sensitivity or responsiveness of quantity demanded to a change in price. The reaction of consumers to an increase or decrease in price depends on the degree of price elasticity.

Price Elasticity of Demand
A measure of the sensitivity or responsiveness of quantity demanded to a change in price.

MEASURING PRICE ELASTICITY OF DEMAND

We will investigate price elasticity of demand by considering three demand curves and measuring their elasticities. In Figure 4–9, for the demand schedule D, 1,600 units would be sold at the price of $10; but if the sale price were only $8, the number of units sold would be 2,000. Elasticity may be measured in either of two ways: the formula method or the total revenue method.

Formula Method

The following formula measures the relative change in quantity demanded against the relative change in price:

$$\text{Price elasticity} = \frac{\text{percentage change in quantity demanded}}{\text{percentage change in price}}$$

$$= \frac{\dfrac{Q_2 - Q_1}{(Q_1 + Q_2)/2}}{\dfrac{P_2 - P_1}{(P_1 + P_2)/2}}$$

This method involves calculating the percentage change by using an average of the beginning and ending values as the base. This makes the percentage change the same, whether we are moving up or down on the price axis. In our example (see Figure 4–9), the $2 absolute change in price is divided by $9 (the average price between $10 and $8), giving us a figure of 22 percent. By using an average base, we find that the relative change in quantity demanded is likewise 22 percent (400/1,800 = 0.22). Consequently, the measure of price elasticity of demand here is 1.0 (0.22/0.22 = 1.0). This means that a given change in price will bring about a proportional change in the quantity sold. For example, a 1 percent decrease in price would result in a 1 percent increase in the quantity demanded, a 3 percent increase in price would result in a 3 percent decrease in quantity demanded, and so forth.

Economists ignore the minus sign and just look at the absolute value of the elasticity coefficient determined by the formula. **Unit elastic demand** exists when a percentage change in price causes an equal percentage change in quantity demanded. It has an elasticity coefficient equal to 1.0 and is the borderline between elastic and inelastic demand. An elasticity coefficient greater than 1.0 indicates an elastic demand, and anything less than 1.0 indicates an inelastic demand. **Elastic demand** exists when a percentage change in price causes a greater percentage change in quantity demanded. **Inelastic demand** exists when a percentage change in price is greater than the percentage change in quantity demanded.

Now let us measure the elasticity for the demand schedule D_1 in Figure 4–9. When the price is changed from $10 to $8, a 22 percent change using the formula, the quantity demanded increases from 1,600 to 2,400 units, an increase of 40 percent ($800/2,000 = 0.40$). In this case, the elasticity coefficient is 1.8 ($0.40/0.22 = 1.8$). Thus, a 2 percent change in price, for example, will result in a 3.6 percent change in the quantity demanded. In short, consumer demand is elastic, and the percentage change in quantity demanded will be greater than the percentage change in price. Demand schedule D_2 shows less consumer responsiveness to a change in price. Here a 22 percent decrease in price from $10 to $8 results in a mere 11 percent increase in quantity demanded. This computes to an elasticity coefficient of 0.5, indicating that the demand is inelastic and that a change in price will bring about a less than proportional change in the amount demanded. Every 1 percent increase in price will result in a 0.5 percent change in the quantity demanded.

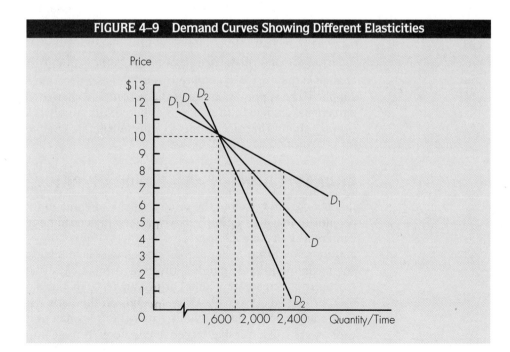

FIGURE 4–9   Demand Curves Showing Different Elasticities

Total Revenue Method

Why is this information about elasticity, inelasticity, and the coefficients of 1.8, 0.5, and 1.0 important? To the seller it is extremely important, because it indicates how total revenue received from the sale of products will be affected as prices increase or decrease. Likewise, it is important to the consumer. After all, the total revenue that sellers receive from the sale of products is nothing other than total expenditures for those products by consumers. From a given consumer's point of view, the more income spent on one good or service, the less there remains to be spent on others.

The total revenue method of measuring elasticity is less precise, but it tells more directly what happens to total revenue. Furthermore, it shows more clearly the importance of a coefficient of elasticity. This method can be summarized in three parts:

1. If price changes but total revenue remains constant, unit price elasticity of demand exists. In this case, the decrease in revenue resulting from a lower price is offset by the increase in revenue resulting from increased sales. If elasticity is 1.0, sales will increase in exact proportion to a price decrease.

2. If price changes but total revenue moves in the opposite direction, demand is elastic. In this case, the decrease in revenue from a lower price is more than offset by the increase in revenue from increased sales. When elasticity is more than 1.0, sales change in greater proportion than price does.

3. If price changes and total revenue move in the same direction, demand is inelastic. Owing to an elasticity of less than 1.0, the increase in revenue from higher sales will not make up for the loss in revenue from a lower price.

The measure of elasticity can be applied to supply, too. If a given percentage change in the price of a good results in a greater percentage change in the quantity supplied, the supply is elastic. If the percentage change in price results in a lesser percentage change in the quantity offered, the supply is inelastic. And if the percentage change in price results in a proportionate change in the quantity offered for sale, unit elastic supply exists.

CHARACTERISTICS AND RANGE OF PRICE ELASTICITY

It is not easy to calculate the price elasticity of demand for a product. First, it may be difficult to gather enough statistical data to determine how much of a good consumers will buy at each of a series of prices. But it can be and is being done more and more by firms. Second, if a price change is made in an effort to observe the change in quantity demanded, the analyst must be certain that no other changes (such as an increase in income) are taking place that also influence the demand.

The degree of price elasticity depends on the nature of the product or service. For example, is it a necessity or a luxury? Is it a small or large expenditure for the consumer? Is it a durable or perishable item? Is it a complementary or substitute

TABLE 4–4 Characteristics Affecting Price Elasticity of Demand	
Tend Toward Elastic Demand	**Tend Toward Inelastic Demand**
Luxuries	Necessities
Large expenditures	Small expenditures
Durable goods	Perishable goods
Substitute goods	Complementary goods
Multiple uses	Limited uses

item? How many uses are there for the item? The effects of these characteristics are summarized in Table 4–4.

The degree of elasticity may range from perfectly elastic to perfectly inelastic demand. Perfectly elastic demand (depicted as a straight horizontal line in Figure 4–10a) indicates that an infinite amount of the product could be sold without a change in price. Perfectly inelastic demand (represented by the straight vertical line in Figure 4–10b) indicates that the same amount would be purchased regardless of price. Most goods and services, of course, have a price elasticity lying somewhere between the two extremes. Perfectly unit elastic demand is shown in Figure 4–10c.

Unfortunately, except in the cases of perfectly horizontal and perfectly vertical demand curves, it is not possible to determine price elasticity by simply looking at the demand curve. In any straight-line, slanted demand curve, certain areas are elastic, others are inelastic, and some spot may be unit elastic. This can be clarified by referring to Figure 4–11. Notice on the demand line that a change in price from $9 to $8, a price change of less than 12 percent, brings about a change in quantity demanded from 10 to 20 units, an increase of 67 percent. At the lower end of the vertical axis, a price change from $2 to $1, a 67 percent change in price, results in an increase in quantity demanded from 80 to 90 units, a quantity change of less than 12 percent.

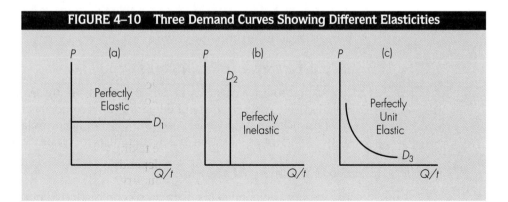

FIGURE 4–10   Three Demand Curves Showing Different Elasticities

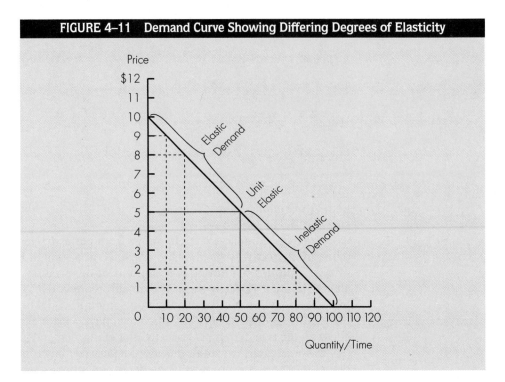

FIGURE 4–11   Demand Curve Showing Differing Degrees of Elasticity

At one end of the scale, we have a price elasticity of demand of more than 5.0; at the other end, we have a highly inelastic measure of less than 0.2. Thus, for any change in price through the range of $10 to $5 demand is elastic, but for any change in price from $5 to $1 demand is inelastic. Observe further that a point of unit elastic demand exists at $5. In fact, on our demand schedule, the point of maximum revenue for the seller is at $5, because both higher and lower prices will result in decreased revenue. For a demand schedule to be unit elastic throughout, it would have to be represented by a rectangular hyperbola, as shown in Figure 4–10c. In such a situation, percentage changes in price and quantity demanded are proportional throughout the curve.

OTHER TYPES OF ELASTICITY

In addition to price elasticity of demand, there are three other important types of elasticity: (1) cross elasticity of demand, (2) income elasticity of demand, and (3) price elasticity of supply. Each uses the same basic formula for calculating the elasticity coefficient as was used in determining price elasticity of demand.

Cross Elasticity of Demand

The quantity demanded of a particular good is affected not only by its price but also by the prices of related goods. If goods are related, they are classified as either substitutes or complements. *Substitute* goods are functionally equivalent goods, such as compact discs and quality tapes. *Complementary* goods are those goods that are used together, such as your economics course and this book. A change in the price of one product, if it is a substitute or complementary product, can affect the quantity demanded of the other. **Cross elasticity of demand** measures the effect of a change in the price of one product on the quantity demanded of another. The formula for calculating cross elasticity is as follows:

Cross Elasticity of Demand
A measure of the responsiveness of the quantity demanded of one product as a result of a change in the price of another product.

$$\text{Cross elasticity of demand} = \frac{\text{percentage change in the quantity demanded of product B}}{\text{percentage change in the price of product A}}$$

The coefficient of cross elasticity can be positive or negative. A positive coefficient implies that goods are substitutes, whereas a negative coefficient indicates that the goods are complementary. The larger the coefficient, the greater the cross elasticity is. Because most goods are unrelated, a coefficient of 0 is not uncommon.

Income Elasticity of Demand

The quantity demanded of a given good is affected by changes in consumer income. As income rises, so does the total demand for goods and services. However, the quantity demanded of individual goods does not necessarily rise proportionally with changes in income. In fact, in some cases the quantity demanded actually declines. **Income elasticity of demand** is a measure of the responsiveness of quantity demanded to a change in income. The formula for income elasticity is as follows:

Income Elasticity of Demand
A measure of the responsiveness of quantity demanded to a change in income.

$$\text{Income elasticity of demand} = \frac{\text{percentage change in quantity}}{\text{percentage change in income}}$$

The demand for most goods varies in the same direction as changes in income. Thus, most goods will have positive coefficients, and these are called *normal goods*. Some goods, however, have negative coefficients; that is, the demand varies inversely with changes in income. These goods are *inferior goods*. Home ownership is an example of a normal good, whereas intercity bus transportation is an inferior good. As before, the larger the coefficient is, the greater the responsiveness of quantity demanded to changes in income and the greater the elasticity. Coefficients of less than 1 are inelastic whether they are for normal or inferior goods.

Elasticity of Supply

Elasticity of Supply
A measure of responsiveness of quantity supplied to a change in price.

Like elasticity of demand, price elasticity of supply is an important tool in analyzing markets. **Elasticity of supply** is a measure of the sensitivity or responsiveness of quantity supplied to a change in price. The formula used to calculate price elasticity of supply is basically the same one used to measure price elasticity of demand. In this case, however, the change in quantity refers to a change in the quantity supplied. Because of the law of supply, you would expect to find a positive relationship between the change in price and the quantity supplied. If producers are responsive to price changes, supply is elastic and the coefficient will be greater than 1. If producers are relatively insensitive to price changes, supply is said to be inelastic and the coefficient will be fractional. The formula for elasticity of supply is

$$\text{Price elasticity of supply} = \frac{\text{percentage change in quantity supplied}}{\text{percentage change in price}}$$

An important factor determining the elasticity of supply is the amount of time that a producer has in which to adjust quantity in response to a change in price. Generally, the elasticity of supply increases the longer the amount of time that a producer has to vary productive resources and employ changes in technology.

TIME AND ELASTICITY OF SUPPLY

The relationship between time and elasticity of supply is shown in Figure 4–12. Assume the demand for the product increases suddenly and permanently from D to D_1. If the producers cannot adjust the quantity supplied on such short notice, the supply curve will be vertical and perfectly inelastic, as in Figure 4–12a. During this period the producer will sell the same quantity, but at a higher price. In agriculture, the farmer may have to wait until the next planting season to adjust the quantity supplied of a particular crop. Figure 4–12b shows the response of the producer who now has sufficient time to vary some productive resources. The supply curve becomes more elastic and the quantity supplied increases, causing the price to fall. The farmer, for example, has allocated more land to this crop. Figure 4–12c shows

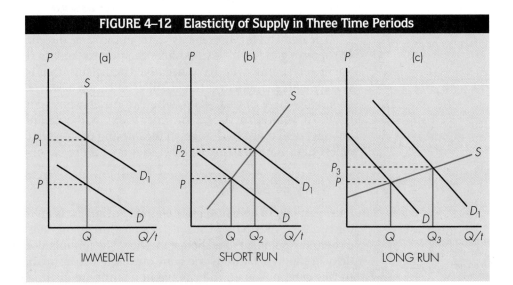

FIGURE 4–12   Elasticity of Supply in Three Time Periods

that over the long run the supply curve becomes still more elastic, because producers can vary all productive resources and make use of new technology. In the case of the farmer, more land and larger machinery can be acquired. The point to remember is that the longer the period of time is, the greater the elasticity of supply.

One last word about the elasticity of supply. This concept does not lend itself to the total revenue approach. The law of supply indicates a direct relationship between price and quantity supplied. Thus, regardless of the degree of elasticity or inelasticity, price and total revenue will always move in the same direction.

AN APPLICATION OF SUPPLY AND DEMAND— A TAX ON CIGARETTES

An example of the effect of supply and demand elasticities on market price and quantity can be seen with the enactment of a tax on cigarettes. Because of growing health concerns over the effects of smoking, the federal government and most state governments have levied increasingly higher sales and excise taxes on cigarettes. Thus, rather than end all subsidies to tobacco farmers or ban cigarette production altogether, public policy has relied on higher prices in the marketplace to curtail consumption. To accomplish this, taxes have been levied on both producers and consumers.

One possibility is shown in Figure 4–13a. Assume that the federal government levies a tax of $1 on each pack of cigarettes produced. This tax affects the cost of

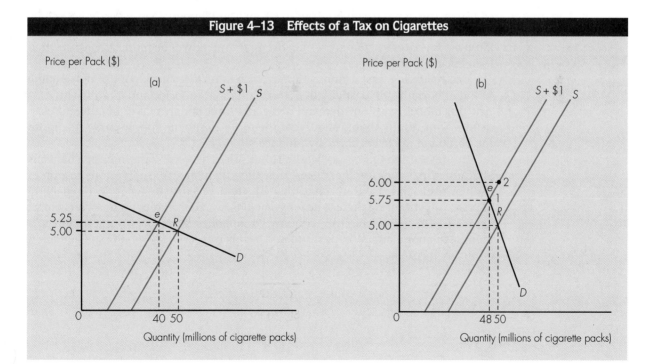

Figure 4–13   Effects of a Tax on Cigarettes

producing cigarettes and results in a shift in the producer's supply curve to the left. The extent to which the tax affects consumers is a function of the elasticity of demand for cigarettes. The original supply curve designated as S has now shifted to S + $1. Sellers must now receive $1 a pack more in order to sell the same amount as before. But their ability to do so depends on the reaction of the consumers to higher prices—the elasticity of demand. The question is, who is going to pay for the tax?

In Figure 4–13a, both supply curves are presented. Note that the vertical distance between the two supply curves is $1, an amount equal to the tax. In Figure 4–13a the demand curve for cigarettes (D) is relatively elastic. The graph indicates that only a small portion of the tax can be passed along to the consumer. The new equilibrium position (e) shows that the price of cigarettes has risen from $5 to $5.25 a pack, and the quantity demanded has fallen by 10 million packs. In this case, consumers have cut consumption, while paying but 25 cents more per pack. But most of the burden of the tax is being borne by producers in the form of fewer sales and less profit per pack.

In Figure 4–13b the demand curve for cigarettes is highly inelastic. In this case, consumers are willing to pay a substantially higher price to continue smoking. Consequently, the quantity demanded falls by only 2 million packs. The new equilibrium position is $5.75, and the equilibrium quantity is 48 million packs. With an inelastic demand, consumers bear the brunt of the tax. If the demand were totally inelastic, 50 million packs would be sold at $6, leaving producers as well off as before.

Given the government's intent to curtail smoking, the tax on cigarettes will be more successful the greater the elasticity of demand is. However, as often happens, if the tax is enacted to raise revenue, the government will be more successful when the demand is inelastic.

Before leaving this section, you may wish to further check your understanding of the importance of elasticity in determining market price and quantity by constructing models with one demand curve and three supply curves of different elasticities. Your results should show that the more elastic the supply curve, the more the portion of the tax is borne by producers.

In previous chapters, we learned that prices serve as rationing mechanisms allocating final goods and services, that they help allocate the various resources to their respective uses, and that they largely determine incomes. The reliability of prices in performing these functions depends to a great extent on how freely market forces function within the economy. Monopolies, strong labor unions, government regulations, and other institutional factors can seriously modify the operation of the price system.

Summary

- In a free market system, the forces of demand and supply determine prices. Demand is a schedule of the total quantities purchasers will buy at different prices at a given time. The two layers of demand are individual and market; market demand is the sum of all individual demands at each price. A change in demand is a change in the amounts of the product purchased at each price; a change in the quantity demanded is caused by a change in the price of the product. In addition to price, determinants of demand include changes in income, changes in taste and preferences, changes in expectations, and changes in the price of other products.

- The supply of a good or service at a given time is the quantity that sellers offer for sale at different prices. A supply curve shows the number of units of a good or service that will be offered for sale at different prices. A supply curve slopes upward to the right because as prices rise, more will be offered for sale. A change in supply produces a shift in the supply curve. Determinants of supply include changes in the cost of resources, changes in technology, expectation of future prices, and prices of related products.

- Equilibrium occurs at the point at which supply equals demand. When the price is above the market price set by demand and supply, the amount of a product that can be sold tends to be lowered. When the price is below the market price, usually more amounts of a product will be sold.

- When demand increases, a higher price usually results; a decreased demand usually lowers prices. When supply increases, the price decreases; when supply decreases, price rises.

- Price ceilings and price floors are forms of price controls that interfere with the impersonal forces of supply and demand. If price ceilings are set below the market price, shortages result. If price floors are set above the market price, surpluses will result.

- Price elasticity of demand measures consumer responsiveness to a change in price. Elastic demand exists when a percentage change in price causes a greater percentage change in quantity sold. Inelastic demand exists when a percentage change in price causes a smaller percentage change in quantity sold. Unit elasticity of demand exists when a percentage change in price causes an equal percentage change in quantity sold.

- Although the total value method of measuring elasticity is not as precise as the formula method, it does tell more directly what happens to total revenue. If price changes but total revenue stays constant, unit elasticity of demand exists. If price changes but total revenue moves in the opposite direction, demand is elastic. If price changes and total revenue moves in the same direction, demand is inelastic.

- Goods having inelastic demand include perishable goods, necessities, complementary goods, small expenditure items, and goods with limited uses. Goods having elastic demand include luxuries, durable goods, substitute goods, large expenditure items, and goods with multiple uses.

- Cross elasticity of demand measures the effect of a change in the price of one product on the quantity demanded of another. If products are related, they are classified as substitutes or complements. Income elasticity of demand measures the responsiveness of quantity demanded to changes in income. Goods are classified as normal or inferior.

- Elasticity of supply measures the sensitivity of quantity supplied to a change in price. Elasticity of supply increases over time.

CHAPTER REVIEW

New Terms and Concepts

Law of demand
Demand
Individual demand
Market demand
Demand schedule
Demand curve
Change in the quantity
  demanded
Change in demand
Supply
Individual supply
Market supply

Supply schedule
Supply curve
Law of supply
Change in the quantity
  supplied
Change in supply
Equilibrium price
Price ceiling
Price floor
Price elasticity of
  demand
Unit elastic demand

Elastic demand
Inelastic demand
Cross elasticity of
  demand
Income elasticity of
  demand
Elasticity of supply

Discussion Questions

1. Explain how the impersonal forces of de-
    mand and supply in the market determine
    prices under most competitive conditions.

2. Define *demand*. What are the three basic ele-
    ments in the definition?

3. Why does a normal demand curve slope
    downward to the right?

4. Distinguish between a change in the quantity
    demanded and a change in demand.

5. Why does a supply curve slope upward to
    the right?

6. Under competitive conditions, why can the
    market price not be higher or lower than the
    price established by the free market forces of
    demand and supply?

7. If both demand and supply increase, but de-
    mand increases more than supply does, what
    happens to price?

8. Define *price elasticity of demand*. If 46,000 units
    of a good can be sold at a price of $22 but
    54,000 units can be sold at a price of $18, is
    the demand for the good elastic or inelastic?
    What is the elasticity coefficient?

9. Define *cross elasticity of demand*. Calculate the
    elasticity coefficient for the following, and in-
    dicate whether the goods are substitutes or
    complements. The price of product X in-
    creases from $7 to $8 and the quantity de-
    manded of product Y decreases from 50,000
    units to 40,000 units.

10. Why does the elasticity of supply tend to in-
    crease over time?

Economic Applications

EconData

To find real-life applications of the role of demand and supply, go to http://econapps. swlearning.com, click on the EconData icon, and select "Supply and Demand" under the Economic Fundamentals heading. This will show you more examples of how supply and demand interact.

4

CHAPTER REVIEW

5

Production, Cost, and Profit

After studying Chapter 5, you should be able to:

1. Define *production function* and explain the principle of diminishing marginal returns.

2. Explain the relationships among total and average fixed cost, variable cost, and total cost.

3. Describe marginal cost and how it changes as output increases; draw a graph showing the relationship of *MC*, average fixed cost, average variable cost, and average total cost.

4. Find the break-even and profit maximizing levels of output on a break-even chart.

5. Define marginal revenue and explain why the output when $MR = MC$ is the maximum profit position for the firm.

6. Explain the difference between normal and economic profits.

Under highly competitive conditions, a firm cannot control its cost for a particular input because that cost is determined by supply and demand in the resource market. Nevertheless, the firm can alter its cost per unit of output by adopting better production techniques, using labor more efficiently, converting to different inputs, and spreading fixed cost over a greater range of output. A firm's cost of production largely determines the quantity of output it offers on the market (and hence its profit), so a further investigation of cost concepts is appropriate.

The Production Function

Production Function
The physical relationship between resource inputs and product output.

The quantity of goods or services offered for sale is affected by costs of production. These costs in turn are affected by relationships between resource inputs and product output. A **production function** is a description of the amounts of output expected from various combinations of inputs. The production function describes only technically efficient combinations and is usually determined by engineers or other experts. *Technical efficiency* is an engineering concept that refers to minimizing the amount of physical units of the inputs to production. The production function has certain properties that determine how cost varies with output.

PRINCIPLE OF DIMINISHING MARGINAL RETURNS

In providing a supply of goods, the entrepreneur's job is to organize land, capital, and labor so that the most efficient combination of these resources will be used. There should not be too much of one resource and too little of another. A farmer, for example, recognizes that a given amount of land must be worked by a certain amount of labor and a specific number of machines. Likewise, an office manager knows that for efficient operation a certain number of computers requires a definite number of employees. In either case, if the resources engaged in production are not in correct proportion, the unit cost of output will be higher than it should be. As a result, the business will not realize the maximum return from their use.

As these examples illustrate, in most cases one of the resources used in the production process is fixed in quantity for the time period under consideration. Other resources, such as labor, are said to be variable because they can be changed. To maximize profits, the firm will choose the least-cost or *economically efficient* combination of resources. This combination is determined in part by the principle of diminishing marginal returns.

As an illustration of the principle of diminishing marginal returns and its effect on cost of production, suppose that an entrepreneur owns a copy and duplicating service with four machines (the fixed input), has adequate space, and ample supplies on hand. If only one worker is hired, the net result will be a limited amount of output. It will be difficult for one worker to operate all four machines, keep production flowing smoothly, remove and package the finished product, maintain the premises, and do other jobs directly or indirectly connected with copying and duplicating. In fact, some of the machines may be left idle a good part of the time.

If a second worker of equal ability is hired, however, total output will increase. In fact, it may more than double because production will benefit from the physical labor of the second worker and from having the machines in operation more of the time. Consequently, total output may rise from 10 to 22 units. This addition to total output is known as the marginal product of labor and is illustrated in Figure 5–1.

A similar increase may take place if the entrepreneur hires a third worker, with output rising to perhaps 36 units. And if a fourth worker is hired so that one person is available to attend each machine, output may rise still further to 52 units. In each case, adding another worker has resulted in an increase in output.

Marginal Product

Marginal Product (MP)
The change in total output resulting from an additional unit of input.

The **marginal product (*MP*)** of any input is the change in total output produced with an additional unit of that input. In our example, the input is labor. But how

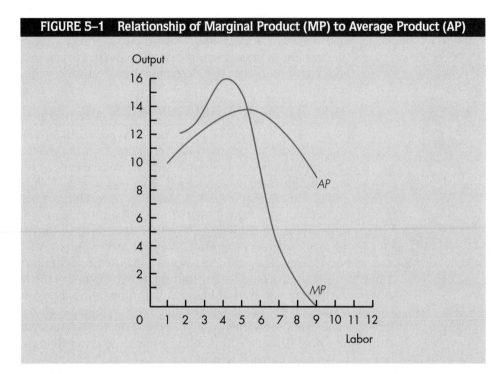

FIGURE 5–1   Relationship of Marginal Product (MP) to Average Product (AP)

long can this marginal product continue to increase? Provided that all other re-sources—space, machines, and materials—remain fixed, a point will soon be reached at which the fixed resources will become overtaxed or reach their maximum level of use. If a fifth worker is hired, for example, output may still rise because this worker can run for stock, package material, and do other jobs that permit the machine tenders to devote more time to their machines. But the increase in output may be less than it was with the addition of the fourth worker. Suppose that when the fifth worker is hired output expands by 15 units, as shown in Table 5–1.

If additional workers are hired, the marginal product will diminish further. Eventually, as the hiring continues, a situation will be reached in which the fixed resources are used to full capacity and there is absolutely no increase in output. In fact, workers may begin getting in each other's way so that a decrease in total output results.

Although it is possible to have increasing marginal returns (especially in the early stages of production) or constant marginal returns over a certain range of output, diminishing marginal returns are more prevalent. The **principle of diminishing marginal returns** is the fact that as more and more units of a variable resource are added to a set of fixed resources, the resulting additions to output eventually become smaller.

Principle of Diminishing Marginal Returns The fact that as more and more units of a variable resource are added to a set of fixed resources, the resulting additions to output eventually become smaller.

TABLE 5–1 Input, Output, Marginal Product, and Average Product			
Units of Labor	Total Output	Marginal Product	Average Product
1	10	—	10
2	22	12	11
3	36	14	12
4	52	16	13
5	67	15	13.4
6	78	11	13
7	84	6	12
8	88	4	11
9	90	2	10
10	90	0	9

Average Product

Average Product (AP)
The total output divided by the number of units of an input used.

The average product, too, affects the per unit cost of production. **Average product** (*AP*) can be defined simply as the total output divided by the number of units of an input used. Thus, in Table 5–1, when 3 units of labor are used to produce 36 units, the average product is 12 units (36/3 = 12).

Like the marginal product, the average product increases, reaches a maximum, and then declines. This follows from the fact that additions to total product (the *MP*) influence the average product. Anytime the *MP* is greater than the *AP*, it increases the *AP*. But when the *MP* is less than the *AP*, it reduces the *AP*. This relationship is shown in Figure 5–1.

Remember that to pull the average product down, the marginal product must be less than the average product, not merely declining. Thus, in Table 5–1, the *MP* with the addition of the fifth unit of labor declined from 16 to 15 units, but the *AP* rose from 13 to 13.4 units because the *MP* of 15, although diminishing, is still larger than the *AP* of 13. Eventually, however, a point is reached where the *AP*, like the *MP*, begins to decline.

RETURNS TO SCALE

The principle of diminishing marginal returns applies when one or a few resources in the input mix are varied and the rest are held constant. But what happens if all resources are changed proportionately? Suppose, for example, that all resources are doubled. Will output increase by 50 percent, by 100 percent, or perhaps even by 150 percent? The answer depends on the type of returns to scale that is in effect.

Constant Returns to Scale
A change in total inputs brings about a proportionate change in total output.

If output changes in a fixed proportion to the change in total inputs, **constant returns to scale** exist. For example, a doubling of all inputs—that is, an increase of

Decreasing Returns to Scale
A change in total inputs brings about a less than proportionate change in total output.

100 percent—in this case will double output. On the other hand, output may increase in a smaller proportion to the expansion of inputs; this is an indication of **decreasing returns to scale.** In this case, if the entrepreneur were to double all inputs, output would not double. In contrast, **increasing returns to scale** imply that a doubling of all inputs would more than double output.

Costs of Production

Increasing Returns to Scale
A change in total inputs brings about a greater than proportionate change in total output.

For all practical purposes the measure of production cost is money, and the cost is figured in terms of payments for labor, capital, materials, and other items directly or indirectly related to production. In addition, in a market economy, an imputed cost allowance is made for the services of the entrepreneur. As we have noted, it is the opportunity for profit that induces the entrepreneur to assume the risks and undertake the production. Once a business is in operation, a certain minimum profit is essential if the entrepreneur is to continue producing a good or service. This amount of profit, therefore, is viewed as a cost of production.

ALTERNATIVE USES AND OPPORTUNITY COSTS

Under a market system, a resource is usually employed for production of a specific good only if it is worth more when used to produce this good than when used to produce something else. For example, if there is competition for labor, a manufacturer of computer chips bids for the labor of technology workers by offering to pay at least as much for their labor as do other employers. Similar competition exists among employers for the labor of workers of all types.

The same principle operates to determine the cost of materials a producer uses. The producer of computer chips and all other users of similar components must pay a price for resources that is at least equal to the value this material has when used for some other purpose. Likewise, the cost of capital goods and borrowed funds in the form of bank loans is largely determined by the value such goods or funds would have if devoted to some other use.

Opportunity Cost of Productive Resources
The amount of payment necessary to attract productive resources away from their next-best opportunities for employment.

In terms of production, the payment necessary to attract a given resource away from the next-best alternative for employment is that resource's **opportunity cost.** (Recall we discussed the opportunity costs associated with choices in Chapter 2.) This cost exists whether or not payment is made in the form of cash expenditures. For example, suppose that you are a farmer and that corn would be the most profitable crop to produce on your farm and wheat would be the next most profitable. If you decide to grow corn, the opportunity cost of producing a corn crop is the value of your land and labor if they had instead been used to produce a wheat crop.

Explicit Costs
Expenditures for production that result from agreements or contracts.

EXPLICIT AND IMPLICIT COSTS

Expenditures for production that result from agreements or contracts are called **explicit costs.** Such costs are always recognized because they are stated clearly in terms of money and are shown in accounting records. A firm's opportunity costs of using its own resources or those provided by its owners without a corresponding cash payment, such as the use of a farmer's own land, are called **implicit costs.** In normal accounting procedure, implicit costs are often ignored. Nevertheless, in determining the true profit of a business, implicit costs must be recognized as a part of the real cost of production. The implicit cost of using one's own productive resource is the resource's opportunity cost.

Implicit Costs
A firm's opportunity cost of using its own resources or those provided by its owners without a corresponding cash payment.

CLASSIFICATIONS OF COSTS

We have seen how productive resources can affect the supply of goods and the general cost of production. Now we can explain and analyze the various costs that economists use to study business firms.

The costs of production in an individual plant may be categorized broadly as either fixed costs or variable costs. **Fixed costs** are costs that remain constant as output varies. Unless the plant capacity is changed, the amount of total fixed cost (*TFC*) in a firm does not vary with the volume of output. *TFC* includes *overhead,* such as interest, depreciation, property taxes, and insurance. In addition, a portion of the salaries paid for executive and supervisory services may properly be regarded as fixed expenses because a minimum managerial staff must be maintained even when the firm is operating at a limited capacity.

Fixed Costs
Costs that remain constant as output varies.

Although the *TFC* remains constant, fixed costs per unit of output decrease with an increase in output. **Average fixed cost (*AFC*)** is calculated by dividing the *TFC* by the number of units produced. For example, if the *TFC* in a given plant is $1 million and if 100,000 units are produced, the *AFC* incurred in producing a single unit is $10. But if output is increased to 1 million units, the *AFC* falls to $1. The *AFC* continues to decrease as the *TFC* is spread over increasingly larger outputs, but

Average Fixed Cost (AFC)
The total fixed cost divided by the number of units produced.

TABLE 5–2 Production Costs and Sales Revenue														
(1)	(2) Total	(3)	(4)	(5)	(6)	(7)	(8)	(9)	(10)	(11)	(12)	(13)	(14)	(15)
Input	Output	MP	AP	TFC	TVC	TC	AFC	AVC	ATC	MC	AR	TR	MR	Profit
1	10	—	10	50	10	60	5.00	1.00	6.00	—	2	20	2	-40
2	22	12	11	50	20	70	2.27	0.91	3.18	0.83	2	44	2	-26
3	36	14	12	50	30	80	1.39	0.83	2.22	0.71	2	72	2	-8
4	52	16	13	50	40	90	0.96	0.77	1.73	0.63	2	104	2	14
5	67	15	13.4	50	50	100	0.75	0.75	1.49	0.67	2	134	2	34
6	78	11	13	50	60	110	0.64	0.77	1.41	0.91	2	156	2	46
7	84	6	12	50	70	120	0.60	0.83	1.43	1.67	2	168	2	48
8	88	4	11	50	80	130	0.57	0.91	1.48	2.50	2	176	2	46
9	90	2	10	50	90	140	0.56	1.00	1.56	5.00	2	180	2	40
10	90	0	9	50	100	150	0.56	1.11	1.67	—	2	180	2	30

Variable Costs
Costs of production that vary as output changes, such as the costs of labor and materials.

Average Variable Cost (AVC)
Total variable cost divided by the number of units produced.

it never disappears entirely. Column 8 in Table 5–2 shows what happens to a $50 *TFC* when it is expressed as an *AFC*.

Variable costs are costs of production that vary with the amount of output produced, such as the costs of labor and materials. The total variable cost (*TVC*) changes as output changes. The **average variable cost (AVC)** is found by dividing the *TVC* by the number of units produced. As long as the prices of the variable resources remain constant, *AVC* decreases as output increases until the point of diminishing marginal returns is reached.

An Example

Column 6 in Table 5–2 indicates that if the cost of a variable unit of input is $10, the *TVC* will increase by $10, each time an additional unit of input is added. Consequently, the *TVC* increases from $10 to $100 as the inputs increase from 1 to 10. The *AVC* in each case can be found by dividing the *TVC* shown in column 6 by the total output shown in column 2. Notice that the *AVC* starts out at $1 per unit of output, drops to $0.75 with 5 input units, and then rises thereafter, reaching $1.11 with 10 inputs. Notice also that the point of lowest *AVC* corresponds to the point of highest average product.

Total Cost (TC)
The sum of total fixed cost and total variable cost at a particular level of output.

Average Total Cost (ATC)
The total cost divided by the number of units produced; also, the average fixed cost plus the average variable cost.

Marginal Cost (MC)
The change in the total cost resulting from production of one more unit of output.

Total cost (TC) is the sum of total fixed cost and the total variable cost at a particular level of output. The **average total cost (ATC)** is found by dividing the *TC* by the number of units produced or by adding the *AFC* and the *AVC*. The *TC* increases as output increases, but not proportionately. The *ATC* decreases, as a rule, until a certain number of units have been produced. Soon after the point of diminishing marginal returns is reached, the *ATC* begins to increase as output increases. This is shown in column 10, Table 5–2, which indicates that the lowest *ATC* is $1.41 with 6 input units.

An exceptionally important concept to the economist is marginal cost. The **marginal cost (MC)** is the change in the total cost resulting from production of one more unit of output. The *MC* is strongly influenced by the principle of diminishing marginal returns, and the shape of any *MC* curve depends on the shape of the corresponding marginal product (*MP*) curve. Column 3, Table 5–2, shows the *MP* schedule, and column 11 shows the *MC* for our hypothetical firm.

Notice that the *MC* values decrease, reach a minimum, and then rise thereafter. Observe further that as the *MP* rises the *MC* declines. Then, when the *MP* starts to decrease, the *MC* begins to increase. The point of lowest *MC*—$0.63 at 4 inputs—corresponds with the point of highest *MP*, also at 4 inputs. This reveals the close but inverse relationship between the *MP* and the *MC*.

In computing the marginal cost, remember that it refers to the change in total cost per additional unit of *output*, not of input. Because the second unit of input cost $10 more but resulted in an increase in total output of 12 units, the marginal cost (or increased cost per unit of output) is equal to $0.83, as shown with 2 inputs in column 11. Similarly, if successive changes in total cost are divided by the corresponding marginal products, the result is the marginal cost for each line.

The Example in Graphic Form

The relationship of these cost values can be seen much more clearly if they are presented in graphic form, as in Figure 5–2. In this case, the *AFC* is represented by a curve that continuously decreases in value as total fixed costs are spread over a larger and larger amount of output. The *AVC* is a curve that decreases, reaches a minimum, and then rises in value, because it, too, is affected by the principle of diminishing marginal returns. The *ATC*, which is a combination of the *AFC* and the *AVC*, likewise drops and then rises. Whenever both the *AFC* and the *AVC* are falling, the *ATC* falls, too. Finally, a point is reached at which the *AVC* starts to rise while the *AFC* is still declining. What happens to the *ATC* at this point depends on the relative strength of the two curves.

In Figure 5–2, the downward pull of the *AFC* is initially stronger than the upward pull of the *AVC*, so the *ATC* continues to drop for a while. But eventually the upward pull of the *AVC* overcomes the downward pull of the *AFC*, and the *ATC* rises thereafter. Graphically, the *MC* decreases, reaches a minimum, and then rises, owing to its close relationship with the marginal product curve. Whenever the *MC* is less than the *AVC* or the *ATC*, it will reduce one or both of them, much as the

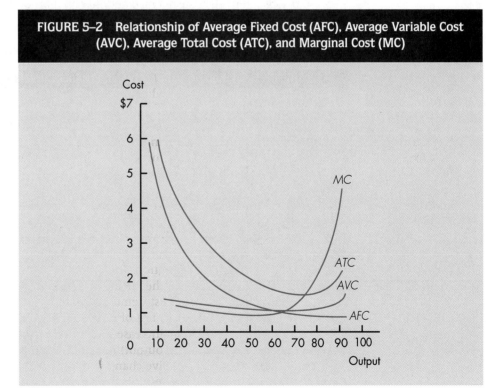

FIGURE 5–2   Relationship of Average Fixed Cost (AFC), Average Variable Cost (AVC), Average Total Cost (ATC), and Marginal Cost (MC)

marginal product affects the average product. Whenever the *MC* is greater than the *AVC* or the *ATC*, it will cause them to increase. Furthermore, by its very nature, the *MC* will intersect the *AVC* line and the *ATC* line at their lowest points.

RELATIONSHIP BETWEEN PRODUCT AND COST CURVES

By this time, you should have surmised that product and cost curves are somehow related to each other. In fact, the shape of cost curves is determined by the behavior of product curves. Thus, the U-shaped nature of cost curves is the result of the same factor that generates the hump-shaped product curves—that is, diminishing productivity.

Figure 5–3 portrays the product and cost curves for a firm in the short run. In Figure 5–3a, output is measured on the vertical axis and the quantity of the variable resource input is measured on the horizontal axis. In Figure 5–3b, output is measured on the horizontal axis and costs per unit of output are measured on the vertical axis. Output measured on the vertical axis in Figure 5–3a is the same output being measured on the horizontal axis in Figure 5–3b. The production model measures outputs from a given amount of inputs, whereas in the cost model, dollar measures are given to the resource inputs needed to produce a given output. The two panels tell us that the average and marginal product curves are mirror images of the average and marginal cost curves.

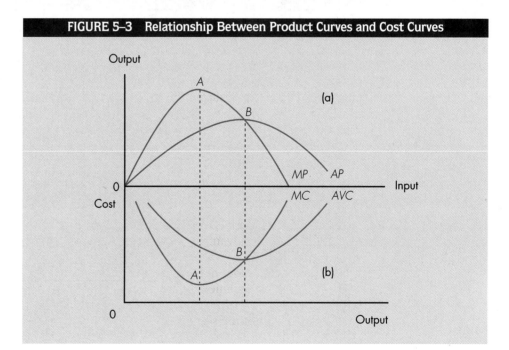

FIGURE 5–3   Relationship Between Product Curves and Cost Curves

The key concept in the analysis is that higher productivity means lower cost, and vice versa. Product curves indicate how much input is needed per unit of output. As average product rises, fewer resource inputs are needed per unit of output, and average cost will decline. Conversely, if average product is falling, a greater number of resource inputs are needed per unit of output, and average cost is rising. Thus, as AP rises, AVC will fall. When AP falls, AVC will rise. When AP is at a maximum, AVC will be at a minimum. The relationship between average product and average cost can be seen by comparing columns 4 and 9 in Table 5–2.

The law of diminishing marginal productivity indicates that marginal product increases, reaches a maximum, and then declines. Diminishing marginal productivity produces a marginal cost curve that falls to a minimum when marginal product is at a maximum and rises as marginal product falls. The marginal product–marginal cost relationship in Table 5–2 is presented in columns 3 and 11. Again, when productivity falls, it is the same thing as saying costs are rising.

LONG-RUN AVERAGE COST

The previous section dealt with the relationships between cost and product curves in the short run. The underlying force accounting for the shape of the short-run average variable and average total cost curves is diminishing marginal productivity. But what about the shape of the average cost curve in the long run when all productive resources and costs are variable? As seen in Figure 5–4, the long-run average cost curve *(LAC)* decreases as output increases, levels out, and eventually begins to rise. Because all costs are variable in the long run, the law of diminishing productivity cannot account for the shape of the long-run average cost curve. The answer lies with economies and diseconomies of scale.

In the long run, all resources can be varied, including such things as plant size, land, and capital equipment. Figure 5–4 shows that as a firm begins production on a small scale and continues to expand, the average cost of production continues to decline. ATC_1 is a short-run average total cost curve for a small-sized firm. Because of its small scale, the firm has relatively high production costs. Over time, when all resources become variable, it may choose to expand to a larger plant size, such as ATC_2. As the firm continues to expand its plant size, the average cost declines even further, as seen by ATC_3. These cost savings are attributed to economies associated with larger-scale operations, or economies of scale. Bigger firms can take better advantage of more highly specialized and more efficient capital and labor. These inputs are more expensive, but they can generate significantly lower production costs.

Eventually, all advantages of bigness disappear, as constant returns to scale are reached. This is the area at the bottom of the average cost curve. In this range, the cost of production does not change with changes in scale. The average cost of production is about the same for each plant size. Constant returns to scale can be seen between ATC_4 and ATC_5.

If the firm continues to expand, diseconomies of scale appear. With a scale of ATC_6, the firm has grown so large that the average cost of production is increasing.

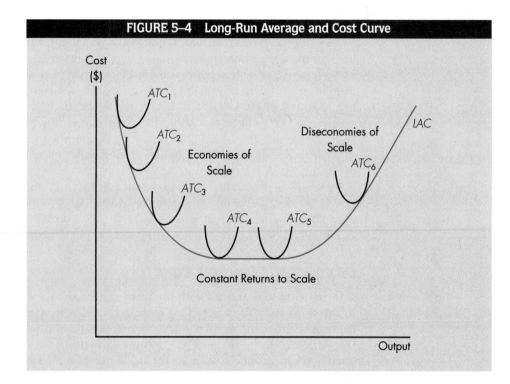

FIGURE 5–4   Long-Run Average and Cost Curve

The basic factor accounting for diseconomies of scale is management inefficiency. As firms grow too large, they become highly bureaucratic as they add layer upon layer of either centralized or decentralized management. This results in costly problems in communication, coordination, and lack of management accountability. In addition, these firms can no longer react quickly to changing market conditions. Efficiency is impaired and costs rise.

Thus, for every plant size there is a different short-run average cost curve. If there were an infinite number of plant sizes to choose from, there would be an infinite number of associated *ATC* curves. The long-run average cost curve, *AC,* envelops the short-run cost curves and forms a U-shaped long-run cost curve that touches each short-run cost curve at only one point.

Economies of scale are most prevalent in industries that are capital-intensive. These industries have a high ratio of fixed to variable costs in the short run. Examples of capital-intensive industries are the electric utility, transportation, and telecommunication industries. But they also exist in a number of other industries—witness the growing number of large retail stores selling specialized consumer goods. Many of these retail firms have grown by means of mergers and acquisitions, as well as by internal growth. Barnes and Noble (books), Home Depot (home improvement), and Staples (office supplies) are examples of large and growing retail specialty stores that are taking advantage of increasing returns to scale. Technology has also spurred the rapid growth of retail firms on the Internet, such as Amazon.com.

In other industries, the record number of company downsizings and restructurings in the past decade reflects diseconomies of scale. To increase efficiency, companies have eliminated thousands of middle-level management positions, at the same time selling off nonessential divisions and product lines.

Revenue and Profit

In Chapter 4 we saw that a demand schedule indicates the quantities of a good or service that will be demanded at various prices. We also saw that under competitive conditions the price is determined by supply and demand. Although conditions are not always competitive, we will suppose for now that the market price is the price at which an individual firm can sell its product. This will permit us to look at some revenue concepts and relate them to cost concepts in order to analyze the profit possibilities for a firm.

REVENUES

Average Revenue (AR)
The revenue per unit of output sold.

Total Revenue (TR)
The amount of revenue or income received from the sale of a given quantity of goods or services.

Marginal Revenue (MR)
The change in total revenue that results from the sale of one more unit of output.

The **average revenue (*AR*),** as used by economists, is the revenue per unit sold. From the viewpoint of the seller, it is the market price; it may be computed by dividing the total revenue by the number of units sold. The **total revenue (*TR*)** is the amount of revenue or income received from the sale of a given quantity of goods or services. It can be calculated readily by multiplying the *AR* (or price) by the number of units sold.

An extremely important and more complicated concept is marginal revenue, which parallels marginal cost. The **marginal revenue (*MR*)** is the change in total revenue that results from the sale of one more unit of output. This value can be calculated by dividing the change in total revenue by the change in total output.

In Table 5–2, the values of the *MR* and the *AR* are identical, but this will not always be the case. Anytime that you are dealing with other than perfectly competitive conditions, the values of the *MR* and *AR* will differ. With a constant price, however, whenever the firm sells an additional unit at the market price of $2, it will add $2 to its *TR*. Therefore, the *MR* will equal the *AR* (or price).

PROFIT

Total profit is the difference between total revenue and total cost. Whether a firm makes a profit and how much it makes depend on the relationship of its revenue to its costs. Even when a firm is not making a profit, the decision of whether to continue to operate or to shut down depends again on its cost–revenue relationships.

A firm can analyze its profit possibilities in many ways. For instance, it may compare its total revenue with its total cost, using a break-even chart. Or it may engage in marginal analysis, relying on marginal revenue and marginal cost concepts.

TOTAL REVENUE VERSUS TOTAL COST

Break-Even Point
The output level at which total revenue equals total cost.

By comparing total revenue with total cost over a given range of output, a firm can determine the levels at which it makes a profit and those at which it suffers losses. Furthermore, it can determine the point at which its losses cease and its profits begin, which is known as the **break-even point.** Some firms calculate the break-even point in terms of the total output, others in terms of total inputs, and still others in terms of capacity (to indicate the level at which they must operate to avoid losses). Naturally, a firm will try not only to reach the break-even point in output or capacity but also to go beyond it as far as is profitable. It must avoid the pitfall, however, of pushing too far beyond, because it may encounter rapidly rising marginal costs at or near full-capacity levels. In such an event, total profits may actually decline, in spite of higher output. The maximum profit position is the level of output at which the greatest vertical gap exists between total revenue and total cost, as shown in Figure 5–5.

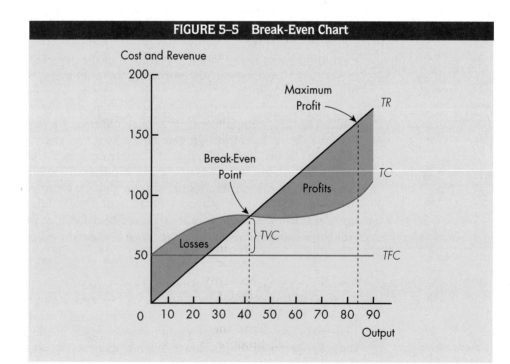

FIGURE 5–5   Break-Even Chart

NET_Link_

To avoid the diseconomies of scale inherent in its corporate structure, IBM restructured and decentralized into six smaller decision-making groups in 1956. Check it out at IBM's Website under "The History of IBM."

http://www.ibm.com/ibm/history

Another advantage of a break-even chart is that cost can be broken down into *TFC* and *TVC*. In fact, if desirable, the variable cost can be segmented into such subcategories as direct and indirect manufacturing costs, material cost, labor cost, and selling costs.

Putting the values from our hypothetical firm into Figure 5–5, we find that the *TFC* of $50 is represented by a straight horizontal line. This indicates that the fixed costs remain constant over the given range of output. Total costs, which continually increase, are represented by a line moving upward to the right. The difference between the *TC* and the *TFC* equals the *TVC*. Because the price at which each unit sells is constant, the total revenue is shown by a line moving upward and to the right at a constant slope. The break-even point is at 42 units of output. Although profits are made at all levels of output beyond this point, maximum profit is made when output is in the vicinity of 84 units. The same information can be inferred from Table 5–2, which we inspected earlier.

MARGINAL REVENUE VERSUS MARGINAL COST

Anytime a firm can add to its total profit by changing the number of units that it produces, it will do so. Consequently, the firm's profit picture is often analyzed in terms of what happens to cost and revenue with the addition of one more unit of output. Whenever the production and sale of a marginal unit add more to revenue than they do to cost, profits are sure to increase or losses diminish, whichever the case may be. If the production of one more unit adds more to cost than it does to revenue, the opposite is true. Two concepts tell us how much is added to revenue and how much is added to cost with each additional unit of output: the *MR* and the *MC*. To determine the point of maximum profit for the firm, all we have to do is observe their relationship.

The marginal revenue (*MR*) measures the change in total revenue per additional unit of output. The marginal cost (*MC*) measures the change in total cost per additional unit of output. Therefore, anytime the *MR* is greater than the *MC*, profits will rise or losses will diminish. On the other hand, if the *MR* is less than the *MC*, profits will decrease or losses will increase. A firm will profit by increasing its output so long as *MR* > *MC*. It will benefit by reducing output whenever *MR* < *MC*.

In most cases, the marginal revenue has a constant or decreasing value, and the marginal cost has a continuously increasing value. Therefore, as a firm adds units of output, it eventually reaches a point at which *MR* = *MC*. This is its maximum profit position, since any lower level of output shows *MR* > *MC* and any greater level shows *MR* < *MC*. In our example firm, for instance, the *MR* has a constant value of $2. Meanwhile, the *MC*, after reaching a low of $0.63, continuously increases to more than $5 as output reaches 90 units. Comparing the *MR* in column 14 with the *MC* in column 11 in Table 5–2, we can see that *MR* > *MC* at all levels of output up to and including the seventh unit of input. Therefore, the firm will continue to produce up to that point. It will not add the eighth unit of input, however, because *MR* < *MC* for the resulting output. Consequently, the firm will maximize profits, according to the marginal analysis, at a level of output in the vicinity of 84 units. This matches the maximum profit indicated on the break-even chart in Figure 5–5.

MINIMIZING LOSSES IN THE SHORT RUN

Thus far we have been dealing with the pleasant situation of a firm making a profit, but what happens if the firm is suffering a loss? Suppose, for example, that in our problem the average revenue the firm received was only $1, as determined by the forces of the market. Assuming that the costs remain the same, we can see from Table 5–2 that the firm will not make a profit at any level of output. It will, however, minimize its losses if it operates at 6 units of input or 78 units of output. What, then, should the firm do—continue to operate or shut down? The answer depends on the relationship of cost to revenue and on whether the action we are talking about covers the short-run or the long-run period.

Short Run
A period of time in which some productive resources are fixed.

Long Run
A period of time in which all productive resources— including machinery, buildings, and other capital items—are variable.

In economics, the **short run** is a period of time in which some productive resources are fixed. The **long run** is a period of time in which all productive resources—including machinery, buildings, and other capital items—are variable. In the short run, for example, it may be possible for a firm to increase its output within a given range by adding more workers, putting on another shift, buying more raw materials, and manipulating other variable resources, without increasing the size of its fixed plant and equipment. In the long run, however, it could increase its output greatly by adding to its capacity by constructing or purchasing new plant and equipment. Thus, in the long run, even the fixed resources become variable. In the long run, there are no total or average fixed costs. The actual length of this loosely defined period varies with different industries.

If a firm is operating at a loss in the short run (and minimizing its losses), the question of whether it should continue to operate or shut down remains. The answer depends on the relationship of its fixed cost to its variable cost and the relationship of variable cost to its total revenue.

Assume that a firm has a *TFC* of $60,000 and a *TVC* of $40,000, for a *TC* of $100,000. At the same time, suppose that its *TR* is $50,000. Obviously, the firm is suffering a loss of $50,000. Nevertheless, it is better for it to continue to operate in the short run rather than to shut down because, by operating, it limits its loss to only $50,000. If it were to close down instead, its total cost would drop by the amount of its variable cost, $40,000, but its revenue would drop to zero. Because it would still have to pay its fixed cost of $60,000, its loss would be $60,000 instead of $50,000.

Economic Profit

New business firms are established in the hope of making a profit, and other businesses fail because of a lack of profit. Starting a business involves a risk, but the opportunity for profit induces tens of thousands of individuals annually to try to become successful entrepreneurs.

Profit is the return to the entrepreneur for organizing, producing, and risk taking in the operation of the business. Profit is what is left after all the other productive resources have been reimbursed. It may be either large or small. If the profit is too small or if the firm suffers a loss, the firm may shut down or go out of business.

Normal Profit
The amount of profit necessary to induce an entrepreneur to stay in business.

Economic Profit
Any revenue in excess of all costs (including a normal profit).

The amount of profit necessary to keep the entrepreneur operating is called **normal profit.** It is equal to the entrepreneur's opportunity cost—what he or she could earn in the next-best alternative employment. Usually, normal profit is considered an economic cost of doing business. If only a normal profit is being made, a position of no economic profit will exist as far as the business operation is concerned. Any amount of profit over and above the normal profit is **economic profit.** Economic profit is income over and above all economic costs (both explicit and implicit) that results from the operation of a business.

Profits are dynamic. That is, their amount is constantly changing. As we will see in Chapter 6, under conditions of pure competition, economic profit is a temporary phenomenon. Put simply, the conditions of pure competition are such that anytime economic profit exists, new firms will enter the industry until the economic profit is eliminated.

Conversely, if an economic profit situation exists for a monopoly, the monopolist may be able to block the entry of new firms into the industry. As a result, economic profit may become a long-term phenomenon. Furthermore, because the output of the monopoly constitutes the total supply on the market, the monopolist can influence the market price by changing output. In this way, the price can be set where it will yield the greatest profit. Under conditions of monopolistic or imperfect competition, which frequently occurs, economic profit may also exist.

Summary

- The marginal product of any input is the increase in total output resulting from an additional unit of that input, such as labor.

- The cost of producing goods and services is affected by physical factors such as the principle of diminishing marginal productivity. The principle of diminishing marginal productivity states that as more and more units of a variable resource, such as labor, are added to a set of fixed resources, at some point the resulting additions to output will become smaller and smaller. The concept of returns to scale applies when all resources are variable.

- In analyzing a firm's costs, economists consider not only explicit costs but also the implicit costs of using the owner's own productive resources, such as labor, land, and capital in the production process. Implicit costs are usually measured in terms of opportunity cost, or the alternative uses to which the productive resources could be applied.

- Costs can also be generally classified as fixed and variable. In the short run, total cost is a combination of both fixed costs and variable costs. Cost may also be broken down into varieties of unit costs, such as average fixed cost, average variable cost, average total cost, and marginal cost.

- Marginal cost is the change in the total cost as a result of one more unit of output. It decreases, reaches a minimum, and then rises because of the law of diminishing marginal productivity. The marginal cost curve is inversely related to the marginal product curve.

- The price received per unit of output, as determined by the forces of supply and demand in the market, is the firm's average revenue. Marginal revenue is the change in total revenue that results from the sale of an additional unit of output. Whenever marginal revenue is greater than marginal cost, profits will rise or losses will diminish with increased output. If marginal revenue is less than marginal cost, profits will decrease or losses will increase. The maximum profit position for the firm is where marginal cost equals marginal revenue.

- A firm's profit position can be analyzed by means of a break-even chart that plots total revenue, total cost, total fixed cost, and total variable cost. The firm's break-even position and its maximum profit position can be determined on such a chart. Break-even and maximum profit positions can also be determined by marginal analysis. A firm will attempt to maximize its profit or minimize its losses by producing that output where marginal cost equals marginal revenue.

- Profit or loss is the difference between the total revenue and total costs that result from production. Even if a firm is suffering a loss, it should continue production in the short run as long as revenue is covering variable cost and making a contribution to fixed cost. In the long run, all costs are variable and the firm's revenue must cover all costs.

- Normal profit is the amount of profit needed to keep the entrepreneur in a given business. Any amount over and above normal profit is considered economic profit.

New Terms and Concepts

Production function
Marginal product (*MP*)
Principle of diminishing
  marginal returns
Average product (*AP*)
Constant returns to
  scale
Decreasing returns to
  scale
Increasing returns to
  scale

Opportunity cost of
  productive resources
Explicit costs
Implicit costs
Fixed costs
Average fixed cost
  (*AFC*)
Variable costs
Average variable cost
  (*AVC*)
Total cost (*TC*)

Average total cost (*ATC*)
Marginal cost (*MC*)
Average revenue (*AR*)
Total revenue (*TR*)
Marginal revenue (*MR*)
Break-even point
Short run
Long run
Normal profit
Economic profit

Discussion Questions

1. Does the size of the marginal product have an effect on the average product? Explain.

2. What is the principle of diminishing marginal returns?

3. Define opportunity cost, and give an example of such a cost in reference to the use of a productive resource.

4. How do explicit and implicit costs differ?

5. Why does the average variable cost decrease, reach a minimum, and then rise again, whereas the average fixed cost continues to decrease as output increases?

6. Is it true that whenever marginal cost is rising the average variable cost and the average total cost must also rise? Why or why not?

7. How is maximum profit position determined on a break-even chart? What components are needed to construct a break-even chart?

8. Why is the output at which marginal revenue equals marginal cost the maximum profit position?

9. What is economic profit, and how is it measured?

10. Why may a firm choose to continue to operate in the short run, even though it is suffering an economic loss?

Economic Applications

EconNews

EconNews carries information about current events in the production and cost area of economics. Go to http://econapps.swlearning.com, click on the EconNews icon, look for the Microeconomics heading and the link titled "Production and Costs." Click here to find the top news stories that apply production and cost issues to our everyday lives.

CHAPTER REVIEW

6

Perfect Competition

After studying Chapter 6, you should be able to:

1. List the characteristics of perfect competition.

2. Understand why the profit-maximizing position of a firm in perfect competition occurs at the output when $MR = MC$.

3. Draw a graph showing ATC, AVC, MC, AR, and MR and indicate the profit-maximizing output for a perfectly competitive firm.

4. Understand and show graphically why a firm suffering an economic loss may continue to operate in the short run.

5. Draw a graph showing long-run economies and diseconomies of scale for a perfectly competitive firm and point out the minimum efficient scale of operation.

6. Understand the concepts of consumer and producer surplus and explain why perfect competition produces the largest combined consumer and producer surplus.

Millions of firms do business in hundreds of industries in the United States. Within this vast field it is possible to find various degrees of competition in a single industry and numerous shades of competition among different markets. Markets may range from near-perfect competition to monopoly. Although there are fundamental differences among types of competition, conditions sometimes enable the market for a firm or an industry to contain elements of more than one type. Furthermore, a firm may find itself in one type of competitive market when selling its products but in a different type of competitive market when buying its raw materials or hiring labor.

The four basic types of market structure are perfect competition, monopoly, monopolistic competition, and oligopoly. Among the distinguishing characteristics of different types of markets are the number of firms in an industry, the presence or absence of product differentiation, and the ability of any or all firms in an industry to influence the market price. Because perfect competition offers a theoretical standard for measuring the economic and social value of other forms of market structure, we shall devote this chapter to analyzing the perfectly competitive industry.

Characteristics of Perfect Competition

Perfect Competition
A market structure that assumes four characteristics: numerous sellers are present in the market, all selling identical products; all buyers and sellers are informed about the market and prices; there is free entry into and exit from the market; and no individual seller or buyer can influence price—instead, price is determined by market supply and demand.

Perfect competition is a theoretical market structure that assumes the following four characteristics:

1. *Numerous sellers are present in the market, all selling identical products.* There are no quality differences, no brand names, no advertising, and nothing else that would differentiate the products of various sellers.

2. *All buyers and sellers are informed about markets and prices.* If one seller offers a product on the market at a lower price than others are charging, all buyers are aware of this action. Furthermore, if one firm can offer a good on the market at a lower price than competitors because of certain cost advantages, other firms will soon learn how to gain these advantages.

3. *There is free entry into and exit from the market.* Anyone who desires to produce and sell goods in a particular market may do so. Perfect mobility of the productive resources is a further feature of this theoretical market system. It also assumes the availability of the necessary productive resources, freedom from government regulations, and the absence of any other conditions that may hinder the production of a particular good or service.

4. *No individual seller or buyer can influence market price; instead, price is determined by market supply and demand.* There must be enough sellers so that the contribution of each to the market supply is minute. Consequently, whether a firm increases or decreases output has no appreciable effect on the market supply. In addition, each seller is a price taker; it must accept the market price as determined by overall demand and supply. A particular seller will not be able to obtain a higher price because all products are identical. This characteristic does not preclude the possibility, however, that the market price could be changed by the actions of many or all firms. If an individual firm were to increase output by 50 or 100 percent, for example, the change in market supply would be insignificant and would not affect the market price. On the other hand, if each of a large number of producers increased output by 10 percent, this action could affect supply enough to cause a change in market price.

NETLink

An example of one of the oldest market mechanisms is the auction. Visit the eBay or Yahoo! online auction Websites at:

http://www.ebay.com/ and
http://auctions.yahoo.com

Price and Profit in the Short Run

Under perfect competition, each firm faces a perfectly elastic demand curve. On a graph, the firm's demand curve is a horizontal line. That is, the firm's entire supply can be sold at the market-determined price. Profit is the difference between the average total cost of production and the selling price, multiplied by the number of units sold. Because firms are in business to make a profit, each firm will try to produce the number of units that will yield the greatest profit when sold.

Acting alone, a producer can do little or nothing to change the market price. Thus, the market price will not be affected whether a given firm sells much or nothing. This is not true, however, for the industry as a whole. If a great many or all firms increase or decrease output, the total market supply will be affected. As a result, assuming that demand does not change, the market price will change.

A case in point is the production of wheat in the United States, where there are more than 500,000 producers. Whether farm owner Dick Worthington increases output from 100 to 1,000 or even to 10,000 bushels will have virtually no effect by itself on a market price of $3 per bushel when the U.S. market supply each year is more than 2 billion bushels. On the other hand, if every wheat farmer in the United States increases output by a mere 2 percent, the total U.S. wheat supply will increase by more than 40 million bushels, and undoubtedly the market price will fall.

In a perfectly competitive industry that produces a standardized good, how much output will each firm produce? This question cannot be answered exactly, but we can analyze the factors that influence how much each one will produce. Within the assumed short-run conditions, each firm will attempt to set an output at which marginal cost is equal to marginal revenue. Remember that in the short run we assume that no new factories will be built in the industry and that existing plants will not be enlarged. The short run is a period too short to allow existing firms to leave the industry. But each firm is free to vary its volume of output from zero to its maximum existing capacity.

ADJUSTMENT OF OUTPUT TO PRICE IN THE SHORT RUN

Just how much will a particular firm want to produce? In most real situations it is probably impossible to say. The firm cannot predict exactly what the cost will be at different levels of output. In addition, the firm may be satisfied with a reasonable amount of profit and will refrain from attempting to squeeze every last cent of profit out of the business.

Nevertheless, we will assume that the firm is motivated by the desire to make as much profit as possible. Therefore, the entrepreneur will produce the amount that maximizes the firm's profit or minimizes its loss. What that volume of output is depends on the firm's cost and revenue relationships.

Let us assume that total cost, average total cost, marginal cost, average and marginal revenues, and total revenue for a certain firm are as shown in Table 6–1 and Figure 6–1. The difference between *AR* (or market price) and *ATC* equals profit per unit. Profit per unit multiplied by output equals total profit. As always, the firm will maximize its profits (or minimize its losses) at the point where marginal cost equals marginal revenue (*MC* = *MR*). Close inspection of Table 6–1 and Figure 6–1 reveals that at a market price of $1.80 per unit an output of 13 units corresponds to the intersection of the marginal cost and marginal revenue curves.

The output level where *MC* = *MR* is called the *equilibrium output* because once the firm reaches that position, it has no incentive to move to any other level of output. On the other hand, if it is not operating at that point, the firm is motivated by

TABLE 6–1   Cost and Revenue Schedule for a Firm in Perfect Competition

Units of Output	TC	ATC	MC	TR	AR and MR	Total Profit or Loss
1	$10.08	$10.08	—	$1.80	$1.80	$8.28
2	11.22	5.61	1.14	3.60	1.80	7.62
3	12.12	4.04	0.90	5.40	1.80	6.72
4	12.84	3.21	0.72	7.20	1.80	5.64
5	13.44	2.69	0.60	9.00	1.80	4.44
6	13.98	2.33	0.54	10.80	1.80	3.18
7	14.52	2.07	0.54	12.60	1.80	1.92
8	15.12	1.89	0.60	14.40	1.80	0.72
9	15.84	1.76	0.72	16.20	1.80	0.36
10	16.74	1.67	0.90	18.00	1.80	1.26
11	17.88	1.63	1.14	19.80	1.80	1.92
12	19.34	1.61	1.46	21.60	1.80	2.26
13	21.12	1.62	1.80	23.40	1.80	2.28
14	23.34	1.67	2.22	25.20	1.80	1.86
15	26.04	1.74	2.70	27.00	1.80	0.96
16	29.28	1.83	3.24	28.80	1.80	0.48
17	33.12	1.95	3.84	30.60	1.80	2.52

the prospect of greater profit to change its output until it attains the equilibrium position. If $MC < MR$, an expansion of output will increase profit. If $MC > MR$, a contraction of output will increase profit. When $MC = MR$, short-run total profit is at the maximum.

In our example, if the market price is $1.80 and fewer than 9 units or more than 15 are produced, the firm will lose money. Only when 9 to 15 units are produced is AR (price) above ATC. Notice that after 13 units are produced MC rises above MR. Although some profit could be realized by producing and selling 15 units, profit cannot be increased by producing more than 13 units, the output for which MC and MR are exactly equal. (If MC and MR did not coincide exactly at an output of a whole unit, it would be most profitable to produce the whole number nearest to where they were equal.)

Now suppose that the market price, instead of staying at $1.80, falls to $1.61, as shown in Figure 6–2. At this price, ATC, MC, AR, and MR_1 are practically equal at the point of intersection of the MC and MR_1 curves. What does this signify? It means that the most the firm can hope for is to break even. By producing 12 units, the firm will end up with an AR that is just equal to ATC. If any more units are produced, ATC and MC will rise above MR_1 and AR_1, and a loss will be incurred. If the firm stops short of producing 12 units, ATC will be greater than AR_1, and again a loss will be incurred.

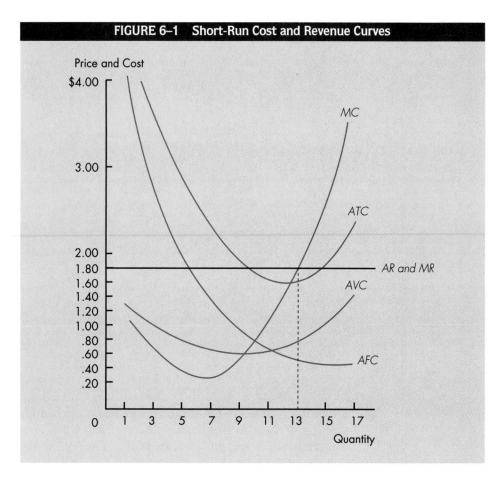

FIGURE 6–1   Short-Run Cost and Revenue Curves

For another example, assume that the market price (AR_2 and MR_2) has fallen to $1.20, as shown in Figure 6–2. How many units should be produced now? We can see that no matter how many units are produced, the firm cannot hope to make a profit. As the figure shows, for any number of units, *ATC* is above AR_2. The point at which the loss can be minimized, however, is at the output of 11 units, the whole number nearest the intersection of *MC* and MR_2. The firm should not produce more than 11 units, however, because beyond that point *MC* rises above MR_2 and losses increase.

In this case, the firm should continue to operate in the short run rather than shut down because it can still recover its variable cost. This can be determined by comparing *AVC* with *AR* at the equilibrium level. If *AR* = *AVC*, the firm will recover its variable cost. If *AR* > *AVC*, it will recover its variable cost and part of its fixed cost or overhead. The amount of its contribution to fixed cost can be observed from the graph. The fixed cost is not drawn on the chart, but, since *ATC* = *AFC* + *AVC*, *AFC*

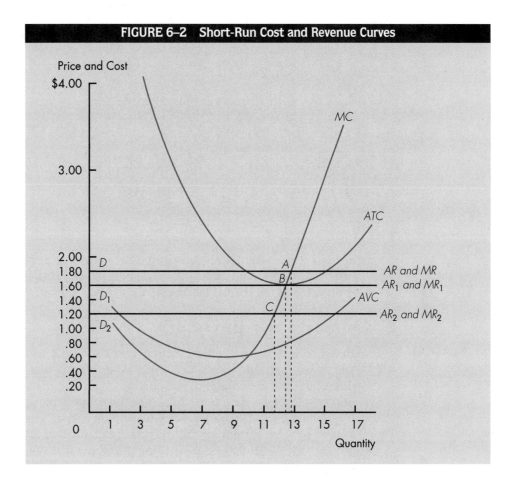

FIGURE 6–2   Short-Run Cost and Revenue Curves

is represented by the difference between the *ATC* and *AVC* curves at the point of equilibrium.

Finally, visualize a situation in which the market price is only $0.60 for the firm in question. Not only will the firm suffer a loss at any level of output but even at the equilibrium output or point of minimum loss, *AR* is less than *AVC*. In this situation, the firm cannot recover any of its variable cost and should shut down rather than operate in the short run. Note, however, that the firm will still need to pay its fixed costs during the short run even if it shuts down and no output is produced.

In analyzing the profit-maximizing and loss-minimizing examples of perfectly competitive firms, it should be evident that individual firms will only offer products to the market at prices above the intersection of the marginal cost and average variable cost curves. At prices below the intersection, the firm will cease supplying the market. Thus, the short-run supply curve of a perfectly competitive firm is that

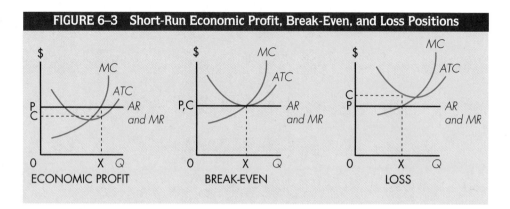

FIGURE 6–3 Short-Run Economic Profit, Break-Even, and Loss Positions

portion of its marginal cost curve that lies above the average variable cost curve. For the industry as a whole, the market or industry supply curve is the horizontal summation of the individual supply curves of all firms in the industry.

SHORT-RUN EQUILIBRIUM

Under perfect competition, all firms pay an identical price for productive resources and all sell their output at a uniform market price. It is still possible, however, for profits among firms to differ. For one thing, even though all firms have the same unit cost for resources, some firms use their inputs more efficiently. In the short run, some may use better production techniques, may spread their fixed costs over a larger range of output, or may use other measures to lower per-unit cost of output. At any given market price, therefore, some firms may be making economic profits, while others are breaking even and still others are suffering losses. This is demonstrated in Figure 6–3.

As the market price moves up or down, the profit status of each firm can be affected. Similarly, a change in the price of resources can affect each firm's profits by altering its average cost curve. In the long run, firms suffering losses must reorganize their productive resources to break even at least, or else they must drop out of business. Perfect competition assumes that all sellers are informed about markets, prices, and costs. Therefore, if one firm is somehow able to produce at a lower cost, others will soon know how it can be done. And, in the long run, adoption of similar production techniques will enable the others to adjust their resources to reduce costs.

Price and Profit in the Long Run

Under perfect competition, competitive forces tend to eliminate economic profits because of the freedom of firms to enter and exit the industry. Short-run economic profits will in the long run attract new firms into the industry and may cause existing firms to expand. Indeed, they have both the incentive and the freedom to do so.

No individual supplier can influence market price under conditions of perfect competition. But if a number of new firms enter the market, the addition of their supplies to the existing total market supply could very well cause a decrease in market price. If economic profits still remain, even at the lower market price, firms will continue to enter the industry (and further lower the price) until a point is reached at which the price equals the average total cost and economic profit is eliminated.

On the other hand, if the market price is below average cost and firms are suffering losses, firms will reduce their scale of operations or drop out of the industry. In the long run, the market supply shrinks, causing price to rise and losses to disappear in the industry. In the long run, the firm must be able to earn enough revenue to cover all costs because all costs are variable costs. If it does not, the firm will exit the industry. Therefore, the perfectly competitive firm's supply curve is that part of its marginal cost curve that lies above the intersection with its average cost curve. This very process took place recently in the computer, telecommunications, and cellular phone industries. Although not perfectly competitive by any means, these industries expanded rapidly during the 1990s as prices and profits rose, but contracted sharply in 2000–2001 as prices and profits fell. Many firms in these industries either went out of business or merged with other firms. The whole process is demonstrated graphically in Figure 6–4.

GRAPHICAL ANALYSIS

Assume that the intersection of demand (D) and supply (S) in Figure 6–4 establishes a market price of $5 per unit. This $5 figure then represents the AR for each firm in the industry. Assuming that the cost and revenue relationships shown in Figure 6–4 are typical for the industry, individual firms are making economic profits. But these economic profits induce new firms to enter the industry. As they do

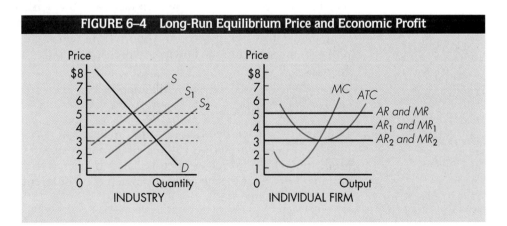

FIGURE 6–4   Long-Run Equilibrium Price and Economic Profit

so, market supply increases (the market supply curve shifts outward), and the market price falls to $4, as shown by the intersection of S_1 and D. The lower market price in turn lowers the AR and MR curves for each firm in the industry, thereby reducing profits. Because economic profits still exist even at this price, however, firms continue to enter the industry, increasing the market supply to S_2 and reducing the market price to $3 per unit.

At an AR and MR of $3, no economic profits remain for the firms in the industry. Consequently, there is no incentive for additional firms to enter the industry. Not only are all the firms in equilibrium (because they are operating at the point where $MC = MR$) but equilibrium exists in the industry as a whole, because there is no incentive for firms to enter or leave. And, there is no economic profit to attract new firms. However, because existing firms can cover all their costs, including a normal profit as a return to the entrepreneur, they will not be inclined to leave the industry.

You can also visualize what happens when the initial market price causes losses to exist in the industry. As firms drop out of the industry, the market supply of goods decreases, raising the market price and the MR and AR of the remaining individual firms. This process continues until the price rises sufficiently to eliminate losses. At that point, there is no further incentive for firms to leave the industry, and equilibrium is again established.

THE ROLE OF RESOURCE COSTS

At the long-run equilibrium, firms in the industry earn a normal profit and all economic profit has been eliminated. Price, marginal cost, and average cost are all equal. The price reflects the cost of production. We have investigated the movement from a short-run economic profit position to a long-run break-even equilibrium through adjustments in market price or average revenue. It is also possible, however, for the long-run profit squeeze to occur sooner because of an increase in the cost of resources. As new firms enter an industry, their combined demand for inputs may substantially increase the market demand for raw materials, labor, capital, and other resources. This in turn may raise the market price of resources and the ATC curve for individual firms, causing a reduction in profits. Consequently, the competitive forces in the economy work from two angles to eliminate economic profits in the long run: the downward pressure on prices and the upward pressure on costs.

THE LONG-RUN COST CURVE

In Chapter 5, we learned that firms in the long run may change their entire scale or size of operation. Because all resources and costs are variable in the long run, there are no fixed resources or costs. The long-run average cost curve, along with various short-run average cost curves depicting different scales of production, is presented in Figure 6–5.

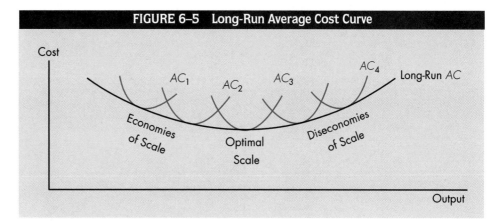

FIGURE 6–5   Long-Run Average Cost Curve

Competition in the long run cuts economic profit to zero. To survive, perfectly competitive firms must adjust their scale of operation until the average cost of production is minimized. As firms grow in size, they can take advantage of **economies of scale.** Failure to expand in size would force these firms out of business because of production costs greater than those of their competitors. Eventually, with increasing plant size, an output level will be reached where the long-run average cost curve no longer decreases. This point is the **optimal scale of operation**—the level at which the long-run average cost is at a minimum. In some industries, the average cost may remain constant over a range of output, so there may be more than one optimal output level. There is no incentive for firms to expand beyond the optimal scale, because production costs would once again be higher than those of competitors due to **diseconomies of scale.** The end result is that each firm in a perfectly competitive industry would have to operate at the optimum scale to remain in business.

CONSUMER SURPLUS AND PRODUCER SURPLUS

Another way to grasp the benefits of perfect competition is by means of the concepts of consumer surplus and producer surplus. **Consumer surplus** is the difference between what consumers would have been willing to pay and what they actually pay for the product. **Producer surplus** refers to the difference between what firms would have been willing to accept as a price for the product and the price they actually receive. Consumer surplus and producer surplus can be viewed as the benefits accruing to consumers and firms from market exchange. Under the condition of perfect competition, total consumer surplus and producer surplus are maximized, as are the benefits to society.

In Figure 6–6, the market or industry demand and supply curves are represented by D_m and S_m, with the corresponding market exchange price being P_e. Because these are market demand and supply curves, we know that the demand

Economies of Scale
Forces that cause long-run average cost to fall as plant size increases.

Optimal Scale of Operation
The level of output at which the long-run average cost is at a minimum.

Diseconomies of Scale
Forces that cause long-run average cost to increase as plant size increases.

Consumer Surplus
The difference between what consumers would have been willing to pay and what they actually pay for the product.

Producer Surplus
The difference between what firms would have been willing to accept as a price for the product and the price they actually receive.

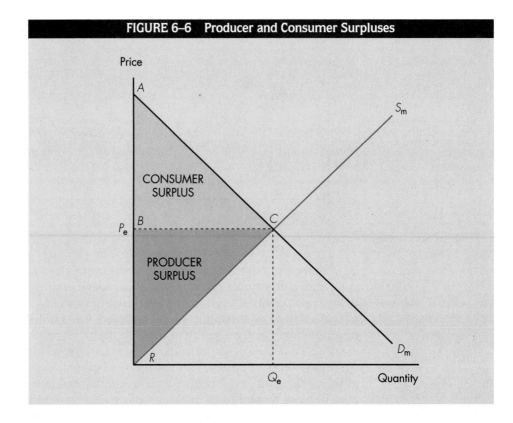

FIGURE 6–6   Producer and Consumer Surpluses

curve D_m represents a number of individual consumers who would be willing to pay prices higher than P_e, but who only have to pay the market exchange price of P_e. Consumer surplus is the area above the equilibrium price and below the demand curve. Hence, area ABC represents a benefit to consumers resulting from perfect competition. Producer surplus is the area represented by the triangle RBC, the area above the supply curve and below the price line of P_e. We have learned that each firm in the industry is willing to sell the product at a price equal to marginal cost and that under perfect competition the sum of the marginal cost curves equals the market supply curve (S_m). But with a market exchange price of P_e, all producers receive a price higher than the supply curve (S_m), and producer surplus results. Perfect competition produces the largest combined consumer and producer surplus area ($ABCR$) of any market structure.

The Social Impact of Perfect Competition

Economic Efficiency
Occurs when firms produce at the minimum point on their long-run average cost curves.

Theoretically, industrywide and economywide perfect competition has two major virtues. First, competition results in **economic efficiency** because firms produce at the minimum point on their long-run average cost curves. Firms whose size or scale is not at the minimum efficient level must either change their scale or leave the industry to avoid further losses. This means all firms have the most efficient size and are using the lowest-cost combination of inputs. Thus, the long-run industry output in perfect competition is produced at the lowest possible cost per unit.

Allocative Efficiency
Occurs when consumers pay a price equal to marginal cost.

Second, at long-run competitive equilibrium, price also equals marginal cost. This means that **allocative efficiency** is being achieved and the productive resources are being allocated exactly as buyers want them to be. If price were greater than marginal cost, it would mean not enough resources were going into production of the good. Consumers would be willing to pay a price greater than what it costs to produce another unit of the good. Just the opposite would be true if price were less than marginal cost. Where price equals marginal cost, the correct amount of resources is being devoted to producing the good.

Perfect competition would serve the consumer very well. It would result in greater output, lower prices, and less economic profit than exist under less competitive conditions. However, competition is not without its disadvantages. It frequently results in an unnecessary duplication of plant and equipment. And although competition benefits the economy as a whole, it can impose financial hardship on individual firms and displace workers if firms are forced out of business by more efficient producers. In some industries (such as public utilities), many firms operating at a small scale may not be able to provide a good or a service as cheaply as a few firms producing at a much larger scale.

Summary

- There are several possible models of economic competition in a market economy, ranging from perfect competition at one extreme to monopoly at the other. In between are monopolistic competition and oligopoly.

- Perfect competition is a market structure in which there are so many buyers and sellers of identical products that no one buyer or seller can influence market price. Both buyers and sellers are well informed about market conditions and prices, and entry into and exit from the market are unrestricted. Supply and demand determine market price.

- Under conditions of perfect competition, each firm operates at its maximum profit position where marginal revenue equals marginal cost. A firm suffering a loss may continue to operate in the short run at the point where marginal revenue equals marginal cost as long as it is covering its variable cost and making a contribution to overhead. In the long run, the firm must cover all costs because all costs are variable.

- Economic forces come into play in the long run to reduce prices and to eliminate economic profits under conditions of perfect competition. Consumers eventually obtain the product at a price equal to the cost of production.

- A long-run cost curve can be constructed from a series of short-run cost curves for firms at different scales of operations. Competitive forces arising from economies of scale in the long run result in a lower unit cost.

- Consumer surplus is the difference between what consumers would have been willing to pay and what they actually pay for the product. Producer surplus refers to the difference between what firms are willing to accept as a price for the product and the price they actually receive. Perfect competition produces the largest combined consumer surplus and producer surplus of any market structure.

- Perfect competition has two theoretical virtues. First, competition results in economic efficiency because firms produce at the minimum point of their long-run cost curves. Second, at long-run competitive equilibrium, price also equals marginal cost. This means that allocative efficiency is being achieved and productive resources are being allocated exactly as buyers want them to be.

New Terms and Concepts

Perfect competition
Economies of scale
Optimal scale of operation
Diseconomies of scale

Consumer surplus
Producer surplus
Economic efficiency
Allocative efficiency

Discussion Questions

1. What four types of market structures may exist?

2. What characteristics or conditions must be present for perfect competition to exist?

3. Why does the individual seller under conditions of perfect competition have no effect on the market price?

4. Explain how, by examining a marginal revenue and marginal cost graph, you can determine: (a) whether a firm is making an economic profit or suffering a loss; (b) if the firm is suffering a loss, whether it should shut down or continue to operate in the short run.

5. If firms in perfect competition all pay the same price for resources and all receive the same price for outputs, how can they have different total profits or different profits per unit sold?

6. How do economic profits disappear in the long run under conditions of perfect competition?

7. What does the optimal scale of operation mean?

8. Total consumer surplus and producer surplus are maximized under perfect competition. If government restricted the quantity that could be brought to market, how would this restriction affect price, quantity, consumer surplus, and producer surplus?

9. What are the social benefits of perfect competition?

Economic Applications

EconData

To learn more about perfect competition, go to the EconData icon at http://econapps.swlearning.com. Find the Microeconomics heading and click on the link titled "Perfect Competition." Learn how "Housing Starts" incorporates perfectly competitive markets.

6

CHAPTER REVIEW

7

Imperfect Competition

After studying Chapter 7, you should be able to:

1. Define *monopoly* and explain why a monopolist has relatively great freedom to establish the price of its product.

2. Draw a graph showing *ATC, MC, AR,* and *MC* and indicate the point of maximum profit for a monopolist.

3. Define *monopolistic competition* and explain why product differentiation enables the seller to influence price.

4. Define *oligopoly* and explain why there is a tendency toward price stability in an oligopolistic market.

5. Explain how market power is measured by the use of concentration ratios and the Herfindahl Index.

6. Show graphically why (assuming identical costs) the market price is higher under imperfect competition than under perfect competition.

7. Understand the major provisions of the Sherman and Clayton acts.

Monopoly

Monopoly
A market structure in which only one producer or seller exists for a product that has no close substitutes.

At the other end of the competitive scale from perfect competition is monopoly. **Monopoly** is a market structure in which only one producer or seller exists for a product that has no close substitutes. The requirement that there be no close substitutes makes it difficult to find a true monopoly. It may be, for example, that Ford Motor Company has a monopoly on the production and sale of Ford cars. But as long as car buyers can turn to Chryslers, Chevrolets, Toyotas, and numerous other makes, Ford is not a true monopoly.

It may appear that a landlord has a monopoly on the location of a certain rental property. After all, the landlord is the only one who has that particular piece of property to rent. But several other choices of similar property may be available near that location, so it cannot be claimed that the landlord is a monopolist. Like perfect competition, monopoly is more of an abstraction than a reality.

A firm may produce a multitude of goods, many of which are sold in the market in competition with identical or similar products. But among its products may be one item for which there is no competition. The firm then has some monopoly power in the sale of that one item. Even if a monopolist did exist, it would still be in competition with other firms—not for the sale of a particular good or service, but for the acquisition of the consumer's dollars. Although various firms have some monopoly power in the U.S. economy today, the only true monopolies that exist are some forms of government-regulated public utilities.

CHARACTERISTICS OF MONOPOLY

The major characteristic of monopoly is the degree of control that the seller holds over price. In perfect competition, the individual supplies of many sellers make up the market supply. But with a monopoly the individual supply of the monopolist coincides with the market supply. On the demand side, because the monopolist is the only supplier, market demand equals the demand for the monopolist's product or service. Therefore, anytime the monopolist increases or decreases supply, it affects the market price. Instead of having to take the market price as given and adjust output to the most profitable position (as under perfect competition), the monopolist can adjust output, within limits, to attain the most favorable market price. The monopolist can be described as a "price maker."

SOURCES OF MONOPOLY

Monopolies may develop from a number of sources. But the essence of obtaining and maintaining a monopoly lies in the erection of barriers to the entry of other firms into the industry. If a monopoly can effectively block the entry of new firms into its business or industry, it can continue to enjoy its economic profits.

Economies of Scale

In some industries, it is not economical for firms to compete. Heavy industries such as steel and large machinery, which require centralized control of vast amounts of capital to achieve the economies of large-scale production, tend to be monopolistic. In such industries, perfect competition is not feasible; if many firms were to supply the market, none could produce enough to take advantage of the low per unit cost associated with economies of scale. Even though most of the largest firms within these industries are not perfect monopolies, they tend to have monopolistic characteristics.

Natural Monopolies: Public Utilities

Some industries, by their very nature, tend to foster monopoly and repel competition. For example, confusion, waste, and inconvenience would result if several natural gas utility companies were to compete for the trade of the same consumers in an urban area. In addition to waste through duplication of assets, just think of what the condition of our streets would be if three or four natural gas companies were periodically tearing them up to repair separate sets of gas lines. And what about the safety of passengers and pedestrians if buses from four different transit companies raced each other from corner to corner to pick up passengers?

In cases where one or two firms can adequately supply all the service needed, it may be desirable to limit the number of firms within a given territory. Under these circumstances, the government may need to regulate services and prices. This regulation is done by granting a monopoly franchise to one or a few firms, subject to control by a public service commission.

Control of Raw Materials

Another effective barrier to entry is ownership or control of essential raw materials. Although it is difficult to gain complete control over raw materials (and in many cases there may be close substitutes for a particular raw material), this method of blocking competition was effective for years in the production of aluminum. ALCOA existed as a monopoly for years through its control of nearly all sources of bauxite, the major ingredient in aluminum production. In Africa and elsewhere, most of the diamond mines are owned by the DeBeers Company of South Africa; and a large portion of the world's molybdenum supplies are controlled by a single company.

Patents

A patent gives the holder the exclusive right to use, keep, or sell an invention for a period of 20 years. In spite of legal safeguards against having an undesirable degree of monopoly arise from the granting of such a temporary exclusive right, the control of patents is an important source of monopoly power for some large corporations.

Procedures for using patents and the patent laws to stifle competition vary. Patents obtained for useless devices or processes increase the likelihood that inventors of worthwhile innovations will encounter lawsuits for infringement. By making slight changes in a patented device or process, the owner may file an amendment to a patent and thus prolong its life. Perhaps the most effective way in which patents allow manufacturers to maintain control is by scaring away new rivals with threats of infringement suits.

Control of patents has played an important role in the development of many of today's well-known giant corporations. Today, nearly two-thirds of all new patents are held by corporations.

Competitive Tactics

A firm may eliminate its rivals or block the entry of new firms through the use of aggressive production and merchandising techniques. Sometimes, unfair tactics are employed to drive out competition. For example, we have seen the use of predatory pricing (temporarily selling below cost) to weed out or bankrupt smaller competitors. Other unfair tactics include defaming competitors' products, pirating competitors' administrative personnel, applying undue pressure on suppliers or financial sources, and sometimes resorting to outright blackmail. Although many of these tactics are illegal, there is still enough aggressive but lawful competition taking place to discourage new firms from entering some industries.

Monopoly Price

The concept of monopoly implies a situation where a single seller offers a good for which there is no available close substitute. Whether monopoly power is used to obtain the highest possible price for what is sold depends largely on whether the monopolist is deterred by fear of possible government regulation or private competition. Another important consideration is the need to gain or maintain the goodwill of the public because this affects sales of the firm's product.

DETERMINING MONOPOLY PRICE

Within limits, a monopolist can maintain supply at virtually any level, assuming that the price is uniform for all consumers and will be set by the monopolist at the point that yields the greatest total profit. The location of this point depends on the demand for the product and the costs of production.

The Monopolist's Demand Curve

Under perfect competition, demand for the output of a single firm is represented by a straight horizontal line. The producer can sell any quantity offered at the current market price. At the same time, the individual producer cannot influence the market price by either increasing or decreasing supply.

The monopolist's situation is different. The monopolist is the only supplier of the good, so the demand curve for the monopolist's product slopes downward to the right *because it is the market demand curve of all consumers.* The less essential the product, the more elastic the demand (see Chapter 4). Hence, the first question the monopolist asks is, "How many units of my good can I expect to sell at various prices?" The number of units to be produced is determined by the answer.

The monopolist's position is reflected in Figure 7–1. There is only one producer, so the demand curve for the individual firm is also the demand curve for the entire industry. *D* is the demand curve and also the average revenue (*AR*) curve for the firm. At 1,100 units, total revenue is $8,800; at 1,000 units, it is $10,000; and

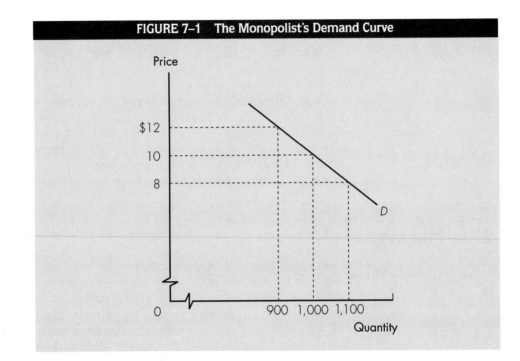

FIGURE 7–1   The Monopolist's Demand Curve

at 900 units, it is $10,800. Thus, the monopolist can obtain a higher price and larger revenue by limiting supply. If sales increase from 1,000 to 1,100, total revenue decreases. Of course, if demand were elastic, the monopolist would make greater revenue by increasing output.

The Monopolist's Cost Curves

As happens with most other producers' costs, the monopolist's cost per unit usually decreases for a while as the number of units produced increases. If production is pushed to the point where the marginal cost (*MC*) begins to increase, however, the average total cost (*ATC*) will soon begin to increase, too. The *ATC* increases when the increase in average variable costs becomes great enough to offset the decrease in average fixed costs. How long the monopolist should continue to increase production after the *MC* begins to rise depends on the number of units that can be produced before the *MC* of the next unit produced is greater than the corresponding marginal revenue (*MR*).

Relationships Between the Monopolist's Cost and Revenue Curves

Assume that the monopolist's cost and revenue situation is as shown in Table 7–1. The level of production at which profit is maximized is reached when 8 units are produced. Because *MC* and *MR* are also equal for 9 units, the same amount of

TABLE 7-1 Costs and Revenues for a Monopoly							
Units of Output	TC	ATC	MC	TR	AR	MR	Total Profit (or Loss)
1	$ 20.00	$20.00	—	$ 16.48	$16.48	—	$ (3.52)
2	34.72	17.36	$14.72	31.48	15.74	$15.00	(3.24)
3	45.12	15.04	10.40	45.00	15.00	13.52	(0.12)
4	52.16	13.04	7.04	57.04	14.26	12.04	4.88
5	56.80	11.36	4.64	67.60	13.52	10.56	10.80
6	60.00	10.00	3.20	76.68	12.78	9.08	16.68
7	62.72	8.96	2.72	84.28	12.04	7.60	21.56
8	65.92	8.24	3.20	90.40	11.30	6.12	24.48
9	70.56	7.84	4.64	95.04	10.56	4.64	24.48
10	77.60	7.76	7.04	98.20	9.82	3.16	20.60
11	88.00	8.00	10.40	99.88	9.08	1.68	11.88
12	102.72	8.56	14.72	100.08	8.34	0.20	(2.64)

profit, $24.48, can be realized if 9 units are produced. But profit decreases if more than 9 units are produced because *MC* rises above *MR*. If 12 units are produced, there will be a loss of $2.64.

Because *ATC* is less at 10 units than at 9 units, and because at 10 units *AR* is still greater than *ATC*, you might at first expect it to be more profitable to produce the larger number. However, this conclusion is not justified. After 9 units, the cost of producing another unit is greater than the amount of revenue received from its sale (*MC* = $7.04, *MR* = $3.16). Thus, the relationship between *MC* and *MR* is the key to determining the point at which the producer should limit output.

The relationships of the cost and revenue curves may be plotted as shown in Figure 7–2. *AR*, the monopolist's demand curve, slopes downward to the right, indicating that as the price decreases, more units are bought. *MR* shows that as the number of units sold increases, the marginal revenue per unit decreases. *ATC* reflects the behavior of average total cost as more units are produced. *MC* indicates the decreasing or increasing costs incurred as additional units are produced by the monopolist. The shapes of these cost curves are the same as those for a competitive firm and are traceable to the law of diminishing marginal productivity.

Because the monopolist is faced with a negatively sloped *AR* (demand) curve, the *MR* curve is always less than the *AR* curve, and the *MR* curve declines at a faster rate. In perfect competition, where the seller has a horizontal *AR* (demand) curve, every time an additional unit is sold at the market price, that same amount is added to the total revenue. Consequently, the *AR* and *MR* curves are equal. The monopolist, however, faces a situation where price must be lowered in order to sell a larger quantity.

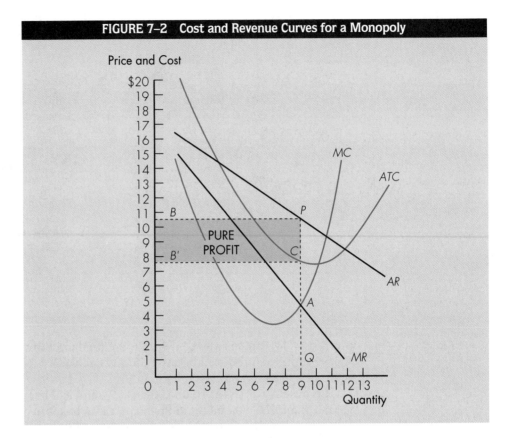

FIGURE 7-2   Cost and Revenue Curves for a Monopoly

For example, the monopolist may be able to sell 1 unit for $10 or 2 units for $9 each. This does not mean that 1 unit can be sold for $10 and two more for $9 each, because one of the two buyers who would pay $9 is the same one who is willing to pay $10. The monopolist's choice, then, is to sell a single unit for $10 or 2 units for $9 each. If the latter option is chosen, AR is $9 but MR is $8. This can be seen in Table 7-2.

In short, the AR of the monopolist declines because a lower price is received on the additional goods sold. The MR declines at a faster rate than the AR because, in selling a larger number of units, the monopolist also takes a lower price on the units that could have been sold anyway at a higher price. Thus, if 3 units are sold for $8 each instead of 2 units for $9 each, total revenue increases by $8 from the sale of the third unit as such, minus $1 less on each of the two previous units that could have been sold for $9 apiece.

Under the conditions represented in Figure 7-2, at a production level of 9 units, MC and MR are exactly equal. Beyond point A, it becomes less profitable to produce an additional unit. The MC of additional units exceeds the MR. Demand

TABLE 7–2 Marginal Revenue: Competition Versus Monopoly							
Perfect Competition				Monopoly			
Quantity	Price	TR	MR	Quantity	Price	TR	MR
1	$5	$ 5	—	1	$10	$10	—
2	5	10	$5	2	9	18	$8
3	5	15	5	3	8	24	6
4	5	20	5	4	7	28	4

being what it is, the price at which 9 units can be sold is $10.56. This is shown by the lines *PB* and *PQ*, which indicate price and quantity, respectively. The total revenue from the sale of 9 units, then, is $95.04. In the figure, the total revenue is represented geometrically by the area 0*QPB*.

The cost of producing 9 units is $70.56. The total cost is represented by the area 0*QCB'*, which is less than the area 0*QPB* by the size of the area embraced within *BPCB'*; this area represents the economic profit of $24.48 ($95.04 − $70.56).

What would happen if additional firms were to enter this industry? The resulting increase in supply and decrease in market price would soon reduce or eliminate economic profits. But if the monopolist could effectively block entry of new firms, the monopolist's prices and economic profits could be maintained. Consequently, it is often said that monopoly results in a higher price, the use of fewer resources, and greater economic profit than would occur under perfect competition.

It is possible that at the optimal output level (where *MC* = *MR*) the monopolist may be only breaking even or actually suffering a loss. This would be the situation in Figure 7–2 if the *ATC* curve were higher than the *AR* curve. Obviously, the monopolist would shut down in the short run to stem the losses, unless it covered its variable costs. If the firm provides an important service, the government may subsidize the monopoly to keep it in business. For example, many local transit systems are subsidized through local income or property taxes.

RESTRAINTS ON MONOPOLY PRICE

People often assume that monopoly implies an exorbitant price. Goods produced by a firm that enjoys a monopoly, or virtual monopoly, may indeed be sold at a price that exploits the public. It would be a mistake, however, to think that monopoly always means an exorbitant price. The monopolist cannot charge more for a product than consumers are willing to pay. Figure 7–1 illustrates that all the monopolist desires to sell cannot be sold at a given price. For example, 1,000 units can be sold at $10 per unit, but 1,200 units cannot be sold at that price. Furthermore, the monopolist cannot raise the price to $12 and still hope to sell as many units as were sold at $10. Even if a firm is a monopoly, it cannot arbitrarily set a price and sell all it wants to sell at that price. It can alter its supply to attain the best possible price for itself, but even so it must price within the limits of consumer demand. In the final analysis, the price that is most profitable to the monopolist may be within the reach of only a small number of consumers, depriving many other consumers of access to the product.

Several other economic considerations may deter the monopolist from selling its goods at the highest possible price. These include the monopolist's lack of specific knowledge about demand, elasticity, and unit production costs; its desire to discourage competition; its desire to maintain good customer relations; and its fear of governmental regulation.

Monopolistic Competition

Monopolistic Competition
A market structure in which relatively many firms supply a similar but differentiated product, with each firm having a limited degree of control over price.

Within the extremes of perfect competition and monopoly are various other market structures, including oligopoly and monopolistic competition. Oligopoly is a market structure that involves relatively few firms. **Monopolistic competition** is a market structure in which relatively many firms supply a similar but differentiated product, with each firm having a limited degree of control over price. *Monopoly* indicates a high degree of control over market supply or price; *competition* suggests that no individual supplier can dictate price. Putting the two terms together, we can conclude that under monopolistic competition, firms retain some control over price, but only a limited amount.

PRODUCT DIFFERENTIATION

Product Differentiation
Establishment of real or imagined characteristics that identify a firm's product as unique.

The major characteristic of monopolistic competition is product differentiation. **Product differentiation** means that the products have either real or imagined characteristics that identify the products as differing from each other. Differentiation permits a limited degree of control over price. There are enough sellers in monopolistic competition that the actions of any one have little effect on the others.

Our review of monopolistic competition will use the sale of coffee as an example. Suppose that a large number of firms sell coffee of identical quality, without brand names or advertising claims, and that the coffee is all packaged in the same type of container. Suppose further that a price of $3.70 per pound has been established by market supply and demand. Under perfect competition, no seller could get more than the market price for its coffee. After all, why would a consumer purchase any one seller's coffee at a higher price when identical coffee for $3.70 per pound could be obtained from many other sellers? On the other hand, if there were only one seller, the market price could be changed by limiting or expanding the monopolist's supply on the market.

In reality, we have a relatively large number of coffee producers supplying a similar but differentiated product. It is different because one coffee is "good to the last drop," another is "mountain grown," another is "heavenly," and another is "the coffee of El Exigente." And quite apart from their names and slogans, some coffees are decaffeinated, others are freeze-dried, and others are espresso style. Many different blends are packaged in a variety of containers. Although these may all sell for about the same bulk line price as determined in the market by the overall demand and supply for coffee, product differentiation (whether real or psychological) permits individual firms to have some degree of control over the price at which their coffee will sell. The similarity among coffees, however, limits this degree of control.

Consumers buy a particular brand of coffee because they like its taste, admire its package, or are swayed by its advertising. Consequently, if the maker of a particular brand—say, Old Judge Coffee—decides to raise the price a little above the market level, not all consumers will be lost, as would be the case under perfect competition. In fact, we can assume that most Old Judge consumers will agree to pay a few cents more than the general market price because of the difference in Old Judge. But the seller cannot raise the price too far above the market price. When the price differential becomes too great, consumers may still feel that Old Judge is different, but not that different! When the price reaches a certain level, they will shift to other brands of coffee.

Substitution Effect
Increased sales at the expense of other firms.

On the other hand, if Old Judge lowers its price by a few cents below the average market price of $3.70, it will probably gain very few new sales by the **substitution effect**—increased sales at the expense of other firms. Consumers buy certain brands because they feel there is something different about them. If their feeling is strong, they will not leave their favorite brand and shift to Old Judge for the sake of a few cents. But if Old Judge reduces its price substantially, many consumers may feel that the quality difference in their preferred brand is not great enough to deter them from switching to the lower-priced Old Judge Coffee. In such a case, a point may be reached where sales of Old Judge Coffee will increase substantially, provided that other coffee producers do not react by lowering their prices.

Product differentiation gives the individual supplier a certain price range within which prices may be raised or lowered without substantially affecting either the supplier's sales or the sales of competitors. This is the monopolistic aspect of monopolistic competition. However, if Old Judge raises its price too high in comparison to other brands, it will lose consumers; and if it lowers its price sufficiently, it can draw consumers away from other brands. This is the competitive aspect of monopolistic competition.

As a result, we usually find products at a variety of prices within a general market price range in monopolistic competition. When many sellers exist, there is less concern about competitors' reactions to a firm's reduction in price. But instead of engaging in strong price competition, firms may stress product differentiation, use heavy advertising, and emphasize packaging to sway consumers. In any event, firms are less likely to engage in collusive practices to fix prices or to limit output when so many of them are in the market.

SHORT-RUN PRICE AND PROFIT

The demand curve faced by a monopolistic competitor is not the horizontal, perfectly elastic demand curve characteristic of perfect competition. Nor is it identical
to the market demand, as is the case with monopoly. Even though there are many
firms, there are far fewer than in perfect competition, and the products that they
offer are differentiated. Consequently, a firm will be able to sell more by lowering
its price. But this degree of control is limited by several things. The firm's supply is
a small portion of the total supply on the market; it has many competitors; and its
product is still similar, although differentiated. Consequently, its demand curve will
slope downward to the right. Furthermore, it will tend to be more elastic than the
demand curve for the total industry. Of course, the more closely monopolistic competition approaches perfect competition, the more horizontal the individual firm's
demand curve will be. The farther market conditions move in the direction of oligopoly or monopoly, on the other hand, the less elastic the individual firm's demand curve will be and the more closely it will approach the industry demand
curve.

Again, when the demand (or average revenue) curve slopes downward to the
right, the marginal revenue curve moves in the same direction, but at a steeper
slope. Typical short-run cost and revenue curves for a firm engaged in monopolistic competition are shown in Figure 7–3. Figure 7–3a depicts the general range of
prices established in the industry around the intersection of total supply and demand. Figure 7–3b shows data for a monopolistic competitor that is making economic profits. The price, although slightly higher than the average price established
by supply and demand in the market, is still within the general price range at
which most producers sell their products. At this price and with the accompanying

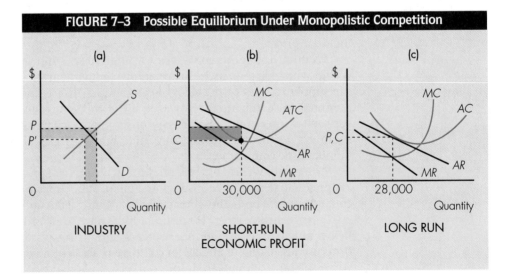

FIGURE 7–3   Possible Equilibrium Under Monopolistic Competition

cost, the firm can produce 30,000 units and enjoy economic profits, as shown in the rectangle.

LONG-RUN EQUILIBRIUM

If short-run economic profits are generally available in the industry, however, they will induce new firms to enter the market. As these new firms attempt to sell their similar but differentiated products, the total supply on the market will increase. This in turn will decrease the market price and lower the average revenue of each firm in the industry. As long as no severe restrictions to entry exist, this process will continue until supply and price eliminate economic profits for the average firm, as shown in Figure 7–3c. Thus, at the point of equilibrium (28,000 units of output), the firm will be making no economic profit in the long run. Furthermore, its total sales will have dropped somewhat as a result of competition, in spite of the total increase of sales in the market.

Of course, if firms in the industry are suffering losses in the short run, the opposite reaction occurs. Firms drop out of business and the total supply on the market decreases, forcing the market price upward. Average revenues for the firms in the industry then rise until losses are eliminated and equilibrium is established at a break-even position in the long run.

Either way, in the long run under monopolistic competition, consumers receive a differentiated product at a price equal to the average total cost of production for the firm. However, this price is not as low as it would be under perfect competition. Because of its slope, the AR curve under monopolistic competition cannot touch the ATC curve at its lowest point, as does the horizontal AR curve characteristic of perfect competition. Hence, even if costs are identical, the equilibrium price under monopolistic competition is higher than the price under perfect competition.

Oligopoly

Oligopoly
A market structure in which relatively few firms produce identical or similar products.

Oligopoly is a market structure in which relatively few firms produce identical or similar products. It might involve two or three firms or a dozen or more, depending on the nature of the industry. However, the firms must be so few that the actions of any one on matters of price and output have a noticeable effect on the others. The two basic characteristics of oligopoly are the ability of individual firms to influence price and the interdependence among firms in setting their pricing policies. If only three firms supply a particular good, any one of them can influence the market price by altering the amount it offers for sale. An increase in supply by any one firm increases total supply and tends to depress the market price. If one firm cuts its price, it gains a larger share of the market at the expense of the other two firms. But the other firms may react by lowering their prices, too. This retaliation again affects all firms' market shares—and may wipe out the initial gain of the original price-cutting firm. Whether or not the firms gain from such price competition depends on the elasticity of demand for the product.

An oligopolist may be reluctant to engage in price competition because of the possible reaction of competitors. Consequently, many forms of nonprice competition—in particular, product differentiation—are found among oligopolists. Oligopolistic structures sometimes lead to collusive practices such as price leadership, pooling, and other techniques designed to fix prices or to limit quantity—especially when market demand is inelastic.

DETERMINING OLIGOPOLY PRICE

Pricing under oligopoly is more difficult than it is under other market structures. The firm may not be able to determine what amount of its product can be sold at various prices. The effect on sales when an oligopolist changes price depends in large part on the reaction of its competitors. In fact, in an oligopoly situation the number of sellers is so few that each must take into consideration the reaction of its rivals. This is a different situation from that of monopolistic competition, where the number of competitors is so large that an individual seller can ignore the reactions of its competitors. Fear of economic retaliation by competing firms can be a strong force limiting price competition under oligopolistic conditions.

Three reactions by rivals are possible when an oligopolist changes supply and/or price. First, competitors may choose to ignore the price change. In this event, the demand and average revenue curve for the individual firm is known with a reasonable degree of accuracy and may appear as D. Second, a change in price may be met by a similar change by rival oligopolists. If they do follow suit, the demand or average revenue of any one oligopolist may appear as D_1. The demand curve D_1 tends to be less elastic because the gain in sales resulting from lower prices is lessened if competitors lower their prices, too. On the other hand, the firm initiating a rise in a price will not lose as many sales as it otherwise would if rivals also increase their prices. In short, the substitution effect resulting from a price change is lessened if other firms adopt the price change themselves.

Third, rivals may follow suit for a decrease in price, but may ignore a rise in price. If one firm reduces its product's price, its increase in quantity sold might be less than anticipated as rivals cut prices, too. This tends to eliminate any substitution effect. The firm that originally introduced the price cut will experience some increase in sales, however, as total industry sales expand in response to the lower price charged by all firms. But if one firm raises its price and its rivals do not, its decrease in sales because of the substitution effect may be greater than anticipated.

In this third case, the oligopolist's demand curve is identical to D for any price above P, but it is identical to D_1 for any price below P. The demand curve will appear as DPD_1, as shown in Figure 7–4, and is termed a *kinked demand curve*. This situation can lead to price stability because the demand curve of the individual firm tends to be inelastic when price moves downward and elastic when price moves upward. Under these circumstances, price P may become the maximum revenue

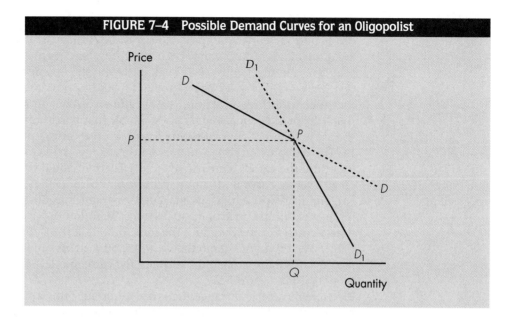

FIGURE 7–4 Possible Demand Curves for an Oligopolist

point for the firm and Q the equilibrium output. There is little incentive for the firm to change its price or output.

PRICE STABILITY

The tendency toward price stability in oligopoly contributes to nonprice competition. Thus, product differentiation is emphasized and advertising is used extensively. Sellers constantly offer a great variety of styles, promotional deals (rebates), guarantees, and the like. But they seldom engage in direct price competition. Witness, for example, the pattern of competition in the production and sale of newspapers, prescription drugs, and steel, where the emphasis is generally on nonprice competition. Sometimes oligopolists practice administered pricing. An **administered price** is a predetermined price set by the seller, rather than a price determined solely by demand and supply in the marketplace.

Administered Price
A predetermined price set by the seller, rather than a price determined solely by demand and supply in the marketplace.

CARTELS

In addition to tacit collusion, firms in an oligopolistic industry may engage in a more formal type of collusion by creating a cartel. A **cartel** is an organization of independent firms that agree to operate as a shared monopoly by limiting production and charging the monopoly price. Cartels are illegal in the United States, for they are in violation of the Sherman Antitrust Act. International cartels, however, are not only common but are even encouraged by some foreign governments.

Cartel
An organization of independent firms that agree to operate as a shared monopoly by limiting production and charging the monopoly price.

Generally, for cartels to be successful, even in the short run, several key ingredients must be prevalent in the industry. Cartels have a greater chance of succeeding if the industry is comprised of a few firms, barriers to entry are substantial, the product is homogeneous, and violations of the agreement are easily detected.

The workings of a cartel agreement can be shown graphically. Let's assume that there are three identical firms in the industry and that each firm agrees to share the market equally and charge a price that maximizes profit for the cartel. As shown in Figure 7–5, the demand curve for the cartel's product is represented by D_c. The demand curve for one of the three identical firms is seen as d_1, which is one-third the cartel's demand schedule. The individual firm's corresponding marginal revenue curve is MR_1, and its marginal cost function is MC_1. As a cartel member, the firm will equate its marginal cost and marginal revenue and charge a profit-maximizing price of P and produce an output of q_1. The three firms are identical, so each firm will produce the same output at the same price. The end result is that the cartel charges a monopoly price and restricts output to the monopoly output (Q_c). Note the similarities between the cartel model and the model of the pure monopolist in Figure 7–2.

In reality, cartel arrangements are inherently unstable because each firm has an incentive to break the agreement if it believes its actions will go unnoticed by

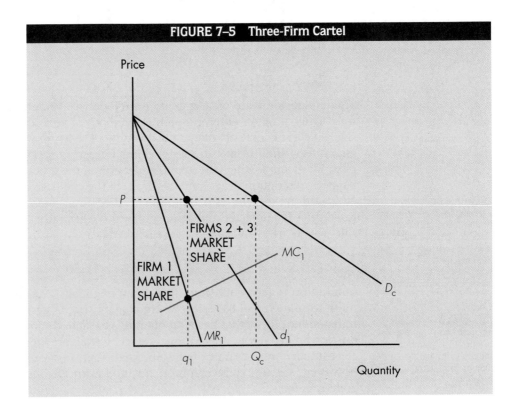

FIGURE 7–5   Three-Firm Cartel

the others. In Figure 7–5, our firm may be tempted to cheat by lowering price by a small amount and gaining market share. The firm will increase its profits as long as its lower price exceeds marginal cost and its rivals ignore its actions. But when the cheating is detected by the other firms, they will retaliate by cutting their prices as well, setting off a price war and bringing an end to the cartel.

Cartels are generally short-lived because of such behavior. Those that are successful usually have a dominant firm (or country) that acts as an enforcer by punishing cheaters. Examples of successful cartels led by prominent players include the oil and diamond cartels.

Saudi Arabia is the dominant firm in the cartel known as the Organization of Petroleum Exporting Countries (OPEC). In 1973, OPEC, led by Saudi Arabia, stunned the industrial nations of the world by restricting the supply of the world's exportable oil. The result was a dramatic increase in world oil prices. The OPEC cartel successfully raised the world price of oil in 1973 from $2.50 per barrel to $11.00 per barrel in a six-month period. OPEC's influence peaked in 1979–1982 when the price of oil imported into the United States reached $36 per barrel. The cartel eventually cracked as individual members cheated on the agreement by producing and selling more than their OPEC quota in order to increase national revenues. In January 2003, the price of oil stood at $31 a barrel. At any point in time the price of oil reflects a number of factors, including the world demand for petroleum, a large-scale war, tension among Middle East countries over the Israel–Palestine hostilities, and the success of the cartel in limiting production.

Another example of a long-lasting cartel arrangement exists in the diamond industry. This cartel has as its dominant firm the DeBeers Company of South Africa. DeBeers controls the mining, processing, and retailing of gem-quality diamonds throughout the world. Diamonds sell for artificially high prices only because DeBeers controls the diamond cartel and determines how many diamonds get to market from an expanding world supply. But even the diamond cartel is being threatened by one of its members. Russia generates 26 percent of the diamonds sold by the cartel and seeks to sell a bigger share. Should the cartel crack, diamond prices would fall sharply, as would the value of jewelry containing diamonds. Diamonds are high-priced only because of the strength of the cartel.

MEASUREMENTS OF CONCENTRATION

Concentration Ratio
A measure of market power calculated by determining the percentage of industry output accounted for by the largest firms.

A common method of examining market power within an oligopolistic industry is through the use of concentration ratios. A **concentration ratio** is the percentage of industry output accounted for by the largest firms. Table 7–3 presents four firm concentration ratios for selected industries. In the case of cigarettes, the four largest firms account for 99 percent of the market, whereas the four largest retail bakeries account for but 3 percent of the market.

Although concentration ratios give a broad picture of industry concentration, care must be exercised in drawing conclusions about market power based solely on this instrument. For example, the concentration ratio does not tell us how the

TABLE 7–3 Concentration Ratios for Selected Industries*	
Industry	4 Largest Firms
Cigarettes	99
Breakfast cereals	87
Breweries	81
Snack foods	63
Cheese manufacturers	57
Wineries	37
Women's dresses	6
Retail bakeries	3

*Based on the percentage of value of shipments.
Source: U.S. Department of Commerce, Bureau of the Census, 1997 Census of Manufacturers, *Concentration Ratios in Manufacturing,*2001.

Herfindahl Index
A measure of market power calculated by summing the squares of the market shares of each firm in the industry.

market is divided among the four firms nor how many firms comprise the entire industry. To overcome some of the shortcomings of concentration ratios, economists employ a statistical tool known as the Herfindahl Index. The **Herfindahl Index** is calculated by summing the squares of the market shares of each firm in the industry. The Herfindahl Index, unlike the concentration ratio, takes into account all firms in the industry and assigns extra weight to firms with the largest market shares. The following example illustrates the use of the formula.

Assume there are five firms in the industry. Firm A controls 75 percent of the market, Firm B has 10 percent, and the three remaining firms each account for 5 percent of the market. Substituting these values in the formula gives the Herfindahl Index in this market:

$$(75)^2 + (10)^2 + (5)^2 + (5)^2 + (5)^2 = 5625 + 100 + 25 + 25 + 25 = 5,800$$

Next assume another five-firm industry in which each firm accounts for 20 percent of the market. In this case, the Herfindahl Index is

$$(20)^2 + (20)^2 + (20)^2 + (20)^2 + (20)^2 = 2,000$$

This example reveals that by squaring each market share, the Herfindahl Index gives much heavier weight to firms with large market shares. Thus, the greater the concentration of output in a small number of firms, the greater the likelihood that, other things being equal, competition in a market will be weak. In contrast, if concentration is low, reflecting a large number of firms with small market shares, competition will tend to be vigorous.

The Herfindahl Index is used by the U.S. Department of Justice. The Department of Justice published formal numerical guidelines for horizontal mergers (those between firms operating in the same product and geographic markets) based on the index. According to the Department of Justice, if the value of the Herfindahl Index is below 1,000, the industry is highly competitive. If the index is between 1,000 and 1,800, the industry is moderately competitive, and if it is over 1,800 the industry is highly concentrated. The Department of Justice has gone on record as saying it will challenge any merger of an industry with an index above 1,800 if the effect of the merger is to raise the index by 50 points or more. In examining each industry, the extent of foreign competition, the number of substitutes, and the financial health of the merging firms are also considered.

Perfectly Competitive Versus Monopolistic Pricing

The weight of economic evidence indicates that a high degree of competition benefits consumers. Under competition, firms tend to have lower prices, use more resources, and obtain fewer economic profits in the long run. In an industry, each firm's amount of economic profit tends to decline to the point where *AR* is equal to *ATC*. This means that the consumer can purchase the good at a price equal to the lowest possible average total cost of production for a given scale of operation.

Under monopolistic competition, a firm's economic profits tend to decline in the long run, and its cost–revenue relationships become adjusted, as shown in Figure 7–6. Because demand (the *AR* curve) for the output of a single firm under monopolistic competition slopes downward to the right, the marginal revenue curve slopes downward, too, but below the average revenue curve. Therefore, the two

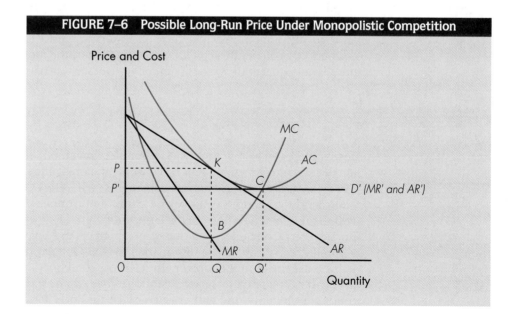

FIGURE 7–6   Possible Long-Run Price Under Monopolistic Competition

cost curves and the two revenue curves cannot all coincide at the point where the average revenue and average total cost curves coincide, as would be the case under perfect competition. Because of the less than perfectly elastic demand, the long-run equilibrium price P under any form of imperfect competition is higher than the long-run equilibrium price P' under perfect competition, for identical cost conditions.

Figure 7–6 shows that under imperfect competition, AC and AR coincide at K, and MC and MR intersect at B. Thus, $0Q$ units are produced with the price at P. If either fewer or more units are produced, a loss results because AR lies below AC for any other quantity.

Output tends to be adjusted to the point where MC and MR are equal. You might think, then, that the result of monopolistic competition in the long run will be the same as that of perfect competition. But this is not so because the price where $MC = MR$ under monopolistic competition is not the same as the price where $AR = AC$.

In Figure 7–6, D' represents the straight-line curves for marginal revenue MR and for average revenue AR', which coincide under perfect competition. The point where MC and MR are equal (point C) is also the point where AC and AR are equal. Thus, the price under perfect competition is at P', and $0Q'$ units are produced. Consequently, the price is lower and the supply is greater under perfect competition than under monopolistic competition.

This analysis assumes, however, that the scale of operation for a small firm in perfect competition is the same as that for a larger firm in some form of imperfect competition. The scale of operation for firms in monopolistic competition may be similar to that for firms in perfect competition, and consequently their cost curves may be nearly identical. But oligopolies and monopolies generally produce at much larger scales of operation. Because of the lower average total cost curve that results, an oligopoly or monopoly may have an equilibrium price lower than is possible under perfectly competitive conditions. Nevertheless, the monopolist's or oligopolist's price is not equal to the lowest point on its average total cost curve (see Figure 7–7).

Competition Among Consumers

Just as there can be different types of competition among sellers, there can be varying degrees of competition among consumers. Pure competition among consumers exists in cases where numerous consumers, who are well-informed about price and market conditions, purchase a commodity under identical conditions and where no individual consumer is large enough to change the total demand or influence the market price. The numerous shoppers in a given locality certainly form a purely competitive consumers' market for the products of the local grocery store.

Monopsony
A market structure in which there is a single buyer.

We use the term **monopsony** to refer to a condition in which there is only one purchaser for a good or service. Monopsonies can be found in local areas where there may be only one granary to service the local farmers. Sometimes a near

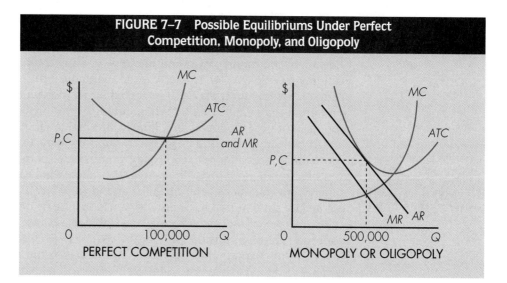

FIGURE 7–7   Possible Equilibriums Under Perfect Competition, Monopoly, and Oligopoly

monopsony will exist when a large-scale employer moves into a predominantly rural area. Such an employer may be the only major consumer of labor in the area. Historically, coal producers operating in the small towns of eastern Kentucky and West Virginia exercised strong monopsony power. However, with greater labor mobility resulting from increased technology and communication, examples of monopsonies are rare today.

Prior to free agency, professional sports leagues acted as monopsonists. When a specific team drafted a player and signed him to a professional contract, that player had no other option than to agree to the team's contract conditions from that time forward. A player could either accept the team's offer or withhold his services. But if he wanted to continue his professional career, he was captive to the monopsonistic control of the team owner. Today, players can play out their options after a certain number of years and offer their services to other teams at market prices.

Oligopsony
A market structure in which there are only a few buyers.

Oligopsony exists when a few buyers dominate the market. In the tobacco market, for example, there are numerous producers but relatively few buyers. It is possible for any of the major producers of cigarettes to influence the market demand and, consequently, the market price for raw tobacco by its decisions to buy more or less tobacco. A similar situation exists in the commercial jet aircraft market, where there are only a few purchasers. The authors of a college textbook also face an oligopsonistic market in the publication of their manuscript.

Monopsonistic Competition
A market structure in which there are many buyers offering differentiated conditions to sellers.

Monopsonistic competition, a condition in which there are many purchasers who offer differentiated conditions to sellers, is very prevalent in the U.S. economy. In any large community, for example, a great number of firms hire labor, offering a variety of working conditions and fringe benefits. Toy manufacturers deal with a monopsonistically competitive market in the distribution of their products.

Market Structure in the United States

The variety and complexity of our markets certainly confirm the notion of a mixed economy (see Chapter 3). Not only is the economy in this sense mixed for the total economic system but it may also be mixed for an individual firm. A firm operating in a purely competitive market when buying its productive resources may have a monopoly or near monopoly in selling its finished product.

Bilateral Monopoly
A situation in which only a single buyer exists on one side of a market and only one seller (the monopolist) exists on the other side.

On the other hand, a **bilateral monopoly** may exist. In this situation, a monopsonist faces a monopolist. Today, professional sports approximate the conditions of bilateral monopoly. Unlike in earlier days when each player was subject to employment conditions determined by an individual team, each player is now represented by a union that bargains with a negotiating committee representing team owners. For example, the National Basketball Association can be viewed as the monopsonist in that it is the only buyer of the services of professional basketball players in the market, and the players union acts as the monopolist because it is the only seller of their services. In 1999, professional basketball players went on strike over a number of contract issues. After much acrimony and a prolonged strike, both parties eventually came to terms and an abbreviated professional basketball season was held.

A seller's influence on supply and price depends on the nature of the market in which the seller operates. The market structure determines the seller's actions regarding price and output, as well as the seller's reactions to changes by others. The type and degree of competition influence the price and output policies and the profit picture of individual firms and of each industry as a whole.

How Much Monopoly Is Tolerable?

A market economy requires that prices be determined by competition whenever possible. Yet many economists and historians have noted a tendency over time for competition to diminish and give way to monopoly, oligopoly, or monopolistic competition.

Is monopoly power increasing? Unfortunately, we have no adequate means of measuring the relative extent of imperfect competition now versus in the past. For example, it is true that there are numerous giant firms. But, at the same time, changing technology, communication, and transportation have enlarged market areas. There is also much more competition from foreign markets today. Nevertheless, the absolute size of some firms and the number of mergers that have occurred in recent years give the impression that in some industries relatively fewer sellers remain. If this view is correct and the tendency continues, what effect will it have on our economic order and on the economic and political welfare of the American people?

Under perfect competition, price tends to equal production costs. However, it is neither possible nor desirable to have enough firms to satisfy the conditions for perfect competition. Moreover, when competition is keen and there are many small firms, prices may be high, because the firms are not large enough to realize the economies of large-scale production. One large plant may thus be able to supply a greater variety and quantity of output at lower prices than can many small competing firms. Therefore, public policy should not aim to eliminate large-scale production merely to guarantee the existence of many firms in an industry. On the other hand, the actions of monopolies and oligopolies over the centuries suggest that when production is controlled by too few producers, the government must stand ready to ensure consumer protection against exploitative practices.

Antitrust Laws

Over the past century, the federal government has enacted a series of antitrust laws. The primary purpose of these laws has been to maintain competition and prevent restraint of trade. They also restrict unfair competitive practices by businesses, both large and small. A few of the more notable laws are described here.

SHERMAN ANTITRUST ACT

Sherman Antitrust Act
A federal law passed in 1890 that outlaws restraint of trade and any attempt to monopolize.

In 1890, Congress passed the first antitrust law, the **Sherman Antitrust Act.** The Sherman Act has two major provisions. Section 1 declares every contract, combination, or conspiracy in restraint of trade to be illegal. Section 2 makes it illegal to monopolize or attempt to monopolize. In addition, the Sherman Act contains a provision enabling private parties who are victims of monopoly under sections 1 and 2 to sue for triple damages. In other words, if a firm is convicted under the Sherman Act, individuals can then file suit to recover three times the damages that they sustained.

The language of the law is strong but vague, and the federal courts took years to determine its scope. In particular, the phrase "in restraint of trade" lacked a legal definition. Under a strict economic definition, any firm with monopoly power (power to restrict output or to increase price) would be guilty of restraint of trade. However, courts have generally held that the restraint must be "unreasonable" before it is illegal. The *rule of reason* states that monopolies that behave well are not illegal. Of course, what is reasonable is a matter of judgment.

The rule of reason was clearly expressed by the U.S. Supreme Court in 1911 in the famous Standard Oil case, in which the Court broke up that company's strong, and often violent, control of the petroleum industry. In the case against the United States Steel Corporation in 1920, the Court held that bigness alone was not a proof of violation. This principle was also used in the International Harvester case of 1927. In subsequent cases, however, courts have held otherwise. For example, in the ALCOA case in 1945, Judge Learned Hand ruled that size alone was enough to establish that a firm enjoyed monopoly power.

Clayton Act
A federal law passed in 1914 that outlaws certain business activities not specifically covered by the Sherman Act.

Price Discrimination
Charging different customers different prices for the same good.

Tying Contracts
Contracts requiring the buyer of one good to purchase another good as well.

Exclusive Dealing
Requiring buyers of goods to agree not to purchase from competing sellers.

Interlocking Directorates
Boards of directors of competing firms with one or more members in common.

Predatory Pricing
Selling at unreasonably low prices to destroy competitors.

CLAYTON ACT

In spite of the Sherman Antitrust Act, the tendency toward corporate combinations continued during subsequent decades. To strengthen the Sherman Antitrust Act, the government passed the **Clayton Act** in 1914. It provides a list of prohibited activities:

1. **Price discrimination:** charging different customers different prices for the same good, which would tend to create a monopoly.

2. **Tying contracts** that require the buyer of one good to purchase another good as well.

3. **Exclusive dealing,** where buyers of goods are required to agree not to purchase from competing sellers.

4. Mergers achieved through acquiring the stock of a competing corporation, if the merger would substantially lessen competition.

5. **Interlocking directorates,** where the same person serves on the boards of directors of competing firms.

In addition, the Clayton Act freed normal labor union activities from coverage by the antitrust laws. The Robinson–Patman Act amended the Clayton Act in 1936 to make predatory pricing illegal. **Predatory pricing** consists of selling at unreasonably low prices to destroy competitors. Unfortunately, the law is often very difficult to apply in particular cases.

Section 7 of the Clayton Act was amended in 1950 by the Celler–Kefauver Anti-Merger Act to outlaw the acquisition of one corporation's assets, as well as its stock, by another company if such acquisition would tend to lessen competition.

FEDERAL TRADE COMMISSION ACT

Federal Trade Commission Act
A federal law passed in 1914 creating the FTC to police unfair business practices.

The **Federal Trade Commission Act** of 1914 set up the Federal Trade Commission (FTC) to police unfair business practices. Initially, the FTC had many powers, but a 1919 Supreme Court decision ruled that only the courts could interpret the laws to determine what practices were unfair. The role of the FTC as a decision-making body was severely limited. The Wheeler–Lea Act of 1938 gave the FTC responsibility for prohibiting "deceptive acts or practices in commerce." The FTC then took on the role of policing false and deceptive advertising.

ANTITRUST ACTION: 1980 TO 2003

Antitrust enforcement throughout the twentieth century was not consistently applied. During some administrations, little regulatory action was taken against big business, whereas during others, the Justice Department was extremely active in filing antitrust charges. In some cases, bigness in itself was a cause for antitrust action; in others, predatory behavior that created or sustained monopoly power triggered lawsuits by the Justice Department.

Since 1980 there have been several major antitrust cases. Perhaps the most notable occurred in 1982 when a landmark decision ended a long, complex suit against AT&T involving charges of monopolistic restraint, price fixing, predatory pricing, and other anticompetitive behavior. The suit was settled in 1982 when AT&T accepted a consent decree requiring it to spin off 22 local divisions into separate companies. Subsequently, the "Baby Bells" were formed. Within a short time, several new companies began competing with AT&T for long-distance service. However, the creation of the Baby Bells resulted in regional monopolies providing local telephone service. Their monopoly powers were drastically reduced with the passage of the Telecommunications Act of 1996. This act required the regional telephone companies to interconnect and exchange traffic with new entrants on nondiscriminatory terms. Today, any new long-distance telephone company, no matter how small, can offer consumers the same telephone network service as a large carrier.

Enforcement of antitrust laws was relaxed considerably through the remainder of the decade, only to resume in earnest in the 1990s. In 1992, a group of Ivy League colleges and other prestigious academic institutions were charged with exchanging and fixing prices on student scholarships, assistantships, and other forms of student aid. Most of them pleaded *nolo contendere* (no contest) and accepted cease and desist orders from the government. The Massachusetts Institute of Technology, however, went to trial and was found guilty. Other price-fixing charges were made against three major cereal producers, two major baby food producers, several milk producers, and even some groups of doctors.

From 1995 on, the Federal Trade Commission and the Justice Department began targeting industry giants that the agencies believed used their market power to eliminate competition and thereby stifle innovation and raise prices. Three notable cases are those involving Microsoft, Visa and MasterCard, and American Airlines.

Microsoft

In 1997, Microsoft Corporation was accused by the Justice Department of using its monopoly power in the computer operating system market to protect its dominance and eliminate competitors. Microsoft controls over 90 percent of the operating system market and over 90 percent of the browser market. The government charged that Microsoft forced PC makers to include the company's Internet Explorer browsing software on each computer that was sold with Microsoft's Windows operating system. By packaging Internet Explorer with its operating system, Microsoft was able to inflict severe damage on the sales of Netscape's Navigator. In response to the government's charges, Microsoft contended that Internet Explorer is an enhancement to the operating system and is an integrated feature of Windows. They are not, the company argued, two separate products. The government believed Microsoft's efforts to monopolize the market for Internet browsers could have a wide-ranging impact on the control of commerce and content of the networked world. After a prolonged trial, Microsoft was found guilty in 1999 of maintaining a monopoly in PC operating systems and engaging in a series of anti-competitive and predatory acts to maintain its monopoly.

In 2001, the court ruled in favor of breaking up Microsoft into a number of separate companies. The appeals court threw out the breakup decision, but once again affirmed the fact that Microsoft was guilty on a number of counts of illegal monopoly behavior. Microsoft agreed to a settlement with the federal government and nine states in which it would cease and desist from anticompetitive behavior by disclosing more technical information to other developers, giving PC makers more leeway in how they implement its software, and offering PC makers uniform contracts. It also agreed to donate over $1 billion in software to schools throughout the country. However, eight states and the District of Columbia refused to accept the penalties and pressed for more restrictions. In 2002, the settlement was upheld again in federal court, rebuffing requests for harsher measures. In rendering its decision, the court specifically rejected the proposal that Microsoft be forced to ship a stripped version of Windows absent Internet Explorer.

However, antitrust action against Microsoft is not over. The European Union has launched an in-depth inquiry into the monopolistic behavior of Microsoft. In separate lawsuits, Netscape Communication, now owned by America Online, has filed for pecuniary damages, claiming it was unable to compete against Microsoft's monopolistic tactics of bundling its Web browser into its operating system. Another competitor, Sun Microsystems, also is seeking damages along with court action to force Microsoft to include Sun's Java programming language with its operating system. Antitrust litigation involving Microsoft is likely to continue in the years ahead.

Visa and MasterCard

In 1999, the Justice Department sued Visa and MasterCard, the nation's two largest credit card networks, for limiting competition in the credit card market. Together, Visa and MasterCard account for 75 percent of all credit card purchases. Both Visa and MasterCard are associations owned, governed, and operated by a group of member banks. The department charged that Visa and MasterCard violated the antitrust laws by placing authority for competitive decisions in the hands of banks that have significant financial interests in both networks. The government's complaint charged that these banks stifled competition by ensuring that Visa and MasterCard did not target each other in advertising campaigns and deterred the development of technology and new card products, such as smart cards. The department also charged that Visa and MasterCard adopted exclusionary rules that prohibited member banks from doing business with other networks, such as American Express and Discover. If a member bank were to issue one or both of these cards, it would lose its right to issue Visa and MasterCard products. In 2001, the decision was made against Visa and MasterCard and in favor of American Express, which had originally filed the complaint. Now banks are free to issue cards under any brand, including more than one brand.

In another alleged violation of antitrust law, millions of retailers joined Wal-Mart, Circuit City, Sears, Safeway, and The Limited in a class-action suit against Visa and MasterCard. Retailers accused Visa and MasterCard of using their monopoly power to force retailers who accept their cards to also accept their more costly signature-based debit cards. The suit charges that the two card companies deceive retailers by designing debit cards that are visually and electronically indistinguishable from credit cards. Retailers contend that they do not know they are receiving a debit card form of payment when a signature is required. Visa and MasterCard charge significantly higher fees for processing a debit card that requires a signature compared with a credit card or a debit card requiring a personal identification number (PIN). The case is scheduled for trial in 2003.

American Airlines

Also in 1999, the Justice Department charged American Airlines with illegally forcing smaller airlines out of its Dallas hub. The suit claimed that after the entry of low-cost carriers, American added flights and slashed fares in these markets with the intent of driving these smaller airlines out of business. After these small carriers exited the market, American then increased fares and reduced service. The government charged American with predatory pricing, while American claimed that it merely met the competition from low-cost carriers. The Justice Department identified several routes out of Dallas in which it believed American was guilty of monopolizing air traffic. One such case involved the airfares between Dallas and Kansas City, Missouri. Prior to the entry of Vanguard Airlines, American charged a one-way nonstop fare of $113. Faced with competition from Vanguard, American lowered its fare to $83. After driving Vanguard from the market, American raised its fare to $125. The case was decided in 2001 in favor of American Airlines. The court conceded that predatory pricing existed on the part of American Airlines, but found it difficult to distinguish it from rigorous price competition. The ruling was based on the fact that American's prices were above its average variable costs, the traditional standard by which monopoly behavior is judged. In ignoring the predatory pricing issue, the ruling in this case could have serious implications, not only in the airline industry but in technology sectors as well.

Airlines are characterized by very high fixed costs and very low variable costs. New Economy industries also have these same characteristics. Most of the cost of making software and computer chips, for example, is in research and development. The same can be said for prescription drug and biotech companies. Once the initial large outlays are made, the marginal cost of providing additional seats, chips, or pills is extremely low. In effect, this ruling may open the door for dominant companies to wage predatory price wars against smaller competitors.

Summary

- A monopoly is a market structure in which only one seller exists for a product that has no close substitutes. The monopolist has the ability to set the price by altering the total supply. Monopolies may arise from various factors, including economies of scale, the nature of the industry, possession of patents, control over raw materials, or certain types of competitive tactics.

- Monopolists maximize profits where marginal cost equals marginal revenue. A monopolist's ability to retain economic profits depends on its ability to erect or maintain barriers to entry of new firms. However, monopolists do not always charge the monopoly price, for they may not know their true costs, they may wish to discourage competition, or they fear government regulation.

- Monopolistic competition is a market structure in which numerous firms produce similar but differentiated products. Product differentiation enables sellers to influence price because the seller's products have real or imagined characteristics that buyers want. Pricing under conditions of monopolistic competition is likely to be higher than under conditions of perfect competition but lower than under monopoly.

- Oligopoly is a market structure in which relatively few firms produce identical or similar products. Because of the limited number of firms, each firm must consider the reaction of its rivals to changes it makes in output and price. A peculiar characteristic of oligopoly is the kinked demand curve, which exists when rivals follow suit if a firm drops its prices, but not follow if a firm raises its prices.

- Cartels are frequently formed within oligopolies for the purpose of maximizing profits. Cartels usually accomplish their goal by limiting production and charging the monopoly price. Cartels are illegal in the United States.

- Concentration ratios measure market power in an oligopolistic industry by calculating the percentage of the market accounted for by the largest firms. The Herfindahl Index calculates market power by summing the squares of the market share of each firm in the industry.

- Market power can also exist on the buyer's side as well as the seller's side of the market. Monopsony, monopsonistic competition, and oligopsony are types of buyer's markets in addition to pure competition. A bilateral monopoly occurs when both the buyers and seller are monopolists.

- Over the years, a series of antitrust laws have been enacted in the United States to promote competition and restrict unfair competitive practices. The Sherman Antitrust Act, the Clayton Act, and the Federal Trade Commission Act are among the notable antitrust laws.

New Terms and Concepts

Monopoly
Monopolistic
  competition
Product differentiation
Substitution effect
Oligopoly
Administered price
Cartel

Concentration ratio
Herfindahl Index
Monopsony
Oligopsony
Monopsonistic
  competition
Bilateral monopoly
Sherman Antitrust Act

Clayton Act
Price discrimination
Tying contracts
Exclusive dealing
Interlocking directorates
Predatory pricing
Federal Trade Commis-
  sion Act

Discussion Questions

1. What is the economic justification for grant-ing a monopoly franchise to a public utility?

2. How can a monopoly exercise control over price? Is this control absolute? Why or why not?

3. What is the relationship between the average revenue curve for a monopolist and the de-mand curve for the product the monopolist sells?

4. Why do the average revenue curve and the marginal revenue curve for a monopolist di-verge, whereas these curves coincide for a firm in perfect competition?

5. How does product differentiation give a busi-ness firm engaged in monopolistic competi-tion a certain degree of control over price?

6. Is it possible for a monopoly or an oligopoly to make an economic profit and still have a lower price than a firm engaged in perfect competition that sells its product at a price equal to its cost of production? Explain.

7. Why does an oligopolist have to be con-cerned about the actions or reactions of its rivals?

8. Describe the kinked demand curve character-istic of oligopoly. How does it tend to cause price stability?

9. What restrictions did the Clayton Act of 1914 place on businesses?

10. Should antitrust laws in the United States be relaxed? Why or why not?

Economic Applications

EconDebate
The EconDebate link, found at http://econapps.swlearning.com, provides many links to informa-tion about monopolies and oligopolies. Look for the Microeconomics heading and click on the links for "Monopolistic Competition," "Monopoly," or "Oligopoly." Under these topics, you will find hot topic debates about competition in the economic market.

CHAPTER REVIEW

8

The Circular-Flow Model

After studying Chapter 8, you should be able to:

1. Describe how the circular-flow model represents a modern economy and note the actions included in leakages and injections.

2. Demonstrate a simple circular-flow model for a stable economy, an expanding economy, and a contracting economy.

3. Explain the effect of government spending on the circular flow when its budget is balanced, in surplus, and in deficit.

4. Illustrate and discuss how international trade fits into the circular-flow model.

Circular Flow of Income
The cyclical operation of demand, output, income, and new demand.

Leakages
Flows out of the circular flow that occur when resource income is received and not spent directly on purchases from domestic firms.

In producing goods and services to satisfy consumer demands and to make profits, firms in the U.S. economy must use the productive resources: land, labor, capital, and enterprise. Because the first three resources are generally owned by someone other than the entrepreneur, the firm must pay the owners of these resources for the services they render. The payments by firms for use of the productive resources become income (and hence purchasing power) to the owners of these resources, which in turn is used to buy goods and services. Likewise, the profits of businesses become purchasing power that can be used to buy goods and services or additional resources. We will refer to the payments to the resources as *resource income*.

The demand for goods and services by the recipients of resource income leads to more output, which in turn brings about additional payments of resource income. This cyclical operation of demand, output, income, and new demand is the **circular flow of income** in the economy. It is the mechanism by which we decide how to use and what to pay the resources. The size of the circular flow measures the level of income and output in the economy.

As we will see later in this chapter, sometimes resource income and spending are not equal. **Leakages** are flows out of the circular flow that occur when resource income is received and not spent directly on purchases from domestic firms.

Injections
Added spending in the circular flow that are not paid for out of current resource income.

Leakages include saving, taxes, and import purchases. **Injections** are added spending in the circular flow that are not paid for out of resource income, such as investment, government spending, and exports bought by foreign buyers.

Circular Flow Demonstrated

We will be referring repeatedly to the concept of circular flow, so let us demonstrate it graphically. At this point, we will divide the economy into two segments: businesses and households. For simplicity, nonprofit institutions are counted as businesses because they usually provide goods and/or services and pay for the resources they use. The role of government will be included later. In the U.S. economy, most households work for firms or are in business for themselves. Households offer their productive services to businesses in exchange for pay in the form of wages, rent, and interest. The owners of businesses receive a profit for their contribution.

Income recipients then use their money to buy goods and services produced by businesses. If all the goods and services produced are sold (and they should be, if households spend all the income they receive), businesses will be induced to produce a second round of goods and services, and the process will start over again. Continuation of this process keeps the economy producing, paying incomes, spending, and allocating goods and services to households according to their demands. Figure 8–1 shows this process.

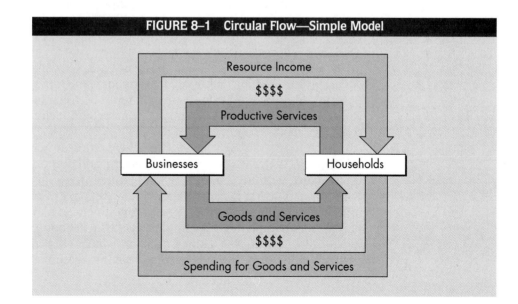

FIGURE 8–1   Circular Flow—Simple Model

Resource Income

$$$$

Productive Services

Businesses   Households

Goods and Services

$$$$

Spending for Goods and Services

In this model, all resource income finds its way to the households shown in Figure 8–1. Note that households include the owners of businesses as well as the owners of the other resources. The value of the goods produced is determined by the cost of production—payments for labor, land, and capital in the form of wages, rent, and interest, plus the profits for the entrepreneurs. Therefore, the total payment of resource income in the economy is equal to the value or cost (including profit) of the output. Households thus should have sufficient income to buy the goods and services the economy produces.

A STABLE ECONOMY

If all the income is spent, businesses will sell all the goods and will be induced to produce the same amount again. But we know from experience that households do not spend all the income they receive. Many people save some of their income, and saving is a leakage from the circular flow. What happens to the circular flow in this case? Unless an injection of additional spending from some source occurs to make up for the amount of saving in the economy, saving may have an adverse effect on the level of economic activity. Suppose businesses produce 500,000 units of goods and distribute $500,000 in resource income. If households spend the $500,000 to buy the 500,000 units of consumer goods, all output will be sold. However, if people spend only $400,000 on consumer goods, not all the output will be sold—unless the other $100,000 is used directly to purchase capital goods or is loaned to businesses to buy capital goods (see Figure 8–2).

Investment
Spending to purchase capital goods.

Investment spending on capital goods is an important injection into the circular flow. As long as planned investment (I) equals planned savings (S), injections will equal leakages, and we have a stable flow of total income and output. In such a case, total spending (which is a measure of total demand) equals total income (which is equivalent to total output or supply). In other words, the demand for goods and services equals the supply.

At any given time, actual investment equals actual savings because output equals income and, by definition, investment is the difference between total output and consumption. Saving is the difference between total income (output) and consumption. Therefore, investment, which could include inventories of unsold consumer goods, has to equal saving.

Sometimes, however, *planned investment* differs from planned savings. When this happens, a change occurs in total income and output until saving comes back into balance with investment. When planned investment (injection) is greater than planned saving (leakage), the economy expands, causing saving to increase until it again comes into balance with investment. If planned investment (injection) is less than planned saving (leakage), the economy contracts, causing saving to decrease until it comes back into balance with investment. As long as planned investment equals planned saving, of course, the economy stays in equilibrium.

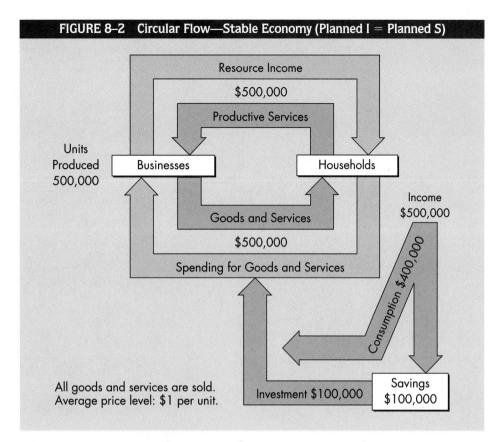

FIGURE 8–2 Circular Flow—Stable Economy (Planned I = Planned S)

Resource Income

$500,000

Productive Services

Units
Produced
500,000

Businesses

Households

Goods and Services

$500,000

Spending for Goods and Services

Income
$500,000

Consumption $400,000

All goods and services are sold.
Average price level: $1 per unit.

Investment $100,000

Savings
$100,000

A CONTRACTING ECONOMY

Anytime injections do not equal leakages, the circular flow of income is disrupted. For example, suppose that out of the $500,000 received by households, $400,000 is spent and $100,000 is saved, but only $50,000 is invested. As a result, leakages are $50,000 greater than injections. In this case, after producing 500,000 units valued at $500,000, producers see only $450,000 returning to buy the output. This results in a decrease in the total income and output due to an accumulation of unsold goods, a reduction in the price of the goods, or both.

Inventory Accumulation

If the price level is maintained at $1 per unit, the $450,000 that flows back to the producers can purchase only 450,000 units. This leaves 50,000 units unsold in inventories (unplanned investment), as shown in Figure 8–3. If the producers of 500,000 units sell only 450,000 units in one period, they may adjust their sales

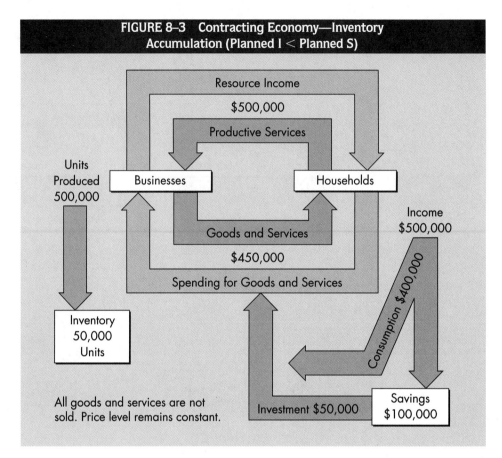

FIGURE 8–3   Contracting Economy—Inventory Accumulation (Planned I < Planned S)

Resource Income

$500,000

Productive Services

Units Produced 500,000

Businesses

Households

Income $500,000

Goods and Services

$450,000

Spending for Goods and Services

Consumption $400,000

Inventory 50,000 Units

All goods and services are not sold. Price level remains constant.

Investment $50,000

Savings $100,000

forecast to 450,000 units for the following period. A reduced output level of 400,000 units plus the inventory of 50,000 units from the previous period yields the desired supply of 450,000 units. Unfortunately, because this move cuts back current output, the producers use less labor and fewer productive resources. As a result, less resource income is paid out, and spending falls accordingly. The net result is a decrease in total income and output in the subsequent period. Output, employment, and income all fall, potentially leading to further declines in business activity, resulting in more inventory adjustment. This may be the beginning of a *recession*, which prevails when a noticeable drop in the level of real output occurs.

Drop in Prices

Under certain circumstances, when $500,000 of resource income is paid out, but consumers are willing to spend only $450,000, the market can be cleared; that is, all the output can be sold if the price level falls. Suppose that the average price falls to $0.90 per unit. In that event, $450,000 buys 500,000 units. In fact, this frequently happens as competition forces prices down when total supply exceeds total demand. If prices begin to fall, however, certain high-cost producers may not be able to make a profit by selling at the lower prices, and all producers make less profit per unit. Consequently, the incentive to produce is weakened. Many firms cut back on output and some go out of business, and total output in the next period is less. This, in turn, means that fewer individual resources are used, less resource income is received, and total demand falls (see Figure 8–4).

Whenever injections are less than leakages, total spending is less than total income, and total demand is less than total supply. This leads to lower output in subsequent periods because of accumulated inventories of unsold goods, falling prices, or a combination of both. As demand slackens and prices fall, producers cut output to get rid of accumulated inventory. As output is cut, incomes fall, reducing employment and income. Hence, the total income and output decrease. Inventory depletion was a contributing element to the recessions of 1980, 1982, 1990–1991, and 2001.

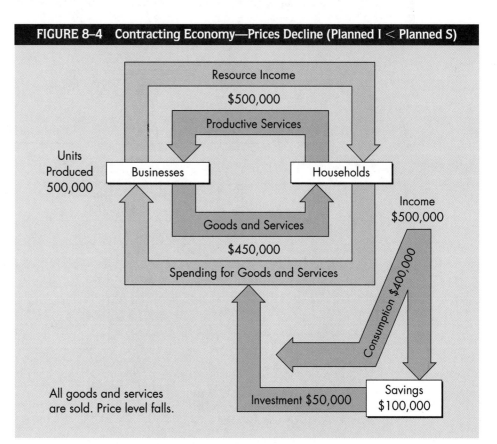

FIGURE 8–4 Contracting Economy—Prices Decline (Planned I < Planned S)

Resource Income
$500,000

Productive Services

Units Produced 500,000

Businesses

Households

Income $500,000

Goods and Services
$450,000

Spending for Goods and Services

Consumption $400,000

All goods and services are sold. Price level falls.

Investment $50,000

Savings $100,000

AN EXPANDING ECONOMY

If planned *I* exceeds planned *S*, injections to the circular flow are greater than leakages. This causes spending to exceed total income, and it causes demand to exceed total output. For example, suppose that 500,000 units are produced and that $500,000 is distributed in resource income. Suppose further that individuals spend $400,000 on consumption and that they save $100,000, which is borrowed and used for investment spending. If businesses borrow $50,000 more from some source (such as a bank) for the purchase of capital goods, total planned *I* becomes $150,000. When this amount is added to the $400,000 in consumer spending, the figure for total spending becomes $550,000. Such action might cause either an increase in total income and output or an increase in the price level, depending on the circumstances (see Figure 8–5).

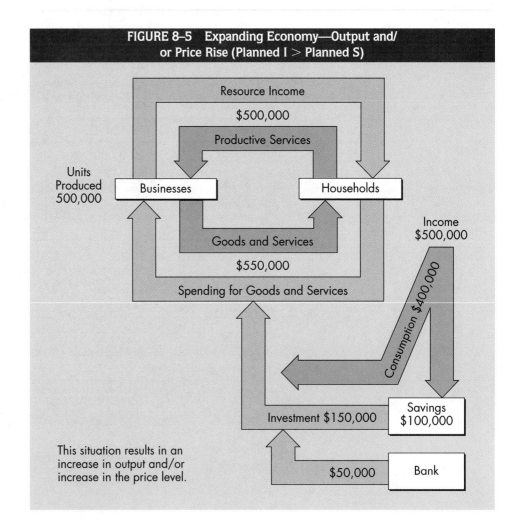

FIGURE 8–5   Expanding Economy—Output and/ or Price Rise (Planned I > Planned S)

Resource Income
$500,000

Productive Services

Units Produced 500,000

Businesses

Households

Income $500,000

Goods and Services

$550,000

Spending for Goods and Services

Consumption $400,000

Investment $150,000

Savings $100,000

$50,000

Bank

This situation results in an increase in output and/or increase in the price level.

More Goods and Services

Naturally, businesses want to increase output to satisfy the additional demand for goods and services. If the economy is in a state of less than full employment—that is, labor, land, and capital are available—output will be increased to satisfy the higher demand. Certainly, if an additional $50,000 appears on the counter, ready to buy goods, some enterprising businesses are going to produce the goods demanded. When they do, total output will increase to 550,000 units. The price level will remain constant because the $550,000 in spending is exchanged for the 550,000 units produced. In turn, the businesses, which must pay for additional productive agents, will pay $550,000 instead of $500,000 in resource income. This will cause spending to increase and bring about more output. As a result, the economy will operate at a higher level of output and employment. Therefore, whenever planned I (injection) exceeds planned S (leakage), total spending exceeds total income, demand exceeds supply, and total income and output increase, provided that we are at less than full employment.

Higher Prices

If the same situation occurs in a period of full employment, the immediate result is higher prices (inflation). Under full employment, businesses are unable to obtain the necessary labor, resources, capital, and capacity to produce additional goods. Of course, some businesses will try to increase production to satisfy the demand for the additional 50,000 units. But the only way they can obtain the necessary resources to increase output in the short run is to bid the resources away from other producers. Their increase in output of 50,000 units is offset by a decrease in output by businesses whose resources were bid away from them. Total output remains at 500,000 units.

This situation forces prices upward as businesses bid against each other for the relatively scarce resources. Furthermore, instead of an increase in total output occurring, the price level rises and the $550,000 is used to buy the 500,000 units of output as households bid against each other for the limited supply of goods available. Although the composition of output (the amount of capital goods compared with consumer goods) may change, the total amount of output does not change, at least in the short run. If, after a while, productivity increases through more efficient use of labor, better use of resources, and expanded capacity, the inflationary pressures tend to be dampened.

Thus, anytime that injections such as planned I are greater than leakages such as planned S, the level of economic activity increases, provided that we are at less than full employment. If we are at full employment, however, this situation merely causes the price level to rise.

SUMMARY OF THE CIRCULAR-FLOW MODEL

We now sum up the foregoing discussion of the relationship of planned investment (I) to planned saving (S) and its effect on the economy. Whenever:

NET_Link_

National and international data, including GDP, can be found at:

http://www.bea.doc.gov

Equilibrium
A stable flow of total output and income.

1. Planned I = planned S (injections = leakages), the result is **equilibrium,** or a stable flow of output and income. The price level tends to remain stable.
2. Planned I < planned S (injections < leakages), total income and output and/or the price level tend to decrease. Income falls, and saving decreases until it comes back into balance with investment.
3. Planned I > planned S (injections > leakages), total income and output tend to increase, if the economy is at less than full employment. However, if the economy is at full employment, total income and output do not increase, and the price level and prices tend to rise. Income rises, and saving increases until it comes back into balance with investment ($I = S$).

Government and the Circular Flow

At one time, the primary function and objective of federal financing was to raise sufficient revenue through taxation to cover the cost of performing necessary government services. Therefore, great emphasis was placed on balancing the budget, even though budget experts were not always able to balance revenue and expenditures. In recent decades, government spending has been used as a means of stabilizing total income and output. At times, we have purposely operated at a deficit.

A BALANCED BUDGET

Because government spending affects the circular flow of income and the price level, we need to inspect it more closely. If the government were to operate on a balanced budget, it would in effect spend the same amount as it collected in taxes. What households gave up in consumption to pay taxes (leakages) would be spent by the government (injection); as a result, the total spending in the circular flow would remain the same. Thus, a balanced budget tends to have a neutral effect on the economy.

For example, in our circular flow, if households (as shown in Figure 8–6) are taxed $50,000 out of their resource incomes of $500,000, they have only $450,000 to spend on consumption. The adverse effect of the tax leakage on the economy, however, is offset by an injection if the government then spends the $50,000 it has received in taxes. Under such circumstances, total spending remains at $500,000, and all the goods and services produced are sold. There may be a change, however, in the composition of the goods and services produced, because government spending is substituted for some of the private spending on consumption and investment.

We noted that a balanced budget tends to have a neutral effect on the economy. This assumes that taxpayers pay their taxes with monies that would otherwise be spent for consumption or investment purposes. However, this is not always the case. A balanced budget may have an other than neutral effect, depending on the source of tax monies and the direction of government spending. For example,

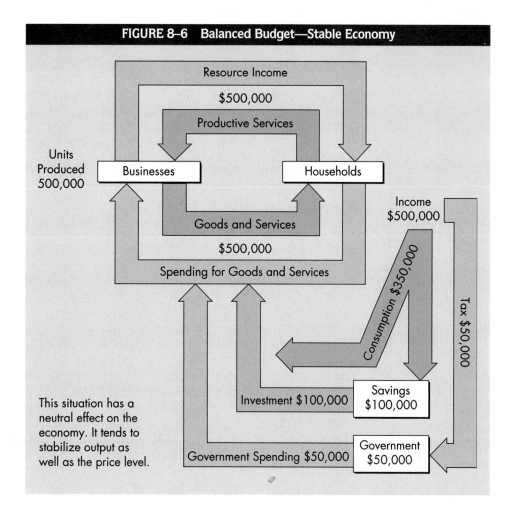

FIGURE 8–6   Balanced Budget—Stable Economy

Resource Income
$500,000

Productive Services

Units Produced 500,000

Businesses   Households

Income $500,000

Goods and Services

$500,000

Spending for Goods and Services

Consumption $350,000

Tax $50,000

This situation has a neutral effect on the economy. It tends to stabilize output as well as the price level.

Investment $100,000   Savings $100,000

Government Spending $50,000   Government $50,000

an expansionary effect could result if the government, in its taxing process, absorbed and spent idle funds that were not going to be used for consumption or investment.

A SURPLUS BUDGET

If the government spends less than it receives in taxes—a surplus budget—injections are less than leakages, and total income and output decrease or prices decline. During a period when strong inflationary forces exist, a surplus budget can be used as a contractionary measure. Because the government spends less than it collects in taxes, total spending in the economy decreases, which, in turn, has a disinflationary effect on the economy.

Rather than the neutral budget depicted by Figure 8–6, let us envision the impact of a surplus budget on the circular flow. If the government had taxed households $50,000, but spent only $25,000, the federal government's surplus budget would have had a contractionary effect on the economy. Total spending of $500,000 would fall to $450,000. This would be offset, however, only to the extent of the $25,000 of government spending. In effect, total spending would be reduced to $475,000 for the economy as a whole. Consequently, spending would be less than income, demand would be less than supply, and either the level of business activity would decrease or the price level would decline.

A DEFICIT BUDGET

If the government spends more than it collects in taxes—a deficit budget—injections are greater than leakages and total income and output increase or prices rise, depending on the circumstances. Because the government spends more than it collects in taxes, the injection of government spending more than offsets the leakages from consumption and investment spending resulting from the taxation.

Again, in reference to Figure 8–6, if the government had spent not only the $50,000 it collected in taxes but also an additional $25,000 (which we will assume it borrowed from banks), total spending would rise to $525,000. The federal government's deficit budget would have had an expansionary effect on the economy. Total spending would rise to $525,000. Because total spending would have exceeded total income by $25,000, demand would outstrip the supply of goods and services available. Thus, a deficit budget tends to increase total income and output if the economy is at less than full employment. If the economy already has full employment, however, a deficit budget merely causes the price level to rise.

So far, our examples have been based on three assumptions.

1. Households always pay taxes out of current incomes.
2. If households did not pay taxes, they would spend the money for consumption or investment.
3. The government borrows from banks instead of from individuals and firms in the economy.

We will see later that if these assumptions do not apply, the analysis must be modified. The economic effects are the same, but less intense. To this point, however, we can sum up the effects of government spending on the circular-flow model as follows: A balanced budget tends to have a neutral effect on total income and output and the price level. A surplus budget tends to decrease total income and output and/or the price level. A deficit budget tends to increase total income and output or the price level, depending on the level of employment.

International Trade and the Circular Flow

Imports and exports greatly affect the circular flow of income. Import purchases are a leakage from the U.S. circular flow, whereas purchases by foreigners of U.S. exports are an injection. Anytime Americans sell exports equal in value to the imports they purchase, injections and leakages are equal. In this case, the circular flow of income remains stable, as shown in Figure 8–7. This is not the usual case, however; most of the time there is an imbalance between exports and imports.

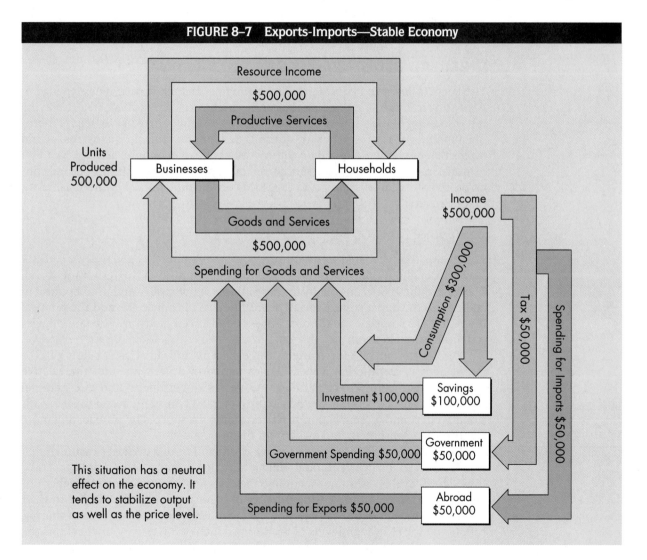

FIGURE 8–7   Exports-Imports—Stable Economy

Resource Income
$500,000

Productive Services

Units Produced 500,000

Businesses   Households

Income $500,000

Goods and Services
$500,000

Spending for Goods and Services

Consumption $300,000

Tax $50,000

Spending for Imports $50,000

Investment $100,000   Savings $100,000

Government Spending $50,000   Government $50,000

This situation has a neutral effect on the economy. It tends to stabilize output as well as the price level.

Spending for Exports $50,000   Abroad $50,000

If the United States buys more from foreigners than it sells to them, imports exceed exports, causing a deficit balance of trade. Leakages are greater than injections to the U.S. circular flow, and not all domestic goods produced can be sold. This can lead to a contraction in total income and output and/or a decline in the price level.

On the other hand, if we sell more to foreigners than we buy from them, export income exceeds import spending, and a surplus balance of trade exists. In this case, the injection of spending by foreigners for U.S. goods and services can lead to an increase in total income and output and/or a rise in prices.

Using Figure 8–7, you can visualize what happens when exports exceed imports (or vice versa) and there is a surplus or deficit balance of payments.

CIRCULAR-FLOW EXAMPLES

The circular flow can be influenced by numerous factors. In fact, when applied to the real world, the simplified model can become very complicated. Before leaving our discussion of the circular-flow model, three examples may prove helpful in understanding the complex nature of the U.S. economy and the many real-world forces that can either expand or contract the level of economic activity. The first example involves the events that occurred on September 11, 2001; the second concerns inventory adjustments; and the third concerns the impact of the Asian crisis on our economy.

September 11, 2001

The events that occurred on the morning of September 11, 2001, caused shock waves throughout the United States and throughout most of the rest of the world. The cost to the U.S. economy from these attacks is not easily measured because in addition to the direct costs associated with the loss of human life and the physical destruction of property, the terrorist attacks have forced many unwelcome changes in the American economy.

Perhaps no outside force affects the economy and our circular flow of economic activity as much as a war. Over a period of time, wars alter the relative demands and incomes of consumers, businesses, government, and international trading partners. Depending on the circumstances, wars usually result in an expansionary effect and a reallocation of the economy's resources by transferring more resources to government and away from the private sector.

In September 2001, the economy was in the midst of a cyclical slowdown that began earlier in the year. Although milder than most contractions, thanks to a continued high level of consumer spending, the economy was experiencing higher unemployment rates, an increasing number of bankruptcies, and a decline in GDP. Investment spending, most notably in the technology sector, had declined sharply. Inflation, thanks to high levels of worker productivity, was well in check. As tax revenues fell and expenditures increased, the federal government's budget surplus was shrinking. Fiscal policy in 2001 also included a tax cut to promote long-run economic growth as well as to stimulate the sluggish economy. The Federal Reserve was doing its part by steadily lowering interest rates throughout the year to prevent a serious recession. In terms of the circular flow of economic activity, the cyclical downturn in 2001 caused the circle to contract. During this time the amount of goods and services produced contracted, investment spending decreased, government expenses rose, and revenues decreased. From the standpoint of international trade, exports did not provide a countercyclical boost because the recession was global in scope, and trading partners were reducing their imports from the United States.

Then came September 11. As an immediate response, the Federal Reserve once again lowered interest rates. Perhaps more importantly, the Federal Reserve provided the critical functions of providing liquidity, clearing checks, processing currencies, and transferring electronic funds in order to ensure the orderly workings of the financial markets and to minimize disruptions in the economy. On the fiscal side, the federal government quickly announced that increased outlays were being directed to the military, domestic security, airlines, individuals and families directly affected by the attacks, and to New York City. In terms of overall economic activity, real GDP contracted for the third consecutive quarter and our circle continued to shrink.

The long-term effects of September 11 on the economy are less clear, for the war against terrorism is a uniquely different war for the United States. Previous large-scale wars have resulted in federal budget deficits, increased production, higher interest rates, full employment, and higher prices for goods and services. In some cases, even wage and price controls and the rationing of goods and services were enacted. Most of these forces serve to increase the size of the circle until full employment of resources occurs. With full employment, growth of the circle becomes largely illusory because only prices are rising and not the production of goods and services. But this promises to be a different kind of war. Should the United States engage in a prolonged and expansive war against nations harboring or supporting terrorists, then the overall economy may experience some if not all of these wartime economic changes.

Inventory Adjustments

One of the key ingredients affecting the circular flow of economic activity is that of inventory adjustments. Inventory adjustments always play a major role in the expansion and contraction of the economy. The most recent business cycle was no exception. In fact, this inventory cycle was the most pronounced since World War II. Throughout the 1990s, business firms invested in plant and equipment at an unprecedented pace. This prolonged period of investment expansion resulted in a huge increase in manufacturing capacity. The circular flow continued to expand as the growth in manufacturing capacity outstripped output growth for several years. This gap resulted in a huge amount of excess capacity, especially in the area of high tech equipment such as computers and semiconductors. For example, while the GDP grew at an annual rate of 4 percent, industrial capacity grew at an 11 percent rate. Capacity growth was even higher in the semiconductor sector. Investment spending was the engine for the economic growth during the period, and the gap between investment spending and output growth was the widest since World War II.

But as the manufacturing sector began to weaken in mid 2000, business firms began to cut inventories aggressively. The pace of investment in high technology capital goods had outstripped the long-term profit expectations of many high tech firms. As expectations were aligned with profit expectations, business fixed investment plunged, inventory reductions continued throughout 2001. Relative to GDP, this inventory correction was the largest in over 50 years. As inventories accumulated, prices were slashed, creating a downward spiral of investment demand and prices. Nowhere was this inventory correction more severe than in the telecommunication and information sectors.

Although more severe than most, this period of inventory accumulation and depletion is part of the normal expansion and contraction of the circular flow of economic activity in a market economy. We will examine these economic forces in greater detail in the analysis of business cycles in Chapter 15.

The Asian Financial Crisis

An example of the impact of international trade and finance on the circular flow can be seen in the shock waves in global economic activity caused by the Asian economic crisis in late 1997. The near collapse of some of the Asian economies stunned developed nations throughout the world. In the United States, the early effects were a sharp decline in financial markets and a drop in exports from U.S. manufacturers because Asian importers no longer had the financial ability to continue buying products from the United States as before. At the same time, because their prices had fallen sharply, increased Asian exports to the United States had a contractionary effect on the circular flow. Coupled with declining profit margins of U.S. multinational companies and layoffs in certain exporting industries, the contractionary effects on the economy were potentially very severe. Some had even predicted that Asia's problems would lead to a recession in the United States. In fact, quite the opposite occurred.

The economy withstood the impacts of the Asian crisis better than most experts had predicted. As investors pulled their money out of foreign economies, cash flowed into the U.S. financial markets. This had the effect of lowering interest rates and borrowing costs for businesses and consumers. As a result of depressed import prices, consumers in the United States continued to spend freely, and, combined with the effects of lower borrowing costs, additional consumption and investment were stimulated.

Summary

- Millions of consumers and business firms make decisions about what and how much to produce. These decisions generate a circular flow of income. Businesses pay to their productive services wages, rent, and interest. The income recipients then spend the money they receive on the goods and services the businesses produce. If all the goods and services produced are sold, businesses will produce a second round of goods and services, and the process starts over.

- Any saving that takes place in the economy disrupts the circular flow, unless the saving is offset by an equivalent amount of borrowing and investment.

- Whenever planned investment is equal to planned saving, equilibrium in total income and output results and prices tend to remain stable. If planned investment is less than planned saving, however, a decrease in total output and/or a decline in the price level results. On the other hand, if planned investment is greater than planned saving, an increase in total output results if the economy is in a state of less than full employment. Otherwise, it leads to higher prices.

- Government spending can also influence total output and the price level. A surplus budget can lead to a decrease in business activity and/or lower prices. A deficit budget can lead to an increase in total output or higher prices, depending on the employment status in the economy. A balanced government budget tends to have a neutral effect on total output and prices.

- Likewise, total output and income and the price level are affected by net exports and by the balance of international payments.

- The circular flow can be impacted by other factors in addition to changes in total output, employment, income, and the price level. Changes in money supply, interest rates, and direct investments abroad can influence the circular flow. In some instances, two or more forces acting together may change the direction or level of the circular flow. At other times, the positive effect of one force may be offset by the negative effect of another force.

New Terms and Concepts

Circular flow of income
Leakages
Injections

Investment
Equilibrium

8

CHAPTER REVIEW

Discussion Questions

1. Describe the relationship of planned investment to planned saving and the effect of that relationship on the circular flow of income.

2. How can the accumulation of large inventories adversely affect the circular flow of income?

3. Why is it necessary to consider the government sector of the economy as part of the circular flow?

4. What effect does a surplus budget have on the circular flow of income?

5. Does a deficit budget always increase the level of business activity? Why or why not?

6. Explain how a deficit balance of payments affects the circular flow of income.

Economic Applications

EconNews

After learning about the circular-flow model, you can read about the equilibrium of real businesses on EconNews Online. Go to the EconNews link at http://econapps.swlearning.com. Look for the "Equilibrium" link under the Economic Fundamentals heading. Click on the link to find news summaries on how current businesses follow a circular flow.

9

Measuring Output and Income in the United States

After studying Chapter 9, you should be able to:

1. Describe how each of the national income accounts is determined.

2. Give an example of a transfer payment, and explain why it does not count as national income, but is part of personal income.

3. Discuss how GDP fits into the circular flow of income.

4. List some of the limitations of using GDP as a measure of economic welfare.

5. Distinguish between current-dollar GDP and constant-dollar or real GDP.

6. Explain how the underground economy affects GDP.

Instead of using hypothetical figures when discussing the circular flow of income (as we did in earlier chapters), we can use actual dollar measurements. The U.S. Department of Commerce keeps a running tab on the dollar value of the total goods and services produced in the economy. This tabulation is broken down into various components, called *national income accounts*, to make it easier to analyze.

National Income Accounts

Let us turn our attention to the national accounting system by which total output is measured in the United States. GDP can be determined either by summing the expenditures made on our nation's goods and services or by summing the incomes earned in producing these same goods and services. The total value of the goods and services produced must be equal to the incomes of those who produced them. We can show the conceptual identity between the value of total output and national income by starting with GDP and making certain adjustments to arrive at national income. Numerical values presented in this chapter for the national income accounts are based on the annual rates of the third quarter of 2002.

GROSS DOMESTIC PRODUCT (GDP)

*Gross Domestic
Product (GDP)*
The current market value
of the total final goods
and services produced
within the United States.

*Gross National
Product (GNP)*
GDP plus the value of
goods and services pro-
duced by U.S. resources
abroad less the value of
goods and services pro-
duced by foreign resources
in the United States.

Gross domestic product (GDP) is defined as the current market value of all final goods and services produced within the United States by both domestic and foreign resources. The 2002 GDP for the United States was $10,504 billion. On the other hand, **gross national product (GNP)** also measures the current market value of the final goods and services produced, but GNP includes the value of goods and services produced by U.S.-owned resources in foreign countries and excludes output produced in the United States by foreign-owned resources. GNP in 2002 was $10,491.

For many years, GNP was used as the standard measure of total output in the United States. In 1992, however, the United States dropped gross national product as the basic measure and substituted in its place gross domestic product. Both GDP and GNP measure the current market value of final goods and services produced, but they differ in how the economy is defined. The United States and most other nations of the world now use GDP as the standard measure.

The dollar value of total output in the United States during a given period is found by adding the values of all the final goods and services produced in this period. Sometimes, however, it is difficult to distinguish intermediate goods (those used in the production of other products) from final goods (those consumed directly). Should we count a tire as a final good, or should we count it as part of the value of an automobile? Is the hard drive of a computer a final good, or is some of it included in the value of the final price of the computer? For an accurate calculation of total output, national income accountants try to eliminate double counting by using only the value of final goods.

Value-Added Approach

Value Added
The change in value of an
intermediate or end prod-
uct attributable to completion of a productive stage.

Another way to obtain the value of total output is by counting the value added in the production of both goods and services. **Value added** is the difference between the cost of raw materials and the price of the final product; it represents the amount that must be paid for wages, rent, and interest, as well as the profit the producer receives. Thus, the sum of the total value added to all products by the various producers plus the value of the services rendered by others will equal the total output of the economy.

Let's use the production of an automobile for a value-added example. Suppose that the iron ore and the other basic raw materials originally cost $600. They might be worth $1,200 after being processed into pig iron and other materials, $2,400 after being refined into steel ingots, and so on, until they finally take the shape of the automobile at a value of $16,900. If we sum the value of the product at the end of each production stage, the total value is $46,100, as shown in Table 9–1. Obviously, there has been much double counting in the process.

However, if we start out with the value of the basic goods and add to this only the extra value added by each productive process, the total value added is equal to the price of the final good, as shown in the third column of Table 9–1. Of course, the total value added represents the total production that has taken place.

TABLE 9–1 Example of Value Added		
Stage of Production	Value at End of Each Stage of Production	Value Added by Each Stage of Production
Iron and other raw materials	$ 600	$ 600 Value of basic commodities
Pig iron and other processed materials	1,200	600 Represents payments for:
Steel ingots, etc.	2,400	1,200 Wages
Sheet steel, etc.	5,500	3,100 Rent
Automobile parts	8,000	2,500 Interest
Assembly	11,500	3,500 Profits
Automobile delivered at showroom	16,900	5,400
	$46,100	$16,900

Likewise, it is equal to the total payments made to the owners of the productive resources.

The value-added approach is not used to measure total output in the United States. It is used, however, in several European countries and is the basis for a value-added tax.

GDP Also Measures Spending

The 2002 GDP of $10,504 billion not only is the value of total output but also indicates the total spending done by consumers, businesses, governments, and international traders on these goods and services. Everything that is produced in a year must be purchased by one of the four buying sectors. We will further discuss the spending of the four sectors later in the chapter.

The first adjustment required in equating GDP and national income is to add (or subtract) the net income received by U.S. productive resources employed in foreign countries. To arrive at this figure, total resource payments to the rest of the world are subtracted from resource income received from the rest of the world. This adjustment produces a figure for gross national product, or GNP, which serves as the basis for a more detailed breakdown of the national income accounts.

NET NATIONAL PRODUCT

In the process of producing goods and services, a portion of capital goods is used up in the production process. Machinery, equipment, buildings, and tools depreciate with use. Some become obsolete and lose their value. A truer picture of the additional production that occurred is found by subtracting this depreciation, or

NETLink

Learn more about the GDP by visiting the Federal Reserve Bank of Chicago's "Economic Research and Data" site at:

http://www.chicagofed.org/ economicresearchanddata/data/ index.cfm

Capital Consumption Allowance
The amount of depreciation and obsolescence in the GNP.

Net National Product (NNP)
GNP minus capital consumption allowances.

capital consumption allowance, from GNP. Also, the capital consumption allowance must be removed because it is included in the price we pay for goods and services but is not earned income to the owners of productive resources. When capital consumption allowances are deducted from GNP, the result is **net national product (NNP)**.

NNP is a more meaningful measure of production than GDP or GNP because it excludes the capital used up in the course of the year's production. However, depreciation is very difficult to measure or estimate accurately, so GDP is more precise and more widely used.

NATIONAL INCOME (NI)

From NNP several additional adjustments are necessary to arrive at national income. We must subtract the costs of production included in final prices that do not represent earned income to productive resources. These costs include indirect business taxes (sales, excise, and property taxes) and business transfer payments (private pensions and bad debts). We must also add payments earned by productive resources that are not included in final prices. These payments take the form of any subsidies to farmers and other businesses. Finally, any current surplus or profit earned by government enterprise is subtracted. Having made these adjustments, we can determine national income.

National Income (NI)
The total productive resource costs of the goods and services produced by our nation's economy. Also, the income earned by the owners of productive resources in producing GDP.

National Income (NI) has a twofold definition. First, it is the total resource costs of the goods and services produced by the U.S. economy. In this sense, it is equivalent to the earnings or income of the owners of the resources used to produce the GDP. Total resource cost and combined earnings are merely two sides of the same coin.

The value of NI can be obtained by adding all the earnings of productive resources in a given period. Alternately, it can be obtained by beginning with GDP and making a series of adjustments, as we have done. In 2002, the value of national income was $8,392 billion.

PERSONAL INCOME (PI)

National income is the income *earned* by individuals. However, the national income figure can be reduced to a concept more appropriate to individuals: personal income. **Personal income (PI)** is the income *received* by persons from all sources. It includes such things as wages, salaries, proprietors' incomes, rental income, interest income, dividend income, and transfer payments received from government and business.

Personal Income (PI)
The current income received by persons from all sources.

Transfer Payment
A payment of money in return for which no current goods or services are produced.

A **transfer payment** is a payment of money in return for which no current goods or services are produced. For example, a retiree may receive $1,000 per month from a business pension plan. This is truly a part of the retiree's personal income, although the retiree produces no current goods or services in exchange for the money. (It is true that the retiree has earned it, but it is nonetheless payment for service in a previous period.) Government transfer payments include Social Security benefits, unemployment compensation, welfare payments, and veterans benefits.

Personal income is found by subtracting corporate income taxes and undistributed profits from NI, because neither of these segments of corporate profit is passed on to individuals. For the same reason, contributions for social insurance (Social Security taxes) and net interest are also subtracted. This leaves only corporate dividends to be counted as part of personal income. Table 9–2 shows this by subtracting all corporate profits (as well as an inventory valuation adjustment) and then adding corporate dividends and personal interest income to the total.

TABLE 9–2 National Income Accounts for 2002 (Billions of Dollars)*		
Gross domestic product (GDP)		$10,503.7
Plus: Productive resource income from the rest of world (less income paid to rest of world)	−12.9	
Gross national product (GNP)		10,490.8
Less: Capital consumption allowance	1,404.8	
Equals: **Net national product (NNP)**		9,086.0
Less: Indirect business tax and nontax liability	807.9	
Business transfer payments	44.5	
Statistical discrepancy	−129.0	
Plus: Subsidies (less current surplus of government enterprises)	29.0	
Equals: **National income (NI)**		8,391.6
Less: Corporate profits and inventory adjustment	770.9	
Contributions for social insurance	691.9	
Net interest	752.2	
Wage accruals (less disbursements)	0.0	
Plus: Government transfer payments	1,082.8	
Personal interest income	437.3	
Personal dividend income	1,263.0	
Business transfer payments to persons	35.3	
Equals: **Personal income (PI)**		8,995.0
Less: Personal tax and nontax payments	1,118.0	
Equals: **Disposable personal income (DPI)**		7,877.0
Less: Personal consumption expenditures	7,360.5	
Consumer interest payments to business	187.2	
Personal transfer payments to foreigners	32.3	
Equals: **Personal saving (S)**		$297.0

*Based on third-quarter annualized rates, preliminary estimates.
Source: Bureau of Economic Analysis (January 2003).

Government and business transfer payments are then added, and a few other minor adjustments must be made. After doing this for 2002, we find that the PI was $8,995 billion. The biggest factors accounting for the difference between PI and NI are government transfer payments and personal interest income.

DISPOSABLE PERSONAL INCOME (DPI)

Disposable Personal Income (DPI)
Personal income minus personal taxes.

We are all well aware that we do not have the opportunity to spend every dollar we earn. Quite a gap exists between our earnings and our take-home pay. The main reason for this difference is that we pay federal and (in most cases) state and local income taxes. What remains of personal income after these deductions are made is **disposable personal income (DPI).** In 2002, the disposable income remaining to persons after personal tax and nontax payments to governments had been deducted was $7,877 billion. Of this total amount, we as individuals spent $7,361 billion on personal consumption, $187 billion on consumer interest payments to businesses, and $32 billion on personal transfer payments to foreigners. As a nation, individuals saved $297 billion.

GDP in the U.S. Economy

The goods and services included in GDP are allocated to four major sectors of the U.S. economy: consumption, investment, net exports, and government. In 2002, 70 percent of the total output of the United States went to consumption—purchases of consumer goods and services. The part of total output devoted to business purchases of machinery, equipment, buildings, and inventories is known as investment; about 15 percent of 2002 output was investment. Net exports (about −4 percent of output, a negative because imports exceeded exports in 2002) represents the difference between exports from and imports to the United States. Government, the fourth sector, must buy goods and services to perform its functions. About 19 percent of the 2002 output went to the government. Breaking government purchases down further, state and local governments accounted for 53 percent of total government spending. The allocation of the GDP to the four sectors of the U.S. economy is shown in Table 9–3.

When the four sectors of the economy purchase goods and services, they must pay for them. Payments to the sellers are in turn used to pay the productive resources for the GDP. As was pointed out in the circular flowcharts in Chapter 8, productive resources are reimbursed in the form of wages, rent, interest, or profit. Table 9–4 shows a breakdown of the payments to the various productive resources. The allocation of GDP and the distribution of NI can also be seen in Figure 9–1.

In summary, GDP is produced by the activity of numerous businesses and individuals, who in turn make payments to the various productive resources for their contributions. Incomes received are used to purchase goods and services. This sets up a circular flow of income, as explained in Chapter 8 and illustrated in Figure 9–2.

TABLE 9-3 Gross Domestic Product for 2002*

Sector	Billions of Dollars	% of GDP
Personal consumption expenditures	7,360.5	70.0
Durable goods	$ 898.3	
Nondurable goods	2,116.4	
Services	4,345.8	
Gross private domestic investment	1,594.2	15.2
Nonresidential structures	259.7	
Producers' durable equipment	850.3	
Residential structures	470.2	
Change in business inventories	14.0	
Net exports of goods and services	−432.6	−4.0
Exports	1,035.4	
Imports	1,468.0	
Government expenditures	1,981.7	18.8
Federal	697.5	
State and local	1,284.2	
Gross domestic product	$10,503.8	

* Based on preliminary third-quarter annualized figures.
Source: Department of Commerce, Bureau of Economic Analysis, December 2002.

TABLE 9-4 Distribution of National Income for 2002*

Income	Billions of Dollars	% of National Income
Compensation of employees	$6,024.7	71.8
Wages and salaries	$5,041.9	
Supplements	982.8	
Rental income of persons with capital consumption	145.0	1.8
Net interest	691.8	8.2
Proprietors' income with inventory valuation and capital consumption adjustments	759.2	9.0
Corporate profits with inventory and capital consumption adjustments	770.9	9.2
National income	$8,391.6	100

*Based on preliminary third-quarter annualized figures.
Source: Department of Commerce, Bureau of Economic Analysis, December 2002.

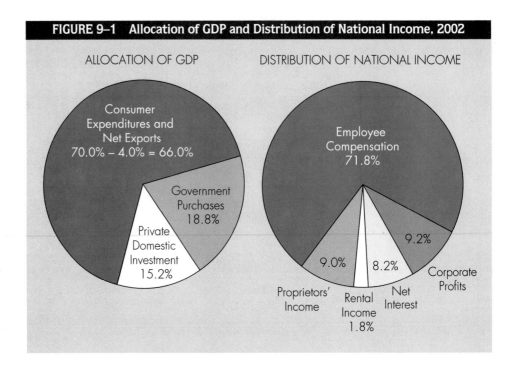

FIGURE 9–1   Allocation of GDP and Distribution of National Income, 2002

ALLOCATION OF GDP

Consumer Expenditures and Net Exports 70.0% – 4.0% = 66.0%

Government Purchases 18.8%

Private Domestic Investment 15.2%

DISTRIBUTION OF NATIONAL INCOME

Employee Compensation 71.8%

Proprietors' Income 9.0%

Rental Income 1.8%

Net Interest 8.2%

Corporate Profits 9.2%

QUARTERLY REPORTS ON THE GDP

To keep citizens informed and to have figures available as a guide for implementing national economic policies, the Department of Commerce publishes quarterly reports on the GDP and related figures. These quarterly reports are expressed in annual rates by adjusting the actual output in any given quarter for seasonal fluctuation and then multiplying the seasonally adjusted figure by 4 to convert it into an annual rate. For example, suppose that actual output for a given quarter is $1,900 billion. If the seasonally adjusted output is $2,000 billion, multiplying by 4 yields an annual rate of $8,000 billion.

The quarterly system makes it easier to analyze movements in the GDP. Any quarter can be measured against another or against the annual total. This method makes it easy to spot the high and low quarters of business fluctuations, especially with constant-dollar (or real GDP) figures. Moreover, downswings and upswings in the economy can be recognized at an earlier date than they would be if the GDP were only published yearly. Table 9–5 presents quarterly figures for GDP for 2002.

The GDP is also revised frequently. A preliminary estimate for a given year usually appears during February of the following year. A more accurate figure is released later in the spring, and a final revision is made available during the summer. A preliminary quarterly figure is given about four weeks after a quarter is completed; it is subsequently revised.

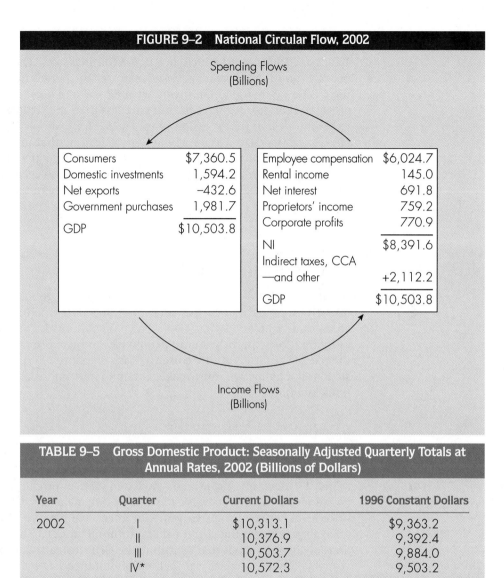

FIGURE 9–2   National Circular Flow, 2002

Spending Flows
(Billions)

Consumers	$7,360.5
Domestic investments	1,594.2
Net exports	–432.6
Government purchases	1,981.7
GDP	$10,503.8

Employee compensation	$6,024.7
Rental income	145.0
Net interest	691.8
Proprietors' income	759.2
Corporate profits	770.9
NI	$8,391.6
Indirect taxes, CCA —and other	+2,112.2
GDP	$10,503.8

Income Flows
(Billions)

TABLE 9–5   Gross Domestic Product: Seasonally Adjusted Quarterly Totals at Annual Rates, 2002 (Billions of Dollars)

Year	Quarter	Current Dollars	1996 Constant Dollars
2002	I	$10,313.1	$9,363.2
	II	10,376.9	9,392.4
	III	10,503.7	9,884.0
	IV*	10,572.3	9,503.2

*Preliminary.
Source: Bureau of Economic Analysis, January 2003.

Frequently, the various accounts of the GDP will not balance when checked against each other because information for various tables is collected from different sources. These differences are usually adjusted by writing them off to statistical discrepancies. In dealing with the GDP and related figures, remember that the data are approximations rather than precise figures.

FINAL SALES AND THE GDP

Tables of GDP data often include a figure for final sales. The difference between final sales and GDP represents *net inventory change*. When final sales are larger than the GDP, a net reduction in inventory took place to meet some of the demand for goods and services. When final sales are less than the GDP, unsold output is added to inventories. In the recession year of 1982, for example, final sales were $3,274 billion and the GDP was $3,259 billion, indicating that inventories were reduced by $15 billion during that recession year. Although the recession of 2001 was short-lived and mild by many standards, final sales exceeded GDP by $60 billion. In that year, the depletion of inventories, particularly in the technology sector, resulted in final sales of $10,142 and a GDP of $10,082.

GDP as a Measure of Economic Welfare

Because GDP is a measure of the total output of goods and services, it is frequently used as a measure of economic welfare. Furthermore, when GDP changes, our incomes change, and a change in our income affects our standard of living. Consequently, many people like to measure the standard of living by the size of the GDP. But if we use GDP as a measure of economic welfare or of the standard of living, we must make certain modifications and keep certain reservations in mind.

CHANGES IN THE PRICE LEVEL

Nominal GDP is the market value in current dollars of the total goods and services currently produced by the U.S. economy. Consequently, GDP can be increased merely by increasing the price of goods and services produced. Comparing one year with another can be very misleading unless we make corrections for changes in the price level between the two years. In effect, we have to remove the element of price changes from the current-dollar or nominal GDP. This is true for all the millions of different goods that constitute the GDP. Instead of adjusting each item individually, however, we adjust them all simultaneously by using the **GDP implicit price deflators,** an index that takes into account not only price changes but also some changes in the quality of various products. By dividing the total GDP for any year by the value of the implicit price deflator for that same year, we can adjust current GDP to a GDP in constant dollars or, as it is often called, a **real GDP.** The Department of Commerce is currently using 1996 as the basis for real GDP, as shown in Table 9–6.

GDP Implicit Price Deflators
An index that converts GDP and related data from current-dollar figures to constant-dollar figures, taking into account some changes in the quality of various products.

Real GDP
The gross domestic product as expressed in constant dollars.

If we were to use the current-dollar GDP as a measure of economic welfare, we would be misled into believing that the GDP had increased by 276 percent between 1980 and 2002. If we look at the GDP in constant dollars, however, we can see that the physical output of goods and services actually increased by 95 percent

	TABLE 9–6 Current-Dollar GDP Converted into 1996 Constant-Dollar GDP		
Year	Current-Dollar GDP (Billions)	Implicit Price Deflators (1996 = 100)	1996 Constant-Dollar GDP (Billions)
1980	$ 2,795.6	59.38	4,872.3
1985	4,213.0	74.05	5,689.8
1990	5,803.2	86.83	6,683.5
1991	5,986.2	89.76	6,669.2
1992	6,318.9	91.70	6,891.1
1993	6,642.3	94.16	7,054.1
1994	7,054.3	96.14	7,337.8
1995	7,400.5	98.19	7,537.1
1996	7,813.2	100.00	7,813.2
1997	8,318.4	101.66	8,159.5
1998	8,781.5	102.86	8,508.9
1999	9,274.3	104.46	8,859.0
2000	9,824.6	107.04	9,191.4
2001	10,082.2	109.36	9,214.5
2002	10,503.7	110.75	9,484.0

Source: Department of Commerce, Bureau of Economic Analysis, December 2002.

during this period. The real GDP tells us what we want to know much better than does the GDP in current dollars.

CHANGES IN POPULATION SIZE

Another modification we should make before using GDP as a measure of economic welfare is an adjustment for population size. The physical amount of goods and services produced in 2002 was much larger than the amount produced in 1980. We must keep in mind, however, that in 2002 more people were sharing the goods and services produced. It is therefore necessary to correct our real GDP to take into account the increase in population. This can be done simply by dividing the real GDP for any year by the total population in that year.

We can obtain an even better measure of the average amount of goods and services received per person by first reducing our GDP to disposable personal income (that is, to spendable income or income after taxes). If we divide total DPI by the total population, we get per capita DPI. This amount can then be adjusted for changes in the price level to give per capita DPI in constant dollars, or **real per capita disposable income.** If other things remain the same, comparing the real per capita DPI for any two years provides a fair indication of what is happening to our

Real Per Capita Disposable Income
Per capita disposable income adjusted for changes in the price level.

	Current Dollar Total DPI (Billions)	Population* (Millions)	Current Dollar per Capita DPI	1996 Constant Dollar per Capita DPI
TABLE 9-7 Current Dollar and Constant Dollar Per Capita Disposable Personal Income				
Year				
1980	$2,019.8	227.7	$ 8,870	$15,944
1985	3,086.5	238.5	12,941	18,120
1990	4,296.3	250.0	17,176	20,058
1995	5,422.6	266.3	20,361	20,798
1996	5,677.7	256.6	21,072	21,072
1997	5,968.2	269.4	21,887	21,470
1998	6,355.6	272.7	23,037	22,359
1999	6,627.4	275.9	23,749	22,678
2000	7,120.2	282.0	25,237	23,501
2001	7,393.2	284.8	25,957	23,692
2002	7,877.0	288.5	27,294	24,562

* Population based on mid-year and includes total population.
Source: Department of Commerce, Bureau of Economic Analysis, December 2002.

standard of living. Still, many people earn less than (and others more than) the value of the per capita DPI.

Table 9–7 shows that current-dollar total DPI increased by about 290 percent between 1980 and 2002. When we divide this total by the population, however, we find that the current-dollar per capita DPI rose by about 207 percent during the period. Finally, after adjusting the current-dollar per capita income for price changes, we see that the real per capita DPI rose by only 54 percent during the period. This is the best measure we have of changes in the standard of living or economic welfare in the United States. It is certainly closer to the truth to say that our standard of living increased by about 54 percent than to say that it more than doubled. Even so, there are other reservations about using GDP figures as a yardstick for the U.S. standard of living and economic welfare.

VALUE OF NONMONETARY TRANSACTIONS

GDP for the most part takes into account only currently produced goods and services supplied in monetary transactions. If you buy a new desk, it is entered in the GDP total, but if you make one yourself out of old lumber, it does not become a part of GDP. Similarly, if you hire a commercial gardener to mow your lawn, the value of the service is entered in the GDP, but if you mow it yourself, it does not go into the GDP. Many goods and services, because they do not involve monetary transactions, never enter the GDP. Nevertheless, they are just as important to the U.S. standard of living as most of the items that are counted in the GDP. This is a substantial defect when we want to use the GDP as an indicator of our economic welfare. For example, even if we took the current minimum-wage value per hour and applied it to a 40-hour week of ordinary household chores done by members of the family, it would add over hundreds of billions of dollars annually to the U.S. gross domestic product.

Underground Economy
The unregulated portion of the economy involving goods and services that are produced and exchanged without the use of monetary transactions.

It is estimated that additional billions of dollars worth of services are exchanged without the use of money in the **underground economy.** A dentist may trade an accountant oral surgery in exchange for financial advice, without any monetary payments involved. A lawyer may perform legal work for a schoolteacher in exchange for tutoring the lawyer's child.

In recent years, some formal barter organizations have been started. These organizations are composed of individuals with various skills—plumbers, lawyers, mechanics, carpenters, dentists, and the like—who perform services for each other in exchange for organization credits instead of cash payments. The earned credits can then be used to obtain services from other members of the organization. The Internal Revenue Service requires barter organizations to issue 1099-B forms for services received. The individuals must count these services as taxable income. It is estimated that activities equivalent to 10 to 15 percent of the reported GDP are currently taking place in the underground economy. (This estimate does not include criminal activities.)

TYPES OF GOODS AND SERVICES PRODUCED

We usually think that the more goods and services we produce, the better our economic welfare will be; but there are exceptions. Sometimes the nature of the goods and services is such that we cannot raise our standard of living through their consumption. For example, the U.S. gross domestic product was $10,503.7 billion in 2002; of that total output, however, $451 billion involved production of military goods and services. Tanks, ships, missiles, and other weaponry may protect our society, but they do not contribute directly to our economic welfare as do food, new homes, autos, clothing, medical care, and numerous other consumer goods and services.

Consequently, in comparing the GDP of various years for an indication of changes in our economic welfare, we may be misled if we fail to consider the type of goods and services produced in each of these years. For the same reason, it is often inaccurate to compare standards of living in two different countries simply by comparing the respective value of their GDPs; if one country is highly militarized while the other is not, a substantial difference in actual standard of living can be masked by roughly equivalent GDPs.

TREATMENT OF DURABLE GOODS

Durable goods are added to GDP in the year when they are produced. When a manufacturer produces an automobile, a refrigerator, a set of golf clubs, a suit, or a bicycle, value is added into the GDP for that product. In subsequent years, although we continue to receive services from the product, there are no additions to GDP. The U.S. national income accountants handle it as though it were entirely consumed in the year when it was produced. Normally, as incomes increase during periods of prosperity, we tend to produce more durable items; but we do not use them up in a single year. This tends to overstate the value of the GDP in a robust economy.

On the other hand, in recessions we tend to decrease our output of durable goods, but we continue to get service out of durable items produced previously. This service is a form of real income. But because there is no accounting in the GDP for the length of service of durable goods bought in previous years, the GDP in recessionary times frequently underestimates our economic welfare. Thus, the treatment of durable goods in the GDP tends to exaggerate the impact of business cycles on our standard of living.

EXTERNAL OR SOCIAL COSTS

Another reservation to keep in mind when using GDP data is the absence of any measure of social cost. When a firm produces goods and services, such internal factors as depreciation are treated as costs of production. Consequently, these costs are subtracted from GDP in calculations of net national product and national income.

In addition to internal costs, however, external or social costs are involved in the production of many goods and services. Effluents discharged from a chemical plant into a stream or river, for example, may pollute the water and make it unsuitable for drinking, swimming, or fishing. This is a social cost to the community. Smoke emitted from a factory may pollute the surrounding air, creating offensive odors or contributing to lung diseases. Noise associated with an airport may create a sound hazard and decrease property values in the area. These costs are associated with the deterioration of our natural environment and of our quality of life.

Because external costs are not borne by the individual firm, they are not included in its total cost or in the value added that enters the GDP. Nonetheless, they are real economic costs that must be borne by society. As GDP increases, these external or social costs tend to become larger and larger. Consequently, the net national product and the national income are overstated by billions of dollars annually because such costs are not subtracted from the GDP.

VALUE OF LEISURE

Finally, the GDP makes no allowance for leisure time. The problem is, even if we wanted to take this into account, how would we value it? For one thing, it means more to some people than it does to others. Still, leisure time should be considered when we attempt to use the GDP as a measure of economic welfare. Today we produce as much as or more than we formerly did per calendar year, even though we now have more holidays and vacation time. Certainly this must be considered a substantial improvement in our standard of living. But this improvement does not show up anywhere in our GDP figures. Shorter work weeks will raise our economic welfare, provided that we maintain the same output of goods and services.

In summary, GDP figures do a fairly good job of indicating the total output of goods and services by the U.S. economy. We can also use them as a measure of economic welfare or standard of living if we are careful. But do not be like the politicians who boast that our total output of goods and services increased by some fabulous amount during their party's administration—or like their opponents who charge that price increases obliterated all the advantages of higher incomes and wages. Get the facts straight, and use them properly. This is important, because the level of the GDP (along with the price level and the level of unemployment) serves as a guide to government efforts to stabilize the circular flow of income.

International Comparisons of Gross Domestic Product

Purchasing Power Parity
The number of units of currency needed in one country to buy the same amount of goods and services that 1 unit of currency will buy in another country.

Table 9–8 presents per capita GDP for the United States and other selected industrialized countries. In order to make such comparisons meaningful, the data have been adjusted to reflect real differences in the volume of goods and services produced in each country. Because market exchange rates do not reflect the relative purchasing power in the various countries, purchasing power parities instead of exchange rates are used to measure real output. **Purchasing power parity** shows how many units of currency are needed in one country to buy the same amount of goods and services that 1 unit of currency will buy in another country.

With the use of purchasing power parity adjustments, it is evident that of the countries presented, the United States has the highest per capita GDP, followed by

TABLE 9-8 Per Capita GDP for Selected Countries, 2001 (Purchasing Power Parity)			
Country	Per Capita GDP	Country	Per Capita GDP
United States	$36,300	United Kingdom	$24,700
Switzerland	31,100	Sweden	24,700
Norway	30,800	Italy	24,300
Denmark	28,000	Australia	24,000
Canada	27,700	New Zealand	19,500
Japan	27,200	Spain	18,900
Austria	27,000	Greece	17,900
Germany	26,200	Argentina	12,000
Belgium	26,100	Hungary	12,000
France	25,400	Mexico	9,000

Source: Central Intelligence Agency, *World Fact Book 2002.*

Switzerland, Norway, and Denmark. Although a high per capita GDP indicates a high level of national income, it says nothing about personal income and how it is distributed. Chapter 14 will focus on personal income distribution in the United States.

National Wealth

Wealth
All goods and resources having economic value, such as machinery, equipment, buildings, and land

Another important concept in the study of economics is wealth. **Wealth** comprises machinery, equipment, buildings, land, and other economic goods. By applying labor and knowledge to this wealth, we can produce additional goods and services, or income. Of course, the greater the base of wealth a nation has to work with, the more goods and services it can produce and the higher its standard of living will be. Consequently, it is advantageous for any nation to add continually to its stock of wealth.

As indicated in Chapter 1, there are various estimates of wealth. The one shown in Table 9–9, calculated by the U.S. Bureau of Economic Analysis, indicates that the net stock of wealth in the United States was about $28 trillion in 1999. Our national wealth and our productive capacity have been increasing continuously.

TABLE 9–9 Net Stock of Fixed Reproducible Tangible Wealth in the United States, 1999 (Billions of Dollars)	
Private	$19,882
Government	5,423
Consumer durable goods	2,561
Net stock of wealth	$27,866

Source: *Statistical Abstract of the United States: 2001.*

Summary

- Gross domestic product (GDP) refers to the current market value of the total goods and services produced by both domestic and foreign resources within the United States over a given period of time. Gross national product (GNP) also measures the current market value of all goods and services produced, but GNP includes the value of goods and services produced by U.S.-owned resources in foreign countries and excludes output produced in the United States by foreign-owned resources.

- The value-added approach to obtaining the value of total output is to count the value added in the production of both goods and services. The total value added is equal to the total payments made to the owners of the productive resources.

- When capital consumption allowances (depreciation and obsolescence) are subtracted from GNP, the result is net national product (NNP). National income (NI) is the total resource costs of the goods and services produced by the nation's economy. NI is also the income earned by the productive resources in producing the GDP. Personal income (PI) is the sum of all current income received by people from all sources. Disposable personal income (DPI) is personal income less personal taxes.

- The categories included in the distribution of national income are total resource costs (money paid for the use of land, labor, capital, and enter-

prise) and earnings (wages, rent, interest, profit) from production of the GDP. The categories included in the allocation of GDP are personal consumption, private domestic investments, net exports, and government.

- Current-dollar GDP is not a true measure of GDP. The real GDP, or constant-dollar GDP, takes into account the changes in the price level between periods. The real GDP is calculated by dividing the total GDP for any year by the value of the implicit price deflator for that year. Thus, real GDP is current-dollar GDP that has been converted to constant-dollar figures.

- Using GDP as a measure of economic welfare has its limitations. Those limitations include the effect of price changes on current GDP figures, the impact of population changes on per capita disposable income, and the exclusion of nonmonetary transactions, social costs, and the value of leisure time. Also, GDP does not distinguish between the types of goods and services produced and their effect on economic welfare. Nor does GDP effectively treat the output of durable goods over the business cycle.

- In order to make international comparisons of GDPs, purchasing power parity of currency is used rather than market exchange rates. Purchasing power parity shows how many units of currency are needed in one country to buy the same amount of goods and services that 1 unit of currency will buy in another country.

9

CHAPTER REVIEW

New Terms and Concepts

Gross domestic product
  (GDP)
Gross national product
  (GNP)
Value added
Capital consumption
  allowance

Net national product
  (NNP)
National income (NI)
Personal income (PI)
Transfer payment
Disposable personal
  income (DPI)

GDP implicit price deflators
Real GDP
Real per capita disposable
  income
Underground economy
Purchasing power parity
Wealth

Discussion Questions

1. How does the gross domestic product give rise to our total personal income?

2. Corporate income must be subtracted from national income to obtain personal income. How is it that personal income can be larger than national income?

3. In 2002, the federal government spent $698 billion on goods and services, according to the GDP accounts. The federal budget, however, shows total expenditures of more than 2 trillion. What is the reason for this difference?

4. Why is it important to convert the GDP and national income to constant-dollar value when using them as measures of economic welfare?

5. How should adjustments for population be included before using GDP figures as a measure of economic progress?

6. Should performance of household chores and other nonmonetary services be included in the gross domestic product? Why or why not?

7. Should GDP include an adjustment for the social (external) costs of production? Why or why not?

8. Does the method of entering durable goods into the GDP moderate or exaggerate the effects of business cycles? Explain.

9. Why are purchasing power parity adjustments made to international comparisons of per capita gross domestic product?

10. As we produce more and more goods and services, do we deplete our wealth? Why or why not?

Economic Applications

EconNews
Check out the EconNews link at http://econapps.swlearning.com to find information on measuring input and output. Look under the Macroeconomics heading and click on "Output, Income, and the Price Level." This will take you to many news articles involving economic measurement issues.

10

Money in the U.S. Economy

After studying Chapter 10, you should be able to:

1. Briefly describe the evolution of currency.

2. Define money, and explain its functions and how it is measured.

3. Understand the quantity theory of money, and show how changes in M and V affect P and Q.

4. Describe the effects of changes in the money supply on total income and output and the price level.

5. Illustrate the multiple expansion of the money supply, using a given initial checkable deposit and reserve requirement.

6. Explain how the Consumer Price Index is constructed and used.

7. Distinguish between nominal wages and real wages, and explain how to convert nominal wages into real wages.

Although classical economists held that money was passive and therefore had little effect on the economy, modern history has shown that the amount and flow of money play a major role in the U.S. economy. This chapter will examine the nature and functions of money, its creation by the banking system, and its effect on the price level.

Nature of Money

Throughout history, money has taken many shapes and forms. In earlier periods, commodity money was largely used as currency. Commodity money is that type of currency in which the commodity itself actually serves as money. Commodities that served as money generally had value in themselves. Many commodities, such as stones, shells, various crops, metal, and paper, have served as monies in various countries of the world. United States history reveals that tobacco, corn, wampum, warehouse receipts, and bank notes, in addition to metal coin and paper currency, have served as money. In fact, many of these monies were given legal tender status, which means they were deemed acceptable in payment of debts, both public and private.

Metallic money is a special type of commodity money in which some metal, such as gold, silver, or copper is used. Most early cultures traded precious metals as money. Egyptians circulated gold and silver coins as money over 2,500 years ago. Greeks and Romans continued the tradition and passed it on to Western civilizations. Coins were appealing because they were storable, easy to carry, and somewhat divisible. Coins were also valuable as commodities, for the value of a coin depended on the amount of gold or silver it contained. Coins issued in the United States no longer contain precious metals. Since 1970, very little silver is contained in nickels, dimes, quarters, half-dollars and dollars. The penny is now almost totally devoid of copper.

The Chinese began using paper money as far back as the tenth century. Paper money is not a form of commodity money insofar as it contains little or no intrinsic value. Paper money can be classified as either representative or fiat money.

Representative Money
Money that is redeemable for a commodity, such as gold or silver.

Representative money served in the place of metallic money and could be exchanged for gold or silver, and in some cases even for commodities such as tobacco. Representative money could be full-bodied or token. For example, a representative full-bodied $5 bill would be backed by $5 in gold or silver. If the $5 bill were a form of representative token money, it might be backed by only $1 in gold or silver. The United States issued representative full-bodied paper money in the form of gold certificates and silver certificates. Gold certificates no longer circulated after 1933, and silver certificates were redeemed beginning in 1968. No representative money is now issued in the United States.

Fiat Money
Money that is not redeemable for a commodity and is accepted on faith.

Fiat money is similar to representative money except it can't be redeemed for a commodity, such as gold or silver. Money in the United States today is entirely fiat money. Over time, the United States has evolved from a monetary system in which commodities, such as gold or silver, served as money to a system that now relies on paper money that is without any commodity backing whatsoever.

Functions and Measurement of Money

Most of us use money every day. We see it, touch it, and spend it. But how many of us can define it adequately? Usually, money is defined too narrowly. Some define it as the currency of a nation; others think of it in terms of legal tender; still others often refer to it as the medium of exchange. To include all segments of the U.S. money supply, we must use a broad definition. Thus, we can say that **money** is anything that is commonly accepted in exchange for other goods and services.

Money
Anything generally accepted in exchange for other goods and services.

FUNCTIONS OF MONEY

Money plays four essential roles in a modern economy: as a standard of value, as a medium of exchange, as a store of value, and as a standard of deferred payment.

Standard of Value

Money serves as a standard of value or as a unit of account, which means that we can measure the value of all other goods and services in terms of money. Without money, it would be extremely difficult to compare the values of different goods and services. How much would one stereo receiver be worth? We might agree, for example, that it would be worth 6 food processors, 20 bushels of wheat, 8 pairs of shoes, or 1/2 cow. Without money we would have to compare the value of the receiver with that of each good or service for which we might trade it. With money as a standard of value, however, we can express the value of the receiver in terms of money. Because the values of all other goods and services are also expressible in terms of money, we can easily compare the value of the receiver with the values of other items by looking at their respective dollar values. If the receiver is valued at $500, we know that it is equivalent in value to any other good or combination of goods whose value is also equal to $500.

Medium of Exchange

In a barter economy, the exchange of goods and services is extremely cumbersome. If a farmer wants to trade a lamb for a pair of shoes, the farmer must first find someone who has a pair of shoes and wants to trade them for a lamb. Thus, a problem of **double coincidence of wants** arises. Under these circumstances, the farmer may be forced to exchange the lamb for two bushels of wheat, the wheat for a set of books, and the books for the shoes.

Double Coincidence of Wants
In a barter economy, the need to find a match between what each of two traders wants to obtain and what each wants to offer in exchange.

In a monetary economy, the farmer could simply sell the lamb for cash and then spend the cash for the shoes. Thus, money serves as a medium of exchange and an economic catalyst. Money eliminates the need for a double coincidence of wants, and it facilitates the exchange of goods and services.

Store of Value

Money serves as a store of value by enabling us to convert excess goods into money and retain the money. It may be difficult to accumulate and hold wealth in the form of goods because some goods are too bulky to store, others are perishable, and others require prohibitively expensive storage. If money is to be a good store of wealth, it must possess stability. People are reluctant to store their wealth as money if they know that the money's purchasing power will decline substantially while being held. When a nation has an unstable currency, its citizens may store their wealth in the form of a foreign currency or of gold or silver. If the value of money declines, people may be prompted to spend the money or convert it into physical assets, such as land or buildings.

NETLink

How is electronic technology changing the use and function of money? Visit the Electronic Banker and ECash sites.

http://www.electronicbanker.com and http://www.ecash.com

Standard of Deferred Payment

In the U.S. economy, a great many purchases are made without immediate cash payment. Instead, the consumer agrees to pay the purchase price over a period of time. Thus, money becomes a standard of deferred payment. When a family buys a home, it may take 20 years or more to pay for it. In this case, the lender trusts that the money to be received from the family over the ensuing years will be usable and that its purchasing power will not decline drastically. As in its role as a store of value, money must be stable if it is to serve as a reliable standard of deferred payment.

Sound money must be able to perform all four functions. The U.S. dollar has done the job reasonably well. Some monies, however, do only a partial job. The currency in some Latin American nations, for example, where price levels have risen drastically over the last two decades, has difficulty fulfilling its functions because of hyperinflation. Even in the United States, during periods when unusually high inflation persists, some holders of U.S. dollars (citizens and foreigners alike) seek to convert their wealth into some other good, such as real property, gold, or a more stable foreign currency.

MEASURING THE MONEY SUPPLY

Although money is broadly defined as anything accepted in exchange for goods and services, the **money stock** or money supply—the quantity in existence at any given time—is more narrowly defined and measured according to its liquidity. The ease with which an asset can be converted into the medium of exchange is called **liquidity. Currency,** which includes paper money and coins, is the ultimate liquid asset because it already is the medium of exchange.

Most often, the U.S. money stock is officially measured by classifying money into three categories: M1, M2, and M3. Table 10–1 indicates the various components that make up each group, as well as their amounts. **M1** consists primarily of currency in the hands of the public, travelers checks, and checkable deposits. **Checkable deposits** are funds held in checking accounts in financial institutions, as well as negotiable orders of withdrawal (NOW accounts) and automatic transfer service (ATS) accounts. NOW accounts are deposit accounts that pay interest and allow check-writing privileges. ATS accounts also pay interest and allow for the automatic transfer of funds from a savings to a checking deposit. Because M1 includes cash and deposits subject to immediate withdrawal for payment purposes, it is the most liquid form of money.

M2 is a broader definition of money, for in addition to M1 it includes savings deposits, small (less than $100,000) time deposits, and money market funds. **Savings deposits** are interest-bearing funds held in accounts that do not allow for automatic transfer services. **Time deposits** are funds that earn a fixed rate of interest and must be held for a stipulated period of time. Early withdrawal of funds, as in the case of certificates of deposit, are subject to penalty. **Money market funds** are

Money Stock
Quantity of money in existence at any given time.

Liquidity
The ease with which an asset can be converted into the medium of exchange.

Currency
Paper money and coins.

M1 Money Stock
Most liquid definition of money; includes currency, travelers checks, and checkable deposits.

Checkable Deposits
Checking deposits at banks and other depository institutions, including demand deposits (checking accounts), NOW accounts, ATS accounts, and share draft accounts.

M2 Money Stock
The total of M1 and savings deposits, small time deposits, and money market funds.

Savings Deposits
Interest-bearing funds held in accounts that do not allow for automatic transfer services.

Time Deposits
Funds that earn a fixed rate of interest and must be held for a stipulated period of time.

Money Market Funds
Deposits held in accounts that are invested in a broad range of short-term financial assets, such as government and corporate bonds.

TABLE 10–1 Money Stock of the United States, December 2002 (Billions of Dollars)		
Currency and travelers checks		$ 637.9
plus		
Checkable Deposits		603.4
	equals M1	$1,241.3
plus		
Money Market Funds		948.2
and Savings Accounts		2,769.5
and Small Time Deposits		
and other smaller components		877.9
	equals M2	$5,836.9
plus		
Large Time Deposits, Including Eurodollars		
and other smaller components		2,726.0
	equals M3	$8,562.9

Source: Federal Reserve Board of Governors.

deposits held in accounts that are invested in a broad range of short-term financial assets, such as government and corporate bonds. Although these funds have check-writing privileges, the investor is limited in the number of checks that can be written and the minimum amount permitted for each check. Money market funds may be held in banks (called money market deposit accounts) or in nonfinancial institutions.

M3 Money Stock
The total of M2, large negotiable certificates of deposit, and Eurodollars.

Eurodollars
U.S. dollars deposited in foreign banks and consequently outside the jurisdiction of the United States.

A still more inclusive classification of money is that of **M3**, which is M2 plus large negotiable certificates of deposit. Also included in M3 are **Eurodollars,** which are U.S. dollars deposited in foreign banks and consequently outside the jurisdiction of the United States. Historically, M1 was most frequently used as the benchmark for the money supply. However, because of the creation and growth of new forms of bank accounts in recent years, such as money market deposit accounts and small-denomination time deposits, most economists see M1 as being too narrow a definition, and M2 is now more frequently used. Thus, throughout this chapter and entire book, money supply will be synonymous with M2.

The Supply of Money and Total Income

What is the effect of money on the economy? From observation and analysis, we can see that changes in the volume of money can definitely affect the level of total income and output and the price level, depending on existing economic conditions. However, changes in the money supply cannot cure all or even most of the weaknesses of a particular economy. What they can do is accelerate or slow down the circular flow of income and/or change the price level.

THE EQUATION OF EXCHANGE

Equation of Exchange
A relationship between the supply of money and the price level.

One way to explain the effects of money on the economic system is in terms of its quantity. The **equation of exchange** expresses a very simple relationship between the supply of money and the price level. It assumes that any money received is generally spent directly or indirectly to buy goods and services. This **transactions approach** can be expressed as the formula

$$MV = PQ$$

Transactions Approach
An analysis of the equation of exchange that assumes that any money received is spent directly or indirectly to buy goods and services.

where M = total money supply (including all types of money)
V = velocity of money (that is, average number of times per year that a dollar is used to purchase final goods and services, found by dividing money supply into total spending in the economy)
P = price level or average price per transaction
Q = total transactions in the economy (total physical units of goods and services produced and sold in the economy over a period of time)

The left side of the equation (MV) represents the total amount spent on goods and services, while the right side (PQ) represents the total amount received by sellers. In effect, the equation of exchange tells us that the amount of final purchases in the economy must equal the amount of money in circulation multiplied by the average number of times per year that each dollar changes hands. The equation of exchange is a truism or tautology because the value of goods purchased is always equal to the value of goods sold.

QUANTITY THEORY OF MONEY

Quantity Theory of Money
A classical view of the nature of money as being passive, so that the quantity of money and the price level are proportional when other conditions are stable.

Being a truism, the equation of exchange is not a predictive tool in itself, but classical economists used this equation as the basis for developing the quantity theory of money. In its simplest form, the **quantity theory of money** states that in equilibrium the price level (P) is exactly proportional to the money supply (M). For this conclusion to hold true, quantity theorists made two very important assumptions. First, they assumed that the national economy is inherently stable and tends to operate at full employment of all productive resources. Thus, with full employment the value of real output or real GDP remains constant. The second major assumption is that the velocity of money is also stable because people's spending habits tend to be constant over time.

Given these assumptions, quantity theorists concluded that, if total output (Q) and velocity (V) are constant, any increase in money supply (M) should lead to a directly proportionate increase in the price level (*P*). For example, by converting the equation of exchange from *MV* = *PQ* to *P* = *MV/Q*, we can more easily see the cause-and-effect relationship between *P* and *Q* according to quantity theorists.

Suppose that the hypothetical value for the money supply is $5 and that of total output is 4. If velocity is assumed to have a value of 4, then the average price per transaction is $5. When these values are used in the formula, they appear as

$$P = \frac{MV}{Q} = \frac{\$5 \times 4}{4} = \frac{\$20}{4} = \$5$$

Now what happens when there is an increase in the money supply? With output and velocity being fixed, *V/Q* will be constant no matter what their values. Under such conditions, if we double the money supply from $5 to $10, the result will be a doubling of the price level. Again, this occurs because at full employment of resources no additional goods and services can be produced and the velocity of money is being held constant. Individuals and firms will use the additional money to bid against each other for existing goods and services, and inflation results. In terms of our formula,

$$P = \frac{MV}{Q} = \frac{\$10 \times 4}{4} = \frac{\$40}{4} = \$10$$

Although economists today agree that there is an important linkage between a nation's money supply and the general price level, they do not see them as proportionately related. The basis for this disagreement lies with the major assumptions contained in the quantity theory. The assumptions of full employment and stable velocity are key to the controversy. Modern economics holds that if the economy is operating at less than full employment, as it often does, increasing the money supply normally leads to an increase in real output, instead of a proportionate increase in prices. Therefore, if the money supply is increased by 10 percent, the additional money may be used to purchase additional goods and services produced by the economy's previously unemployed workforce, unused resources, and idle capacity. Rather than increase proportionately, the price level may remain stable or increase only slightly.

As for the assumption of constant velocity, this, too, is challenged by modern economists based on empirical evidence. In some periods, people tend to spend their incomes faster or save smaller portions of their income. When this occurs, the turnover of the money supply is greater and total spending increases. This can lead to an increase in total output and/or a price increase, depending on existing economic circumstances. If, on the other hand, people are inclined to spend their incomes at a slower rate or save a greater share of their incomes, total spending will fall. In this case, declining velocity may exert downward pressure on prices and output.

Interest rates and expected price changes are examples of two factors that can cause velocity to change. Higher interest rates can induce people to save more, reducing the amount available for spending and therefore increasing the velocity of the remaining stock of money in circulation. Conversely, velocity may decrease as interest rates fall as a greater amount of money is allocated to consumer spending and away from savings. Velocity may also change if people anticipate a change in inflation. Velocity tends to increase if higher inflation is expected, as people spend money faster to beat future price increases. But if lower prices are expected, velocity may fall as households postpone purchases to take advantage of lower prices in the future. History has shown that dramatic changes in economic conditions can have a substantial short-term impact on the velocity of money.

MONEY AND THE CIRCULAR FLOW

Clearly, the amount and flow of the money supply can affect business activity in the economy. This was demonstrated in the discussion of circular flow in Chapter 8. Whenever planned investment is greater than planned saving, the result is an increase in total output or a rise in prices. Absent a change in velocity, however, an increase in the money supply is necessary to give businesses the means to increase their investment. The increased investment may come about through an increase in the amount of currency or through an increase in the creation of other forms of money by banks.

Likewise, government deficit spending is often financed by means of an increase in the money supply generated by banks. On the other hand, a decrease in investment or a government surplus may trigger a decline in the money supply.

There appears to be some relationship between investment–savings decisions and the status of the government budget, on the one hand, and changes in the money supply on the other. Furthermore, a change in any of these may affect the GDP and the price level. These relationships are summarized in Table 10–2.

TABLE 10–2 Relationships of Investment, Savings, the Government Budget, and the Money Supply		
Conditions Tending Toward Stable Total Output and Stable Price Level	Conditions Tending Toward Decrease in Total Output and/or Decline in Price Level	Conditions Tending Toward Increase in Total Output and/or Increase in Price Level
Planned I = planned S	Planned I < planned S	Planned I > planned S
Balanced government budget	Surplus government budget	Deficit government budget
Exports = imports	Net imports	Net exports
Stable money supply	Decrease in money supply	Increase in money supply

Creation of Money

In this chapter we have learned how money is defined and measured, the functions it must serve, and the importance of changes in the money supply on output and income. We can now address the role of financial institutions in changing the money supply through the expansion and contraction of checkable deposits. Although numerous types of financial institutions can now offer checkable deposits and thus affect money supply, we will refer to the expansion and contraction of checkable deposits in terms of the banking system.

Although checkable deposits compose a large part of the U.S. money supply, they remain the most mystifying part of it. To understand the important role played by checkable deposits, we must determine how banks actually create deposits and what restraints limit the process of deposit creation.

Banks today provide a wide variety of income-producing services, but their major functions are to provide loans and, as a group, create money. Thus, in seeking to maximize profits, banks will try to make as many loans as they can with reasonable safety. Let's begin by assuming that you have been saving money in your desk drawer from holidays and birthdays and that you have $1,000 in cash. You now visit your neighborhood bank and set up a new checking account with your $1,000 deposit. Note that this action has no immediate effect on the money supply (M1), for you have merely converted currency into checkable deposits. However, to earn a profit on your deposit, the bank will have to put your money to work by lending it out to a borrower. The key question is how much, if any, of your $1,000 deposit your bank can loan out. The answer to this question lies with existing state and federal banking regulations that require reserve backing for deposits, and these requirements limit a bank's ability to make a loan.

If reserve requirements were 100 percent of deposits, the bank could not lend any of your money because your $1,000 deposit would have to serve as its own reserve. In practice, however, banks are required to hold only a fraction of your $1,000 deposit in reserve and can loan out the remainder, and it is through this fractional reserve system that banks create money.

If, by law, the legal reserve requirement is 10 percent, the bank must place $100 in legal reserves and have $900 in excess reserves to loan out to other customers. When the bank loans out the $900, the result is an increase in the money supply, since you still have your checkable deposit for $1,000 and the bank's borrower has a new one for $900. Although your bank increased the money supply to only a limited degree, the cumulative action of all banks can increase the money supply by a multiple of your original deposit.

To illustrate this point, suppose the borrower of the $900 purchases a new refrigerator from Sears and that $900 is then deposited in Sears' account in another bank. This bank can then hold $90 as legal reserves against Sears' $900 deposit and loan out the remaining $810. This process can continue until the total loans outstanding equal $9,000 and the original $1,000 is held as reserves in various banks.

At that point, the banks can lend no more money from the original deposit. This process is known as the multiple expansion of the money supply. As long as no-body withdraws cash and no excess reserves are allowed to sit idle, the amount by which the money supply changes is determined by the money multiplier.

The **money multiplier** equals the reciprocal of the reserve ratio. That is,

Money Multiplier
The reciprocal of the reserve ratio.

$$\text{Money multiplier} = \frac{1}{\text{Required reserve ratio}}$$

In our example, the money multiplier is the reciprocal of $1/10$ (10 percent $= 1/10$), or $10/1 = 10$. In other words, the value of the total deposit expansion was 10 times the value of the original deposit. The two big factors determining the size of the money multiplier are the size of the original deposit and the required reserve ratio. For example, had the reserve requirement been 20 percent, your $1,000 deposit could have supported only $4,000 in loans and resulted in $5,000 in total deposit expansion.

Another way of looking at this process is in tabular form, as shown in Table 10–3. This table shows how $1,000 deposited in a bank (Bank A) can be expanded into $10,000 in checkable deposits through loans of $9,000. To meet its 10 percent reserve requirement, Bank A will hold $100 against the original deposit of $1,000. It thus has $900 in cash to lend. People who borrow this money spend it and circulate it in the community until it finally ends up in other banks as recipients make deposits. If all these deposits are made in Bank B, that bank will hold a $90 reserve against its deposits of $900 and lend the remaining $810. This process continues until all the initial deposit is tied up in reserves in various banks. At such time, the

TABLE 10–3 Expansion of the Money Supply							
10% RESERVE REQUIREMENT				**20% RESERVE REQUIREMENT**			
Bank	Deposit	Reserve	Loan	Bank	Deposit	Reserve	Loan
A	$ 1,000	$ 100	$ 900	A	$1,000	$ 200	$ 800
B	900	90	810	B	800	160	640
C	810	81	729	C	640	128	512
D	729	73	656	D	512	102	410
E	656	66	590	E	410	82	328
F	590	59	531	F	328	66	262
G	531	53	478	G	262	52	210
H	478	48	430	H	210	42	168
I	430	43	387	I	168	34	134
J	387	39	348	J	134	27	107
etc.	etc.	etc.	etc.	etc.	etc.	etc.	etc.
	$10,000	$1,000	$9,000		$5,000	$1,000	$4,000

total deposits will equal $10,000, the reserves $1,000, and the total loans outstanding $9,000. Table 10–3 also shows the effect of the multiple expansion of the money supply with a 20 percent reserve requirement.

Just as we can observe the multiple expansion of the money supply when a bank experiences a net increase in deposits, we can also see a multiple contraction of the money supply when it experiences a net withdrawal of deposits. When reserves are withdrawn, the bank must recall loans to replenish its reserves.

We can relate the relationship of the money supply to the level of total income and output by using circular flow analysis. We have seen that the reserve requirement on checkable deposits can alter banks' ability to extend the money supply. If changes in the money supply can alter the circular flow, then we can accelerate or slow down the circular flow by changing the reserve requirement. This is exactly what happens in the U.S. economy. The reserve requirement is used, along with several other monetary measures, as tools to stabilize total income and output and the price level. A similar process of money expansion takes place in most industrial nations of the world.

Changes in the Price Level

Prices constantly move up or down, depending on business conditions. In general, prices may all be moving in the same direction. But some may be rising, some declining, and others remaining stable. In fact, individual price changes are of no great consequence. It is more valuable to have a device for measuring the general or average movement of all prices in the economy. For this reason, we construct price indexes.

The Producer Price Index (PPI), the Consumer Price Index (CPI), the GDP Implicit Price Deflators, and many other price indexes calculated by various government agencies have the same basic makeup. A **price index** compares the average price of a group of goods and services in one period of time with the average price of the same group of goods and services in another period. Prices are determined for a base period, and the prices in all subsequent years are measured in relation to the base-period prices. In calculating price indexes, it is essential that the items whose prices are to be measured remain constant both in quantity and in quality.

Price Index
A measuring system for comparing the average price of a group of goods and services in one period of time with the average price of the same group of goods and services in another period.

A HYPOTHETICAL PRICE INDEX

Now we will calculate a hypothetical price index for a group of goods and services that might be purchased by a young adult. The group includes five items: (1) rent and utilities for an apartment, (2) transportation, (3) food, (4) clothing purchases and upkeep, and (5) recreational activities. Table 10–4 presents a hypothetical set of figures for this market basket of goods and services.

Assume that the market basket cost $807 per month to buy in 1983. The price index in column 3 represents a comparison of the price of the market basket in

		TABLE 10–4 Price Index Using a Hypothetical Market Basket		
(1) Year	(2) Price or Cost	(3) Price Index, Base Period 1983	(4) Price Index, Base Period 1990
1980	$ 670	83	64
1983	807	100	76
1985	863	107	82
1987	920	114	87
1989	1,000	124	95
1990	1,057	131	100
1996	1,267	157	120
1999	1,340	166	127
2001	1,429	177	135
2002	1,445	179	136

any year with its price in the base period 1983. The formula for finding the price index is

$$\frac{\text{Price of market basket in given year}}{\text{Price of market basket in base period}} = 100\%$$

The index for 1983 must be 100 because the price of the market basket in 1983 was 100 percent of its price in the base period (1983). By 1989, however, the price of the market basket was $1,000. Therefore, the index for 1989 was 124; that is, its price was 124 percent of what it was in 1983 ($1,000/807 \times 100 = 1.24 \times 100 =$ 124 percent), which means that the price of these goods and services increased by 24 percent over the intervening six years. By 2002, the market basket cost $1,445, 179 percent of its price in 1983, or 79 percent more.

The index gives us a way to compare the level of prices at any time with the level that existed in the base period. The index for any given year can be obtained by dividing the prices in the given year by the prices in the base period. The data for any one year can be compared with those for another by noting the change in the index.

It is necessary to change the base period occasionally because spending habits change over the years, new products enter the market, and the comparison of current prices with prices from a much earlier period may become meaningless. For example, if we were to use the same market basket in 2003 that we did in 1983, a number of goods and services that today constitute an important part of consumer expenditures would be excluded. Digital cameras, CDs, DVDs, personal computers, hand-held computers, mobile phones, and laser printers are just a few of the products that were not included in the 1983 basket. A change in the base period does not change the actual prices; it merely changes the identity of the year with which all other years' prices are compared. For example, if the base period for the index in Table 10–4 were changed to 1990, the cost of buying the market basket in 2002 would still be the same, but the index would read (1,445/1,057 $\times$ 100 = 136 percent) instead of 179, as it did when the index was based on 1983 prices.

Changing the base period is a fairly simple matter; the difficulties arise when the products being analyzed change. Constructing a new index to handle a revision of current index numbers is not a simple task. Changing the items included in the market basket and the weights of the various goods and services will certainly yield a price for the new market basket that differs from the price of the former market basket.

THE CONSUMER PRICE INDEX

Consumer Price Index (CPI)
An index that compares the price of a group of basic goods and services as purchased by urban residents.

The **Consumer Price Index (CPI)** compares the price of a group of basic goods and services as purchased by urban residents, including professional employees, the self-employed, the poor, the unemployed, and retired persons, as well as urban wage earners and clerical workers. These items are weighted according to the percent of total spending that is applied to each of several categories, including food, rent, apparel, transportation, and medical care. The CPI is calculated by the Bureau of Labor Statistics (BLS), which is part of the U.S. Department of Labor. A separate index is calculated for each category, as well as a composite index for over 200 categories. Indexes are calculated for each of 29 metropolitan areas, for several non-metropolitan urban areas, and for the United States as a whole. The BLS has used a number of different base periods for the CPI, but it now uses 1982–1984 as the base period.

Components of the CPI

The CPI market basket consists of various goods and services purchased by consumers in urban households. The current categories and their weights are as follows: all items (100 percent), food and beverages (16.4 percent), housing (40.5 percent), apparel (4.2 percent), transportation (16.7 percent), medical care (6.0 percent), recreation (5.9 percent), education and communication (5.4 percent), and other goods and services (4.9 percent).

Because the prices of some goods and services rise faster than the prices of others, it is essential to identify the appropriate geographic areas and item categories when using the index for specific purposes. Figure 10–1 depicts the annual change in overall prices, the annual change in the price of medical care, and the value of the CPI for the years 1980–2002. Medical care price changes have far exceeded the rise in overall prices throughout the period. Because the medical care component carries a weight in the CPI of but 6.0 percent, it does not pull the index upwards in the same way as a comparable rise in housing, which has a much greater weight.

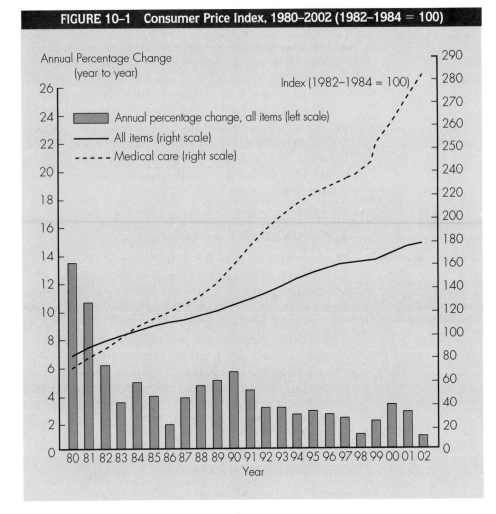

FIGURE 10–1   Consumer Price Index, 1980–2002 (1982–1984 = 100)

Nevertheless, because of their steep ascent and their impact on specific population groups, medical care prices are under constant scrutiny by public policymakers.

Limitations of the CPI

The CPI merely measures relative change in the cost of living. It does not measure the actual cost of living. A higher index in one city may not mean that prices are really higher in that city than elsewhere. It simply means that the cost of living has increased more rapidly in that city than it has elsewhere since the base period.

	1982–1984		2003	
City	Cost of Market Basket	Base Period CPI	Cost of Market Basket	Current Year CPI
A	$1,500	100	$2,100	140
B	$1,800	100	$2,400	133

TABLE 10–5 Sample Cost of Living and CPI Figures for Two Cities

Suppose that the actual monthly dollar cost of living and the Consumer Price Index for two cities are shown in Table 10–5. If 1982–1984 is selected as the base period, both the $1,500 figure for city A and the $1,800 figure for city B receive an index value of 100 for the base period. The actual monthly cost of living in both cities increased by $600 between the 1982–1984 base period and 2003. But the CPI rose more in city A, which has the lower dollar cost of living. Thus, it is possible for a city with a lower actual cost of living to have a higher Consumer Price Index number than a city with a higher cost of living. For example, according to the Bureau of Labor Statistics, average annual expenditures of consumer units in 1999 was $50,945 in Anchorage, Alaska, and $44,016 in the New York City Metropolitan Area. But the CPI in 1999 was 168.9 for Anchorage and 177.0 for New York.

Another limitation of the CPI is that it is not a completely pure price index. The BLS admits that certain elements of quality improvement may be reflected in the index. Determining the extent to which an increase in the price of a good or service represents an improvement in quality is difficult. An upward bias in the collection and processing of data for the index does seem to exist. Various studies indicate that its size amounts to roughly 1 or 2 percentage points annually.

The CPI, COLA, and Indexation

In recent years, much attention has been focused on the composition, structure, and measurement of the CPI. As inflation erodes purchasing power, the CPI is often used to adjust consumers' income payments. Today the wages of some 2 million workers covered by collective bargaining agreements are tied to the CPI through cost-of-living adjustment (COLA) clauses. In addition, the CPI affects the income of almost 80 million persons as a result of statutory action. These include 48 million Social Security beneficiaries, approximately 22 million food stamp recipients, and about 4 million military and Federal Civil Service retirees and survivors. Changes in the CPI also affect the cost of the school lunch program for 27 million children. Another example of how dollar values are adjusted by the CPI occurs with the federal income tax structure. Federal income tax payments are adjusted by the CPI to prevent "bracket creep," which produces inflation-induced increases in tax rates.

COLAs can be inflationary, because they increase wages or salaries without necessarily increasing productivity. It is detrimental to a worker's wages to move the base year forward in inflationary times while retaining the same indexation factor, because a larger absolute increase in the cost of living would be required to equal the same percentage increase in the new CPI.

Consumer Price Indexes of Other Countries

Consumer price indexes are maintained by developed nations throughout the world as a measure of inflation. However, the construction and use of consumer price indexes vary among countries. Countries also place different weights on the various categories that comprise their indexes. Thus, as is the case whenever international statistics are used, care must be exercised in comparing inflation rates between countries. The Bureau of Labor Statistics has converted the consumer price indexes of a select number of countries to conform with the CPI of the United States. Table 10–6 contains the average annual percent change in the consumer price indexes of six countries, including the United States, for the years 1990 through 2001. In examining the table, it is evident that over the time period spanning over a decade, annual price changes in these countries have followed the same downward trend. The table also shows that the United States had the highest inflation rates during the past three years. On the other hand, Japan experienced

TABLE 10–6 Consumer Price Indexes, Six Countries Average, Annual Percent Change, 1990–2001					
Period	United States	Canada	Japan	Italy	United Kingdom	France
1990	5.4	4.8	3.1	6.5	9.5	3.4
1991	4.2	5.6	3.3	6.3	5.9	3.2
1992	3.0	1.5	1.6	5.2	3.7	2.4
1993	3.0	1.8	1.3	4.5	1.6	2.0
1994	2.7	0.2	0.7	4.0	2.5	1.7
1995	2.8	2.2	−0.1	5.2	3.4	1.7
1996	2.9	1.6	0.2	4.0	2.4	2.0
1997	2.3	1.6	1.7	2.0	3.1	1.2
1998	1.6	0.9	0.6	1.9	3.4	0.7
1999	2.2	1.7	−0.3	1.7	1.5	0.5
2000	3.4	2.7	−0.7	2.5	3.0	1.7
2001	2.8	2.6	−0.7	2.8	1.8	1.7

Source: International Monetary Fund, Washington, D.C., *International Financial Statistics.*

the condition known as *deflation* during 1999 through 2001. Deflation occurs when there is an actual decrease in a nation's price level.

OTHER PRICE INDEXES

The CPI measures changes in the prices of consumer goods only. Because these account for only about two-thirds of total spending, the CPI does not give a full account of what is happening to prices. It does not take into consideration changes in the prices of industrial machinery, equipment, buildings, or raw material. The **Producer Price Index (PPI)** measures changes in producer prices. In other words, it is a measure of the average prices received by producers and wholesalers. Because the PPI includes the prices of important raw materials, such as steel, that are used to produce many other producer and consumer goods, the PPI is a widely followed index. Like the CPI, the PPI is also based on the constant basket approach, but it is more volatile than the CPI. Because higher prices at the producer level usually result in higher prices at the consumer level, the PPI is often used as a forecasting tool to predict changes in consumer prices.

Producer Price Index (PPI)
A measure of the average prices received by producers and wholesalers.

A broader measure than either the CPI or the PPI is the *GDP Implicit Price Deflator,* which takes into account the prices of all final goods and services produced by the economy. The GDP deflator is an index of the price level of aggregate output. It measures the average price of the components of the gross domestic product compared to a base year. In effect, the GDP deflator is a current-weight index in that the weights assigned to the various components are the proportions sold in the current year, as opposed to prices existing in the base year. Because the GDP is a broader index, it is the inflation index most favored by economists. Unfortunately, the index is difficult to compute and is published only quarterly. Inflation rates as measured by the CPI, the GDP deflator, and the PPI for finished goods for the years 1990–2002 are shown in Table 10–7.

THE VALUE OF MONEY

In addition to their usefulness for measuring changes in the price level, price indexes are useful for determining the value of money. The value of money is based on the goods and services that a given amount of money will buy. An increase in the price level is the same as a loss in purchasing power. Conversely, if the price level falls, the value of money increases because a given amount of money buys more. Changes in the price level have caused the value (or purchasing power) of money to change substantially over recent years.

The value of the U.S. dollar at any time can be determined by dividing $1.00 by the price index and multiplying by 100. Thus, the value of the dollar in 1982–1984, using an index value of 1982–1984 = 100, was $1.00 ($1.00/100 × 100 = $1.00). In 2002, the dollar was valued at $0.56 ($1.00/179 × 100 = $0.56) compared to its 1982–1984 value. That means that a 2002 dollar would purchase only 56 cents worth of goods as measured in 1982–1984 dollars.

TABLE 10-7 Comparison of Inflation Rates: Consumer Price Index, GDP Deflator, and Producer Price Index, 1990–2002			
Year	Inflation Rate CPI (Percent)	Inflation Rate GDP Deflator (Percent)	Inflation Rate PPI (Percent)
1990	5.4	3.9	4.9
1991	4.2	3.6	2.1
1992	3.0	2.4	1.2
1993	3.0	2.4	1.2
1994	2.7	2.1	0.6
1995	2.8	2.2	1.9
1996	2.9	1.9	2.7
1997	2.3	1.9	0.4
1998	1.6	1.2	0.9
1999	2.2	1.1	1.8
2000	3.4	2.3	3.8
2001	2.8	2.4	2.0
2002*	1.6	1.3	−1.4

*Preliminary.
Source: Department of Labor, Bureau of Labor Statistics.

REAL INCOME

Real Income
The constant-dollar value of goods and services produced; also, the purchasing power of money income.

Although the purchasing power of the dollar has declined in recent decades, we obtain many more dollars in income today than we did previously. As a result, the total purchasing power, or **real income,** of the average person has changed irregularly in the past several decades. Total purchasing power increased in the 1950s and 1960s, when income rose faster than the price level. It has declined since the latter part of the 1970s because the level of prices has risen faster than incomes have grown.

We can obtain some idea of the total change in purchasing power for the average person from Table 10–8. In this table, the nominal wage (column 2) represents average gross weekly earnings in all private nonagricultural industries. Column 4 is the real wage—that is, the purchasing power of the nominal wage in 1982 dollars. The real wage in column 4 is determined by dividing the nominal wage in column 2 by the Consumer Price Index for Urban Wage Earners and Clerical Workers (1982–1984 = 100).[1] Column 5 is the percent change in real wage in each year.

1   Throughout this book we have been using the Consumer Price Index for All Urban Consumers as the measure of inflation. However, the Bureau of Labor Statistics also constructs the Consumer Price Index for Urban Wage and Clerical Workers. Although more limited in use, this index is better suited for determining real wages.

TABLE 10–8	Nominal Weekly Wages Versus Real Weekly Wages in Nonagricultural Industries, 1982–2002			
Year	Nominal Wage	Annual % Increase in Nominal Wage	Real Wage (1982 $)	Annual % Change in Real Wage
1982	267.26	—	267.26	—
1983	280.70	5.0	272.52	2.0
1984	292.86	4.3	274.73	0.8
1985	299.09	2.1	271.16	1.3
1986	304.85	1.9	271.94	0.3
1987	312.50	2.5	269.16	1.0
1988	322.36	3.0	266.79	0.9
1989	334.24	3.8	264.22	1.0
1990	345.35	3.3	259.47	1.8
1991	353.78	2.5	255.64	1.6
1992	363.95	2.7	255.47	0.2
1993	373.64	2.8	254.87	0.0
1994	385.86	3.3	256.73	0.7
1995	394.68	2.3	255.29	0.6
1996	406.61	3.1	255.73	0.3
1997	424.89	4.5	261.31	2.2
1998	442.19	4.1	268.32	2.7
1999	456.78	3.3	271.25	1.1
2000	474.38	3.9	272.36	0.3
2001	489.74	3.3	273.45	0.5
2002*	503.20	2.7	277.50	1.5

* Preliminary.
Source: *Economic Indicators* (January 2003) and Bureau of Labor Statistics.

Some interesting observations can be made from Table 10–8. For instance, the nominal wage increased substantially in the period from 1982 to 2001, but because of price increases, the real wage actually rose very little. In effect, price increases ultimately offset most of the advantages of higher wages for the average worker during that period. Although the average worker had $236 more in weekly pay in 2002 than in 1982, the purchasing power of that pay was only $10 more in 2002 than in 1982. Although not shown in the table, the average real wage as measured in 1982 dollars peaked in 1972 at $315.44. This means that real wages have declined about 12 percent since then, despite substantial increases in nominal wages.

EFFECTS OF CHANGES IN THE PRICE LEVEL

Inflation benefits those whose incomes rise faster than increases in the price level. For example, business profits and salespersons' commissions are very susceptible to increases or decreases in output and prices. When the price level is increasing, that may be an advantage to businesses and salespeople on commission. But since their incomes usually decrease faster than do prices, they are at a disadvantage when the price level decreases. Others, such as most employees, some executives, schoolteachers, and pensioners, whose incomes remain relatively stable despite changes in the price level are at a disadvantage in periods of rising prices. These people suffer from inflation, but they gain during a period of deflation, provided that they maintain their income and their jobs. It thus seems that whenever prices move substantially in either direction inequities develop.

Changes in the price level also affect creditors and debtors, each in a different manner. Inflation is beneficial to debtors but detrimental to creditors. Deflation works a hardship on debtors and enhances the value of creditors' dollars. For example, suppose you borrowed $50,000 to build a home in 1977 with the stipulation that you would repay the entire amount plus interest in one lump sum in 2002. In 1977, the creditor gave up $50,000 (the equivalent of a good three-bedroom home), but when you repaid in 2002, the $50,000 the creditor received would purchase only about one-third of the same type of house, because the cost of such homes had risen to more than $150,000. The money repaid to the creditor in 2002 had less purchasing power than the money lent in 1977. On the other hand, you would be making repayment with dollars that had less purchasing power than those that you borrowed. The increased income that accompanied rising prices also made it easier for you to repay the loan. If prices had fallen, the situation would have been reversed. You would have had to repay the loan with dollars of greater value than those that you initially borrowed.

Summary

- Over time, the United States has evolved from a monetary system that used commodities as money to an economy that uses coins and paper. The United States has issued both representative and token monies. Representative gold certificates were retired in 1933 and representative silver certificates were no longer issued after 1968. All currently issued money in the United States is fiat money.

- As a *standard of value*, money can be used as a measure of the value of all other goods and services. Money is a medium of *exchange* that eliminates the need for a double coincidence of wants and facilitates the exchange of goods and services. Money serves as a *store of value* by enabling us to convert excess goods into money and retain the resulting money. Money is a *standard of deferred payment* when consumers agree to pay the purchase price over time rather than paying the entire amount immediately with cash.

- In the equation $P = MV/Q$, P is the price level, MV is the velocity of the total money supply, and Q is the total of the transactions in the economy. If M increases but V stays the same, P will increase. If M increases but V decreases (such as with saving money), P decreases. If M increases and V increases, P increases. If M increases and Q increases, P decreases. If M increases and V increases, P increases. If M increases and Q increases, P decreases. If M increases but V and Q remain the same, P will increase. If M decreases but Q and V remain the same, P will decrease.

- Investment and saving, the status of the government budget, the supply of money, and net exports are related to total income, total output, and the price level in the following ways. Total output and price level remain *stable* when planned investment equals planned saving, the government budget is balanced, exports equal imports, and the money supply is stable. Total output and/or price level *decline* when planned investment is less than planned saving, there is a surplus government budget, imports exceed exports, and the money supply decreases. Total output and/or price level *increase* when planned investment is greater than planned saving, there is a deficit government budget, exports are greater than imports, and there is an increase in the money supply.

- Multiple expansion of the money supply occurs with a deposit and a given reserve requirement. Banks make loans in the form of checkable deposits. Banks will hold a certain reserve against the original deposits and lend the rest of the money in the form of cash or checkable deposits. Because of the money multiplier, banks can lend out more money than the amount of the original deposit.

- Reserve requirements limit the amount of checkable deposits a bank may issue. If the reserve requirement decreases, banks can create more money; if the reserve requirement increases, banks can create less money. Changes in the reserve requirement affect business activity and prices.

- A price index is constructed by comparing the average price of a group of goods and services in one period of time with the average price of the same group of goods and services in another period. The prices are determined for a base period; the prices in all subsequent years are measured in relation to the base-period prices. The items whose prices are being measured must remain constant in quantity and quality.

- The most commonly used price index is the Consumer Price Index constructed by the Department of Labor. The CPI currently uses 1982–83 as the base year. The CPI can be used to determine the real income of workers and the value of a dollar compared to a previous year. Two other widely used indexes are the Producer Price Indexes and the Implicit Price Deflators.

- Changing price levels bring about a redistribution of income. Changing price levels affect both creditors and debtors. Price increases benefit debtors, while price dereases benefit creditors.

New Terms and Concepts

Representative money	Currency	M3 money stock	Price index
Fiat money	M1 money stock	Eurodollars	Consumer Price Index
Money	Checkable deposits	Equation of exchange	(CPI)
Double coincidence of	M2 money stock	Transactions approach	Producer Price Index
wants	Savings deposits	Quantity theory of	(PPI)
Money stock	Time deposits	money	Real income
Liquidity	Money market funds	Money multiplier	

Discussion Questions

1. Would it be possible for some physical good to serve as money in a modern economy? If so, how and under what circumstances?

2. What effect does a rapidly rising price level have on the function of money as a store of value?

3. Distinguish among M1, M2, and M3. Which is the best measure of the money supply? Why?

4. Assume the following: $M = \$2,000$, $V = 10$, and $Q = 1,000$. Using the transactions approach formula, find the value of P. If the amount of money doubles, what is the new price level according to the quantity theory of money?

5. Under what conditions does an increase in the money supply have more influence on total output than on the price level?

6. Should the money supply be increased each year in order to finance normal increases in business activity and to stabilize total income and output? Why or why not?

7. How do reserve requirements on bank deposits affect a bank's ability to create money? What would happen to the money supply if a 100 percent reserve requirement were established?

8. Is there any relationship between the multiple expansion of the money supply and the velocity of money? Explain.

9. In evaluating the cost of living for a particular city, can a person rely on the CPI as a specific indicator of how much it costs to live in that particular city? Why or why not?

10. Distinguish between nominal wages and real wages. Are real wages today higher or lower than they were in 1990?

Economic Applications

EconData

Find the EconData link at http://econapps.swlearning.com. Click on "Money and the Financial System" under the Macroeconomics heading. Here, you can find information on the Consumer Price Index and more.

11

The Federal Reserve and the Money Supply

After studying Chapter 11, you should be able to:

1. Outline the structure of the Federal Reserve System and explain the makeup of the Fed's Board of Governors.

2. Describe the role of the 12 Reserve Banks and the characteristics of member banks.

3. Explain under what conditions the Fed will engage in open-market operations.

4. Explain why changes in reserve requirements can have a major effect on the economy.

5. Explain the effects of changes in the discount rate.

6. Analyze the reasons for recommendations for changes in the structure and policies of the Federal Reserve.

7. Discuss the structural changes that have occurred recently in the banking and financial services industries.

8. Briefly discuss the status of deposit insurance.

A few banks existed in the United States during colonial days, but the first real attempt at centralized banking occurred when the federal government chartered the First Bank of the United States in 1791. The primary functions of this central bank were to provide commercial bank services for individuals and businesses, to act as a banker's bank, to serve as a fiscal agent for the federal government, and to maintain some order in the banking business by exercising restraints on state banks. Political and business opposition to the bank led to the defeat of its recharter in 1811. For the following five years, only state banks existed.

In 1816, however, the Second Bank of the United States was chartered for a 20-year period. Although it was designed to perform functions similar to those of the First Bank, it had more capital stock and operated on a broader scale. Despite its efficient operation, many people opposed the Second Bank. Some opponents disliked the idea of central authority, others objected to its strict regulations, others were alarmed by the fact that foreigners owned a certain amount of the bank's stock, and still others thought the bank was unconstitutional. Political tensions between the bank's officials and the presidential administration of Andrew Jackson were instrumental in defeating its recharter in 1836.

Between 1836 and 1863, an era known as the wildcat banking period, there was no central authority in the U.S. banking system, and abusive banking practices were prevalent. The National Banking Act of 1864 brought some order to the chaos by creating a National Banking System. Its stringent requirements and provisions for note security ended many unsound operations of private commercial banks. The system had several noticeable weaknesses, however, such as the perverse elasticity of the money supply, the gravitation of reserves toward the money center, and the lack of assistance to the farm sector of the economy because real estate could not be used as collateral for loans. After several years of research and study of foreign central banks, such as the Bank of England and the Bank of France, lawmakers replaced the National Banking System in 1913 with the Federal Reserve System by passing the Federal Reserve Act. This established a central-type banking system for the United States.

Structure of the Federal Reserve System

Federal Reserve System
A system composed of various bodies, organizations, and committees for regulating the U.S. money supply.

The **Federal Reserve System** (or Fed) is a complex and intricate system composed of a Board of Governors, a Federal Advisory Council, a Federal Open Market Committee, 12 reserve banks, 25 branch banks, many member banks, and several minor organizations. It is an instrument of the government and yet is not owned by the government. Instead, it is owned by the member banks; however, its most important officials are appointed by the president of the United States. Each body within the Fed has its own individual function, but the functions of all bodies are interrelated. Figure 11–1 summarizes the organization of the Federal Reserve System. Because the United States was larger geographically than any of the other countries with central banks, Congress decided to create 12 separate banks instead of one, each with a certain amount of autonomy.

THE BOARD OF GOVERNORS OF THE FEDERAL RESERVE SYSTEM

At the top level of the Fed is the Board of Governors, headquartered in Washington, DC. Its primary function is to formulate monetary policy for the U.S. economy. The board is an agency of the federal government, but it has considerable autonomy. It consists of seven members, who are appointed by the president of the United States with the consent of the Senate. Each member must be selected from a different Federal Reserve district. Each member is appointed for 14 years and is ineligible for reappointment after having served one full term. Appointments are

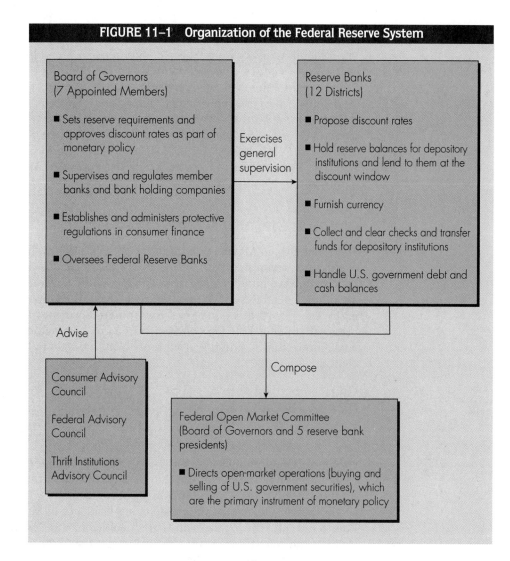

FIGURE 11-1 Organization of the Federal Reserve System

Board of Governors
(7 Appointed Members)

- Sets reserve requirements and approves discount rates as part of monetary policy
- Supervises and regulates member banks and bank holding companies
- Establishes and administers protective regulations in consumer finance
- Oversees Federal Reserve Banks

Exercises general supervision

Reserve Banks
(12 Districts)

- Propose discount rates
- Hold reserve balances for depository institutions and lend to them at the discount window
- Furnish currency
- Collect and clear checks and transfer funds for depository institutions
- Handle U.S. government debt and cash balances

Advise

Consumer Advisory Council

Federal Advisory Council

Thrift Institutions Advisory Council

Compose

Federal Open Market Committee
(Board of Governors and 5 reserve bank presidents)

- Directs open-market operations (buying and selling of U.S. government securities), which are the primary instrument of monetary policy

staggered so that a new appointee is assigned every two years. The president of the United States selects the chairman and the vice-chairman of the board from among the seven members for a four-year term each.

The board has numerous responsibilities, including supervising the 12 reserve banks. It must approve each reserve bank's officers and has the right to suspend or to remove officers if necessary. It authorizes loans between reserve banks, reviews and determines discount rates established by the reserve banks, establishes reserve requirements within legal limits, regulates loans on securities, and performs many other functions.

FEDERAL ADVISORY COUNCIL

The Federal Advisory Council is a committee of 12 members, one from each Federal Reserve district, selected annually by the board of directors of each Federal Reserve Bank. The council serves primarily an advisory role, conferring with the board on business conditions and other matters pertinent to the Fed.

In addition to the Federal Advisory Council, various other committees and conferences assist the board. Among the most important of these is the Conference of Presidents of the reserve banks, which convenes periodically and meets with the Board of Governors once or twice a year. Each president reports on economic conditions within his or her district.

FEDERAL OPEN MARKET COMMITTEE

The Federal Open Market Committee (FOMC) is also composed of 12 members, including the seven members of the Board of Governors and the president of the Federal Reserve Bank of New York. The remaining four members of the committee are other Federal Reserve Bank presidents, who serve one-year terms on a rotating basis. The FOMC buys and sells government securities in the open market expressly to influence the flow of credit and money. Its actions help stabilize the price level, interest rates, and the growth of economic activity. The FOMC meets about eight times a year.

RESERVE BANKS

The Fed divides the United States into 12 geographic districts. Each district has a reserve bank named after the city in which it is located. The districts reflect the concentration of financial activity. As a result, the St. Louis district geographically is about one-half the size of the Kansas City district, but it does as much financial business as the latter. Most of the districts also have branch banks. The Federal Reserve Bank of Cleveland, for example, has branches in Pittsburgh and Cincinnati. Puerto Rico and the Virgin Islands are included in the New York district for check clearing and collection. Figure 11–2 delineates the 12 districts, and Table 11–1 lists the reserve banks and branches.

Reserve banks supervise member banks in their districts and conduct periodic examinations of banks' operations. If any member bank chronically engages in unsound banking practices, the reserve bank has the authority to remove its officers and directors. Although this power is seldom exercised, its existence helps keep member banks in line.

In addition to serving as central banks (or bankers' banks), the reserve banks also serve as fiscal agents for the federal government. They handle the detailed work of issuing and redeeming government securities, they hold deposits and disburse funds for the Treasury, and they perform many other fiscal duties. They supply money for the business community in the form of Federal Reserve notes, and

NETLink

After reading about the Federal Reserve System, visit the Federal Reserve Bank of New York for data and information.

http://www.ny.frb.org/introduce

FIGURE 11–2 The Federal Reserve System

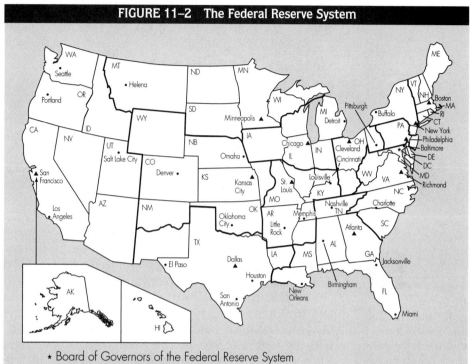

★ Board of Governors of the Federal Reserve System
▲ Federal Reserve Bank Cities
• Federal Reserve Branch Cities

TABLE 11–1 Federal Reserve Districts and Banks

District	Reserve Bank	Branches
1	Boston	None
2	New York	Buffalo
3	Philadelphia	None
4	Cleveland	Cincinnati, Pittsburgh
5	Richmond	Baltimore, Charlotte
6	Atlanta	Birmingham, Jacksonville, Miami, Nashville, New Orleans
7	Chicago	Detroit
8	St. Louis	Little Rock, Louisville, Memphis
9	Minneapolis	Helena
10	Kansas City	Denver, Oklahoma City, Omaha
11	Dallas	El Paso, Houston, San Antonio
12	San Francisco	Los Angeles, Salt Lake City, Portland, Seattle

they regulate their member banks' ability to create money in the form of checkable deposits. The branch banks help carry out the functions of the reserve bank.

FEDERAL RESERVE MEMBER BANKS

When the Federal Reserve System was established, all national banks were required to join. Membership is also open to qualified state banks, but many state banks cannot qualify because of the high minimum capital requirement. Some banks simply do not like the Fed's restrictions and regulations; others are reluctant to join because as nonmembers they are permitted to use the Fed's major facilities anyway. Although less than one-half of all commercial banks belong to the Fed, these **member banks** hold a majority of the total deposits in the United States.

Each member bank is required to buy stock in the Federal Reserve Bank of its district. As a result, the member banks completely own the reserve banks, but most of the regulation or control of reserve banks resides with the Board of Governors. Although the member banks are operated for profit, the reserve banks are operated strictly in the public interest. The Fed pays a 6 percent dividend on its stock. Any profits over this amount are turned over to the U.S. Treasury.

In addition to purchasing reserve bank stock, each member bank must maintain sufficient monetary reserves to meet the requirements set by the Board of Governors. Member banks are required to maintain most of their required reserves with the reserve banks, and they are subject to examinations and regulations by the reserve banks. All member banks must insure their deposits with the Federal Deposit Insurance Corporation. In addition, member banks must comply with various federal laws, regulations, and conditions regarding adequacy of capital, mergers, the establishment of branches, and loan and investment limitations.

Member Banks
Commercial banks that belong to the Federal Reserve System.

NET*Link*

Interested in how your money will be redesigned or in steps the United States is taking in counterfeit protection? Visit the Federal Reserve Bank of Minneapolis.

http://www.minneapolisfed.org/econed/curric/counter.cfm

Federal Reserve Control of the Money Supply

Through its control over bank reserves, the Fed can affect the money supply. Thus, its actions influence the level of economic activity and/or the price level. The Fed can use many instruments or measures to control bank deposit creation. Some are referred to as *general controls* because they affect the overall supply of money. Others are referred to as *selective controls* because they affect the use of money for specific purposes in the economy.

OPEN-MARKET OPERATIONS

Open-Market Operations
The Fed's continuous purchase and sale of government securities on the open market.

The most important instrument of monetary management is the Federal Reserve open-market operations. **Open-market operations** are the Fed's continuous purchases and sales of government securities on the open market to affect bank reserves. The securities used are primarily U.S. Treasury bills (T-bills) with a maturity of one year or less. Most banks hold government securities, and the Fed can induce banks to sell or buy government securities by offering to buy them at a premium price or to sell them at a discount.

Purchase of Securities

If the FOMC wants to encourage expansion of the money supply, it can direct the Fed's open-market account manager at the trading desk located in the Federal Reserve Bank of New York to buy securities from banks and individuals. When the Fed purchases securities, it increases bank reserves, which in turn enables the banks to expand checkable deposits and make more loans.

Suppose that at a particular time banks have no excess reserves and therefore cannot extend any additional loans via checkable deposits (see Figure 11–3). If the Fed buys $50,000 worth of government securities from banks, it puts the proceeds directly into the banks' reserve accounts. This increases excess reserves and expands the banks' ability to make loans by $500,000 (see Figure 11–4).

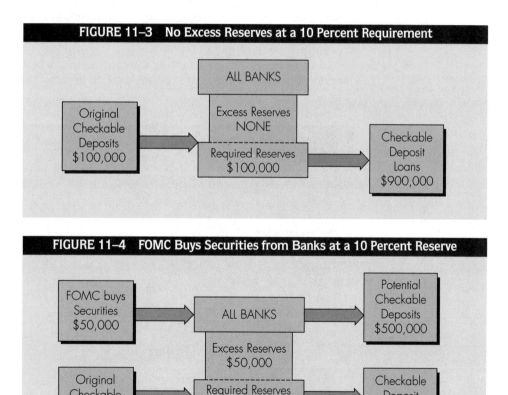

FIGURE 11–3   No Excess Reserves at a 10 Percent Requirement

ALL BANKS

Original Checkable Deposits $100,000

Excess Reserves NONE

Required Reserves $100,000

Checkable Deposit Loans $900,000

FIGURE 11–4   FOMC Buys Securities from Banks at a 10 Percent Reserve

FOMC buys Securities $50,000

ALL BANKS

Potential Checkable Deposits $500,000

Excess Reserves $50,000

Original Checkable Deposits $100,000

Required Reserves $100,000

Checkable Deposit Loans $900,000

Practically the same result can be accomplished by purchasing securities from individuals or businesses because these sellers usually deposit the money received from the sale of securities in banks or have it credited directly to their accounts. These deposits increase bank reserves and potentially increase the money supply (see Figure 11–5). The potential expansion of the money supply is somewhat less in this case than it is when the Fed buys government securities directly from banks, however, because (at a reserve requirement of 10 percent) the banks must hold $5,000 in required reserves against the new deposits of $50,000 made by the individuals and businesses that sold the securities.

Sale of Securities

During times of rising price levels, the Fed may want to absorb some of the existing excess reserves. It can do so by selling government securities to the banks. To buy securities, banks must give up some of their excess reserves, which in turn decreases their ability to expand checkable deposits. When the Fed sells securities to individuals or businesses, they usually withdraw funds from banks to pay for the securities, which reduces excess reserves and decreases the banks' ability to increase the money supply.

Most of the Fed's open-market operations are, in fact, transacted with about two dozen specialized security dealers located in New York City. The Federal Re-

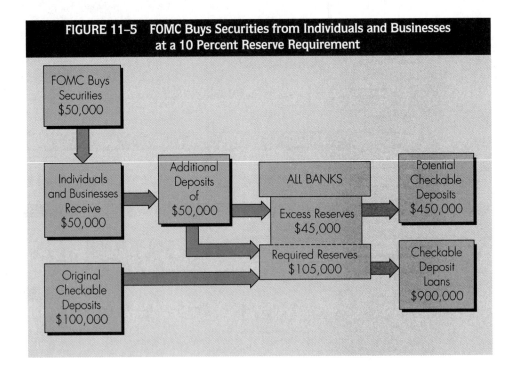

FIGURE 11–5   FOMC Buys Securities from Individuals and Businesses at a 10 Percent Reserve Requirement

serve Bank of New York serves as the Fed's agent for the purchase and sale of securities. Billions of dollars—mostly in short-term government securities—change hands daily in this market.

Key Role of Excess Reserves

The Fed's ability to influence the money supply through its open-market operations is restricted. Although purchasing government securities from banks does increase bank reserves, banks are not obligated to make loans and businesses are not obliged to borrow. Conversely, selling securities cannot prevent an expansion of the money supply unless enough are sold to absorb all the excess reserves. The effectiveness of the Fed's efforts to limit expansion of the money supply depends on the status of excess reserves. In any case, however, the purchase of securities in the open market by the Fed increases the member banks' ability to expand the money supply, whereas the sale of securities decreases the member banks' ability to create money.

RESERVE REQUIREMENTS

Required Reserves
The amount of reserves that member banks must hold against checkable deposits.

We saw in Chapter 10 that a bank's ability to create money is affected by the amount of reserves it must hold for its checkable deposits. An increase in the reserve requirement decreases the bank's ability to increase the money supply, and vice versa. The Board of Governors of the Federal Reserve has the authority to determine, within limits, the amount of reserves that banks must hold against checkable deposits. These moneys, as designated by the Fed, are referred to as **required reserves.** Any reserves over and above this amount that a bank may have are **excess reserves.** Both are important to the potential size of the money supply.

Excess Reserves
Any reserves that a bank may have over and above the legally established required reserves.

Transaction Accounts
The various forms of checkable deposits, including regular checking accounts, NOW accounts, ATS accounts, and share draft accounts.

Before 1980, the Fed could regulate only member bank deposits and reserves, but the Monetary Control Act of 1980 made all depository institutions subject to the Fed's reserve requirements. With respect to reserve requirements, deposits are divided into two broad categories: transaction accounts and nonpersonal time accounts. **Transaction accounts** include the various forms of checkable deposits: regular checking accounts, NOW accounts, automatic transfer service (ATS) accounts, share draft accounts in credit unions, and accounts that permit payment by automatic teller, telephone, or preauthorized transfer. **Nonpersonal time accounts** include negotiable (and transferable) certificates of deposit (CDs) and large CDs that require at least 14 days' notice before withdrawal is made.

Nonpersonal Time Accounts
Negotiable CDs and large CDs that require notice before withdrawal is made.

Required reserves against transaction accounts are 3 percent on deposits over $5.7 million but less than $46.5 million and 10 percent on deposits in excess of that amount. Breaking points can be adjusted annually. The Monetary Control Act authorizes the Fed to impose a supplemental reserve requirement of up to 4 percent under certain conditions. The Fed pays interest on such supplemental reserves. Reserve requirements against nonpersonal time deposits are set (again by the Fed) at between 0 and 9 percent. Table 11–2 shows the current reserve requirements.

TABLE 11–2 Reserve Requirements Established by the Monetary Control Act of 1980			
Type of Accounts	Minimum Requirement (%)	Maximum Requirement (%)	Requirements (%) (as of July 2002)
Net transactions accounts			
$5.7 million to $46.5 million	3	3	3·
Over $46.5 million	8	14	10
Nonpersonal time accounts	0	9	0

Effect of Lower Reserve Requirements

The Fed may decrease the reserve requirements during periods of low production, income, and employment to increase the money supply and expand business activity. To see how this is accomplished, consider an example in which the banking system as a whole has no excess reserves to use as a basis for expanding checkable deposits. The situation at the beginning (assuming a 10 percent reserve requirement) is depicted in Figure 11–6.

The banks are holding $100,000 in cash reserves (10 percent) against total deposits of $1 million ($100,000 in primary deposits and $900,000 in loans in the form of checkable deposits). In this situation the banks cannot create any more checkable deposits. If the reserve requirement is decreased to 5 percent, however, the banks need hold only $50,000 in required reserves against the $1 million in checkable deposits. Therefore, if the remaining $50,000 is left on deposit with the Fed, it constitutes excess reserves. On the strength of these reserves, the banks can extend another $1 million in checkable deposits (see Figure 11–7).

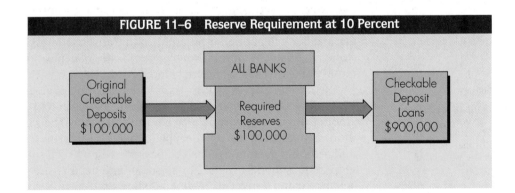

FIGURE 11–6   Reserve Requirement at 10 Percent

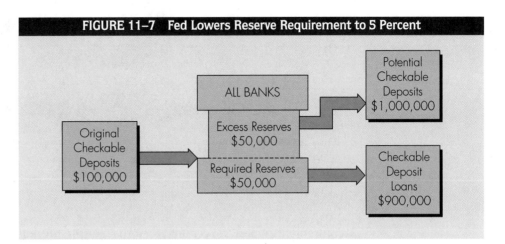

FIGURE 11–7   Fed Lowers Reserve Requirement to 5 Percent

A decrease in the reserve requirement thus increases the banks' ability to expand checkable deposits and thereby effectively increases the money supply. Reduction of the reserve requirement does not necessarily increase checkable deposits or the money supply, however; it merely enables the banks to increase checkable deposits. There can be no increase in the money supply until businesses or others actually borrow from banks in the form of checkable deposits. Frequently, in a period of recession the Fed lowers the reserve requirement, but businesspeople are reluctant to borrow and spend money anyway because of the poor return on capital investment. Therefore, lowering the reserve requirement may not result in an increase in the money supply.

Effect of Higher Reserve Requirements

The Fed can decrease the banks' ability to expand the money supply by raising the reserve requirement. Assume once again the situation depicted in Figure 11–6, in which the banks have no excess reserves. If the Fed increases the reserve requirement from 10 percent to 20 percent, the banks will be short of required reserves. As a result, they must either increase their reserves or recall some of the loans outstanding to bring their reserves up to 20 percent of their checkable deposits (see Figure 11–8). The action of the banks in recalling loans reduces their checkable deposits to $400,000. Thus, the increase in the reserve requirement effectively decreases the money supply by $500,000.

In reality, the Fed never increases the reserve requirement by a large amount because doing so would seriously disrupt business activity. The Fed is more inclined to use its power to prevent undesirable conditions from developing. For example, it may ease the money supply by lowering reserve requirements when the economy appears to be entering a period of declining business activity, in the hope that it will prevent a recession. Or it may tighten the money supply by raising reserve

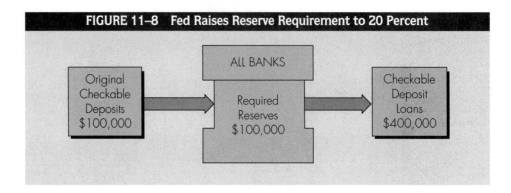

FIGURE 11–8   Fed Raises Reserve Requirement to 20 Percent

requirements when the economy approaches the full-employment stage of business activity because further increases in the money supply under these conditions are likely to produce higher prices.

DISCOUNT RATE

Discount Rate
The interest rate at which depository institutions borrow funds from the reserve banks.

The **discount rate** is the interest rate at which depository institutions may borrow funds from the reserve banks. If you as an individual wished to borrow $100 at 10 percent from a bank for one year, you would have to sign a note payable to the bank (which thus becomes a note receivable for the bank). The bank would then discount your note for you. Instead of giving you the face value of the note, the bank would deduct the interest and give you $90. However, you would still have to repay $100 to the bank. The difference, $10, represents the interest or discount.

Discounting Process

Discounting is very short term borrowing that banks can use to replenish their reserves (that is, to bring them up to the required level). If a bank is short of reserves, it can obtain funds by recalling loans, selling government securities or other assets, or borrowing from its reserve bank. Suppose that the bank is making 10 percent interest on its loans or other assets. If the discount rate is also 10 percent, it will not matter much whether the bank recalls loans, sells assets, or borrows from the reserve bank's discount window. But rather than disrupt its operations, it will probably prefer to go to the discount window and obtain a direct credit to its reserve account. Moreover, if the discount rate is only 5 percent, the bank will find it cheaper and more profitable to borrow from the reserve bank. On the other hand, if the discount rate is 8 percent, the bank will be less likely to borrow from the Fed.

Even if a bank is not short of required reserves, the discount rate affects the bank's action. For example, if the discount rate is lower than the rate of interest that the bank can make on loans, the bank may be encouraged to extend additional loans, knowing that it can borrow at a lower rate at the discount window if it runs short of required reserves. On the other hand, when the discount rate is higher, the bank will be reluctant to expand loans.

Lowering the discount rate provides a signal that the Fed wants to encourage an expansion of the money supply. Raising the discount rate gives the opposite signal. When business activity is falling, the Fed may lower the discount rate, encouraging banks to discount and increasing their ability to expand the money supply. In turn, the banks encourage businesses to borrow by lowering the commercial loan rate. During full-employment inflationary periods, the reserve banks raise the discount rate to discourage discounting, which restrains the expansion of the money supply and discourages borrowing by pushing up commercial loan rates.

The discount rate is usually changed in small increments—one-fourth or one-half a percentage point at a time—so that the change does not seriously disrupt business activity. This action is primarily preventive, rather than remedial. Sometimes, in fact, changes in the discount rate lag behind changes in the commercial loan rates. In such cases the Fed may raise or lower the discount rate simply to reduce the spread between the two rates.

The discount rate for each district is determined by its reserve bank, with the approval of the Board of Governors. Although the reserve banks themselves initiate changes in the discount rate, the board retains authority to review and determine discount rates. The discount rate often varies slightly for short periods among districts because of differences in the money markets. When a district changes its rate, the others usually follow suit because factors of national scope are generally responsible for the change.

It is important to remember that a decrease in the discount rate generally encourages banks to expand their checkable deposits and encourages businesses to borrow, thus tending to increase the money supply. An increase in the discount rate discourages banks from expanding their checkable deposits and discourages businesses from borrowing, thus tending to limit increases in the money supply.

Commercial Loan Rates

Prime Rate
The rate at which individuals and firms with the best collateral can borrow.

Changing the discount rate has a secondary effect as well. The commercial loan rate is greatly influenced by the bank discount rate. For example, the **prime rate**—the interest rate at which individuals and firms with the best collateral can borrow—is usually a few percentage points above the discount rate. Thus, if the discount rate in Atlanta is 3 percent, the prime rate may be 5 or 6 percent. Usually, when the discount rate is lowered, the commercial loan rates are lowered too, encouraging businesses to borrow. But if the discount rate is raised, the commercial loan rates may also be increased, which tends to discourage businesses from borrowing. The funds may still be available, but at a higher cost.

Federal Funds Market

Federal Funds Market
A fairly well organized
market where interbank
borrowing takes place.

Besides borrowing from the reserve bank, a bank can adjust its reserve position by borrowing from other banks that have surplus reserves. Such interbank borrowing takes place in a fairly well organized market known as the **Federal Funds Market.** The federal funds rate (over which the Fed has some influence) is the rate at which banks are willing to borrow or to lend immediately available reserves on an overnight basis. It is a very sensitive indicator of the tightness of bank reserves. The federal funds rate may be higher or lower than that prevailing at the discount window, depending on the status of excess reserves. By facilitating the transfer of the most liquid funds between depository institutions, the Federal Funds Market plays a major role in the execution of monetary policy. The interest rate on federal funds, the federal funds rate, is highly sensitive to Federal Reserve open-market operations that influence the supply of reserves in the banking system. For example, if the Federal Reserve wishes to increase the growth rate of the money supply, it may purchase securities in the open market, thereby increasing the availability of bank reserves and decreasing the federal funds rate. Sales of securities by the Fed in the open market tend to have the opposite effect.

The Federal Reserve does not announce its policy intentions, so observers of monetary policy pay careful attention to the open-market desk's reserve operations in conjunction with the federal funds rate to capture signals of changes in monetary policy. Changes in the money supply and movements in the federal funds rate have important implications for the loan and investment policies of all financial institutions, especially commercial banks. Financial managers compare the federal funds rate with yields on other investments before choosing the combinations of maturities of financial assets in which they will invest or the term over which they will borrow.

U.S. Foreign Exchange Intervention

Foreign exchange intervention is the process by which the U.S. monetary authorities attempt to influence market conditions and/or the value of the U.S. dollar on the foreign exchange market. This is done to try to promote stability by countering disorderly markets or in response to special circumstances. Foreign exchange rates are of particular concern to governments, because changes in exchange rates affect the value of financial instruments all over the world and, as a result, might affect the health of countries' financial systems. In addition, rate changes can also affect a nation's international investment flows and terms of trade. These factors, in turn, can influence inflation and economic growth.

Although the U.S. Treasury has overall responsibility for foreign exchange policy, its decisions are made in consultation with the Federal Reserve System. Intervention is conducted by the Federal Reserve Bank of New York on behalf of the U.S. monetary authorities. If a decision is made to support the dollar's price against a currency, the foreign trading desk of the New York Fed will buy dollars and sell foreign currency; to reduce the value of the dollar, it will sell dollars and buy foreign currency. In addition, traders at the New York Fed observe market trends and developments to provide information to policymakers. Although the Fed's trading staff may operate in the exchange market at any time and in any market in the world, the focus of activity usually is the U.S. market.

OTHER CONTROLS

Moral Suasion
A number of different measures that the Federal Reserve Board uses to influence the activities of banks.

Moral suasion is a term applied to a number of different measures that the Fed uses to influence the activities of banks in one way or another. For example, it may send banks letters in which it encourages or discourages the expansion of the money supply. At other times it may issue public statements revealing the status of the economic situation and urging businesses and banks to expand or to restrain the money supply. During personal interviews, Fed officers may warn against speculative loans or may suggest that banks become more liberal with their loans. The Fed may ration credit and suspend the borrowing privileges of banks if necessary. In general, moral suasion affects the money supply only to the extent that banks and businesses are willing to cooperate.

At various times the Fed has also been given discretionary control over certain specific uses of money and credit in the economy. These controls are known as selective controls. For example, the Fed currently has the authority to set stock market margin requirements. The margin requirement is the portion of a stock purchase that may be made on credit (usually with a loan from the brokerage house). The higher the margin requirement, the greater the down payment required to purchase shares of stock, which reduces the opportunity for speculation in the stock market, holds down the demand for stocks, and moderates stock prices. At one time the Fed also had control over the conditions or terms of installment sales. The controls set the percentage of the down payment and the length of time in which an installment loan had to be repaid, and they had the effect of limiting total demand. For a short time in the late 1970s, the Fed also had the authority to impose restrictions on purchases made via credit cards.

Recent Federal Reserve Policy

The Fed is an independent organization within the government, not apart from it. As such, it exercises a considerable amount of autonomy. Because the Fed is responsible only to Congress, it may or may not agree with the economic policies of a given presidential administration. But because both have the same objectives (economic growth and high employment, along with a stable price level), their actions usually complement each other.

The 1990s were a period of sustained economic growth, low inflation, and high levels of employment. On several occasions, the Fed acted to preempt inflationary pressures by raising the discount rate by a quarter-percent or more and pressuring the federal funds rate upwards. But the Federal Reserve's stance for most of the decade could be characterized as neutral to expansionary. Because the federal government began experiencing record budget surpluses toward the end of the decade, while the Fed was pursuing an accommodating monetary policy, there were few if any conflicts between monetary and fiscal authorities. However, the Fed became increasingly concerned about inflation in mid-1999, and as a result of a series of interest rate hikes, the federal funds rate rose to 6.50% by June 2000.

Shortly thereafter, evidence of a slowdown in the economy began to surface, as businesses began to slash investment spending in response to weakening final demand, an oversupply of some types of capital, and declining profits. Many firms in the manufacturing sector were struggling with high levels of inventories and were sharply cutting production. At the same time, foreign economies were also slowing, further reducing demand for U.S. production. A slowdown gripped the U.S. economy in 2001. As signs of continuing deterioration of the economy became more widespread, the Federal Reserve quickly shifted into an easy money policy. In January 2001, the Fed initiated the first of many interest rate cuts that would occur throughout the year. By the time the year was out, the Fed had reduced interest rates a total of 11 times. The federal funds rate, which began the year at 6.75%, had fallen to 1.75% by December 2001, while the discount rate had declined from 6.0% to 1.25% by December 2001—its lowest level since 1948. The prime rate followed along the downward path, dropping from 9.50% to 4.50%. The Fed cut the federal funds rate again in November 2002, dropping the rate to 1.25%. In addition to these steps, the Fed used its powers of moral suasion in an attempt to increase the money supply.

Although the Federal Reserve usually works hand-in-hand with the administration to stabilize the level of economic activity and the price level, attempts at coordinated efforts sometimes fall short. Coordination among monetary and fiscal policies can be difficult for several reasons. First, the Fed is more autonomous and can act more quickly. Because monetary policy is more flexible, the Fed can also reverse course quickly if need be. Fiscal policy is more difficult to implement because it occurs in the political arena. Consequently, the time required to enact change can be lengthy. Unlike monetary policy, once a change is enacted in fiscal policy, it is politically difficult to eliminate when the desired results of that policy change are no longer needed. Finally, monetary and fiscal authorities may disagree with one another and the results may be counterproductive.

However, the coordination of monetary and fiscal policies can effectively work together over longer periods, as witnessed in the 1990s. But in 2001, although many economists and political leaders called for additional tax cuts over and above the marginal income tax rate cuts previously enacted, these efforts stalled. Congress debated the fiscal impact of such cuts on the federal deficit and federally sponsored socioeconomic programs, and questioned the benefits of proposed cuts to lower- and middle-income families. Consequently, additional tax cuts did not occur in the year, despite support from the administration.

Critics of the Federal Reserve

There have been numerous critics of the Federal Reserve System's structure and policies. Much of their criticism centers on the belief that the Fed's independent status allows it to exercise too much power over the economy and consequently over the economic well-being of households and businesses. Many of these critics contend that any institution with this amount of power should be placed under the direct control of Congress. Defenders of an independent Federal Reserve worry that putting the Federal Reserve directly under congressional control would mean that decisions concerning monetary policy would be driven by political considerations. These individuals favor a monetary authority that is independent of the political process.

Although for entirely different reasons, even a group of economists seeks to restrict the autonomous decision-making powers of the Fed. These economists, known as monetarists, believe that the Fed only worsens economic conditions when it attempts to stabilize the economy by pursuing either a tight money policy or an easy money policy. Their solution is to have the Fed increase the money supply at about the same annual rate as the long-run growth rate of the economy. This approach would strip away the Fed's discretionary powers to deal with economic fluctuations.

In response to such criticism of the Fed's independence, Congress passed the Full Employment and Balanced Growth Act of 1978. Known as the Humphrey–Hawkins Act, this legislation required the Federal Reserve chairman to appear before Congress twice a year. These meetings, anxiously awaited in economic and financial circles throughout the world, constitute a forum in which the Fed keeps Congress informed as to the nature of the monetary policy it intends to pursue. Although the Humphrey–Hawkins requirement no longer exists, the Fed chairman continues the tradition by appearing before the Congress twice each year to present the Monetary Policy Report.

Issues and Concerns in Banking

The banking industry is no longer a sleepy association of small-town banks, savings and loans, and credit unions. It has become a highly competitive, technologically oriented spectrum of financial services. The marketplace has grown nationwide, even worldwide, and some of the players are well-known names in other fields. But these changes in the banking industry have not prevented bank failures, nor have they dampened enthusiasm for greater competition and less regulation.

DEREGULATION

For most of the twentieth century, the basis for the structure of financial institutions in the United States can be traced back to the Glass–Steagall Act of 1932. The

Great Depression drove many banks out of business. The worst casualties were small banks, in part because they were unable to survive the vigorous competition that preceded the financial collapse. To guard against ruinous competition in the future, Congress passed the Glass–Steagall Act, which increased regulation and decreased competition in the banking industry. Historically, the Glass–Steagall Act created distinctions among depository institutions, the securities industry, and the insurance industry. Each of these three groups was subdivided into constituent compartments. Depository institutions, for example, included separate compartments for commercial banks, savings and loans, mutual savings banks, credit unions, and industrial banks. The securities industry was subdivided into brokerage firms, securities dealers, underwriters, and rating agencies. As long as these compartments were separate and noncompeting, each compartment could be regulated independently and, in fact, they were for many decades.

These regulations were designed as if banks did not compete with other types of financial institutions. But, over the years, any natural walls separating financial institutions have largely fallen away, despite regulatory restrictions regarding price, location, and product.

In general, price restrictions are no longer important in banking. Maximum interest rates on time and savings deposits were dismantled between 1980 and 1986 in compliance with the Monetary Control Act of 1980. Statutory prohibition of interest payments on demand deposits is also irrelevant today. The 1980 act also expanded the use of Fed services to nonmember banks, increased insurance coverage on deposits, and expanded the availability of checking accounts. By mid-1985, deregulation at the state level further increased competition because more and more states were permitting branch banking. **Branch banking** allowed banks to have branches throughout a state. Branch banking was followed by the emergence of **interstate banking**, which permits a bank in one state to conduct banking operations in other states. Following the passage of state laws, Congress passed the Riegle–Neal Interstate Banking and Branch Efficiency Act in 1994. This act permitted interstate branch banking on a national scale for the first time since the Great Depression years. Banks no longer have to create subsidiaries or holding companies to operate across state lines. Branch banks can be extended regionally and even nationally. In addition, foreign banks now operate branches in various cities in the United States.

With pricing and location restrictions removed, only the regulations pertaining to product competition remained. However, the 1999 Financial Services Modernization Act eliminated many of these product restrictions from regulation. For all intents and purposes, the 1999 act served as the death knell of the Glass–Steagall law.

The Financial Services Modernization Act removed the long-standing separations between banks, brokerage firms, and insurance companies. Today, brokerage firms and insurance companies can buy banks, and banks can underwrite insurance and securities. With the 1999 law, consumers have the opportunity to shop for almost any financial service, from certificates of deposit to life insurance to online stock trading, in one place.

Branch Banking
The practice of operating multiple outlets of a single depository institution throughout a state, a region, or the nation.

Interstate Banking
The practice of conducting banking operations across state lines.

The Financial Services Modernization Act did not eliminate banking regulations. The legal framework of finance and commerce remains, including laws that discourage fraud and misrepresentation, guard against anticompetitive practices, and require timely release of accurate information. In addition, the law gave the Federal Reserve umbrella authority over bank affiliates that engage in risky business activities, such as insurance underwriting and real estate development. The Treasury Department's Office of the Comptroller of the Currency now has the authority to regulate bank subsidiaries.

Deregulation, the expansion of foreign bank branches in the United States, the impact of foreign interest rates, and the globalization of money flows make it much more difficult today than previously for the Fed to control domestic interest rates and the money supply and to influence domestic economic activity.

INDUSTRY CONCENTRATION

The banking industry is going through substantial changes in market structure as a result of deregulation and technological innovations. Both factors have the potential to produce long-lasting effects, not only in the banking industry but also in the entire financial sector. However, uncertainty exists as to whether or not these changes will result in greater concentration of market share by the largest banks, or whether overall competition will increase.

Deregulation of the banking industry has contributed to numerous mergers among banks. The number of banks has been declining for several decades, even before the passage of recent legislation. In 1983, for example, there were 14,800 commercial banks in the United States. Of those, 37 percent (5,400) belonged to the Federal Reserve System. Although the number of commercial banks continued to decline with the passage of time, the 1994 Reigle–Neal interstate banking legislation increased the rate of consolidation. Today, there are 8,149 commercial banks remaining, of which 3,152 are members of the Federal Reserve System.

The fewer number of banks has undoubtedly increased concentration in the industry. Following deregulation, some of our nation's oldest and largest banks successfully merged. Citicorp has merged with the Travelers group, Nations Bank with Bank of America, and Chase Manhattan with J.P. Morgan. Most financial assets held in banks are concentrated in a relatively small number of banks. Currently, the 80 largest banks control about 71 percent of all banking assets.

Branch banking and interstate banking have undoubtedly played roles in shrinking the number of banks, but so too has the drive to achieve larger, more cost-efficient organizations. For example, mergers often eliminate duplicate services such as branches, automated teller machines, and information technology services. Although the number of commercial banks has fallen, the total number of banking offices has increased more than 23 percent since 1983. Today, banking offices can be found in shopping malls, large supermarkets, airports, and hotels. Interstate branch banking continues to grow, although unevenly across regions. Most analysts suggest that consolidation will likely help create a single, unified financial market.

In addition to legal reforms, another new source of competition may lie in the Internet. The Internet is creating considerable competition to traditional banks from both within and outside of the financial sector. New entrants have had relatively easy access to the market, but survival rates have not been strong. If many of the new entrants succeed, then the Internet will actually strengthen competition. But early signals are that the Internet competition will be coming from large companies in the nonfinancial sector in terms of account aggregation. Account aggregation refers to the ability to view all one's financial accounts on a single Web page. Most portals, such as Yahoo, and financial Websites, such as Quicken.com, offer account aggregation. In the future, industry concentration could lessen if traditional banks face intense competition sparked by new technology and the Internet. However, the long-term viability of these new forms of competition remains uncertain.

Mergers will lead to fewer banks that compete vigorously across national markets. The broader scope of these large banks may spur new, smaller competitors at the local level. Also, the effects of consolidation may also be more than offset by the increased competition stemming from the Internet as well as new technologies that make it easier for both bank and nonbank firms to compete with more traditional banks.

ELECTRONIC BANKING

An important part of the Federal Reserve's mission is to ensure that the nation's payments system evolves to meet the needs of a dynamic economy. One reason that Congress created the Fed in 1913 was to establish a coherent national system for clearing checks. Today, one of the Fed's major priorities is developing an orderly transition from a payment system based on currency and checks to one based on electronic banking. The important role of electronic banking is evident by the fact that electronic transfers now account for nearly 90 percent of the dollar value of all transactions in the United States.

Electronic banking is not new. The Fed and the nation's banking community have long operated using electronic transfers. But, until recently, electronic banking was an activity largely invisible to the general public. More than anything else, it was the Debt Collection Improvement Act of 1996 that created a heightened awareness of electronic banking. Wherever possible, the 1996 law required the federal government to make all payments electronically by 1999. Today, payments made by the federal government for such things as wages, salaries, food stamps, welfare, pensions, Social Security, and the purchase of goods and services are made electronically by means of direct deposit. As a result, millions of Americans have been introduced to at least one form of electronic banking. The Fed processes approximately 80 percent of all electronic payments. Although electronic banking is not new, what is new are the different types of electronic payments available to government, business, and the consumer.

Electronic Banking
Financial transactions that entail the electronic transfer of funds.

Electronic banking is a general term that refers to various forms of financial transactions that entail the electronic transfer of funds in and out of accounts. The most common form of electronic banking transfer is the *automated teller machine* (ATM), which allows us to make deposits, obtain cash, and transfer funds between accounts. Another form of electronic banking is *preauthorized electronic bill payment* and its companion *direct deposit payment*. Preauthorized bill payments are automated debits or reductions to the account. Electronic bill payment is most commonly used for recurring payments such as rent, utility bills, loans, and insurance payments. Direct deposits, on the other hand, are automated credits or increases. Direct deposits are increasingly used by employers, government agencies, and organizations that make regular payments, such as wages and dividends to individuals. Today, over 60 percent of U.S. households receive their wages by direct deposit. The U.S. government is the largest single user of direct deposit. The Social Security Administration alone uses direct deposit to make payments to 5 million recipients every month. Both preauthorized electronic bill payments and direct deposits are usually cleared through the Fed.

Stored-value and *smart cards* are two other forms of electronic banking that are becoming increasingly popular. Stored-value cards provide a convenient substitute for cash and checks. The cards contain a magnetic strip that records a dollar balance that is established when the card is purchased. Most of these cards can be used only for a single purpose, such as for public transit systems, university food service, and public telephones. Smart cards are similar to stored-valued cards except that they contain a computer chip instead of a magnetic strip. When the balance is at zero, a smart card can be reloaded with funds by using an ATM.

Home banking is also being offered by more and more financial institutions. Software packages now allow customers to debit or credit accounts, confirm balances, and even apply for a loan. The Internet is expected to be a major factor in home banking in the next few years.

These new technologies are constantly changing the way we make payments. Figures 11–9 and 11–10 show the number of payments by type and the dollar value of these payments in 2000. Cash accounts for 45 percent of the total number of transactions made by consumers in the United States, while personal checks account for another 26 percent. Figure 11–10 shows that on the basis of the dollar value of transactions, cash comprises 19 percent and checks account for 44 percent. It should be noted that check totals reflect only direct purchases by check, not checks used to prepay or repay another form of payment, such as to pay a credit card bill.

All indications point to the fact that consumers are embracing electronic money more than ever before, despite their historical reluctance to forgo the use of currency and checks and move to a cashless society. However, there are still millions of households without banking accounts, and many millions more that have fears about the security and privacy of electronic banking. Countless others simply refuse to use new technology. Consequently, the shift to electronic banking has been evolutionary. But this shift will undoubtedly accelerate as college graduates who have grown up with computers, ATMs, and the Internet move into the economic mainstream.

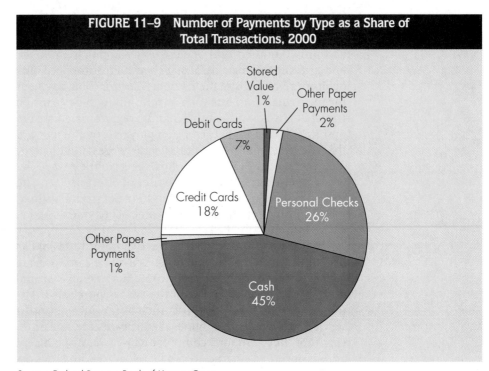

FIGURE 11-9   Number of Payments by Type as a Share of Total Transactions, 2000

Source: Federal Reserve Bank of Kansas City.

The benefits to society from electronic banking are clearly seen. Processing checks is a labor-intensive, relatively inefficient process. Americans write about 65 billion checks every year. The Federal Reserve estimates that the costs of processing these checks are equal to 1 percent of the gross domestic product. As economic incentives to change intensify and as we become more familiar with new banking systems, electronic banking may eventually equal or exceed cash or checks as the convenient and accepted means of paying for goods and services.

DEPOSIT INSURANCE

An issue that is a major controversy in the banking community is that of the federal deposit insurance program. In 2002, the Federal Deposit Insurance Corporation supported legislation in Congress to increase the maximum insurance coverage of deposits. At the present time, the FDIC insures individual accounts for amounts up to $100,000. Proposed legislation calls for insurance coverage of $130,000 on individual accounts and up to $200,000 for retirement accounts. Supporters of the bill claim that insurance hasn't kept pace with the size of individual bank accounts and retirement funds. Nor has it kept pace with inflation. Because of inflation, the constant dollar value of the insurance coverage has declined by

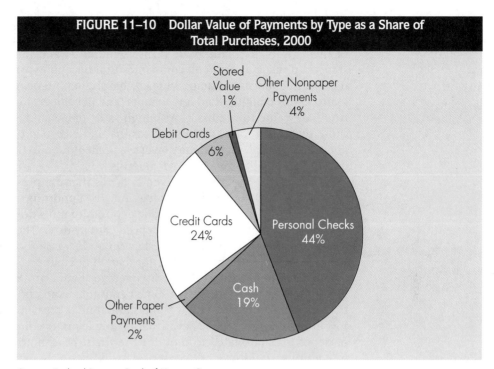

FIGURE 11–10   Dollar Value of Payments by Type as a Share of Total Purchases, 2000

Source: Federal Reserve Bank of Kansas City.

some 50 percent since 1980. The Federal Reserve Board of Governors is opposed to the proposed increase in insurance limits.

The United States has the oldest deposit insurance system in the world. The system was established in 1934 to put an end to the devastating bank runs that shut down businesses and contributed to the Great Depression. Since that time, the federal deposit insurance program is clearly the most recognized component of the public's financial safety net and has helped insure the public's confidence in the banking system. Since its inception, it has deterred liquidity panics, forestalled bank runs, and avoided instability in the economy. Insurance coverage has been at the $100,000 level since 1980. It was increased from $40,000 in that year to $100,000 in order to instill public confidence following the savings and loan crisis in the late 1970s and 1980s.

During this period, competition from the newly created and less restrictive money market funds caused banks and savings and loans to lose deposits to higher-paying accounts or securities. Soon, many of them found that the interest rate they had to pay to maintain old depositors was higher than the interest rate that they were receiving on their existing loans and investments. This created a cash outflow from the banks. To remain afloat, many of them began making more speculative loans seeking higher returns. But with the collapse in oil prices and the recession of 1982, many borrowers could not pay the interest or the principal on their loans. In addition to cash flow problems, banks saw a sharp decline in the market value of their assets, particularly in Texas, Oklahoma, and Louisiana. Banks in these states had made loans to oil companies that became worthless when the price of oil collapsed. Prices of homes dropped sharply, and homeowners defaulted on their loans. Office buildings had few tenants, and developers abandoned buildings with no resale value to the bank. Although most banks and S&Ls remained healthy, those that failed rolled up huge losses that far exceeded the financial resources of deposit insurance. The U.S. taxpayer was called upon to pay in excess of $130 billion to clean up the savings and loan crisis.

The Federal Reserve, however, believes that the present insurance coverage limit of $100,000 is more than adequate. To support its position, the Fed reports that about 98 percent of all domestic deposit accounts are currently fully insured, and 71 percent of total domestic deposits are insured. The Fed argues that raising the ceiling now would extend the safety net, increase the government subsidy to banking, and reduce the incentive for market discipline.

Increasing maximum account coverage would protect more depositors and might increase the amount that some depositors would hold in any one bank, particularly smaller banks, while at the same time decreasing the number of depositors at risk. But the Fed believes that raising insurance limits reduces the number of depositors motivated to monitor the financial conditions of their banks. Too much protection lowers the cost of risk taking on the part of banks, particularly large ones. Some banks may fund projects that might not otherwise be viable without full or near-full deposit guarantees. After all, any losses will be fully reimbursed for most people. Consequently, the actions of these banks lead to a misallocation of credit, which is costly to the economy as a whole because it reduces economic efficiency. In the 1980s, 100 percent insurance protection of all depositors, and in some cases even creditors, became a common practice and banks behaved as predicted, resulting in one of the worst financial debacles in U.S. history.

Concern over deposit insurance may seem to be occurring at an unlikely time, at least as far as the U.S. banking industry is concerned. Banks are performing well and the industry is stable. But banks are consolidating in record numbers and the size and complexity of banks are growing. The loss of just one of these very large banks will pose an even greater systemic risk than before. Yet too much depositor protection can result in such banks taking too much risk.

Summary

- The Federal Reserve System is composed of a Board of Governors, a Federal Advisory Council, a Federal Open Market Committee (FOMC), 12 reserve banks, 25 branch banks, member banks, and several minor organizations. It is owned by the member banks, but its most important officials are appointed by the president of the United States. The Board of Governors, whose main function is to formulate monetary policy for the U.S. economy, consists of seven members appointed by the president of the United States with the approval of the Senate. Each member must be selected from a different Federal Reserve District and is appointed for 14 years. The chairman and the vice-chairman are selected from the seven members by the president of the United States.

- The Federal Reserve uses general and selective controls to affect the money supply by regulating the reserve requirements, thus influencing the level of economic activity and/or the price level. The general controls affect the overall supply of money; the selective controls affect the use of money for specific purposes in the economy.

- The reserve requirement is a powerful tool of the Federal Reserve. By changing the reserve requirement, the Fed can greatly affect a bank's ability to loan money. Increasing the reserve requirement tends to constrict the money supply, while decreasing the requirement tends to increase the money supply.

- A change in the discount rate affects the money supply by influencing the borrowing that banks and businesses engage in. Generally, an increase in the discount rate discourages banks from borrowing to increase their reserves and discourages businesses from borrowing, because an increase usually forces up the commercial loan rate.

- The Fed will engage in open-market operations when it wants to affect bank reserves. To expand the money supply, the FOMC will order securities to be purchased. When price levels are rising, the Fed will sell government securities to the banks to absorb some of the existing excess reserves.

- The Depository Institutions Deregulation and Monetary Control Act of 1980 lessened regulation and promoted competition among depository institutions (commercial banks, savings banks, S&Ls, credit unions, etc.). Many of the differences between commercial banks and other depository institutions were diminished by the act. The 1999 Financial Modernization Act eliminated many of the product restrictions that were in place in the financial industry. With this act, brokerage firms and insurance companies can now buy banks, and banks can underwrite insurance and securities.

- Recent structural changes in the banking and financial services industries include branch and interstate banking; new types of accounts, such as NOW accounts; money market mutual funds; expansion of foreign bank branches in the United States; the globalization of money flows; and the increased use of electronic banking.

- The banking industry is undergoing substantial changes in market structure as a result of deregulation and technological innovations. Questions exist as to whether deregulation and technology will produce greater banking competition in the future, or whether the largest banks will increase their share of the market at the expense of smaller banks.

- The United States has the oldest deposit insurance system in the world. In 2002, the Federal Deposit Insurance Corporation insured individual accounts up to $100,000. Because this ceiling has not been increased since 1980, the FDIC sought to increase the maximum insurance limit. The Fed opposed increasing the limit.

CHAPTER REVIEW

New Terms and Concepts

Federal Reserve System
Member banks
Open-market operations
Required reserves
Excess reserves

Transaction accounts
Nonpersonal time
   accounts
Discount rate
Prime rate

Federal Funds Market
Moral suasion
Branch banking
Interstate banking
Electronic banking

Discussion Questions

1. Other nations have but one central bank. Why is it that the U.S. has multiple central banks?

2. Should all commercial banks be required to become members of the Federal Reserve System? Why or why not?

3. Since the federal government owns no stock in the reserve banks, why should the government appoint the Federal Reserve Board of Governors?

4. Does the lowering of reserve requirements automatically increase the money supply? Why or why not?

5. The Fifth National Bank has total deposits of $20,000,000 and has legal reserves of $5,000,000. If the legal reserve is 10 percent, is this bank loaned up? What is the maximum

loan that the bank can make and what is the maximum increase in the money supply?

6. How can a change in the discount rate affect commercial loan rates?

7. What is the effect of the FOMC's purchasing securities from individuals versus its purchasing them from banks, insofar as the expansion of the money supply is concerned?

8. What role does the Fed play in foreign exchange markets?

9. Should the independence of the Fed be modified in any way? Explain.

10. What does the globalization of money and banking do to the Fed's ability to stabilize domestic prices?

Economic Applications

EconDebate

Go to http://econapps.swlearning.com and click on the EconDebate icon. Then, click on "Money and the Financial System" under the Macroeconomics heading. This will take you to debates about the U.S. financial market.

12

Macroeconomic Models and Analysis

After studying Chapter 12, you should be able to:

1. Explain briefly the aggregate supply and aggregate demand framework.
2. Explain the major ideas of classical economic doctrine and understand Say's law.
3. Define *aggregate expenditure* and name its components.
4. Demonstrate an equilibrium position according to Keynesian analysis.
5. Explain the relationship between the multiplier and changes in income resulting from a change in aggregate expenditures.
6. Discuss the various opinions concerning the shape of the aggregate supply curve.
7. Distinguish between the monetarist and the new classical theories.

In Chapter 9 we saw that the GDP is allocated to four major sectors of the economy: consumption, investment, net exports, and the government. These sectors must pay for the goods and services they receive, and such payments are eventually distributed to the productive resources that contributed the goods and services to produce the GDP. Thus, in exchange for the physical goods and services the four sectors receive, monetary payments are made to the productive resources.

As we learned in Chapter 1, each resource—land, labor, capital, and entrepreneurship—contributes toward the total product, and the owners of these factors are paid in the form of rent, wages, interest, and profits, respectively. It is reasonable to assume that the total demand by the four sectors determines the size of the GDP and that the size of the GDP determines our earned income.

This sets up the circular flow of income, with the flow of goods and services to the four sectors occurring in proportion to their economic contribution. The greater the demand by consumers, investors, foreign buyers, and the government, the greater the amount of income distributed to the productive resources. The less the demand, the smaller the income payments. The demand for goods and services by these four sectors thus determines the total output, employment, and income in our economy. But how is the equilibrium level of activity determined for the economy?

Aggregate Demand and Aggregate Supply

Before looking at the details of macroeconomic theory, we need a general model or framework. The framework we will use to explain the levels of national income, output, employment, and prices is the aggregate supply and aggregate demand model. This framework is general enough to accommodate a variety of macroeconomic viewpoints. Once we have established the framework, we will use it to introduce different macroeconomic schools of thought whose competing ideas will recur in this and later chapters.

AGGREGATE DEMAND

Think back to the supply and demand curves for individual products developed in Chapter 4. Your first thought about how to obtain aggregate supply and demand curves might be to add up the supply curves and demand curves for all individual products in the marketplace. Unfortunately, this method is incorrect. There are technical problems with adding different goods (such as cars, shampoo, and movies) on the horizontal axis and the prices of each good on the vertical axis. What units do we use to combine such different products, and how do we construct an aggregate price that represents all these prices appropriately?

Aggregate Demand (AD) Curve
The total amount of real output that buyers in an economy will purchase at various alternative price levels.

Real Output
Output adjusted for changes in the price level.

The **aggregate demand (*AD*) curve** shows the total amount of real output that buyers in an economy will purchase at various alternative price levels. On the vertical axis, P represents the price level, measured by a price index. On the horizontal axis, Y represents **real output,** or output adjusted for changes in the price level. Economists often casually use the symbol Y to stand for a variety of different concepts related to the flow of income and output. However, if we overlook some of the smaller differences between GDP and national income, Y can represent both concepts: the flow of output and the flow of income.

Economists generally believe that the aggregate demand curve has a negative slope, for several reasons. First, if the price level rises, so does nominal income, and when nominal income increases, so do income taxes. Therefore, disposable income does not rise as much as prices because higher taxes reduce people's ability to buy at higher prices. Second, higher price levels in the United States relative to price levels in the rest of the world discourage exports and stimulate imports, reducing the net exports component of aggregate demand. Third, a higher price level also reduces the real purchasing power of assets or wealth that people own. As a result, people may cut back on spending while they try to rebuild the value of their asset holdings. Fourth, higher price levels are associated with higher interest rates. Higher interest rates increase the cost of borrowing by businesses for planned investment, by households for autos and consumer durables, and by state and local governments to finance construction.

AGGREGATE SUPPLY

Aggregate Supply (AS) Curve
A plot of various quantities of total real output that producers will offer for sale at various price levels.

The **aggregate supply (AS) curve** is a plot of various quantities of total real output that producers will offer for sale at various price levels. The shape of the aggregate supply curve is a matter of much debate among economists. Because time plays an even more important role in aggregate supply than in aggregate demand, much of the controversy is really about the difference between what *AS* looks like in the short run and what it looks like in the long run and about how long the short run and the long run are. Much of the controversy relates to how firms and owners of productive resources respond to changes in the price level and how quickly. We will continue our discussion of the shape of the *AS* curve later in the chapter.

The intersection of the aggregate supply and aggregate demand curves determines the equilibrium level of average prices and total output in the economy. The equilibrium level or price is shown as P_1. This equilibrium level of output is shown as Y_1 in Figure 12–1. Next we will consider two theoretical viewpoints concerning equilibrium in the economy: classical and Keynesian.

Classical Analysis

The most critical classical assumption is that the economy can be in equilibrium only at full employment. If the economy is not at full employment, according to classical analysis the situation will correct itself. The market economy is thus self-regulating: Competition helps maintain or move the economy toward equilibrium at full employment. If unsold inventory exists, competition forces prices down to

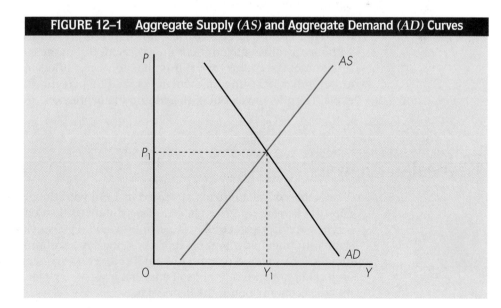

FIGURE 12–1 Aggregate Supply *(AS)* and Aggregate Demand *(AD)* Curves

ensure that all goods are sold. Competition likewise ensures that all saving is invested because it forces the interest rate down. The lower interest rate causes planned saving to decrease and borrowing to increase until businesses have invested all available funds. If workers are unemployed for any reason, they will compete for jobs against each other, and against those still employed, by offering to work for lower wages. As a result of this competition, wages are forced down. As wages decline, it becomes profitable for firms to hire more workers.

Thus the normal tendency of the economy, the classical economists believed, is to move toward full employment. Temporary deviations may be caused by any of several factors, such as monopolistic restrictions, labor unions, and government intervention in the economy.

According to the classical economists, all income is spent. People use their incomes to buy the current goods and services they need. What they do not spend on current consumption, they spend to build up their inventories of consumer goods or to invest in capital goods. If anything is saved, it is borrowed by others and spent in various ways, especially for capital goods investment. Thus, any decrease in planned consumption is offset by an increase in planned investment. Fluctuations in the interest rate ensure that all the planned saving is borrowed.

The classical theory holds that production, which creates supply, also creates an equivalent amount of monetary purchasing power (demand). And because all the income is spent, supply and demand are always equal. This conclusion is often referred to as **Say's law.** (Jean Baptiste Say was a French economist who, along with others, espoused the theory that supply creates demand. He explained the theory in his book *A Treatise on Political Economy,* published in 1830.) If supply creates its own demand, then all goods offered for sale must be purchased. According to the classical presentation, there is no reason why the economy should not move right to equilibrium at full employment.

Classical theory was widely accepted until the Great Depression of the 1930s. Although economic downturns had occurred previously, recovery came about without any direct government intervention. But in the early 1930s, the economic situation of the country went from bad to worse; prices and interest rates fell, yet in December 1933 unemployment was at 24.9 percent. Classical theory could not explain or offer a way out of the continuing depression.

Say's Law
The classical view that if supply creates its own demand, then all goods offered for sale must be purchased.

Keynesian Analysis

A new theoretical approach appeared in 1936 with the publication of *The General Theory of Employment, Interest, and Money* by the British economist John Maynard Keynes. Keynes argued that the economy could get stuck at an equilibrium with significant unemployment of labor and other factors of production and that no automatic forces would operate to help it recover. His conclusion was that the economy could not take care of itself and that it was the government's responsibility to pull the economy out of the depression.

The Keynesian approach, also known as income–expenditure analysis, is an alternative to the classical view that the economy is in equilibrium only at full employment. Keynes contended that purchasing power does not automatically become demand for goods and services. People may have the purchasing power, or potential demand, and yet not use it. After producing goods and earning income, individuals may decide to hold some of their money as savings instead of spending it. Therefore, the total demand for goods and services may be less than the supply, and goods produced may not be sold. In such a case, firms will reduce production and employment will decline.

In explaining what determines the actual level of output and employment at any given time, Keynes focused on aggregate expenditure. **Aggregate expenditure (AE)** is total planned spending for goods and services by consumers, businesses, government, and foreign buyers. Total output—and therefore total employment and income—is determined by *AE*. The income derived from the output of goods and services in turn determines *AE*. If spending for consumer and capital goods is high, *AE* will also be high. Thus, a continued high rate of spending will ensure a strong *AE*, which in turn will ensure high levels of production, employment, and income. This action gives us the circular flow of income described in Chapter 8. Since the cause of unemployment is inadequate *AE*, the Keynesian model concentrates its efforts on the analysis of *AE* and its four sectors: consumption, investment, government spending, and net exports.

Consumption plus government spending plus net exports is generally less than total output. As a result, planned investment is necessary to absorb the difference between what is produced and what is consumed by households and government. Furthermore, as output increases, planned consumption does not increase by as much. This means that the higher the output is, the greater the gap between output and planned consumption. Moreover, the higher the levels of output and employment are, the greater the amount of planned investment required to maintain a given level of employment. Finally, the theory contends that, because of the relative stability of the consumption function, *AE* will shift primarily according to changes in planned investment. Keynes felt that increased government spending must be used to raise total aggregate expenditure when planned consumption, planned investment, and net exports are inadequate to maintain a satisfactory level of production and employment for the economy.

Aggregate Expenditure (AE) Total planned spending for goods and services by consumers, businesses, government, and foreign buyers.

A TWO-SECTOR ECONOMY

In a simple economy with no government and no foreign trade, there are just two sectors of *AE*: consumption and investment. We will start with these two sectors to develop a simple model of income determination, and then we will add the others to make the model more realistic.

Consumption

Keynes challenged Say's law by arguing that it is demand (or planned spending) that determines how much is produced. The largest single component of spending is consumption, so Keynes began building his model by examining the behavior of consumption. He argued that the amount consumers spend depends primarily on their disposable income. Keynes called this relationship the *consumption function* and made it a key part of his theory.

Consumption Function
Any equation, table, or graph that shows the relationship between the income that consumers receive (disposable income) and the amount they plan to spend on currently produced final output.

The **consumption function** is any equation, table, or graph that shows the relationship between income received by consumers (disposable income) and the amount they plan or desire to spend on currently produced final output. Notice that the Keynesian consumption function relates consumer spending to disposable income—not to national income.

Keynes believed that consumers were creatures of habit. When disposable income changed, he expected that consumer spending would change by a constant fraction of the change in income. Keynes called the ratio of the change in consumption spending to the change in disposable or after-tax income the **marginal propensity to consume (MPC)**. This ratio corresponds to the slope of the consumption function. The *MPC* is always a positive value between 0 and 1. Keynes believed that it would be relatively constant for a moderate income range. As income increases beyond that range, Keynes felt the *MPC* would decline somewhat. To simplify our graphical analysis, *MPC* will be held constant, and the consumption function will be a straight, upward-sloping line.

Marginal Propensity to Consume (**MPC**)
The ratio of the change in consumption spending to the change in disposable or after-tax income; the slope of the consumption function.

Keynes also disagreed with the classical economic belief that planned saving depended entirely on the interest rate. He felt that consumers saved for many reasons—an emergency reserve, a future large purchase, retirement—other than to earn interest. Keynes believed that consumers' saving habits were based mostly on their income. The **saving function** shows the relationship between the amount of disposable income that consumers receive and the amount they save. Recall from Chapter 8 that saving is a leakage from the circular flow of income.

Saving Function
The relationship between the amount of disposable income consumers receive and the amount they save.

The **marginal propensity to save (MPS)** describes how planned saving responds to income changes. The *MPS* is the ratio of the change in planned saving to the change in disposable income and in the slope of the saving function. The *MPC* and the *MPS* always add up to 1, whatever the value of the *MPC*, because all consumer income that is not spent on final goods and services must be saved.

Marginal Propensity to Save (**MPS**)
The ratio of the change in planned saving to the change in disposable income; the slope of the saving function.

Although the absolute amount of consumption increases with higher income, consumption decreases relative to income. Therefore, as the economy expands, the difference between the amount of production (which is equivalent to income) and the amount of planned consumption increases. Therefore, there may be less *AE* than is necessary to sell all the goods the economy is capable of producing. In that case, inventories will grow beyond the size that firms desire to hold. Firms will respond by cutting output, and employment and income will fall as a result.

Investment

Investment spending is an injection into the circular flow of income and product. How do we explain the behavior of planned investment demand (*I*)? Classical economists believed that the most important determinant of planned investment spending was the interest rate: When the interest rate got low enough, businesses would borrow money to invest in capital goods. Keynes did not agree. He argued that profit expectations are the most important single determinant of planned investment spending by businesses. Other important influences are the interest rate, the size and age of the existing stock of capital, changes in corporate taxes, and changes in technology. Some of these factors can change suddenly and by large amounts.

Keynes assumed that planned investment demand would shift so frequently that the relationship between planned investment spending and the level of income, or the rate of interest, would not be as important as the other factors that make it shift. In the Keynesian model, the level of planned investment spending is what matters. To simplify our presentation here, we will treat planned investment as having a given value that is determined by factors outside the model.

Equilibrium in a Two-Sector Economy

Let us return to our two-sector economy, where $AE = C + I$. Notice the reference line sloping upward to the right at a 45° angle in Figure 12–2. A 45° line is a straight line that cuts through the origin and divides the graph diagonally into two equal sections. At any point on the 45° line, the value measured on the vertical axis (aggregate expenditure) equals the value measured on the horizontal axis (real income or output Y).

Line C is the consumption function representing planned consumption at various levels of output. As output increases, planned consumption will increase, too, but not as much as income. Therefore, planned consumption can be represented by a line sloping upward to the right at less than a 45° angle. The MPC is the slope of the consumption function. At very low levels of output, planned consumption may actually exceed income. This can occur if people borrow money in addition to their regular incomes in order to buy goods and services.

At the point where line C crosses the 45° line, planned consumption is equal to total income and output. In an economy that has only planned consumption spending, Y_1 is the equilibrium output. In most instances, however, planned consumption spending is less than output. At every level of output, the vertical difference between the 45° line and C represents planned saving, as shown at output level Y_2 in the lower part of Figure 12–2.

Sufficient planned investment is needed to fill the gap between output and C if all goods and services are to be sold. If planned investment is not large enough to fill the gap, some inventory will remain unsold and production will be cut. The level of economic activity, then, is determined by the amount of planned investment.

Our example economy has a given constant level of planned investment I. When planned investment spending is added to planned consumption spending, the resulting function $C + I$ is a line parallel to line C. Real output will adjust to the point where $C + I$ crosses the 45° line. At this equilibrium point, AE will equal total output, and all the goods and services produced will be sold. This is shown as output Y_3 in Figure 12–3.

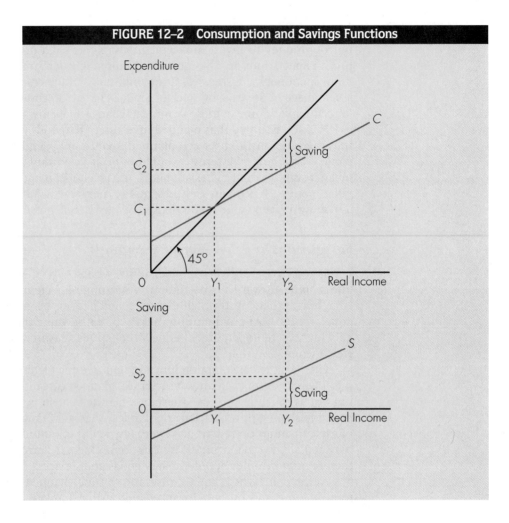

FIGURE 12–2　Consumption and Savings Functions

At any lower output level, *AE* will be greater than output. Planned investment (the difference between total output and *C*) will be greater than planned saving, as illustrated by output Y_2 in Figure 12–3. Thus, if the economy were at output Y_2, production and output would increase as firms expanded to supply the excess demand until the equilibrium output Y_3 was reached. At output Y_3, *AE* equals total output and planned investment equals planned saving. At any higher level of output, such as output Y_4, *AE* is less than output. Thus, not all the goods produced are sold. As we noted earlier, firms will respond to this situation by cutting production until output again reaches equilibrium output Y_3. There, planned investment fills the vertical gap between the 45° line and *C*, planned investment is equal to planned saving, and *AE* is equal to total output and income. In terms of the circular flow, equilibrium occurs when injections (investment) and leakages (saving) are equal.

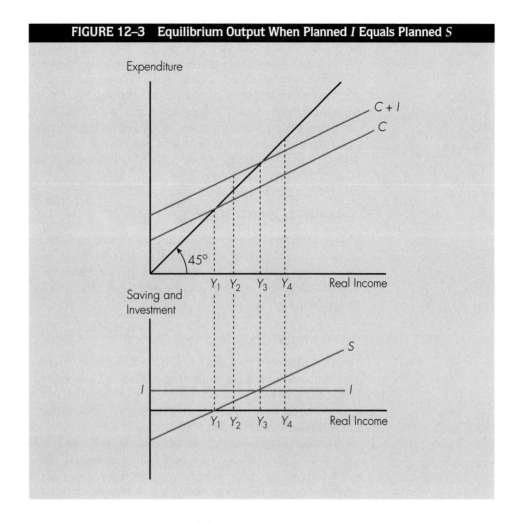

FIGURE 12–3   Equilibrium Output When Planned *I* Equals Planned *S*

Relationship of Planned Investment to Planned Saving

In analyzing Figure 12–3, keep in mind that the difference between the 45° line and the *C* line at each level of output represents planned saving. At output Y_2 in Figure 12–3, for example, the amount of planned investment (as shown by the vertical difference between *C* + *I* and *C*) is more than that necessary to fill the gap between the 45° line and *C*. Therefore, as shown in the lower portion of the figure, planned investment (injections) is greater than planned saving (leakages). This means that *AE* is greater than output. As a result, production will increase to satisfy the excess demand. As output increases, income and planned saving increase. The economy comes into equilibrium at output Y_3, where planned saving is equal to planned investment. Therefore, *AE* is equal to total output. All goods produced will be sold, and the economy will be in equilibrium.

There is no incentive to move to a higher level of output because it would not be profitable to do so. At Y_4 in Figure 12–3, planned investment is insufficient to fill the gap between the 45° line and C. Therefore, planned investment (injections) is less than planned saving (leakages). This means that AE is less than total output and inventory will remain unsold. As a result, businesses will curtail production, bringing about a decline in output, employment, and income. As output decreases, the gap between total output and $C + I$ becomes smaller, until output Y_3 is reached, at which point planned investment just fills the vertical gap between the 45° line and C. Here, once again, planned investment equals planned saving, AE equals total output, and the economy is in equilibrium.

A FOUR-SECTOR ECONOMY

The two-sector economy consisting of consumption and investment gave us a basic understanding of how the equilibrium level of national output is determined. A more complete Keynesian model includes all four sectors from the circular flow and the national income accounts. Adding government and net exports gives us all the participants.

Government Spending and Taxes

The first addition is the government, which causes increases in aggregate expenditure in the form of government spending and decreases in aggregate expenditure in the form of taxes (T). Government expenditures (G), like planned investment expenditures, are assumed to be determined by factors other than income. Thus, G has a constant value in our model.

Government spending—at the federal, state, or local level—provides another injection into the circular flow and another source of demand for output. Taken by itself, the addition of G to aggregate expenditures simply increases the equilibrium level of output. However, there is a downside to adding government spending; government purchases must be paid for, at least in part, by taxes. For simplicity, we will assume that taxes are equal to government spending, that taxes are equal to a fixed amount of income, and that all taxes are paid by consumers. We noted earlier that consumers have only two choices of what to do with their income: spend it or save it. Because paying taxes is not a direct way of purchasing any goods or services, economists classify taxes as a form of saving.

Taxes are a leakage from the income flow because they are an (involuntary) addition to planned saving. An increase in taxes causes the saving function to shift up by the amount of the tax increase. A decrease in taxes causes the saving function to shift down. Taxes (T) are not directly part of the AE equation because they do not represent planned spending for output. Taxes are incorporated into aggregate expenditure through the consumption function. A rise in taxes reduces disposable income and causes the entire consumption function to shift down. A fall in taxes increases disposable income and causes the consumption function to shift upwards.

Net Exports

The last component of aggregate expenditure is the foreign sector. Purchases by foreigners are exports (*X*) and add to aggregate expenditures. The spending of consumers, businesses, and government for imports (*IM*) reduces the level of *AE* for domestic output. The foreign sector is very large for some countries, accounting for more than half of all sales or purchases in the circular flow. For the United States, exports of goods and services currently are about 10 percent of total GDP, and imports are slightly larger.

Exports are an injection into the domestic flow of income and product, whereas imports are a leakage from the flow. Thus, we add exports and subtract imports to arrive at *AE*. For now, we will assume that both export and import spending are determined by factors outside the model, just as we did for planned investment and government spending. Thus, net exports (*X − IM*) can be treated as a given constant. With the foreign sector added into the model, the complete *AE* relationship is

$$AE = C + I + G + (X - IM)$$

Changes in exports or imports, like changes in any aspect of domestic spending, can shift the *AE* function and change the level of real income and output. Suppose, for example, that a drought in another country leads to a large increase in exports of grain from the United States. How will this change in net exports influence the equilibrium level of output? If imports remain unchanged, there will be an increase in (*X − IM*), which shifts the *AE* schedule up and causes an increase in equilibrium output. A decrease in (*X − IM*) has the opposite effect: The *AE* schedule will shift down, and equilibrium output will decrease.

Equilibrium in a Four-Sector Economy

Equilibrium occurs at an output level where output is exactly equal to the sum of planned purchases by the four sectors. At lower levels of output, aggregate expenditure (*AE*) is greater than output (*Y*). At higher levels of *Y*, output is greater than aggregate expenditure. Adding a government with a balanced budget and positive net exports will increase the equilibrium level of income compared to the two-sector model. The increased number of buyers for output more than offsets the negative effects of imports on *AE* and of taxes on consumption and *AE*.

Once again, when aggregate expenditures equal total output, planned leakages from the circular flow equal planned injections. However, there are now three leakages—saving, taxes, and imports—and three injections—investment, government purchases, and exports. Again, leakages and injections are only equal at the equilibrium level of income. Below that level, injections exceed leakages, causing income and output to rise; above that level, leakages exceed injections, causing income and output to fall, just as we saw in the circular flow analysis in Chapter 8.

EQUILIBRIUM WITH UNEMPLOYMENT

If an economy were in equilibrium at less than full employment of productive resources, the classical economists felt that employers and employees merely had to wait for the competitive factors to make the adjustments necessary to move the economy to a full-employment position. According to Keynes, however, there may be no automatic adjustment toward the full-employment level of output. Rather than letting the economy stagnate with unemployment and uncertainty, the Keynesian analysis suggests stimulating the economy to move to a higher position by using various measures designed to increase the level of spending. Some of these measures are mentioned here; they will be discussed in detail in Chapter 16.

Increased Consumption and Net Exports

The Keynesian approach does not deny the possibility of increasing the level of employment through increased consumption. Because planned consumption spending depends primarily on income, however, it is unlikely that the consumption function could be changed sufficiently to raise the level of economic activity. Net exports are a relatively small share of total spending in our economy. Thus, even a huge increase in exports would not have a significant impact on total employment.

Increased Investment

Because planned consumption and net exports are not likely to increase, increased planned investment may provide a way to move the economy to a higher level of employment and output. Unfortunately, if the business sector is discouraged by poor profit expectations and high unemployment, it may not be willing to increase planned investment spending by a large amount.

Increased Government Spending

NETLink

How would the present economic report affect government spending? See economics data at:

http://www.bea.doc.gov or
http://www.bls.gov

When $C + I + G + (X - IM)$ is not large enough for high employment, Keynesians suggest that government spending be increased to bolster the economy. Increased government spending has the same effect as an increase in the spending of any other sector. As a means to reach a given level of output and employment, increased government spending can be used to absorb the difference between output and AE. Additional government spending that is undertaken to stabilize the economy is called *discretionary government spending*. Keynes felt that the government should intervene even if doing so meant having a deficit budget (spending more than the revenue received through taxes).

Figure 12–4 illustrates the use of discretionary government spending, where G and $(X - IM)$ have been added to the $C + I$ function. The initial equilibrium position Y_1 is at an output with less than full employment. However, if discretionary government spending were used to fill the vertical gap Y^* between total output and AE at full employment, injections (planned investment plus government spending plus exports) would equal leakages (planned saving plus taxes plus imports). As a

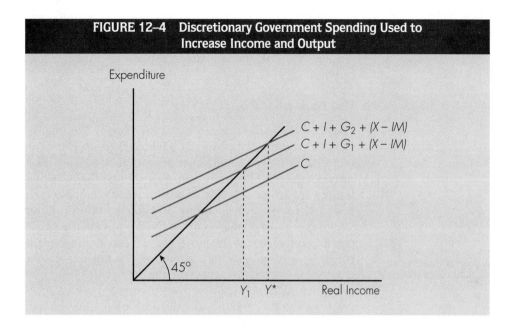

FIGURE 12–4 Discretionary Government Spending Used to Increase Income and Output

result, *AE* (including discretionary government spending G_2) would equal total output. All goods and services produced would be sold, and equilibrium would occur at the higher level of output, income, and full employment.

EQUILIBRIUM WITH INFLATION

If *AE* continues to increase once the economy has reached the full-employment level, prices will be pushed upward as investors and consumers bid against each other for the use of scarce labor, raw materials, and capital. A continued rise in the price level means that inflation will set in. If inflation occurs, measures should be taken to discourage aggregate expenditure, because increased spending will lead to still higher prices. Although inflation was not a pressing issue in Keynes's time, he had suggestions for government intervention in this area if it were needed. To combat inflationary tendencies, government spending can be decreased, taxes can be increased (to lessen consumption), and interest rates can be pushed upward (to discourage investment).

AGGREGATE EXPENDITURE AND THE MULTIPLIER

Throughout this section of the chapter, we have been discussing the effect of changes in aggregate expenditure on output, income, and employment. To be effective, a net change has to occur. For example, if planned investment increases by $20 billion while planned consumption decreases by $20 billion, there is no substantial change in total income. If planned investment increases by $20 billion, however, and planned consumption, net exports, and government expenditure remain the same, the increase in spending will also increase the level of economic activity.

The Multiplier Effect

What would be the result of a net increase of $20 billion in planned investment? Would it increase output by $20 billion? Actually, it would increase the GDP and our total income by some larger amount than $20 billion. When one person spends money, it becomes income to the recipient; when the recipient in turn spends the money, it becomes income to a third party; and so on. The total income resulting from the continual respending of a given amount of money is thus considerably larger than the actual amount of money initially spent. The **multiplier** is the relationship between a change in aggregate expenditure (planned investment, planned consumption, government spending, or net exports) and the resulting larger change in national output or income.

Multiplier
The relationship between a change in aggregate expenditure and the resulting larger change in national output or income.

As an example, suppose that investors spend $20; this may result in an increase in income of $20, $40, $60, and so on, as it is respent. The only limiting factor on the creation of income by respending the original $20 is the possibility of a failure somewhere along the line to respend the money that is received. This would be the case if a person used some of the money to pay taxes, or saved a portion of the money, or spent it on imported goods. In other words, any time we withdraw money (create leakages) from the circular flow, that money will not be available for respending and for creating more income.

Relationship to Consumption and Saving

Planned saving constitutes the biggest leakage factor from the income stream. Thus, the size of the multiplier depends on the relationship of planned saving (or of planned consumption) to income. For example, suppose that people spend four-fifths of their income and save one-fifth. The multiplier in this case will be 5, which means that a net increase in planned investment of $20 will increase output and income by $100. This effect is demonstrated in Table 12–1.

According to this table, an increase in planned investment of $20, when originally spent, becomes income of $20 to individual A. If A saves one-fifth of this ($4) and spends the rest, the $16 respent by A becomes income to individual B. When B in turn spends four-fifths of the $16 income, it creates $12.80 in income for individual C. This process of receiving income and then respending the money, which creates incomes for others, continues until the original amount of money is all held in saving by the various individuals. At that time, no more income will be generated. Through this process, the original planned investment of $20 brings about an increase of $100 in income and output. Thus, the multiplier has a value of 5. The change in output is the result of respending, so the level of planned consumption has a direct influence on the size of the multiplier.

TABLE 12–1 Multiplier Effect Example				
Net Increase in Investment		Increased Income	Increased Spending (Spend 80%)	Savings (Save 20%)
$20	A	$20.0	$16.0	$4.0
	B	16.0	12.8	3.2
	C	12.8	10.2	2.6
	D	10.2	8.2	2.0
	E	8.2	6.6	1.6
Multiplier effect	F	6.6	5.2	1.4
	G	5.2	4.2	1.0
		etc.	etc.	etc.
		$100.0	$80.0	$20.0

The more money people respend, or the less they save, the larger the multiplier will be. For example, if individuals and businesses were inclined to save only one-tenth of everything they received in income, the multiplier would be equal to 10. In this case, an increase of $20 in planned investment would bring about a $200 increase in output, because the money would turn over more times before it was all saved. Conversely, the lower the marginal propensity to consume, the less the multiplier will be. If income recipients were to save one-half of everything they received, this would result in a multiplier of only 2.

Calculating the Value of the Multiplier

As you study Table 12–1, you will notice that the multiplier depends on the spending and saving habits of the individuals and businesses in the economy. In fact, the size of the multiplier directly depends on the marginal propensity to consume, that is, on the relationship between income and planned consumption. The marginal propensity to consume is used to calculate the multiplier k.

$$k = \frac{1}{1 - MPC} = \frac{1}{MPS}$$

When the marginal propensity to consume is subtracted from 1 (the total increase in income), we get the marginal propensity to save (MPS). Dividing the MPS into 1 gives us the multiplier. Thus, the multiplier is equal to the reciprocal of the MPS. If consumers spend three-fourths of any additional income they receive, the MPC is 0.75. Putting this information into the multiplier equation, we find that

$$k = \frac{1}{1 - MPC} = \frac{1}{1 - 0.75} = \frac{1}{0.25} = 4$$

The size of the multiplier is 4. Evidently, the multiplier is related directly to the *MPC* and inversely to the *MPS*. Various estimates of the actual multiplier for the United States place it somewhere between 2 and 3, depending on the nation's level of employment and business activity.

AGGREGATE EXPENDITURE AND AGGREGATE DEMAND

At the beginning of this chapter, we considered the aggregate supply and aggregate demand model as a framework for the study of macroeconomics. Then we discussed the Keynesian model, which uses an aggregate expenditure function to derive the equilibrium quantity of real income and output. The aggregate supply and aggregate demand model shows the equilibrium output at various price levels, while the Keynesian model shows the equilibrium output at various levels of income. How are the two models connected?

Figure 12–5 shows the relationship between the aggregate demand curve and the aggregate expenditure curve. The *AE* function is drawn for a given price level. For each price level, a specific aggregate expenditure function yields a unique equilibrium output. Higher price levels are associated with a lower *AE* at every level of income. The same reasons that explained why aggregate demand slopes down from left to right also explain why a different *AE* function exists for each different price level. Thus, AE_1 is associated with a high price level P_1; AE_2 is associated with a lower price level P_2; and AE_3 is associated with the lowest price level P_3.

The graph in Figure 12–5b derives an *AD* curve from the graph in Figure 12–5a by plotting the various *P* and *Y* combinations derived from the set of *AE* curves shown there. For example, along AE_1, price level P_1 is associated with equilibrium real income level Y_1. Remember, the *AE* line shows the amount consumers and business firms will spend on planned consumption and planned investment at various alternative income levels. The *AD* curve obtained by plotting these points in the graph in Figure 12–5b shows the amounts of real output (*Y*) that consumers, businesses, government, and foreign buyers will demand at various alternative price levels.

Both the *AE* curve and the *AD* curve represent demand for total output, but *AE* shows the relationship between demand and income, whereas *AD* shows the relationship between demand and price level. In both models, the equilibrium level of national income occurs at the point where total output and aggregate expenditures are equal.

Aggregate Supply and Aggregate Demand Again

We reviewed two opinions concerning economic equilibrium in this chapter. The classical economists believed that equilibrium in the economy would always be at the level of output associated with full employment and that any deviation from this would be temporary. In terms of the aggregate supply and aggregate demand

FIGURE 12–5 Deriving an Aggregate Demand Curve from Aggregate Expenditure Curves

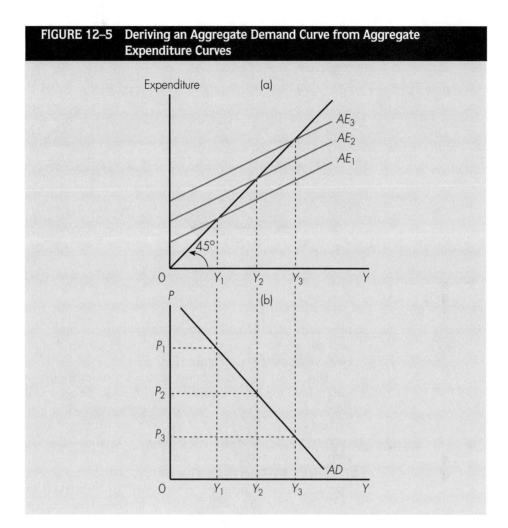

framework, the classical economists described both the short- and the long-run aggregate supply curves as vertical at the full-employment level of output, Y^*. Where the aggregate demand curve is located determines the price level in the economy, as shown in Figure 12–6a. An increase in aggregate demand from AD_1 to AD_2 simply results in a higher price level, because no more output can be produced.

Keynes agreed that the long-run aggregate supply curve would be vertical at the full-employment level of output, but he disagreed about the short-term situation. Keynes felt that equilibrium could easily be reached at an output level involving less than full employment, and he argued that the situation could continue for a long time. He described a horizontal aggregate supply curve based on the possibility of increasing output without raising prices—simply by using the unemployed

FIGURE 12–6   Classical and Keynesian Views of Aggregate Supply

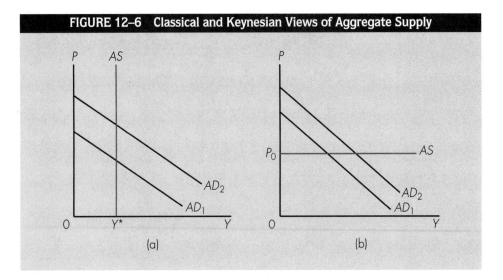

resources. (Recall that he was writing during a lengthy depression.) In the Keynesian model, aggregate demand determines the level of income and output in the economy, as shown in Figure 12–6b.

Obviously, the classical and Keynesian views are the two extremes. Most economists hold the more moderate opinion that the aggregate supply curve is upward sloping (but not vertical), because higher prices will encourage producers to try to expand output. As a result, the cost of resources will increase, and these increased costs will be reflected in higher prices. If all these differing ideas are presented together, a composite *AS* curve can be drawn.

Figure 12–7 depicts a composite *AS* curve and several levels of aggregate demand. If national income is lower than Y_2, any increase in aggregate demand—for example, AD_1 to AD_2—will generate increased real output and employment without increasing the price level. If the level of income is between Y_2 and Y^*, an increase in aggregate demand—say, AD_3 to AD_4—will generate some increase in real output and employment along with an increase in the price level. Finally, any increase in *AD* beyond the full-employment level Y^* will result in a higher price level, but no increase in either real output or employment.

Monetarists and New Classicals

The debate over the extent to which monetary and fiscal policies affect the economy continues among theoreticians. Before leaving this chapter, a brief description of the monetarist and new classical schools of thought may provide greater insight

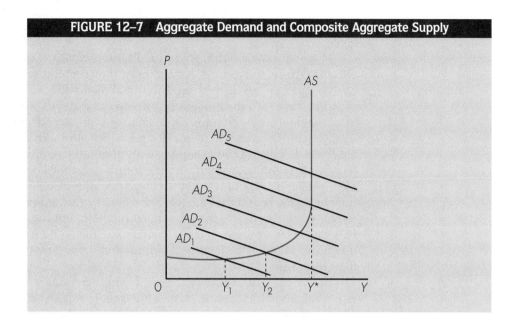

FIGURE 12–7   Aggregate Demand and Composite Aggregate Supply

into the differing views of economists as to the workings of the economy and the implications for economic policy. Unlike Keynesian theory, which focuses on fiscal policy and its impact on unemployment and recession, both the monetarists and new classicals focus on monetary policy and have inflation as their chief economic concern. Both these schools trace their roots to the classical theory and both became popular during periods of inflation.

THE MONETARIST SCHOOL

The monetarist school emerged in the 1950s and 1960s and became popular in the 1970s. Like the classical economists of the nineteenth century, monetarists rely on the market system to bring the economy to its peak of efficiency. Both wages and prices are seen as highly flexible and adjusting quickly to supply and demand conditions. While Keynesians believe that the economy is subject to periods of disequilibrium requiring government intervention, monetarists believe that the economy automatically tends toward full-employment equilibrium. Consequently, the economy is fundamentally stable according to monetarists, and government intervention is not needed.

Monetarists focus on the role of money as being the most important variable in determining aggregate demand. Monetarists concede that changes in monetary policy can have a powerful impact on the economy in the short run, but the long-run effects of these changes are inflationary. For, in the long run, increases in the money supply do not increase employment or output, but only the price level.

Monetarists argue that government intervention worsens, not alleviates, the effects of the business cycle. For example, they contend that inflation follows periods of rapid money growth and that recessions follow periods of slow money growth. The key to the monetarists' argument is the important time lags inherent in changing the money supply. The first lag is in recognizing that a problem exists in aggregate demand and formulating a policy approach to correct it. The second lag occurs because of the extensive amount of time required for the policy to work its way through the economy. By the time it does, the economy may be in a completely different situation, and the corrective policy decisions made previously may now be totally counterproductive. For example, the Fed may implement measures to tighten the money supply to combat inflation, but the effects of tighter money may not be felt until much later. At that time, the economy may be sluggish or in a downturn and may in fact need stimulation toward monetary expansion rather than contraction.

To eliminate the destabilizing effects of discretionary economic policy, monetarists call for monetary and fiscal authorities to follow a fixed set of rules. Specifically, they call for the government to produce a balanced budget over the business cycle and for the Federal Reserve to maintain a constant rate of growth in the money supply, regardless of interest rates, the level of economic activity, or any other economic variables. Monetarists suggest that the money supply be increased at a rate of 3 to 5 percent annually. This monetary rule, they believe, would stabilize economic activity and the price level more successfully than the current policy of tampering with the money supply in reaction to business and price fluctuations.

THE NEW CLASSICAL SCHOOL

The new classical school first became popular in the late 1970s and early 1980s. Like the monetarists, the new classicals hold that the economy is essentially stable and that price and wage flexibility are self-correcting properties. Market forces tend to move the economy toward full employment and are responsive enough to keep it there in the face of shifting economic conditions. Deviations from full-employment equilibrium are mild and short-lived.

The new classical theorists also believe that active monetary policy has no place in the economy. New classicals hold that economic intervention is ineffective, not because of the time lags involved in policy changes, but because of rational expectations. By *rational expectations*, the new classicals mean that people learn not only from their past experiences but, with access to the vast amount of economic information available, are able to correctly foresee the future. This information includes an understanding of the structure of the economy, economic forecasts, the likely actions taken by monetary and fiscal authorities, and the long-run response to their policies. Armed with this knowledge, people will correctly anticipate changes in monetary and fiscal policy and change their behavior accordingly. As they change their behavior prior to the enactment of public policy, the effects of public policy become ineffective. Instances where monetary policies alter employment or output levels are occasional, random events and must catch people by surprise.

If, for example, the economy is sliding into a recession, prices and wages would normally be expected to fall without an expansionary policy. But if market participants correctly expect the introduction of an expansionary policy, they will not lower prices because they anticipate an increase in future demand. With prices remaining high, the increased money supply will result in inflation.

Therefore, the new classicals conclude that activist monetary policy has no place in a world in which households and firms automatically deploy resources fully and efficiently. For market forces to work properly, new classical economists, like the monetarists, recommend a stable growth in the money supply and as small a role for the government as possible. Expansionary policies by the government can only lead to inflation and will have no effect on aggregate demand.

Summary

- The aggregate supply and aggregate demand framework can be used to explain the levels of national income and output. Aggregate demand (*AD*) shows the total amount of real output that buyers will purchase at various alternative price levels. Aggregate supply (*AS*) shows the various quantities of total real output producers will offer for sale at various price levels. The intersection of the aggregate supply and aggregate demand curves determines the equilibrium level of average prices and total output in the economy.

- The most critical assumption of the classical economists was that the equilibrium output is normally the full-employment output. When this is not the case, the situation is temporary and will correct itself. Say's law states that supply creates its own demand. That is, when resource income is received, it will be spent on the goods and services produced by the productive resources.

- Aggregate expenditure is the total planned spending for the economy. It is made up of consumption, investment, government expenditure, and net exports.

- Keynes said that the level of economic activity is determined by the size of aggregate expenditure. Graphically, equilibrium income occurs at the point where the aggregate expenditure curve crosses the 45° line (representing output). At that point, aggregate expenditure is equal to total income and output. However, the equilibrium output may well not be the full-employment output.

- If an initial increase in spending by any of the four sectors occurs, it will increase national income and output—not simply by the initial increase but by some multiple thereof. The size of the multiplier varies directly with the marginal propensity to consume and inversely with the marginal propensity to save.

- There is much debate about the shape of the aggregate supply curve. The classical view is that the short-run *AS* curve is vertical, while Keynes viewed it as horizontal. The middle view is that the *AS* curve is upward sloping. When all three views are consolidated, the resulting composite short-run *AS* curve is horizontal over a range of output, then upward sloping, and finally vertical at the full-employment level of output.

- Unlike Keynesian analysis, the monetarist and new classical schools of thought are largely concerned with the effects of inflation on the economy. Both schools of thought hold that the economy is essentially stable and that market forces automatically provide equilibrium. The monetarist and new classical schools support a stable rate of growth in the money supply and the elimination of expansionary policies by the federal government.

New Terms and Concepts

Aggregate demand (*AD*) curve

Real output

Aggregate supply (*AS*) curve

Say's law

Aggregate expenditure (*AE*)

Consumption function

Marginal propensity to consume (*MPC*)

Saving function

Marginal propensity to save (*MPS*)

Multiplier

Discussion Questions

1. Why does the aggregate demand curve slope downward from left to right?

2. What are the merits of the classical economists' assumption that full employment is the normal equilibrium level for the economy?

3. What does the statement "supply creates its own demand" mean?

4. Recent empirical data indicate that the marginal propensity to consume may not decline as much with rising income as Keynes and others assumed it would. If this is true, how does it affect the validity of the income–expenditure approach as a tool of analysis?

5. Why does a high level of planned consumption make it easier to maintain a high level of employment?

6. Why does the marginal propensity to consume determine the size of the multiplier?

7. What are the similarities and differences between the multiplier and the velocity of money? (Refer to Chapter 10 for a review of the velocity of money.)

8. Find the value of the multiplier when (a) $MPC = 0.40$; (b) $MPS = 0.25$; (c) $MPC = 0.67$; (d) $MPS = 0.50$; (e) $MPC = 0.90$; and (f) $MPC = 0.75$.

9. How does Keynes's famous remark, "In the long run we are all dead," relate to the debate between classical and Keynesian economists?

10. What are the similarities and differences between the monetarist and new classical theories?

Economic Applications

EconData

This chapter reviews aggregate supply and aggregate demand. To find current data on these topics, go to http://econapps.swlearning.com and click on the EconData icon. Look under the Macroeconomics heading and select the "Aggregate Demand/Aggregate Supply" link. You can find data on many topics that apply demand and supply concepts.

12

CHAPTER REVIEW

13

Employment

After reading Chapter 13 you should be able to:

1. Define *labor force* and describe its related concepts.
2. Recognize the changing trends in the labor force.
3. Explain the purpose of the Employment Act of 1946.
4. Define the full-employment unemployment rate and differentiate between unemployment and underemployment.
5. Explain how the Full Employment and Balanced Growth Act of 1978 differs from the Employment Act of 1946.
6. Describe how increases in the federal minimum wage impact employment.

A definite relationship exists between the level of employment and the size of the GDP. When real GDP decreases, unemployment usually increases. In fact, as we shall see, unemployment may develop even when the GDP remains constant or increases moderately over an extended period of time. Unemployment is detrimental to the economy because it decreases incomes, which in turn reduces consumer spending, which further decreases demand and eventually GDP.

In referring to full employment previously, we were considering full employment of all productive resources. In this chapter, however, we are concerned primarily with employed and unemployed labor. In this sense, unemployment causes individual hardship to workers and their families. As Table 13–1 indicates, the United States has had periods of full employment and periods of widespread unemployment. In recent years the size of the labor force has grown, making the problem of maintaining full employment more complex.

The Labor Force

Customarily, our labor force consists of between 45 and 50 percent of our total population. This percentage seems to be the norm for industrial nations throughout the world. However, the size of the labor force is limited by definition. Many individuals who work just as much as do those in the labor force are excluded from it because of the nature of their work or because they receive no payment for it.

SIZE AND COMPOSITION OF THE LABOR FORCE

To understand the problem of maintaining full employment, let us look more closely at our labor force and our population. In 2002, the United States had a total population of 287 million. Of this total, 214 million fell into the category of noninstitutional population, that is, all persons 16 years of age or older, including members of the resident armed forces, but excluding persons in prisons and mental institutions.

Total Labor Force

Total Labor Force
All persons in the noninstitutional population who are either working or seeking work.

The **total labor force** consists of all persons in the noninstitutional population who are either working or seeking work. Thus, it includes the unemployed as well as the employed. It also includes proprietors, the self-employed, and members of the resident armed forces. However, it excludes persons under the age of 16, members of the armed forces stationed overseas, persons engaged in unpaid work (less than 15 hours per week) in a family business, and persons engaged exclusively in housework in their homes or in attending school. Thus, students as such are not members of the labor force. If they work or look for work during the summer vacation period, however, they become members of the labor force for that time. Likewise, when they graduate, they generally become members of the labor force.

Civilian Labor Force

Civilian Labor Force
All persons in the total labor force except members of the resident armed forces.

Labor Force Participation Rate
The civilian labor force expressed as a percentage of the civilian noninstitutional population.

Employed Labor Force
All employed workers, including persons who did not work at all during the census week because of illness, bad weather, vacation, or labor disputes.

By definition, the **civilian labor force** consists of all persons in the total labor force except members of the resident armed forces. In 2002, the civilian labor force was 142 million. The **labor force participation rate** describes the civilian labor force as a percentage of the civilian noninstitutional population. It indicates what portion of the eligible population is in the labor force. Table 13–1 shows that over 66 percent of the civilian noninstitutional population was in the labor force in 2002.

The **employed labor force** consists of all employed workers, including persons who did not work at all during the census week because of illness, bad weather, vacation, or labor disputes. It includes part-time as well as full-time workers. In 2002, the number of employed was 134 million, (3 million in agricultural work and 131 million in nonagricultural employment). Nonagricultural employment included 3.7 million people who were working part-time.

	TABLE 13-1 Population, Civilian Labor Force, and Unemployment			
Year	Noninstitutional Population (Millions)*	Civilian Labor Force (Millions)	Participation Rate (%)	Unemployment Rate (%)
1933	NA	51.6	NA	24.9
1940	99.8	55.6	55.7	14.6
1945	94.0	53.9	57.2	1.9
1950	105.0	62.2	59.2	5.3
1960	117.2	69.6	59.4	5.5
1970	137.1	82.7	60.4	4.9
1980	167.7	106.9	63.8	7.1
1990	189.2	125.8	66.5	5.6
1997	203.1	136.2	67.0	4.7
1998	205.2	137.6	67.1	4.3
1999	207.7	139.4	67.1	4.2
2000	209.7	140.9	67.2	4.0
2001	211.8	141.9	66.9	4.8
2002	213.9	142.5	66.6	5.8

*Includes resident armed forces.
Sources: *Economic Report of the President* (2003) and Bureau of Labor Statistics.

Unemployed Labor Force
All persons in the labor force who are not currently working but are actively seeking work.

The **unemployed labor force** includes all persons in the labor force who are not currently working, but *are actively seeking work*. In 2002, 8.4 million members of the civilian labor force (5.8 percent) were unemployed.

Approximately 74 million persons in the noninstitutional population were not in the total labor force. The largest part of this group is unpaid full-time homemakers. Although homemakers certainly work hard and provide extremely valuable services, they are not included in the labor force. Another portion of those not in the labor force are students in high school, college, or elsewhere. Another sizable group is made up of people who are unable to work, usually for health reasons. The remainder includes retirees, individuals who do not want to work, and individuals who do not have to work. There is an important group of people who are not in the labor force because they have become discouraged at not finding employment and are not currently seeking jobs. People not seeking jobs are not counted as being in the labor force.

TRENDS IN THE LABOR FORCE AND IN EMPLOYMENT

The U.S. labor force has definite characteristics, but some of these characteristics have changed over time. Some of the most pronounced trends that have developed in the labor force in recent decades include the following.

Older Workers

The percentage of the civilian labor force made up of people 65 years old and over has decreased over the last 30 years. This decrease is the result of the growth and expansion of Social Security and private pensions. Today, the participation rate of males 65 years and over is about 19 percent, compared with about 27 percent in 1970. The participation rate for females 65 years and over is close to 10 percent. In recent years, participation rates of men and women 65 years of age and older has leveled off. Legislation restricting compulsory retirement, changes in Social Security benefits, and longer and healthier life expectancies of both men and women have affected the downward trend in participation rates. Many senior citizens are employed or are seeking employment as part-time workers.

Female Workers

NETLink

After reading about the changing trends in the labor force, examine the *Statistical Abstracts of the United States*. What trends do you see in the employment status of women?

http://www.census.gov/statab/www/

The number and percentage of women in the U.S. labor force have increased. The participation rate for women has grown significantly over the years since World War II. Increased employment of women in service industries and light manufacturing (occupations in which women historically had been employed) has led the way to increased demand for female labor throughout the United States. In addition, equal employment opportunity laws have resulted in a continuing increase in the number of women at the managerial and professional levels. Currently, about 46 percent of the employed civilian labor force consists of women. Approximately 60 percent of all women in the noninstitutional population are members of the labor force. In 2002, both the husband and the wife were employed in 53 percent of all married-couple families. Figure 13–1 presents information about the composition of the labor force according to sex. The changing role of women in the labor force over the past few decades can be seen by the fact that women are comprising a growing share of the labor force. This trend is expected to continue at least through the year 2006.

Skilled and Unskilled Workers

The percentage of unskilled laborers in the U.S. labor force has decreased because the number of unskilled jobs has decreased. Workers have had to learn how to operate complex machinery and equipment. As a result, the percentage of semi-skilled workers has increased, while the percentage of skilled workers has remained relatively constant. The U.S. labor force has also experienced substantial increases in the percentage of professional and technical workers (which consist primarily of skilled and semiskilled workers) and an increase in the percentage of clerical workers.

Service-Oriented Jobs

Another pronounced trend in employment is the growing number and percentage of service-oriented jobs. Today, approximately 50 percent of our total output is in

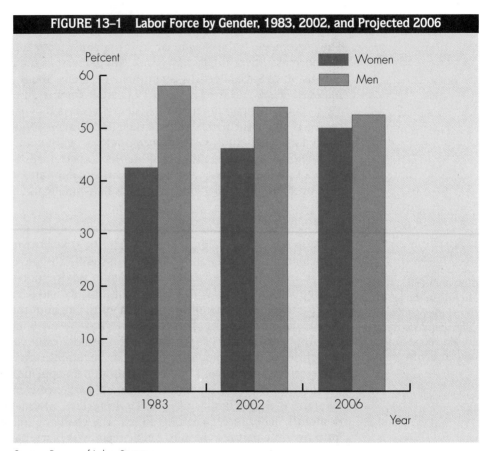

FIGURE 13–1   Labor Force by Gender, 1983, 2002, and Projected 2006

Source: Bureau of Labor Statistics.

the form of services. The demand for workers in goods-producing industries, such as manufacturing, construction, and mining, is declining, while the demand for workers in service-producing industries is growing in both absolute and relative terms. Today, only 19 percent of all nonagricultural workers are engaged in the production of goods, as compared with 34 percent in 1970. On the other hand, the percentage of workers in service-producing industries has risen from 66 to 81 percent during the same period. This trend can be observed in Table 13–2. The services category includes workers in the recreation and travel industry, in financial services, in the medical and legal professions, and in certain educational services.

Agricultural Employment

There has been a definite move away from agricultural occupations. As a result of increased productivity, we produce more and more agricultural commodities with fewer and fewer agricultural workers. In 1930, for example, 10.3 million agricul-

TABLE 13–2 Percentages of Nonagricultural Employees in Goods-Producing and Service-Producing Industries				
Industry	1970	1980	1990	2002
Goods-producing				
Manufacturing	27	22	17	13
Construction and mining	7	6	6	6
Total Goods-producing	34	28	23	19
Service-producing				
Transportation and public utilities	6	6	5	5
Wholesale and retail trade	21	22	24	23
Finance, insurance, and real estate	5	6	6	6
Services	16	20	25	31
Government	18	18	17	16
Total Service-producing	66	72	77	81

Source: *Economic Indicators* and Bureau of Labor Statistics.

tural workers provided food for 122 million Americans. Today, 3.1 million agricultural workers provide more than enough food for nearly 290 million Americans. Thus, less than one-third the number of agricultural workers needed in 1930 are feeding over twice as many people, and the United States remains the world's largest agricultural exporter.

Although direct employment in agriculture is relatively small, millions of other people are employed indirectly in the manufacture of farm equipment and supplies or in the processing and selling of food and other agricultural commodities.

Organized Workers

A substantial increase occurred in the number and percentage of organized workers in the labor force between 1935 and 1955. For a few decades, labor union membership remained fairly stable at about one-fourth of the total labor force. Since 1970, however, union membership has decreased as a percentage of the civilian labor force. This stabilization and then decline have resulted largely from the fact that, in percentage terms, the labor force has been declining in occupations where workers traditionally have been organized, such as the unskilled, semiskilled, and craft occupations. The increase in the labor force has been primarily in professional, technical, sales, clerical, and other white-collar occupations not traditionally organized by labor unions.

A dramatic drop in union membership occurred between 1980 and 1984. During that time, the organized labor movement lost 2.7 million members. This accompanied a severe drop in employment in the durable-goods-producing and transportation industries, which are highly organized. Competition from imports caused job losses in auto, steel, appliance, and other heavy industries. Moreover, the movement of some firms from highly unionized areas of the country to less unionized areas contributed to the decline in union membership. Government deregulation of transportation brought competition from increased numbers of nonunionized firms. Widespread layoffs and job terminations in these industries also occurred during the early 1990s as many industries downsized and restructured. After 14 years of decline, the number of union members in the United States increased in 1993 and again in 1994 according to the Labor Department. Since 1994, however, union membership has resumed its steady decline. Union membership now totals 16 million wage and salary workers and accounts for approximately 14 percent of all such workers.

Today, 40 percent of all government employees are unionized compared to but 9 percent of private sector employees. Local government has the highest unionization rate with 43 percent of all workers organized. Unionization at the local government level reflects the heavy concentration of occupations traditionally unionized, such as teachers, police officers, and firefighters. Half of all union members live in six states—California, New York, Illinois, Michigan, Ohio, and Pennsylvania.

Diversity

As our nation's population becomes more diverse, so too does the labor force. In addition to women accounting for a relatively larger share of the labor force, Hispanics, blacks, and Asians are also growing in number. Figure 13–2 presents the distribution of the labor force by race in 1996, along with the projection for 2010. The figure indicates that non-Hispanic white members will continue as the largest component of the labor force, although their share has been declining and is expected to fall from 75 percent in 1996 to 69 percent in 2010. Despite their declining share of the labor force, whites will experience the largest numerical increase of any racial group. The relative share of the labor force held by blacks is expected to increase by 1 percent over the period, whereas Hispanics are expected to show a growth rate of approximately 65 percent by 2010. But because Hispanics' share of the labor force is still relatively small, this increase translates into only a 3 percent gain (from 10 percent to 13 percent). The smallest component of the racial groups presented by the Bureau of Labor Statistics is that of Asians and other minorities, a group that comprises about 6 percent of the labor force.

Types of Unemployment

Frictional Unemployment
Unemployment that arises from normal operation of the labor market—job terminations by employees, discharges, or relocation.

There are several categories of unemployment. **Frictional unemployment** is due to workers being temporarily between jobs or new entrants to the labor force. Workers are constantly being hired, being fired, quitting, leaving the labor force to return to school or receive special training, taking time off from entering or reentering the labor force to search for the right job, and relocating (often interstate) from one job to another. Frictional unemployment is usually short term.

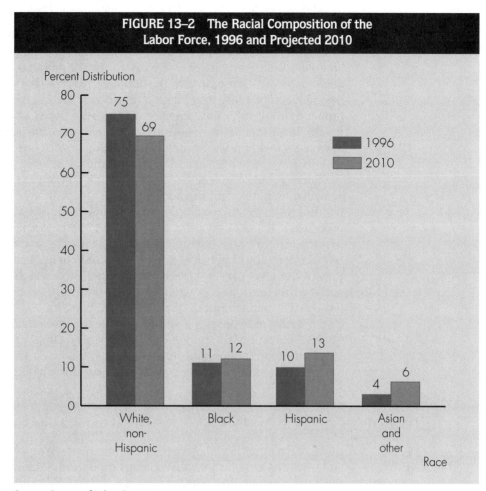

FIGURE 13–2   The Racial Composition of the Labor Force, 1996 and Projected 2010

Source: Bureau of Labor Statistics.

Cyclical Unemployment
Unemployment that arises from less than full use of productive capacity in an economy due to a recession or depression.

Structural Unemployment
Unemployment caused by an imbalance between the skills possessed by workers and the skills demanded in the labor markets.

Cyclical unemployment is the result of a decline in the level of total output, usually due to a recession. It is traceable to insufficient aggregate demand in the economy. If the aggregate demand can be strengthened by an increase in consumption, investment, or government spending, the level of output can be increased and the cyclical unemployment perhaps reduced. Much of the rise in unemployment associated with the recessions over the past 20 years was cyclical in nature. Cyclical unemployment may be short or long term, depending on the length of the recession.

Structural unemployment is caused by an imbalance between the skills possessed by workers and the skills demanded in the labor markets. Structural unemployment tends to be long term. Some experts argue that a substantial portion of our present unemployment is structural, insofar as we have an imperfect adaptation of workers to jobs. In short, unemployed workers are often unqualified to fill available job openings. For example, workers may be rapidly displaced because of technological development and automation. The need for new skills arises, and old skills are no longer as important (or the demand for them is no longer as great) as before. Consequently, the displaced workers—nearly 2 million annually—have difficulty finding new jobs. Some workers are unemployed because they lack proper training; others are unemployed because they lack the geographic mobility to take advantage of job opportunities. Some groups have suggested that we ought to expect a higher rate of structural unemployment in our growing, dynamic economy than we have been accustomed to in the recent past.

Some people also feel that some unemployment is a consequence of subsidies provided by public and private socioeconomic programs. One source of induced unemployment is the unemployment compensation system in the United States. Although it serves as an automatic stabilizer and has many other benefits, the system tends to increase unemployment. In many cases the minimal difference between unemployed persons' unemployment benefits and what they may be able to earn from working at other jobs may deter their search for new jobs. This is especially true in situations where laid-off workers, such as those in the auto industry, receive supplementary unemployment benefits (SUB) from their employers. Unemployment benefits, plus SUB, provide the workers with an income equal to 90 to 95 percent of their regular take-home pay. Other programs, such as welfare payments, food stamps, and rent subsidies, can cause a similar upward bias on the rate or duration of cyclical and even structural unemployment.

The Employment Act of 1946

It was feared that trouble would arise after World War II when veterans returned and began looking for jobs. Lawmakers thought that many wartime entrants into the labor force would hesitate to leave, which would result in a surplus labor force as the veterans returned, especially with the decline of war production. Many women, however, left their factories and offices to manage their homes. In addition, young people reluctantly returned to school, and elderly citizens also left the labor force. Nevertheless, the civilian labor force did rise by 6.5 million within two years after World War II.

Some economists and government officials anticipated that we might have between 6 and 8 million unemployed workers in 1946, mainly because of the termination of wartime industries. However, the economy made a quick transition from wartime to peacetime production. Even though government defense spending decreased by more than $50 billion from 1945 to 1946, the slack was taken up by massive consumer spending, expanded business investments, and strong foreign demand for our products. As a result, the GDP fell only moderately in 1946. Unemployment averaged 2.3 million for the year and never exceeded 4 million in any month.

Still, the fear that widespread depression and chronic unemployment might recur with the cessation of war production spurred the passage of the Employment Act of 1946. With the long and deep depression of the 1930s fresh in their minds, many individuals, organizations, and public officials supported the act, which was introduced shortly after the end of World War II.

PURPOSE OF THE EMPLOYMENT ACT

In its original form, the Full Employment Bill would have made the government directly responsible for maintaining full employment and would have mandated a planned federal budget designed to take up any employment slack in the economy. However, those provisions were not enacted. Instead, the Employment Act of 1946 merely declared that it was the government's policy to use the measures at its disposal to promote maximum production, employment, and purchasing power. Section 2 of the act reads:

> *The Congress hereby declares that it is the continuing policy and responsibility of the Federal Government to use all practicable means consistent with its needs and obligations and other essential considerations of national policy, with assistance and cooperation of industry, agriculture, labor and State and local governments, to coordinate and utilize all its plans, functions, and resources for the purpose of creating and maintaining, in a manner calculated to foster and promote free competitive enterprise and the general welfare, conditions under which there will be afforded useful employment opportunities, including self-employment, for those able, willing, and seeking work, and to promote maximum employment, production, and purchasing power.*

The Employment Act of 1946 also set up a Council of Economic Advisers (CEA), to be appointed by the president with the advice and consent of the Senate. Specifically, it is the function of the Council of Economic Advisers to develop and recommend to the president national economic policies to foster and promote free competitive enterprise; to avoid economic fluctuations or to diminish the effects thereof; and to maintain employment, production, and purchasing power. The CEA also analyzes existing programs and activities of the federal government to determine whether they are consistent with the express purpose of the act, which is to maintain maximum employment. Another function of the council is to work with the president in preparing the *Economic Report of the President.*

MEANING OF FULL EMPLOYMENT

The Employment Act of 1946 says nothing about guaranteeing jobs, but it does oblige the government to take steps to maintain a high level of employment. Nowhere, however, does the act define the term *full employment.* In addressing this oversight, the 1953 *Economic Report of the President* stated specifically that under the Employment Act full employment means more than jobs. It means full utilization of our natural resources, our technology and science, our farms and factories, our business brains, and our trade skills.

We will always have some unemployment because of job terminations by employees, discharges, and relocations. Included in this group are people who are chronically unemployed because of certain mental or physical disabilities. In the late 1950s, a number of organizations, committees, and government agencies studying the problem of unemployment concluded that the amount of this normal unemployment should be about 4 percent of the total civilian labor force.

In the early 1970s, various authorities suggested that our full-employment standard of 96 percent employment and 4 percent unemployment was outmoded. The structure of the labor force was changing, and these experts argued that a new unemployment figure might be more appropriate as a measure of full employment. The labor force had come to include larger numbers of young people, women, and minority workers than before, and these groups have usually had higher rates of unemployment than the labor force as a whole. Consequently, if more weight were given to these categories in establishing a normal unemployment figure, the current rate would be perhaps 4.5 to 5 percent. Thus, a 4.6 percent figure was suggested in the 1974 *Economic Report of the President,* and a 5.1 percent rate was used as a benchmark in the 1979 *Economic Report.* Today, government economists and others generally agree that 5 percent is an acceptable **full-employment unemployment rate.** The full-employment unemployment rate is the rate of unemployment that can be expected from normal frictional unemployment in an otherwise fully employed economy. Unemployment rates from the period 1989–2002 are presented graphically in Figure 13–3. Using a 5 percent unemployment figure as the definition of full employment, the U.S. economy experienced full employment from 1997 through mid-2001. If, as in the Humphrey–Hawkins legislation (to be discussed later in this chapter), a 4 percent unemployment figure is used, only in 2000 did the economy reach full employment.

But unemployment rates have to be viewed with certain reservations. With any given unemployment rate, some categories of workers will be experiencing significantly higher unemployment rates than others. Table 13–3 indicates that in 2002, when unemployment was 5.8 percent, the unemployment rate among black workers was 10.7 percent and among teenagers it was 17.6 percent. On the other hand, unemployment among non-Hispanic white workers was only 5.2 percent and among married men with a spouse present only 4.1 percent. Thus, the average unemployment rate can mask a wide range of unemployment rates within various groups.

Not only is it important to hold unemployment to a minimum, it is also desirable to reduce underemployment. What is the difference between unemployment and underemployment? **Unemployment** occurs when workers are not employed at all. **Underemployment** occurs when a worker is employed but not working to full capacity. It is thus possible for the economy to be in a state of full employment and yet be underemployed. Such would be the case if large numbers of workers were employed in jobs that did not require their full skill or productivity. For example, situations occur in which engineers drive taxis, artists paint signs,

Full-Employment Unemployment Rate
The rate of unemployment that can be expected from normal frictional unemployment in an otherwise fully employed labor force.

Unemployment
A condition in which workers in the labor force are not currently working at all.

Underemployment
A condition in which a worker in the labor force is employed but not working to full capacity.

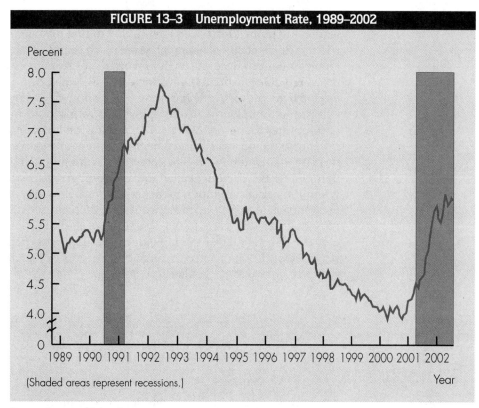

FIGURE 13–3   Unemployment Rate, 1989–2002

Percent

(Shaded areas represent recessions.)   Year

Source: Bureau of Labor Statistics.

TABLE 13–3   Unemployment Rates for Various Categories of Workers

Category	Unemployment Rates 2002*
Married men, spouse present	4.1%
Adult male	6.1
Adult females	5.7
Women who maintain families	8.2
White workers (non-Hispanic)	5.2
Black workers	10.7
Hispanics	7.4
All teenagers	17.6
Full-time workers	6.1
Part-time workers	5.0
Total civilian labor force	5.8

*Preliminary.
Source: Bureau of Labor Statistics.

mechanics sweep floors, or skilled secretaries do filing work. Annually, many individuals are trained for skilled jobs but fail to find job openings. Often, college graduates with tremendous potential never reach their full productive capacity. Underemployment can occur also when workers for some reason or another (such as a recession) do not work a full work week. Although much has been done to prevent unemployment, very little has been done nationwide to reduce underemployment.

The full-employment unemployment rate should not be confused with the natural rate of unemployment. The **natural rate of unemployment** corresponds roughly to the sum of frictional unemployment and structural unemployment. It is the rate that would occur if the economy were producing at its full potential. The natural rate is sometimes called the *inflation threshold rate of unemployment* because when the actual unemployment rate drops below the natural rate, inflationary pressures build up in the economy. As a result, labor markets tighten and employers face greater pressure to raise wages in order to keep or obtain qualified workers. The natural rate of unemployment is subject to change with changes in the structure of the labor force. A surge of teenagers or unskilled workers into the labor force, for example, could cause it to rise.

Natural Rate of Unemployment
The rate of unemployment that would occur if the economy were producing at its full potential.

The Full Employment and Balanced Growth Act of 1978 (Humphrey–Hawkins Act)

After nearly a year of debate, revision, and compromise, Congress enacted the controversial Humphrey–Hawkins Bill under the official title of the Full Employment and Balanced Growth Act of 1978. This act amended and embellished the Employment Act of 1946. In particular, it included specific numerical targets and timetables regarding full-employment and inflation rates.

The Humphrey–Hawkins Act was broader in coverage than the Employment Act of 1946. Instead of calling for maximum production, employment, and purchasing power, the act established goals of full employment and production, plus increased real income, balanced growth, a balanced federal budget, and reasonable price stability. The Humphrey–Hawkins Act also required the president to spell out in the *Economic Report* measures designed to accomplish the objectives of the act.

For example, the act set a goal of 3 percent or less unemployment among adult workers (20 years of age or older) and 4 percent unemployment for the total labor force by the end of 1983. It also required that the rate of inflation be reduced to at least 3 percent by that same time. In directing the federal government to achieve these goals, the act gave some preference to full employment, stating that "the policies and programs designed to reduce the rate of inflation shall not impede the achievement of the goals for the reduction of unemployment." The long-term goal for reasonable price stability was to reduce the rate of inflation to zero by 1988. Subsequently, the target date for full employment was postponed indefinitely.

According to the act, a balanced budget and balanced economic growth are to be sought after the goals regarding unemployment have been reached. Moreover, the act calls for a narrowing of the differences in unemployment rates among various categories of the unemployed.

Two major items included in the original Humphrey–Hawkins Bill did not survive to be included in the final Full Employment and Balanced Growth Act of 1978. First was the concept of using the federal government as an "employer of last resort" for the unemployed if unemployment were not reduced to target levels within the initial five-year period. This item would have required the federal government to provide or find jobs for the excess of unemployed who could not find work. The second item would have established a broad and specific planning system for the U.S. economy. The Humphrey–Hawkins Act expired in 2000, but one feature of the act remains. Twice each year, the Fed chairman delivers a report on the economy and monetary policy to Congress. While they are no longer officially Humphrey–Hawkins reports, they are colloquially called that.

Unemployment Rates in the United States and Elsewhere

At this point it may be informative to compare unemployment rates in the United States with those of several other developed countries. Figure 13-4 presents unemployment rates for April 2002 for seven countries. Because of stronger economic growth rates in the United States during the decade of the 1990s, unemployment was lower than in each of these nations except Japan.

Even in 2002, after more than a decade of experiencing an economic recession, deflation, and little in the way of economic growth, Japan's unemployment rate remained below that of the United States. There are several differences in the definitions of unemployment between Japan and the United States, but after adjustment of the Japanese data for these differences, the resulting rates are about the same as the published rates. Many of these differences are the result of different customs and traditions. For example, large numbers of Japanese women who are temporary or casual workers withdraw from the labor force when they lose their jobs rather than becoming unemployed. Such workers generally bear the brunt of labor market adjustments in Japan. In this way, Japanese employers have some degree of flexibility in their workforces during economic recessions, enabling regular workers, predominantly men in larger Japanese enterprises, to be virtually assured of employment until they retire. Although lifelong employment is no longer universally assured, the tradition remains in many Japanese industries.

In Europe, many European Union members have had to make difficult, but necessary, adjustments in monetary and fiscal policies to be in compliance with European Monetary Union rules. These adjustments have proven difficult in light of

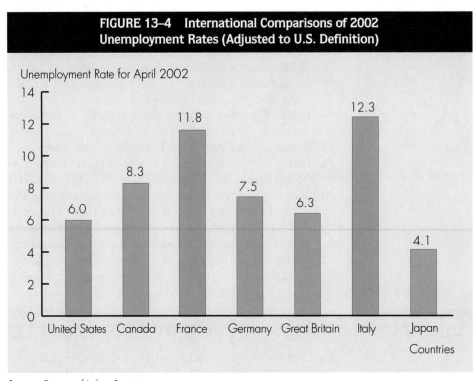

FIGURE 13–4   International Comparisons of 2002
Unemployment Rates (Adjusted to U.S. Definition)

Source: Bureau of Labor Statistics.

the long-standing regulations on wage negotiations, working hours, part-time employment, and worker dismissal. European nations, as well as Canada, also have very generous unemployment insurance systems. Hence, Germany, Italy, and France have had unemployment rates appreciably higher than that of the United States for the past 20 years.

Varying degrees of labor mobility is another factor accounting for the differences in unemployment rates among countries. The United States has an extraordinarily mobile labor force. In 2000, the Census Department reported that 41 million U.S. residents moved to a new home. Sixteen percent of these moves were work related. The percentage of people who moved for work-related reasons increased in tandem with their educational level and many were moves of long distance. The same can be said for occupational mobility. In the United States, it is not uncommon for individuals to work for a number of employers during their worklife. Many of these jobs require different skills and experiences. This degree of mobility is absent in many European countries where one's work experience may be limited to but one job in one locale. The loss of one's job may result in lifetime unemployment, supported by generous unemployment insurance.

Minimum Wage and Employment

A public policy issue that is politically controversial and impacts a large number of young people in the labor force is the federally mandated minimum wage. Although it is commonly viewed as simply a wage issue, one of its more controversial aspects is the impact the minimum-wage law has on employment in general and teenage employment in particular.

In 1996, Congress raised the federal hourly minimum wage rate from $4.25 to $5.15. This 90-cent increase was implemented in two steps, with the final 40-cent hike occurring in 1997. The purpose of the minimum wage is to provide a floor for the payment for labor services and to ensure workers of a decent standard of living.

The United States has had a federal minimum-wage law since 1938, with the passage of the Fair Labor Standards Act. The 1938 law set the minimum wage at 25 cents per hour. Since that time, Congress has amended the act numerous times in order to increase the minimum-wage rate. The implicit goal associated with these periodic minimum-wage adjustments is to maintain the purchasing power of the wage. But, despite these wage adjustments, there has been a decline in the purchasing power of the minimum wage.

Because most working Americans earn more than the minimum hourly wage, relatively few are directly affected by changes in the law. Those who are affected tend to be found in low-wage industries, such as in the service and retail sectors. Minimum-wage workers are primarily women, part-time workers, and a disproportionate number of minorities. Classified by age, teenagers account for 31 percent of all minimum-wage workers, and it is this group of workers who are at the center of the minimum-wage controversy.

The minimum wage is a form of price support in that it creates and maintains a wage higher than the impersonal forces of supply and demand would establish. If the minimum wage is not higher than the market wage, then the minimum wage serves no purpose. Figure 13–5 graphically shows the effects of the minimum wage on employment. Assume the supply and demand for entry-level and unskilled workers results in a market wage of W_e and an employment level of Q_e. The minimum wage, W_m, is above the market wage, with the result being that a gap exists between the quantity of labor demanded at the minimum wage and the quantity supplied at that wage. Because the supply of workers exceeds the demand for workers, the effect of the minimum wage is to create a labor surplus of $Q_d - Q_s$. Figure 13–5 indicates that the minimum wage will result in layoffs equal to $Q_d - Q_e$ and attract additional entrants seeking the work at the higher wage, $Q_e - Q_s$ (law of supply), but who now become unemployed members of the labor force.

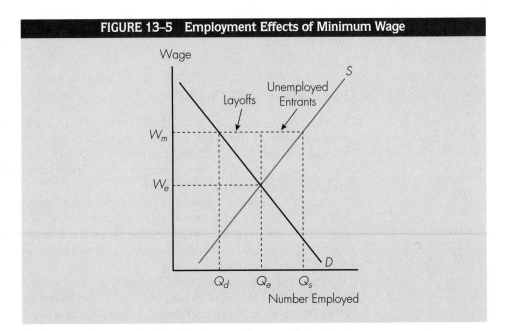

FIGURE 13–5   Employment Effects of Minimum Wage

Increases in the minimum wage benefit workers who maintain their jobs, but the net effect is a loss of jobs. Empirical studies support this conclusion, despite problems distinguishing the effects of the minimum wage per se from other developments in the economy. One such study conducted by the congressionally mandated Minimum Wage Study Commission in 1981 concluded that an increase of 10 percent in the minimum wage reduces teenage employment by 1 to 3 percent. Additional studies conducted in the late 1990s also support this conclusion. If so, the increase in the minimum wage from $4.25 to $5.15 per hour has eliminated between 130,000 and 400,000 jobs.

Not everyone agrees, however, that a reduction in teenage employment is an inevitable result of increases in the minimum wage. Supporters of higher minimum-wage levels contend that as long as any single minimum-wage hike is not too high, there is no resulting decline in employment. The impact on employment also depends on the level of the minimum wage prior to an increase. For example, they would argue that the current hourly minimum wage of $5.15 is low enough to comfortably sustain an increase to $6.15 without causing unemployment. To eliminate future difficulties with increasing the minimum wage and to protect the purchasing power of minimum-wage workers, they support indexing future increases in the minimum wage to changes in the Consumer Price Index or changes in the average annual wage rate. Congress is reluctant to index the minimum wage for a number of reasons, not the least of which is the uncertain effects of indexing on employment.

Future Employment

This chapter has presented an overview of employment, the labor force, and unemployment. Of particular concern to students today are the opportunities for employment in the years ahead and the expected earnings associated with various occupations. This section will focus on expected changes in the labor force and employment opportunities.

The primary source of information on future trends in the labor force and employment is the Bureau of Labor Statistics. In a recent study, the bureau has projected labor force and employment trends forward to the year 2010. The study indicates that total employment will increase to 168 million in 2010, a 15 percent increase from the 146 million in 2000. The 22 million jobs that will be added to the economy over this period will not be distributed evenly across major industrial and occupational groups.

Professional and professionally related occupations, along with service occupations, will grow the fastest and add the most jobs by 2010. These occupational groups, although situated at opposite ends of the educational attainment and earnings spectrum, are expected to provide more than half the entire job growth over the period.

In the professional and professionally related occupational category, nearly 75 percent of the job growth is projected for three subcategories—computer and mathematical occupations; health care practitioners and technical occupations; and education, training, and library occupations.

The demand for computer-related jobs will continue to increase as a result of the rapid advances in computer technology and the continuing demand for computer applications, including those on the Internet. Health care practitioners and technical occupations are also expected to grow rapidly. The growth in this sector can be attributed to an aging population, which will continue to require increased medical technology as well as greater health care services. Registered nurses continue to show the most potential for job growth, but the number of self-employed health professionals is expected to decline as more individuals join group practices. Another industry expected to benefit from increased population is the education industry. Rising enrollments are anticipated for elementary, secondary, and postsecondary schools. Employment in the education industry will provide employment not only for teachers but for teacher aides, counselors, and administrators as well.

The service sector is expected to show the second-highest growth rate among major occupational groups, reflecting the continuing shift from a goods-producing economy to a services-producing economy. More than 30 percent of the job growth in the service occupation group will be created in retail trade, particularly at eating and drinking establishments. The number of jobs in the health care support category of services is also expected to grow rapidly.

TABLE 13–4   Occupations with the Fastest Growth in Total Employment, 2000–2010 Projected

Occupation	EMPLOYMENT		CHANGE		Quartile rank by 2000 median annual earnings[1]	Most significant source of education or training
	2000	2010	Number	Percent		
Computer software engineers, applications	380	760	380	100	1	Bachelor's degree
Computer support specialists	506	996	490	97	2	Associate degree
Computer software engineers, systems software	317	601	284	90	1	Bachelor's degree
Network and computer systems administrators	229	416	187	82	1	Bachelor's degree
Network systems and data communications analysts	119	211	92	77	1	Bachelor's degree
Desktop publishers	38	63	25	67	2	Postsecondary vocational award
Database administrators	106	176	70	66	1	Bachelor's degree
Personal and home-care aides	414	672	258	62	4	Short-term on-the-job training
Computer systems analysts	431	689	258	60	1	Bachelor's degree
Medical assistants	329	516	187	57	3	Moderate-term on-the-job training
Social and human service assistants	271	418	147	54	3	Moderate-term on-the-job training
Physician assistants	58	89	31	53	1	Bachelor's degree
Medical records and health information technicans	136	202	166	49	3	Associate degree
Computer and information systems managers	313	463	150	48	1	Bachelor's or higher degree, plus work experience
Home health aides	615	907	291	47	4	Short-term on-the-job training
Physical therapist aides	36	53	17	46	3	Short-term on-the-job training
Occupational therapist aides	9	12	4	45	3	Short-term on-the-job training
Physical therapist assistants	44	64	20	45	2	Associate degree
Audiologists	13	19	6	45	1	Master's degree
Fitness trainers and aerobics instruction	158	222	64	40	3	Postsecondary vocational award

[1]The quartile rankings of Occupational Employment Statistics annual earnings data are presented in the following categories: 1 = very high ($39,700 and over), 2 = high ($25,760 to $39,699), 3 = low ($18,500 to $25,760), and 4 = very low (up to $18,490). The rankings were based on quartiles using one-fourth of total employment to define each quartile. Earnings are for wage and salary workers.
Source: U.S. Department of Labor.

Table 13-4 shows the 20 individual occupations with the fastest projected employment growth rates from 2000 to 2010. In addition to projecting employment opportunities for occupations, the Bureau of Labor Statistics has separated out individual occupations by earnings potential. Not all of these occupations are associated with strong earnings potential. Of the 20 occupations presented, 9 offer average earnings in the highest quartile ($39,700 and over), while 5 are concentrated in the second quartile ($25,760 to $39,669), and 6 are in the third quartile ($18,500 to $27,760). None are in the fourth quartile, which includes occupations with average earnings below $18,500. In examining the table, you can see that half of the fastest-growing occupations are computer related. Of the remaining occupations, most are health related. All but 6 require a postsecondary degree or award.

Summary

- The labor force is defined in terms of the total number of people who work or are seeking work, including members of the resident armed forces. Related concepts include the civilian labor force, the labor force participation rate, the employed labor force, and the unemployed labor force.

- The changing trends in the labor force include older workers (the percentage has decreased), female workers (an increase in the number and percentage), skilled and unskilled workers (the percentage of unskilled laborers has decreased), service-oriented jobs (a definite increase in the number and percentage), agricultural employment (a move away from agricultural occupations), and union membership (a decrease), as well as a continuous increase in the size of the labor force

- The purpose of the Employment Act of 1946 was to ensure the government's policy of using the measures at its disposal to promote maximum production, employment, and purchasing power

- The role of the President's Council of Economic Advisers is to study the economy in light of the objectives of the Employment Act and to make reports and recommendations to the president of the United States, who is required to transmit an annual Economic Report to Congress. The president also recommends to Congress, based on information received from the CEA, a program to promote a high level of employment.

- The full-employment unemployment rate is the rate of unemployment that can be expected from normal unemployment (job terminations by employees, discharges, relocations, and chronically unemployed people because of their mental or physical handicaps) in an otherwise fully employed labor force. Unemployment refers to workers in the labor force currently not working at all; underemployment refers to workers in the labor force who are employed but are not working to full capacity, such as recent college graduates hired to do fairly routine or menial work.

- The Full Employment and Balanced Growth Act of 1978 differs from the Employment Act of 1946 in that it is much broader in coverage. It established specific unemployment and inflation rate goals for the nation's economy, and it required that measures be taken to reduce adult unemployment to 3 percent and total unemployment to 4 percent, and to reduce the inflation rate to 3 percent annually by 1983.

- An ongoing important public policy issue affecting employment is the federal hourly minimum wage, which in 1997 was raised to $5.15. Although retained workers benefit from the higher wage rate, the general view is that increases in the minimum wage create unemployment.

New Terms and Concepts

Total labor force
Civilian labor force
Labor force participation rate
Employed labor force
Unemployed labor force
Frictional unemployment

Cyclical unemployment
Structural unemployment
Full-employment unemployment rate
Unemployment
Underemployment
Natural rate of unemployment

Discussion Questions

1. Why are homemakers not included as members of the labor force? Should they be included?

2. Should everyone who is seeking work be classified as an unemployed member of the labor force? Explain.

3. Should there be a nationwide compulsory retirement age to increase opportunities for young people coming into the labor force? Why or why not?

4. Should unemployed persons whose spouses are still working be counted as unemployed as far as our national employment figures are concerned? Why or why not?

5. Technological development and automation displace more than 2 million workers annually. Does this mean that all these individuals become unemployed? Explain.

6. Would the Council of Economic Advisers function better if it were responsible to Congress, or if it were an independent agency, rather than being part of the president's administration? Why or why not?

7. Should the federal government act as "employer of last resort," as stated in the original Humphrey–Hawkins Bill? Why or why not?

8. Some commentators have suggested that we should consider the economy to be at full employment as long as job vacancies are equal to or greater than unemployment. Do you agree? Explain.

9. Is 4.0 percent unemployment a sustainable goal? Why or why not?

10. Should the federal hourly minimum wage be indexed to the CPI to maintain its value?

Economic Applications

EconDebate

For some interesting debates on employment issues, go to http://econapps.swlearning.com and click on the EconDebate icon. Find the Macroeconomics heading and click on "Employment, Unemployment, and Inflation." This link leads to a variety of hot topic debates on employment.

CHAPTER REVIEW

13

14

Income Distribution

After studying Chapter 14, you should be able to:

1. Describe the distribution of income in the United States.
2. Understand the use of the Lorenz curve and the Gini coefficient as measures of income inequality.
3. Analyze the causes of income inequality.
4. Compare equal and equitable distributions of income.
5. Define *poverty* and indicate the incidence of poverty in the United States.
6. Describe the current status and future challenges facing the welfare system.

Prosperity in the 1990s lifted the wealth and incomes of most American households. Unemployment, poverty rates, and the number of people on welfare fell as a result of the sustained economic growth during the decade. Along with high- and middle-income households, incomes of those at the bottom of the pay scale accelerated as well. This welcomed outcome served to quell criticism of income inequality.

Although evidence shows that the incomes of the poor and middle classes did increase, their share of the total money income received in the United States continues to decrease. Thus, although the poor and middle classes are not getting poorer, the rich have gotten much richer. There are a number of causes for the existing income inequality, some of which can be attributed to the economic rewards received by those employed in the New Economy. During the New Economy boom, every measure of income inequality got worse. Although many of the individual gains derived from the excesses of the 1990s have dissipated as a result of bankruptcies, unemployment, the stock market crash, and smaller increases in income, the New Economy has created a powerful force for the accumulation of wealth and higher incomes. High-level executive salaries, stock options, and the appreciation of equity holdings have resulted in an unprecedented number of millionaires. Consequently, the income and wealth gaps between the rich and everyone else are getting larger. Those working in the Old Economy did not enjoy anything like these gains.

Although information in this chapter supports the view that inequality is increasing, the inherent time lag associated with the use of government statistics hides the full effects of growing disparities. This is particularly true of statistics pertaining to the accumulation of wealth. It should be noted that income inequality is not a bad thing per se, as long as economic growth is strong and poverty is low. The gap between rich and poor must also be perceived as being in accordance with the norms of fairness and social justice. These norms were violated in those cases where corporate CEOs committed unmitigated acts of fraud to enrich themselves at the expense of workers and investors. Public indignation and political reaction to these scandals have resulted in extensive debates about the subject of income inequality.

Individual, Family, and Household Income

Family
A group of two or more persons who live in the same dwelling and are related by birth, marriage, or adoption.

Household
Includes all persons, related or unrelated, who occupy a housing unit, including individuals living alone.

The Bureau of the Census collects and records figures for distribution of income based upon individuals, families, and households. A **family** is a group of two or more persons who live in the same dwelling and are related by birth, marriage, or adoption. A **household** includes all persons, related or unrelated, who occupy a housing unit. A person living alone is counted as a household. The U.S. median family income (the amount that one-half of all families receive less than and one-half of all families receive more than) in 2001 was $52,275 per year. The median income for households was $42,228.

DISTRIBUTION OF INCOME

Distribution of income refers to the way income is divided up among households or families. The Bureau of the Census presents the distribution of income by dividing all households into five income classes or quintiles, low to high, and indicating the percentage of total or aggregate income received by households in each quintile. Table 14–1 reveals some interesting facts about the distribution of income in 2001.

According to the Bureau of the Census, households in the lower income brackets received a relatively small percentage of total income. For example, households with incomes under $17,900 received only 3.5 percent of the nation's aggregate income. At the other extreme, households earning in excess of $83,500, the highest quintile, received 50 percent of total income. The table also shows that the top 5 percent of households garnered about 22 percent of aggregate income. Census data are somewhat incomplete in that they do not include noncash transfer benefits or include capital gains.

Figure 14–1 indicates that the relative distribution of income received by households in each of the first four quintiles has decreased between 1970 and

TABLE 14–1 Money Income of Households 2001 (Percentage of Aggregate Income Received by Each Fifth)		
	Money Income	Share of Aggregate Income
Lowest fifth	Under $17,900	3.5
Second fifth	$17,901–33,314	8.7
Middle fifth	$33,315–53,000	14.6
Fourth fifth	$53,001–83,500	23.1
Highest fifth	$83,501–and over	50.1
TOTAL		100.0
Top 5 percent (Over $150,499)		22.4

Source: U.S. Census Bureau, *Current Population Reports: Money Income in the United States: 2001.*

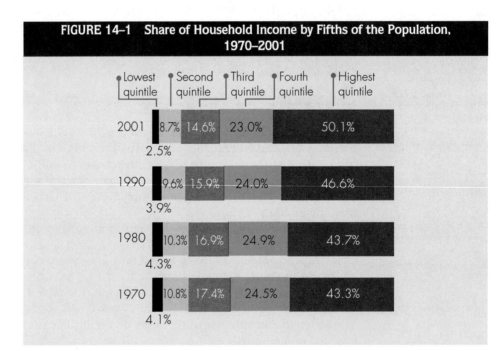

FIGURE 14–1   Share of Household Income by Fifths of the Population, 1970–2001

Source: U.S. Census Bureau. *Current Population Reports: Money Income in the United States: 2001*

2001, whereas the highest fifth has increased its share from 43 percent to 50 percent. Numbers such as these should leave little doubt as to the inequality of income in the United States.

LORENZ CURVE

Lorenz Curve
A graph that traces the percentage relationship between the portion of total income received and the portion of all households or families in the economy.

Economists often illustrate the distribution of income by using a graph called the Lorenz curve. A **Lorenz curve** traces the percentage relationship between the portion of total income received and the portion of all households or families in the economy. Figure 14–2 shows an economy with a perfectly equal distribution of income and the actual distribution of 2001 income in the United States. A perfectly equal distribution of income is represented by a diagonal line, since any given percentage of households receive the same percentage of income. On this diagonal line, 20 percent of the households receive 20 percent of the income, 40 percent receive 40 percent, 60 percent receive 60 percent, and so on. When incomes are not distributed equally, the Lorenz curve diverges from the 45-degree line of perfect equality. The greater the difference between the 45-degree line and the Lorenz curve is, the greater the inequality of income distribution. The Lorenz curve presented in Figure 14–2 is constructed from the information contained in Table 14–1.

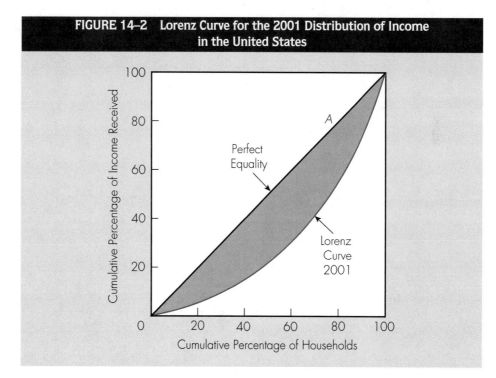

FIGURE 14–2   Lorenz Curve for the 2001 Distribution of Income in the United States

GINI COEFFICIENT

Gini Coefficient
An index that summarizes the inequality revealed by the Lorenz curve in a single number.

Another method of expressing the degree of income inequality is through the use of the Gini coefficient. The **Gini coefficient** index summarizes the inequality revealed by the Lorenz curve in a single number. The index is computed by dividing the area between lines *A* and *B* (the shaded area in Figure 14–2) by the total triangular area under line *A*. If income were distributed equally, the Lorenz curve (line *B*) would lie on top of line *A*. With only one line, the coefficient of the Gini index would equal 0. On the other hand, if a single household received all income, there would be maximum inequality. In this hypothetical case, the Lorenz curve would lie along the horizontal and vertical axes and look like a backward L. This would occur because none of the households would receive any income whatsoever until the last household, which would receive all of society's income. In this case, the Gini coefficient equals 1, because the areas between the Lorenz curve (*B*) and the line of perfect equality (*A*) and the area under the line of perfect equality are equal. Thus, the values of the Gini index range between 0 and 1, with larger values indicating greater inequality.

Coefficients of the Gini index for the 1969–2001 period are presented in Figure 14–3. The Gini coefficients shown in the figure indicate that the long-run

FIGURE 14–3   Gini Index, Household Income Distribution, 1969–2001

Source: U.S. Census Bureau. *Current Population Reports: Money Income in the United States: 2001.*

trend toward income inequality did not occur smoothly over the period. The trend was somewhat gradual from 1970 to 1979, but grew rapidly between 1979 and 1993, except during the recession years of 1990 and 1991. Since 1993, the Gini co-efficient increased each year except for 1995 and 1998, rising from 0.454 in 1993 to 0.466 in 2001.

INTERNATIONAL COMPARISON OF INCOME DISTRIBUTION

It may be informative at this point to compare the distribution of income in the United States with that of other nations. Figure 14–4, based on research conducted by the World Bank, compares the household income distribution of the United States to those of Sweden and Brazil. The Lorenz curve for Brazil is the farthest away from the line of equal distribution. In the case of Brazil, significant income inequality is linked to its developing-nation status. Most developing nations have a higher degree of income inequality than industrialized nations.

As for Sweden, it has a homogeneous population, a highly progressive income tax, and a long-standing government policy of redistributing income. This produces a more equitable distribution of income. Of the three countries, Sweden's Lorenz curve is closest to the line of perfect equality distribution. The Lorenz curve for the United States lies between those of Sweden and Brazil.

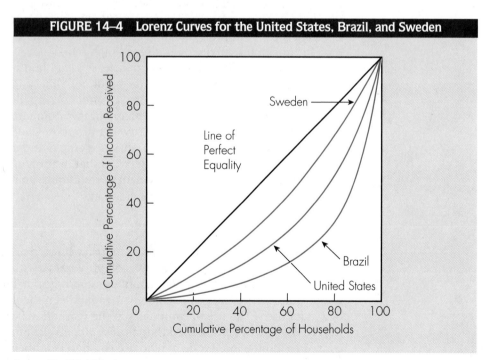

FIGURE 14–4   Lorenz Curves for the United States, Brazil, and Sweden

Source: The World Bank.

If a Lorenz curve were drawn for world income, it would show much greater income inequality than the curve for a given country. The disparity of incomes between rich nations and poor nations is not only huge but growing. Wealthier nations are generally those in the Northern Hemisphere, while poorer nations are generally found in the Southern Hemisphere.

CAUSES OF INCOME INEQUALITY

In virtually all economies, and especially in market economies such as the United States, variations in earnings among individuals and households exist. Some earnings disparity is desirable, for it creates an incentive for individuals to invest in education and training and to take employment and investment risks for greater rewards. However, given the growing degree of income inequality depicted by the Lorenz curve and Gini index, serious concerns are being voiced as to the causes and extent of income inequality in the United States. Among numerous factors contributing to the unequal distribution of income, the following are seen as having the greatest impact.

Education

Differences in income are often based on differences in educational attainment. In 2001 the median income of a high school dropout was $18,445, compared to $24,645 for a high school graduate and $40,939 for an individual with a bachelor's degree. People with professional degrees earn an estimated $5 for every $1 in lifetime income of those who do not finish high school. Over a worklife, those with a bachelor's degree can expect to earn at least $1 million more than a high school dropout, based on 2001 dollars. For the amount of time and money a person spends obtaining an education, it is hard to find a better investment. The increasing rewards from education reflect the shift in demand in favor of more educated workers. Employment opportunities have shifted away from those goods-producing sectors that have disproportionately provided high-wage employment for blue-collar men toward medical, business, and other services that disproportionately employ college graduates. Rapidly growing employment in restaurants and retailing also help to explain the lower wages of high school graduates.

Technology

In addition to shifts in demand across industry lines, there continues to be a shift in demand for educated and highly skilled workers within the same industries. These changes are being brought about by economywide technological changes in how work is performed. One major change has been the use of computer technology in industry. The use of computers in the workplace has increased significantly in recent years. It is estimated that almost 50 percent of the labor force now use computers on the job. Workers who use computers in their jobs are shown to earn an average 10 to 20 percent higher wages than those who do not. Highly educated employees are more likely to adjust to the complexities of computers than their less educated counterparts. Consequently, income inequality is increased at the same time that the economy is becoming more technologically efficient.

Even many occupations traditionally held by the skilled and educated are falling behind in wage gains. It now matters very much in what sector of the economy people work. Jobs in the retail, construction, health care, and education industries, for example, are paying higher wages, but real wages in these industries are either falling or barely rising. These industries are now seen as part of the Old Economy. The Old Economy is comprised of industries that produce tangible goods or personal services, but if a worker's main product or service is information, income has soared. The New Economy of information is attracting college graduates in record numbers. This phenomenon also provides opportunities for training in computer-related jobs on the part of workers without a college degree. If the best and brightest individuals head to the New Economy, the income gap may widen.

Unions

The decline in the number of workers belonging to labor unions has contributed to the increase in income inequality. Through collective bargaining, unions have bargained for wages higher than the competitive wage that would be paid in a highly competitive market. The effect of collective bargaining has been to equalize wage rates within a given firm and to stabilize wage rates across firms that have unionized workforces. Because of the successful use of market power, unions have historically diminished the income differential between white-collar and blue-collar workers.

As a percentage of the labor force, union membership has undergone a marked decline. The reasons for this precipitous decline are numerous, and several of the most important were identified in the previous chapter. This decline in union membership is largely tied to the decline in manufacturing. Manufacturing provides high-paying work opportunities for millions of workers. But the steady reduction in U.S. manufacturing jobs has resulted in fewer jobs for the unskilled and semiskilled worker. Many of these individuals are forced into the lower-paying service jobs, adding to income disparity.

Abilities

A number of individuals are gifted with talents that command large incomes in the marketplace. Some inherit the mental qualities necessary to enter high-paying fields, such as medicine and law, while others move up the corporate ladder to become chief executive officers of large multinational companies. Extraordinary physical abilities enable star athletes, such as Barry Bonds and Tiger Woods, to become millionaires many times over. In the entertainment industry, certain entertainers, such as Britney Spears and Jenifer Aniston, are gifted with artistic talents that command large sums for their services. Although these talents enable some individuals to make substantial contributions to total output, their extraordinary high incomes have become highly controversial during a time of growing income inequality. This is particularly true of those corporate executives who earn tens of millions of dollars in salary, bonuses, and stock options annually, while simultaneously laying off thousands of workers.

Wealth

Household Wealth
The value of a household's total assets minus its liabilities. Also known as net worth.

Income from wealth is more unevenly distributed than income from labor. **House-hold wealth,** or net worth, is the value of a household's total assets minus its liabilities. The median net worth of households in 1995 was $40,200. This figure includes the four major assets that comprise household wealth. Asset classes include home equity; liquid assets, such as cash, bank deposits, money market funds, and savings in insurance and pension plans such as IRAs and Keogh accounts; real estate and unincorporated businesses; and corporate stocks and bonds. It does not include the value of equities in employer-sponsored pension plans. Over 44 percent of today's net household wealth is in the form of home equity. Ownership of wealth also generates income in the forms of rents, interest, and profit. Wealth can be generated by its current owners as well as by previous generations through inheritance. The Bureau of the Census estimates that 84 percent of the nation's wealth is held by 20 percent of the households.

Figure 14–5 shows the net worth of households in 1995 by type of household and by age. These values exclude the value of home equity. The 1995 data presented in Figure 14–5 were published in 2001 and constitute the most current government information available. The rising prosperity of the 1990s has undoubtedly created an even greater concentration of wealth in the hands of the wealthiest households. Despite the sharp fall in the value of equities in 2001 and 2002, the wealthiest households have reaped unprecedented gains in their portfolios over the period.

Census figures do not reflect the unprecedented gains in the stock market that have occurred throughout the decade. Despite the notion that most households now have a stake in the stock market because of increased participation in mutual funds, equity ownership has remained the privilege of a relatively small but growing group of households. Various studies undertaken by economists and research organizations support this view. Research conducted by Edward Wolff, professor of economics at New York University, indicates that only 48 percent of households owned any stock whatsoever in 1998. Most of these holdings were relatively small and were held in retirement accounts. On the other hand, nearly 75 percent of all shares were held by the top 10 percent of households, and 42 percent were held by the richest 1 percent. Ownership in stocks by the highest 10 percent served to raise their share of the national wealth to 75 percent.

Figures depicting income distribution mask the rise in capital gains received by the wealthiest households. Although interest and dividends are included as income, capital gains are not. With stock options, mutual funds, and direct stock ownership, the economy produced a record number of paper millionaires in the 1990s. For

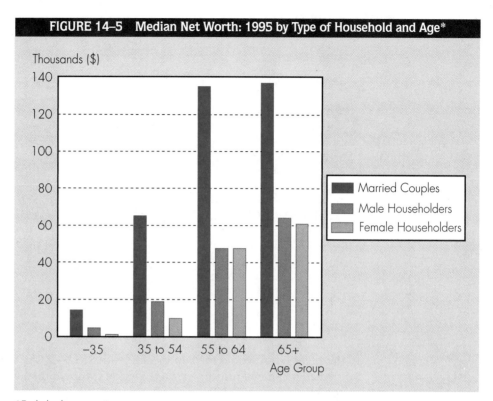

FIGURE 14–5   Median Net Worth: 1995 by Type of Household and Age*

Legend:
- Married Couples
- Male Householders
- Female Householders

*Excludes home equity.
Source: U.S. Census Bureau. *Current Population Reports: Household Net Worth and Asset Ownership: 1995, March 2001.*

some, however, this standing was short-lived due to the subsequent correction in the equity market.

Discrimination

Labor Market Discrimination
Discrimination that occurs if the employment and earnings practices are based on factors unrelated to worker productivity, such as race, sex, age, or national origin of the worker.

Discrimination in labor markets is a complex problem, the effects of which are not easy to measure. **Labor market discrimination** occurs if the hiring, promotion, firing, or wage payment is based on factors unrelated to worker productivity, such as the race, sex, age, or national origin of the worker. There is compelling evidence based on numerous economic studies that discrimination is responsible for a sizable share of the income inequality between the races and sexes.

There are substantial differences in the average incomes of households according to race, age, and sex. Statistical information presented in Table 14–2 indicates that in 2001 the median income of all white, non-Hispanic households was $46,305, while the median income for black households was $29,470, and for Hispanic households the corresponding figure was $33,565. Asian and Pacific Islanders had

TABLE 14–2 Household Median Income, 2001	
Households	Median Income (Dollars)
All Households	$42,228
White, non-Hispanic	46,305
Black	29,470
Hispanic	33,565
Asian and Pacific Islanders	53,635
Type of Household	
Family households	52,275
Nonfamily households	25,631
Earnings of Year-Round, Full-Time Workers	
Male	38,275
Female	29,215

Source: U.S. Census Bureau. *Current Population Reports: Money Income in the United States: 2001.*

the highest household median income with $53,635. The table also shows that the median income of full-time female workers who worked year-round was $29,215, compared to $38,275 for male workers. Although women earn less than males, women's earnings have been rising more rapidly than those of men. Figure 14–6 depicts women's earnings as a percentage of men's earnings for the period from 1960 to 2001. Since 1960, women's earnings have climbed from 61 percent to 76 percent of men's earnings.

Since we now know that a number of factors account for the inequality of incomes in the United States, how much of the income inequality between the races and sexes can be attributed to discrimination? As a result of numerous economic studies, there is enough evidence to conclude that about half of the earnings differences between the races and sexes are caused by discriminatory practices.

Labor market discrimination on the basis of sex or race does not normally take the form of discriminating between two workers doing the same job. More often than not, labor market discrimination is of a more institutional nature, based on channeling groups of people into occupations for which they are considered suitable. Channeling people into occupations according to sex or race is known as **occupational segregation.** For example, until recently women were barred from being fighter pilots in the military because it was considered an occupation better suited for men. Women were thought to be better suited for paperwork and other less dangerous assignments. In the commercial airline industry, men were pilots and women were flight attendants. The channeling of the sexes has been obvious in the medical profession, where men were considered more suitable as doctors

Occupational Segregation
Channeling people into occupations according to sex or race.

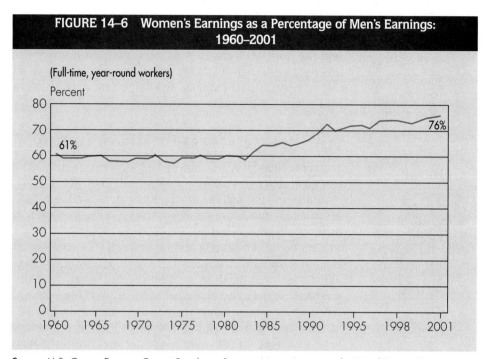

FIGURE 14-6 Women's Earnings as a Percentage of Men's Earnings: 1960–2001

(Full-time, year-round workers)

Source: U.S. Census Bureau. *Current Population Reports: Money Income in the United States: 2001.*

and women more suitable as nurses. College professors were largely male, and elementary schoolteachers were largely female. Men became leaders in business, while women were channeled into secretarial functions. Black males were barred from jobs in police and fire departments and were channeled into the sanitation and public transportation departments. Black females were not considered suited for the nursing profession; instead, they worked at hospitals as orderlies.

Channeling may be the result of the employee's own preferences. Many women want to be schoolteachers, nurses, or secretaries and nothing else. If so, this does not constitute labor market discrimination. However, the one obvious result of channeling is that women and minorities have been crowded into occupations reserved for them. Crowding increases the supply of labor in these fields, driving wages down. At the same time, wages are higher in the restricted fields because the supply of labor is reduced. Again, witness the wage differentials between flight attendants and pilots in the airline industry. Low-paid occupations are still largely female and minority occupations.

Income inequality between the sexes is also a function of the childbearing role of women. Many women leave employment in order to bear and raise children at a time in which males are acquiring the experience and training that lead to career advancement. Women also assume greater responsibility for child care than men and are likely to seek employment that provides greater flexibility in hours, is in relatively close proximity to home, and requires little if any travel. More often than not, the trade-off for such working conditions is lower earnings. In preparation for this role, women historically were channeled into courses of study and occupations that provided such flexibility. To a large extent, the pattern continues today on college campuses across the country.

THE INCOME DISTRIBUTION QUESTION

Is income inequality necessarily bad for the economy? This is a question of normative economics and calls for a value judgment. The answer is both yes and no, depending on the degree of inequality. If most families lack sufficient income to provide for the basic necessities of life, it is detrimental to the welfare of society and disruptive to the operation of the economic system.

On the other hand, a certain amount of income inequality is beneficial to the economic system. First, income serves a functional purpose, because it is how individuals are paid for their productive efforts. One way to recognize differences in productivity is by paying higher incomes to those who produce the most. If people received the same income regardless of their productivity, much of the incentive to increase productivity would disappear. Would people sacrifice to attend college or to learn a trade if they could not better their income? Would entrepreneurs undertake the type of risky business ventures that eventually enrich our standard of living if society removed the incentive of large profits as a reward for success?

Second, savings are essential to the development of capital formation, which is responsible for most of the increased productivity in the economy. The higher a person's income is, the greater his or her ability to save. Thus, high incomes that generate savings are beneficial. If we had perfect equality in the distribution of income, the result would be a minimum of personal saving and a dampening of economic growth.

EQUAL VERSUS EQUITABLE INCOME DISTRIBUTION

Equal Distribution of Income
An income distribution in which all households receive the same income.

Equitable Distribution of Income
An income distribution based on the application of some objective standard.

An **equal distribution of income** is a distribution in which all households receive exactly the same income. An equal distribution of income may differ from an equitable distribution. An **equitable distribution of income** implies distribution according to some objective standard. Equity, however, means different things to different people. For example, some individuals believe that the only equitable distribution of income is an equal distribution of income. Others consider an equal distribution of income inequitable, arguing that such a system rewards those who contribute the least to the economy just as much as those who contribute the most.

In our market system, an equitable distribution is generally considered one in which income distribution is made according to the perceived contribution of the individual. Consequently, we are sure to have some diversity in the distribution of in-

NETLink

What effect does homelessness have on the income distribution of the United States? Visit the National Coalition for the Homeless.

http://nch.ari.net/jobs.html

come. But under this system our main task is not to eliminate income inequality. Instead, it is to keep the inequality from becoming too great. The condition of poverty is one such income extreme and is the subject for the remainder of the chapter.

Poverty

The federal government's primary interest in the distribution of income in the economy is centered on poverty. Poverty first became a national issue under the Kennedy administration. Because of his concern about the number of families in the economy that were living on substandard incomes, Kennedy instructed his Council of Economic Advisors to undertake a study of poverty in the United States. This study was the basis for designing President Johnson's War on Poverty program instituted by passage of the Economic Opportunity Act in 1964. Since that time, billions of dollars have been spent on a number of different federal programs designed to reduce, if not eliminate, poverty.

DEFINING POVERTY

Relative Measure of Poverty
A definition of poverty based on the average annual incomes earned by other households.

Absolute Measure of Poverty
A definition of poverty based on a specific level of annual income for a given-sized household.

Poverty is not easily defined. The choice of definition is important, for it will determine the number of poor people and the success of government programs in reducing poverty. Some analysts define poverty in terms of a relative standard; others prefer to define it in terms of an absolute standard. A **relative measure of poverty** defines poverty in terms of the average annual incomes earned by other households. If a relative definition of poverty is used, poverty will always be among us because in a market economy some portion of the population would always be classified as poor. The only way to eliminate poverty is to have an equal distribution of income. An **absolute measure of poverty** is one that defines poverty as an annual income below a specific level for a given-sized household. According to the absolute approach, a household is impoverished if its income is not high enough to enable it to acquire a certain quantity of goods and services deemed essential for a minimum standard of living.

In the early 1960s, the federal government rejected the relative measure of poverty and defined poverty according to an absolute standard. The U.S. government established the official poverty level as three times the annual cost of the Department of Agriculture's nutritionally sound food budget. The poverty level was based on evidence that the typical family spent one-third of its income on food. In 1963, the Council of Economic Advisers adopted a poverty threshold line of $3,000 for a family of four. Any family of four earning less than $3,000 was classified as being part of the poverty population. The **poverty threshold line** refers to the established annual income level that separates the poor from the nonpoor. The official definition of poverty contains numerous classifications based on family size and age, and the poverty threshold line is adjusted upward every year or so to account

Poverty Threshold Line
The established annual income level that separates the poor from the nonpoor.

for changes in the general price level. In 2001, the poverty threshold line for a family of four (husband, wife, and two children under the age of 18) was $17,960.

INCIDENCE OF POVERTY

In 1960, more than 40 million people, consisting of 22 percent of the population, were officially classified as being in poverty. By the late 1960s, the number of people in poverty had declined to approximately 25 million, a number that remained fairly constant until 1978. Between 1978 and 1983, however, the number of people in poverty increased sharply to 35 million. In 2001, the number of people below the official poverty level was 32.9 million, a number that comprised about 11.7 percent of the nation's population. Thus, although the total number of people in poverty has changed relatively little since 1960, as a percentage of the population poverty has declined significantly. Figure 14–7 graphically portrays the total number of people in poverty and their percentage of the population for the period 1959 to 2001.

Poverty is a condition that affects some groups in society more than others. One way of measuring the unequal distribution of poverty is by examining the in-

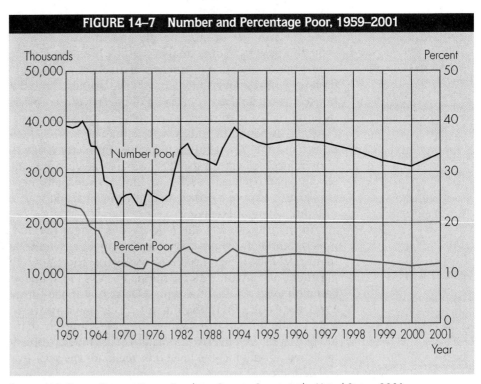

FIGURE 14–7   Number and Percentage Poor, 1959–2001

Source: U.S. Census Bureau. *Current Population Reports: Poverty in the United States: 2001.*

TABLE 14–3 Demographic Characteristics of the Poor, 2001		
Characteristics	(Millions)	Percentage
Persons		
Total	32.9	11.7
White, non-Hispanic	15.2	7.8
Black	8.1	22.7
Hispanic	8.0	21.4
Asian and Pacific Islanders	1.3	10.2
Under age 18	11.7	16.3
65 years and over	3.4	10.1
Female householder, no husband present	3.5	26.4
By Region		
Northeast	5.7	10.7
Midwest	6.0	9.4
South	13.5	13.5
West	7.8	12.1

Source: U.S. Census Bureau. *Current Population Reports: Poverty in the United States: 2001.*

Incidence of Poverty
The percentage of persons in a particular group who are officially classified as having income below the poverty threshold line.

cidence of poverty. The **incidence of poverty** refers to the percentage of persons in a particular group who are officially classified as having income below the poverty threshold line. Table 14–3 presents the incidence of poverty for various demographic groups in 2001. As can be seen from the table, the poor are disproportionately comprised of nonwhites, the young, and households headed by women. The group with the highest incidence of poverty was women living in a household with no husband present. The table indicates that 26 percent of all such women lived in poverty. Blacks and Hispanics have a much higher incidence of poverty relative to their populations compared to whites. In 2001, approximately 23 percent of all blacks and 21 percent of all Hispanics fell below the poverty threshold, whereas about 8 percent of non-Hispanic whites were officially classified as poor. By age, 16 percent of children under the age of 18 were in poverty, as well as 10 percent of all individuals over the age of 65. Geographically, poverty is more prevalent in the West and South than in the Northeast and Midwest.

A major shortcoming inherent in the official poverty line measures is that only pretax income is included. No consideration is given to income received from cash transfers and in-kind benefits from government. In-kind benefits from the federal government include such things as food stamps, subsidized housing, and medical care. Tax credits such as the Earned Income Tax Credit are also excluded. The Census Bureau estimates that by including cash and in-kind benefits and credits, the percentage of the population in poverty would be reduced to about 10 percent of the population.

Welfare to Work

Historically, the redistribution of income to the poor has been primarily directed through public assistance or welfare programs. These programs are jointly funded by the federal government and state governments.

LEGISLATION

During the 1990s, growing dissatisfaction occurred with welfare programs throughout the country. The center of the political storm over welfare is the incentive to work issue and the perceived lack of desire on the part of welfare recipients to move off welfare roles. Critics of the welfare system contended that for many recipients welfare had become a way of life. The system itself created disincentives for people to seek work, and staying on welfare in many situations was an economically rational decision.

The biggest disincentive to employment is the implicit tax trap that awaits recipients as they enter the workforce. This is due to the fact that transfer programs are similar to progressive income taxes, in that as income rises benefits decrease. When people begin earning income from employment, the implicit tax rate on welfare benefits is high and eventually reaches 100 percent. This will occur at the level of income at which welfare benefits are eliminated.

A second disincentive is the fact that for a good number of welfare recipients, taking a job results in a decrease in income. Because many welfare recipients have limited education and skills, they would enter the workforce as minimum-wage workers. Their annual income for 52 weeks at $5.15 an hour would be $10,500. But these earnings are taxable, whereas welfare benefits are not. In addition, a person leaving welfare and going to work not only must give up leisure but must now absorb the expenses associated with working, such as clothing, transportation, and child care.

Given these disincentives to work, the increasing calls for overhauling the welfare system at both the state and national levels were not surprising. The hardening of attitudes toward welfare reached a peak in 1994 when the percentage of welfare recipients hit an all-time high of 5.5 percent of the population. This occurred despite a growing economy with increasing employment opportunities.

In response to the nation's cry for welfare reform, President Clinton signed into law the Personal Responsibility and Work Opportunity Reconciliation Act of 1996. This law was seen as a serious attempt at encouraging welfare recipients to leave welfare and go to work. The passage of this act resulted in the elimination of the previous welfare system, comprised of Aid to Families with Dependent Children (AFDC) and the Job Opportunities and Basic Skills Program (JOBS). In their place, a new system was created, the Temporary Assistance for Families (TANF). The law set a lifetime limit of five years of welfare for each family. It requires all able-bodied adults to work after two years of welfare.

Welfare-reform legislation made several important modifications to existing laws to achieve its goals. Among the many changes, it transformed cash assistance to the able-bodied poor from an entitlement to a block grant with time limits for cash aid. It also gave states wide-ranging authority to require welfare recipients to participate in work-related activities. It allowed states to impose sanctions for noncompliance, to change benefit levels, and to change the way benefits are reduced as families attempt to work themselves off welfare.

To further support the effort of the 1996 act, the Balanced Budget Act of 1997 included provisions for the Welfare-to-Work program. The Balanced Budget Act allocated $3 billion in grants to states for this purpose and included tax credits to business firms who hired welfare-to-work individuals. Tax credits were based on wages paid and the length of time employed with the firm. The Welfare-to-Work legislation focused on transitioning the hardest-to-hire welfare recipients to permanent, unsubsidized employment and economic self-sufficiency.

PRELIMINARY RESULTS

The Personal Responsibility and Opportunity Act is widely seen as a success. Figure 14–8 presents the number of people on welfare for the period from 1992 to 2001. The graph shows that in absolute terms welfare caseloads reached a peak in 1993. In that year, 14.2 million people were on welfare. By 2001, this number had declined by over 8 million recipients to stand at 5.5 million. Relative to the population, Figure 14–9 shows that the percentage of people on welfare has also dropped sharply. Less than 2 percent of the population was on welfare in 2001, compared to 5.5 percent during the peak years of 1993 and 1994.

Reports from states indicate that most recipients who leave welfare find jobs. Most of these jobs are in the retail or services sectors of the economy. However, many of these jobs pay between $5.15 and $8.00 an hour, a rate equal to or higher than the minimum wage, but not high enough to raise a family out of poverty. Consequently, many who leave welfare cash assistance continue to receive other forms of public assistance, such as Medicaid and food stamps.

But successes in the TANF program are likely to prove far more difficult to match in the Welfare-to-Work program. Welfare to Work was created to help employ the hardest-to-hire individuals. The population eligible for this program consists of people who face two or three labor market deficiencies. Included as deficiencies are such things as the lack of a high school diploma or GED, low reading or math skills, the need for substance abuse treatment, or a poor work history. Also eligible for the Welfare-to-Work program are long-term welfare recipients, those who

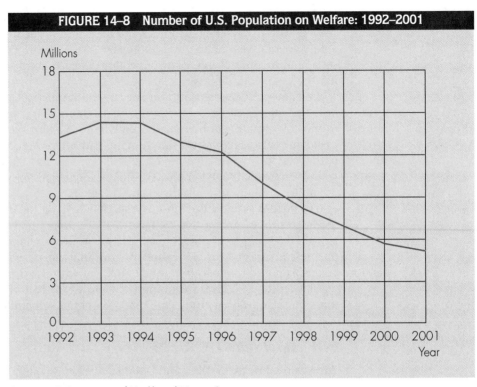

FIGURE 14–8   Number of U.S. Population on Welfare: 1992–2001

Source: U.S. Department of Health and Human Services.

face termination from TANF, and noncustodial parents meeting the criteria. Given the fact that the target population for the Welfare-to-Work program is markedly different than that of the more general TANF program, to hold Welfare to Work to the same expectations for success seems unrealistic.

Another concern is that welfare caseloads normally fluctuate with the business cycle, rising in periods of high unemployment and falling in periods when employment is high. The tight labor market in the mid- and late 1990s undoubtedly accounted for some of the increased hiring of welfare recipients. But a major test of recent welfare reform measures will come with economic downturns, as large companies lay off thousands of workers and many small companies struggle to survive. Because former welfare recipients were among the last hired during the economic expansion, they are likely to become the first fired as the economy sinks into a recession. At that time, the gains made in recent years in reducing welfare caseloads will be put to the test. With a recession, state governments will have to bear the brunt of increased welfare caseloads with increasingly scarce resources, for state revenues rise and fall with the business cycle as well. If the downturn proves lengthy, states will have to make difficult choices. After deplet-

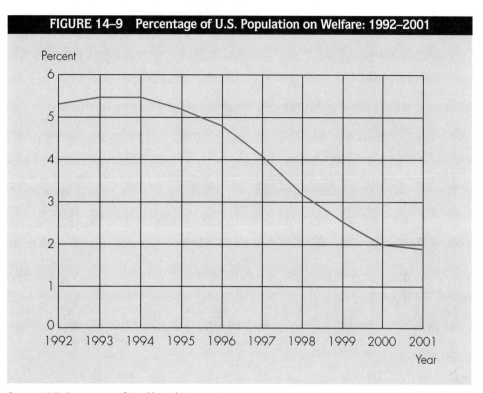

FIGURE 14–9   Percentage of U.S. Population on Welfare: 1992–2001

Source: U.S. Department of Health and Human Services.

ing unspent balances, states will have to either cut benefits or seek additional help from the federal government.

The 1996 act expired in 2002 and was extended by the Bush Administration in 2003. Although the original act underwent a significant number of changes, the basic tenets of the original law were retained.

Summary

- Although the United States has one of the highest per capita incomes in the world, the distribution of income in the United States is becoming more unequal. Recent figures indicate that the lowest-ranking quintile of households receive 3.5 percent of all income, while the highest receive over 50 percent of income.

- The Lorenz curve is a tool that can be used to illustrate income equality. The greater the difference between a 45-degree line and the Lorenz curve, the greater the income inequality. The Gini coefficient is an index that summarizes the inequality of incomes in a single number.

- Among the numerous factors accounting for the unequal distribution of income are education; technological change; the decline of unionism; differences in the intellectual, physical, and artistic abilities among individuals; and discrimination.

- The number of people in poverty in the United States is determined by the definition given to poverty. The federal government uses an absolute standard for measuring poverty. The poor are disproportionately comprised of nonwhites, the young, and households headed by women.

- Historically, the redistribution of income to the poor has been primarily directed through public assistance or welfare programs. These programs created disincentives on the part of many welfare recipients to seek gainful employment.

- Responding to growing concerns over the welfare issue, President Clinton signed into law the Personal Responsibility and Work Opportunity Reconciliation Act of 1996. The resulting Welfare-to-Work program is intended to encourage people to leave the roles of public assistance and enter the labor force.

New Terms and Concepts

Family
Household
Lorenz curve
Gini coefficient
Household wealth
Labor market
  discrimination

Occupational
  segregation
Equal distribution of
  income
Equitable distribution
  of income

Relative measure of
  poverty
Absolute measure of
  poverty
Poverty threshold line
Incidence of poverty

Discussion Questions

1. How might equality of income not be equitable?

2. Does our current progressive income tax (which requires those in higher income brackets to pay a higher tax) tend to heighten or lessen the unequal distribution of income in the economy? Explain.

3. How is it possible to raise the income level of all families and individuals in the economy without substantially changing the distribution of total income?

4. Is the incidence of poverty in the United States ever likely to drop below 5 percent? Why or why not?

5. Do you consider the minimum wage a poverty wage? Why or why not?

6. Given the investment returns from education, is it logical to believe that everyone is better off by completing a college degree?

7. The per capita GDP of Mozambique is less than $100. A Mozambique family of four earning $10,000 per year might fall into the highest fifth or quintile in that country. Is this family poor?

8. What causes the great disparity of income among various nations of the world?

9. "Statistics show that women earn approximately 76 percent of the income earned by men. This, in itself, proves the case for sex discrimination." Evaluate this statement.

10. Describe how the Welfare-to-Work program is working in your state.

Economic Applications

EconNews

Go to the EconNews icon on http://econapps.swlearning.com. Find the "Income Distribution and Poverty" link located under the Microeconomics heading. Here, you will find news articles about poverty as well as questions for further studies.

14

CHAPTER REVIEW

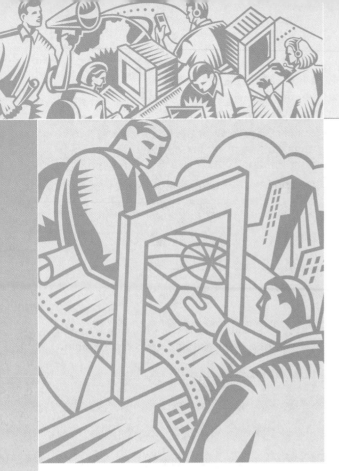

15

Business Cycles

After studying Chapter 15, you should be able to:

1. Define a *business cycle* and differentiate between major and minor cycles.

2. Describe each of the four phases of the business cycle.

3. Identify internal and external factors that may modify the business cycle.

4. Distinguish among leading, lagging, and coincident cyclical indicators and describe how they are used.

5. Compare and contrast the major theories concerning the causes of the business cycle.

The expansion of the economy from 1991 until 2001 was the longest cyclical economic growth period in our nation's history, surpassing the record previously held by the 1982–1990 expansion. During the 1990s, the question was raised once again about whether the conventional business cycle was a thing of the past. This question was also raised during the prolonged economic expansions in the 1970s and 1980s. It arises whenever there are long periods of economic prosperity. Usually, critics of the existence of the business cycle base their views on new structural or innovative changes taking place in the economy that are thought to preclude future economic downturns. In the expansion of 1991–2001, it was thought to be information technology. However, in 2001, as with each cyclical expansion preceding it, the economy once again slid into a recession.

There are no doubts that real changes are occurring in the economy, and these changes do affect the business cycle. Many of these recent changes can be attributed to the revolution in information technology, which is affecting the business cycle in ways not clearly understood. However, despite these changes, business cycles are not likely to disappear, although they are getting milder and of shorter duration. Consequently during expansionary periods, it is not a matter of whether there will be a recession, but rather when the next recession will occur. Not only the United States, but countries throughout the world experience the cyclical ups and downs that are reflected by swings in unemployment, real GDP, and capacity utilization. This chapter explains the nature of the business cycle and presents several theories that seek to explain its intrinsic causes.

The Business Cycle

Business Cycle
The rise and fall of economic activity relative to the economy's long-term growth trend.

National output is subject to various types of disturbance, but the most pronounced of these is the business cycle. The **business cycle** is the rise and fall of economic activity relative to the economy's long-term growth trend. As the cycle progresses, all parts of the economy display marked changes in activity as they move through distinctive periods usually called *peak, contraction, trough,* and *expansion.* Production, prices, income, and employment activities all show characteristic changes during the cycle; in fact, no part of the economy is immune to the cycle. Extensive studies have shown that these cyclical fluctuations are found in economies throughout the world.

TYPES AND LENGTHS OF CYCLES

A study of past economic data reveals that our economy has experienced many and varied business cycles. Some cycles have been long, others short. Some have been severe, while others have been mild. In general, business fluctuations may be classified as minor cycles or major cycles.

Minor cycles are cycles of relatively mild intensity in which the fluctuations are noticeable but not severe. They are shorter but more numerous than major cycles. Since the end of World War II, we have experienced ten such downswings in the economy: in 1949, 1953–1954, 1958, 1960–1961, 1970, 1974–1975, 1980, 1982, 1990–1991, and 2001. The durations of business cycles since World War II are presented in Figure 15–1. Although still only a minor cycle, the 1982 recession was the deepest and most prolonged downswing since the Great Depression of the

Figure 15–1 Duration of Business Cycles Since World War II	
Number	10
Average duration	56 months
Longest cycle	120 months (1991–2001)
Shortest cycle	28 months (1980–1982)
Average expansion	57 months
Shortest expansion	12 months (1980–1981)
Longest expansion	120 months (1991–2001)
Average recession	11 months
Shortest recession	6 months (1980)
Longest recession	17 months (1981–1982)

Sources: *Survey of Current Business* and *Economic Report of the President,* 1993.

1930s. The recession of 1990–1991 lasted eight months, and the 2001 recession lasted nine months.

Major cycles are cycles that show a wide fluctuation in business activity and are usually characterized by serious contractions or depressions. This translates into widespread unemployment, lower output, and low profits or net losses in many cases. Since World War II, we have experienced no major cycle, perhaps due to our use of modern monetary, fiscal, and other measures and to our economy's automatic stabilizers and the built-in stimulus of large-scale defense outlays.

Other types of cycles or fluctuations, including long-wave (of 50 to 60 years' duration) building cycles, commodity price fluctuations, and stock market price fluctuations have been revealed by research and economic analysis.

PHASES AND MEASUREMENT OF CYCLES

Today, business cycles are considered to have four distinct phases: peak, contraction, trough, and expansion. A **peak** exists whenever an overall high level of economic activity prevails. A **contraction** occurs whenever the level of business activity drops noticeably. The **trough** is the period when the level of business activity has dropped as far as it is going to drop in a particular cycle. **Expansion** occurs when the level of business activity begins to rise. Figure 15–2 illustrates the four phases of the business cycle.

It used to be customary to refer to the contraction phase of the business cycle as a *recession* and to the trough as a *depression*. But in the late 1960s and the early 1970s, it became conventional to define a recession as a period in which the real GDP declines in two consecutive quarters. This effectively changed the previous meaning of recession, but left us without a specific definition of a depression. Some analysts consider the combined downswings of 1980 and 1982—often referred to

Peak
The highest level of economic activity in a particular cycle.

Contraction
A noticeable drop in the level of business activity.

Trough
The lowest level of business activity in a particular cycle.

Expansion
A rising level of business activity.

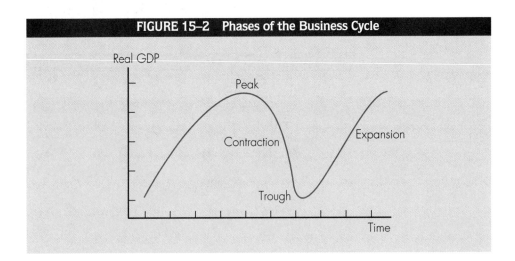

FIGURE 15–2   Phases of the Business Cycle

as a *double-dip recession*—a depression. This period was marked by an unemployment level exceeding 10 percent, a drop in the use of industrial capacity to less than 70 percent, and a record number of bankruptcies.

Although we can make more or less definite measurements of the length of the total cycle and even the length of the expansion and contraction periods of the average cycle, it is difficult to obtain a conclusive measurement of the average length of each of the four phases of the cycle, mainly because analysts disagree about exactly when we leave one phase of the cycle and go into another.

It is a bit easier to measure the severity of a business cycle. In measuring the business cycle, however, we must make allowances for any forces affecting business activity other than those inherent in the business cycle. The level of business activity at any time is affected by four forces or types of economic change: (1) the trend, (2) seasonal variations, (3) random fluctuations, and (4) cyclical fluctuations.

The **trend** is the directional movement of the economy over an extended period of time, such as 20 to 30 years. It represents the long-run average change (growth or decline) in real GDP. **Seasonal variations** are recurring fluctuations in business activity over a given period, usually one year. The cause of the fluctuations may be natural or artificial. For example, we produce more farm products in the summer than we do in the winter because of a natural cause, the weather. On the other hand, retail store sales increase substantially during November and December because of an artificial phenomenon, holiday shopping.

Random fluctuations in business activity result from unexpected or unusual events. A serious flood or drought can affect certain portions of the economy or even the economy as a whole. **Cyclical fluctuations** are changes in the level of business activity that come about regardless of the trend, seasonal variations, or random forces. Business cycles may occur because of inherent forces in the economy. Nevertheless, they may be strongly influenced by external forces, such as wars, changes in the monetary system, and changes in population.

PATTERN OF CYCLES

Some business cycles are short and others long; some are intense and others mild. Even so, the cycle appears to have a definite pattern. Once a contraction has started, a cumulative action among several elements in the economy tends to augment the downswing. During the trough, however, other forces eventually arrest the contraction and start an upward movement. Once this upward motion begins, reactions of individuals and businesses tend to augment the expansion. During the peak, however, forces build up that eventually cause a new contraction.

Two kinds of elements or forces bring about business cycles: internal and external. **Internal forces** are elements within the very sphere of business activity itself and include such things as production, income, demand, credit, interest rates, and inventories. **External forces** are elements outside the normal scope of business activity and include population growth, wars, basic changes in the nation's currency, and national economic policies, as well as floods, droughts, and other catastrophes

Trend
The directional movement of the economy over an extended period of time, such as 20 to 30 years.

Seasonal Variations
Recurring fluctuations in business activity over a given period, usually one year.

Random Fluctuations
Changes in economic activity from unexpected or unusual events.

Cyclical Fluctuations
Changes in the level of business activity that come about regardless of the trend, seasonal variations, or random forces.

Internal Forces
Elements within the very sphere of business activity itself.

External Forces
Elements outside the normal scope of business activity.

that have a pronounced effect on business activity. We will first analyze the internal forces. To see how the relationships among various elements change and how these changes cause business activity to oscillate, let us look at each phase of the cycle individually.

Trough

The bottom of the cycle is called a *trough*. During a trough, output, employment, and income are at low ebb. Prices, costs, and profits have declined to the extent that little investment in plant and equipment occurs. Although banks can extend loans at low interest rates during a trough, businesses are reluctant to borrow because profit expectations are dim.

Although many claim that during a trough is the ideal time to replace capital because of low prices, relatively few firms follow this policy. Because excess capacity is available, there is no need to replace worn-out machinery and equipment to meet current demand. Lack of funds and uncertainty about the future discourage firms from doing so. In addition, many firms that would like to borrow are poor risks, and banks are not eager to accommodate them. These factors result in a sizable reduction in the output of capital goods.

Consumers tend to repair and keep their durable goods during a trough instead of replacing them. Because of high unemployment and corresponding reductions in household incomes, consumers postpone purchases of durable goods. Even those who maintain employment and income levels will cut spending on durables because of the uncertainty of future employment. Instead of buying new homes, automobiles, and appliances, consumers are more inclined to remodel and redecorate existing homes and repair older automobiles and appliances. In many cases, consumers use discretionary income to pay off debts.

Given such conditions, a pessimistic attitude inevitably prevails. Only when the economy shows signs of recovering will business firms and consumers resume their investment and spending levels. Although corrective and expanding forces may be slow to materialize, recovery always comes sooner or later.

Expansion

What leads the economy out of a trough and onto the road to expansion and prosperity? It may occur as a result of external forces such as technological innovations, war, or changes in monetary and fiscal policies. Even without such external factors, however, the relationship among certain basic elements of the business cycle may eventually shift to a more favorable position and initiate an upward movement in the economy. Any combination of internal factors may start the expansion.

One likely starter is a better cost–price relationship. Depending on the extent of industry competition, prices either remain stable or actually decline during the contraction phase. Costs, however, fall slower than prices. Production costs are less flexible than prices because they are the result of existing contracts. In time, the prices of productive resources will begin to fall as contracts expire and producers are able to vary the use of labor and materials. Costs per unit will continue to decline and eventually will fall below the prices of final goods. At this point, there is an incentive to increase production, because final sales will once again generate profits. Production costs at this stage of the cycle will remain low, as wages, rents, and interest rates are being held in check by the competitive forces of supply and demand.

The replacement of depleted inventories can also jump-start the economy. Inventories can satisfy existing demand until a point is reached when increased output is needed to replenish inventory stocks. Also, low interest rates make borrowing more attractive. With loanable funds available at low interest rates and sales increasing due to depleted inventories, an incentive exists to replace old machinery and worn-out equipment. As prices begin to show signs of upward pressure and costs remain stable, the incentive to invest in capital equipment increases, resulting in increased profits, output, and employment. Consumer demand also provides support as consumers begin to replace worn-out consumer goods.

Regardless of what causes it, the force that leads the economy out of the trough is the increase in output. When output increases, employment and income naturally increase as well. And with higher incomes, consumers begin to increase their demand for goods and services. Prices remain fairly constant during the early part of the expansion, but begin to rise with increasing demand. On the other hand, cost remains low because of the abundant supply of available resources. With increasing demand, rising prices, and low cost, profits increase with higher sales, and larger inventories are maintained in the expectation of even higher sales. Increased profits bring about increased investment and still higher levels of employment and income. The general outlook is now more favorable, and with increased optimism the expansion is on its way. Figure 15–3 presents the lengths of expansions since World War II. The most recent expansion is now the longest one on record.

Peak

As output, employment, and incomes begin to rise, internal forces work together to augment the expansion. As output increases, the economy eventually reaches the bottleneck stage. Some goods become relatively scarce, and less efficient and higher-cost facilities are pressed into service. This stimulates an upward price movement, which may trigger a general rise in prices. Because prices increase faster than costs, expansion results in higher profits, because, in addition to greater sales, large profit margins exist. Higher profits in turn provide further incentives for investment. This investment is augmented by the multiplier effect, and it can further activate the expansion.

The buildup or accumulation of inventories also plays an important role in the peak of the business cycle. Most producers and merchants keep inventories at a certain ratio to sales. Therefore, when sales increase, the size of inventories decreases, which means that output must increase not only to satisfy the greater

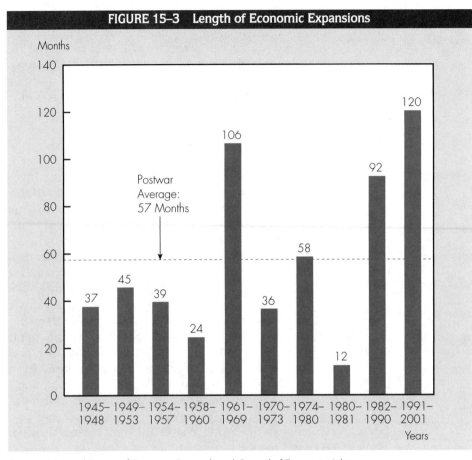

FIGURE 15–3   Length of Economic Expansions

Postwar
Average:
57 Months

37   45   39   24   106   36   58   12   92   120

1945– 1949– 1954– 1958– 1961– 1970– 1974– 1980– 1982– 1991–
1948   1953   1957   1960   1969   1973   1980   1981   1990   2001
Years

Sources: National Bureau of Economic Research and Council of Economic Advisors.

demand by consumers but also to build up inventories. In addition to building up inventories, firms tend to replace worn-out capital goods at an accelerated pace. When this action is multiplied by the hundreds of thousands of producers, wholesalers, and retailers who keep inventories, output obviously increases considerably beyond the actual consumer demand.

During the business cycle peak, the levels of output, employment, and income are high, and high income means a large demand. As demand continues to increase, prices rise. Costs continue to move upward because of the competitive bidding for labor, resources, and capacity. The decrease in excess reserves and the shortage of loanable funds force interest rates upward.

When the general outlook is optimistic, as it usually is during a peak period, further encouragement is given to consumption and investment in the economy. The level of economic activity may increase until we reach the stage of full employment. At this time, further increases in demand, investment, loans, and the like can only lead to inflation. Although expansion may extend beyond the peak of the business cycle, it too will eventually end.

Contraction

The peak does not last forever. Downswings are certain to occur, although exactly when or to what extent is not easy to predict. But during peak periods, internal factors change in a way that leads to a contraction in the economy. While output, employment, and income are still at their peak, consumer demand may begin to taper off or increase at a slower rate. Sales resistance begins to level out prices, and inventories begin to increase. Meanwhile, costs continue to increase as businesses bid against each other for relatively scarce resources, and profit margins diminish.

When demand slackens and prices stabilize, business firms reduce excess inventories. Output is cut as a result, as are employment and income. Idle capacity appears in the economy and inventories accumulate. Prices may not decline at first, but eventually they will decline and reduce profits further. Investment is now discouraged, pushing output, employment, and income down even more.

In general, declining output, employment, income, profit, demand, and prices become cumulative. Under such conditions, the general outlook becomes pessimistic, exerting an adverse psychological effect on both investors and consumers. The contraction continues until it reaches a trough and the business cycle is completed. The pattern is similar in each cycle, although each cycle may differ somewhat in cause, amplitude, and duration.

Factors That May Modify the Business Cycle

The duration and intensity of these fluctuations can be modified through the use of monetary and fiscal policies, as we shall see later. In fact, we know the pattern so well that we can take action to avoid the two extremes of the cycle: widespread unemployment and runaway inflation.

Various external forces also affect the level of economic activity and often generate business fluctuations. For example, a war has a profound effect on a nation's level of economic activity. The requirements for war and defense materiel necessitate increased production and employment. Additional attempts to increase production may lead to inflation unless definite measures, such as materiel and wage–price controls are used to combat rising prices.

Population growth, changes in the money supply, or government deficit spending may provide similar impetus to the economy. On the other hand, terminating a war can have an unfavorable effect on the economy as production is cut back, unless a substantial increase in consumer demand and private investment offsets the decrease in defense spending. Adverse effects can also result from natural catastrophes that force a reduction in production and income.

NET*Link*

Learn more about business cycles by creating your own graphs from historical financial and economic data.

http://www.globalfindata.com

The fact that all internal elements may not move or act in precisely the fashion described is no indication that the pattern is invalid. In any particular cycle, one or more of the elements may act contrary to their usual tendency. But, generally, enough of them act in the prescribed manner and with sufficient strength to overcome any countervailing force of a few maverick elements. This has been the case in recessions since 1980, when institutional factors have caused the general price level to continue to rise instead of declining.

Through the use of various monetary, fiscal, and other economic measures, the United States has been able to prevent wide swings in production, employment, and income. Measures and powers to stabilize the level of economic activity and to keep it expanding at a satisfactory rate have improved over the years. Underlying the need for these stabilizing measures, however, is the fact that in a free economy fluctuations do occur. Stabilizing measures do not eliminate the business cycle; they merely modify its effects. Furthermore, the occurrence of contractions, nagging unemployment, inflation, and stagflation in the economy in the past 25 years certainly indicates that business cycles are still with us.

Leading Indicators
A group of 11 indexes whose upward and downward turning points generally precede the peaks and troughs of general business activity.

Business Cycle Indicators

Changes in business activity are reflected in different areas or sectors of the economy. In many cases, statistics and indexes are used to keep track of these changes. Although some indexes measure changes in particular activities in the economy, they also represent activity in the economy as a whole. Other statistics measure composite types of economic activity that pervade the economy. Therefore, they reflect the general status of the economy. Some analysts of business cycles have combined several different indicators in an effort to develop a general indicator for the entire economy.

Roughly Coincident Indicators
A group of 4 indexes whose turning points usually correspond to the peaks and troughs of general business activity.

Lagging Indicators
A group of 7 indexes whose turning points occur after the turning points for the general level of business activity have been reached.

Economists rely on a series of business cycle indicators to develop forecasts of the economy. Included in this series are three separate groups: the **leading indicators,** which consist of 11 indexes whose upward and downward turning points generally precede the peaks and troughs of general business activity; the **roughly coincident indicators,** a group of 4 indexes whose turning points usually correspond to the peaks and troughs of general business activity; and the **lagging indicators,** made up of 7 indexes whose turning points occur after the turning points for the general level of business activity have been reached. The three groups of indicators are shown in Figure 15–4.

By following the business cycle indicators closely, a business cycle analyst or business executive may be able to anticipate pending changes in the overall level of business activity. Armed with this knowledge, he or she may adjust production schedules, employment, inventories, and financing to compensate for expected changes in business activity.

NET*Link*

Check the current economic indicators for the United States and other nations.

http://www.bea.doc.gov

FIGURE 15–4   Economic Indicators

Leading Indicators
Average workweek for production workers in manufacturing
Rate of layoffs in manufacturing
New orders for consumer goods and materials
New business formations
Contracts and orders for plant and equipment
Vendor performance, measured as a percentage of companies reporting slower
    deliveries from suppliers
Number of new building permits issued for private housing units
Net changes in inventories
Change in sensitive prices
Change in total liquid assets
Changes in money supply

Coincident Indicators
Number of employees on nonagricultural payrolls
Personal income less transfer payments
Industrial production
Manufacturing and trade sales volume

Lagging Indicators
Average duration of employment
Change in labor cost per unit of output
Average prime rate charged by banks
Commercial and industrial loans outstanding
Ratio of consumer installment loans outstanding to personal income
Change in the CPI for services
Ratio of manufacturing and trade inventories to sales

Causes of the Business Cycle

Business cycles are complex phenomena, and many forces are active in changing the level of business activity. During the past 50 years, numerous theories have been offered as explanations of business fluctuations. But, to date, no one theory completely and satisfactorily explains the cause of business cycles. Nevertheless, studying various theories permits a better understanding of the possible causes of cycles and of the complexities involved in analyzing them.

Although the theories disagree on some points, the differences are frequently only a matter of emphasis. However, one theory may clearly be more suitable than others to a particular situation. At times, a cycle may reflect elements of several theories. For the sake of simplicity, we can classify these theories into four major categories: real or physical causes, psychological causes, monetary causes, and spending and saving causes.

REAL OR PHYSICAL CAUSES

Innovation Theory
The theory that business cycles are caused by breakthroughs in the form of new products, new methods, new machines, or new techniques.

A traditional explanation of why cycles occur is the **innovation theory.** This theory is associated with Joseph Schumpeter, who did extensive business cycle research during the 1930s and 1940s. Schumpeter believed that business cycles are caused by breakthroughs in the form of new products, new methods, new machines, or new production techniques.

Innovation leads to increased output, employment, and income in the economy. As businesspeople borrow to finance innovations, they set up new factories, buy raw materials, and hire workers. The increased income that results from their spending increases the total demand in the economy. If their ventures are profitable, other investors will imitate them. But as additional firms begin and continue to produce, a point of overexpansion is eventually reached. The reaction to this overexpansion triggers a contraction in the form of declining output, employment, and income. As long as the decline is smaller than the expansion, the economy will experience a net gain in activity as a result of the innovation.

According to this theory, the intensity and duration of the cycle depend on the nature of the innovation. A simple innovation will result in a short, mild cycle. A series of innovations may occur in such an integrated manner, however, that the cycle is more pronounced and continues over a longer period. Historically, major innovations—the rise of the corporate form of business enterprise, the development of the steamboat, the perfection and use of electric power and the automobile, the development of computers, and the advances in telecommunications produced increased business activity on a larger scale.

Agricultural Theories
Theories of the business cycle that relate the general level of business activity to the weather.

Early in this century, **agricultural theories** of the business cycle were very popular. They tried to relate the general level of business activity to the weather as the main factor influencing the volume of agricultural output; this output, in turn, has a definite effect on the level of business activity, even though the proportion of agricultural production in the gross domestic product has declined dramatically in the last 100 years. A larger volume of agricultural output requires more labor and equipment to harvest and handle the crop, more transportation facilities, increased storage facilities, and an increased amount of credit to finance these operations. Such activity should give a positive impetus to the total economy.

Similar phenomena occur in the durable consumer goods industries and in the handling of business inventories. Consequently, fluctuations in the output of capital and durable consumer goods are of greater intensity than fluctuations in the economy as a whole.

PSYCHOLOGICAL CAUSES

Psychological Theory
The theory that when investors and consumers react according to some belief about future conditions, their actions tend to transform their outlook into reality.

Although the psychological theory is seldom offered as a complete or independent explanation of what causes business cycles, it is incorporated in some way in nearly every other theory. In brief, the **psychological theory** holds that when investors and consumers react according to some belief about future conditions, their actions tend to transform their outlook into reality. Thus, if investors think that economic conditions in the immediate future are going to be good, they will increase their investment in machinery, equipment, and buildings in an effort to increase their total output and make more profit. Likewise, consumers who foresee good times ahead will spend money more readily and perhaps seek additional credit to increase their spending power. Such actions tend to boost the level of economic activity.

On the other hand, if investors expect sales and prices to be lower in the future, they will rein in their investments. Similarly, businesspeople will allow their inventories to dwindle and will be cautious about hiring additional workers. If consumers observe that jobs are difficult to obtain, that overtime is no longer available, and that some workers in the plant are being laid off or are being put on a short workweek, they may become pessimistic about the immediate future. In such a case, they may limit spending, hesitate to take on new debt, and perhaps even try to save in preparation for a possible layoff. The actions of both the investors and the consumers tend to bring about a slowdown in the economy.

The psychological theory also holds that the actions of some business leaders influence other businesspeople and consumers to act in the same way. If certain high-profile business leaders exude optimism and back it up with actual investments, their action may influence the thinking of smaller businesses about the prospects for the economy. If these smaller businesses follow suit with increased investment, the economy will be stimulated.

Competition exerts another potent psychological force on the economy. Several firms competing for trade in a given area may misjudge their respective shares of the market. Undue optimism, for example, may lead them to overestimate their individual shares. If so, business activity will substantially increase for a time, but as the grim realities of the marketplace unfold, some or all of the firms may have to retrench on production. This in turn means a cutback in the demand for materials, labor, credit, and capital. In such a case, a decline in the general level of business activity will set in.

Rational Expectations Theory
An economic theory suggesting that individuals and businesses act or react according to what they think is going to happen in the future after considering all available information.

During the 1970s, the **rational expectations theory** emerged as yet another explanation of changes taking place in the economy. It is based on the belief that businesses and individuals act or react according to what they think, based on all available information, is going to happen to the economy. The theory further contends that the expected results of the federal government's anticyclical policies and measures are often discounted or offset by the actions of businesses and individuals.

More recently, some economists have been talking about "real business cycles"—cycles resulting from unexpected (as opposed to anticipated) changes in the economy. A major tenet of this group is that adjustments can readily be made for anticipated changes, but not for unanticipated changes or shocks to the economy. The steep oil price hikes by OPEC in the 1970s provide a case in point. This effect may not differ much, however, from the effect of what we previously referred to as random fluctuations in business activity.

MONETARY CAUSES

Monetary Theories
Theories that the business cycle is caused by the free and easy expansion of the money supply.

Most **monetary theories** are based on the premise that the banking system in a typical developed economy provides an elastic money supply through the creation of checkable deposits. According to these theories, the free and easy expansion of the money supply by banks permits an overexpansion of investment. Therefore, the expansion of the money supply modifies the forces exerting pressure on the interest rates. As a result, interest rates do not rise quickly, so more investment takes place than would take place in the absence of an expanded money supply. Eventually, a point is reached at which the economy has excess productive capacity and abundant inventories. Readjustment then follows as businesspeople slacken their investment, prices begin to fall, production schedules are cut back, unemployment increases, and a contraction commences. Retraction of loans by the banks during this period augments the downswing.

Monetary theorists maintain that business cycles can be eliminated only by eliminating the banks' ability to create money. The banks, on the other hand, argue that they do not cause business cycles because they do not force loans on anyone and that they merely service the business community when it needs money. Although complete elimination of banks' ability to create money might eliminate the business cycle, it would also eliminate whatever amount of healthy expansion and growth in the economy is made possible by the use of bank loans.

SPENDING AND SAVING CAUSES

Underconsumption Theories
Theories that the business cycle is caused by the failure to spend all national income, resulting in unsold goods, reduced total production, and consequent reductions in employment and income.

Spending and saving theories fall into two broad categories. The first consists of **underconsumption theories.** Some underconsumption theories hold that the economy does not distribute enough income among the productive resources to permit purchase of all the goods and services produced by the economy. The more widely accepted theory, however, is that the economy does distribute enough purchasing power to buy the total goods and services produced, but that not all the income or purchasing power is used. Hence, some goods will be produced and not sold. As a consequence, total production must be reduced, which in turn reduces employment and income.

Some leading underconsumption theorists maintain that the underlying problem is the unequal distribution of income in modern society. They suggest lessening that inequality to eliminate or modify business cycles. This can be accomplished to some degree by using steeply progressive income taxes, by increasing the number of privately and federally sponsored income-maintenance programs, by strengthening labor unions, by regulating monopolistic pricing, and by nationalizing certain industries. The first three of these recommendations are already operating to some extent in our economy.

The other important spending and saving theory is the underinvestment theory. The **underinvestment theory** holds that income in the economy is equal to total production and that to clear all goods off the market, spending equivalent to current income must take place. Because spending on consumption is less than total income, however, the difference must take the form of investment—that is, spending on machinery, equipment, and buildings. Whenever investment spending is equal to the gap between income and consumer spending, the economy will be in a stable position. But whenever investment spending is insufficient to fill the gap between consumer spending and total income, surpluses will exist in the markets, which will initiate a downswing in the economy. If for some reason investment spending exceeds the amount needed to fill the gap between consumer spending and total income, the total demand for goods and services will be greater than the total output, which will tend to increase the level of business activity. Because business cycles are caused by variations in investment, the cycles can be modified or eliminated by maintaining an adequate amount of investment. As we saw in Chapter 12, this is the crux of modern Keynesian analysis.

Underinvestment Theory
The theory that recessions occur because of inadequate investment in the economy.

The 1991–2001 Business Cycle

This was the longest cyclical expansion on record in U.S. history, and the subsequent recession was one of the mildest. It was the National Bureau of Economic Research (NBER) that initially declared that the economic expansion had ended in March 2001 and that the economy was in a recession. NBER uses peaks and valleys of the cycle to measure cyclical activity. Monthly data, not quarterly data, are used to determine economic activity. Simply put, if the economy has declined off its cyclical peak in any one month, it is in recession. NBER data can be quickly released and easily understood, but one month's data may be misleading and lacking in detail.

Data provided by the Bureau of Economic Analysis (BEA) initially contradicted NBER's pronouncement that the economy was in recession. It stated that a recession was avoided in 2001 because real GDP had declined for only one quarter. This downturn in the cycle did not meet the widely accepted yardstick that a recession must entail a declining real GDP for two consecutive quarters. The BEA's measure of inflation is more widely accepted because it is more detailed and examines the economy over quarters rather than months. However, it suffers from possible numerous revisions that make its numbers suspect. In August 2002, the Bureau of Economic Analysis revised its GDP figures for 2001 and reported that the economy had actually experienced not one, but three consecutive quarters of declining GDP. Thus, regardless of which measure is used, the economy experienced a recession in 2001, albeit a relatively mild one by historical standards. The decline in real GDP is clearly seen in Figure 15–5.

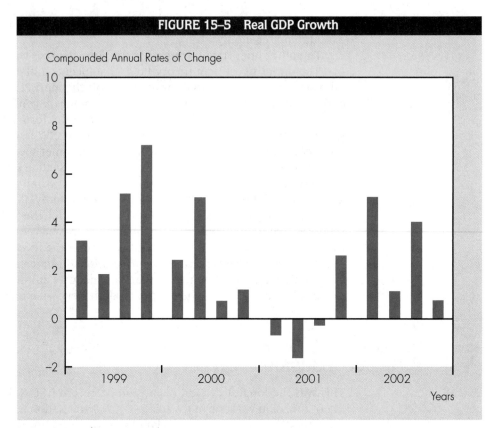

FIGURE 15–5   Real GDP Growth

Compounded Annual Rates of Change

Source: Bureau of Economic Analysis.

What caused the 1991–2001 business cycle? Again, a number of factors were responsible, some of which were unique to this cycle, while many were present in previous ones.

Coming out of the recession of 1990–1991, the economy exhibited many of the usual ingredients for a cyclical recovery. Among other factors, unemployment was falling, prices were stable, and employment, profit expectations, and consumer confidence were rising. Monetary and fiscal policies were also conducive for the stimulation of economic growth. Rapid introductions of new applications of innovations in communication and in computer technology, not the least of which occurred with the wide acceptance of the Internet, helped launch what turned out to be ten years of economic prosperity. The economy exhibited an average real economic growth rate of 3.6 percent from 1993 to 2000, and in five of these years, real economic growth exceeded 4 percent. Productivity gains averaged over 2.5 percent during the same time span. This remarkable growth was aided not only by increased applications of technology but also by low energy costs, an accommodating monetary policy, low rates of inflation, and federal budget surpluses that served to hold down long-term interest rates. Unemployment during the period fell to 4 percent, the level previously targeted by the Humphrey–Hawkins legislation. Equity markets produced unprecedented wealth creation for millions of people as stock prices soared to record levels. As in previous periods of sustained economic prosperity, many believed that the business cycle was a thing of the past. It was thought that the information-based New Economy was inherently different and could keep growing indefinitely.

By 2000, optimism still prevailed, but there were signs that once again the business cycle was at work. Manufacturing output was declining, inventories were piling up, the stock market was becoming highly volatile and increasingly speculative, and real economic growth was slowing. In 2001, despite repeated cuts in short-term interest rates by the Federal Reserve, along with mid-year income tax cuts, the economy slid into recession. Unemployment increased, corporate earnings declined sharply, and real economic growth was negative. The recession of 2001 began before September 11, but the attacks on the World Trade Center and the Pentagon served to deepen the economic decline that had set in earlier in the year and made recovery more difficult. Airlines, cruise lines, hotels, and most travel-related companies and their employees were particularly hard hit. After the initial shock waves from these attacks subsided, the economy rebounded during the fourth quarter and recorded the only positive quarterly growth in GDP for the year.

But unemployment in 2002 continued to rise, reaching 6 percent by the end of the year. The collapse of several major companies such as Enron, WorldCom, Adelphia Communications, and Global Crossing, along with continued declines in corporate earnings, destroyed enormous sums of individual wealth. Approximately $9 trillion dollars in financial wealth was stripped away from investors as equity markets dropped to lows not seen in years. The lack of a robust economic recovery fueled fears of a double-dip recession.

Summary

- A business cycle is the rise and fall of economic activity relative to the economy's long-term growth trend. Business cycles are major, minor, or long-wave. Major cycles show a wide fluctuation in business activity and usually are characterized by serious contractions or depressions. Minor cycles are relatively mild, with noticeable but not severe fluctuations. Long-wave cycles last 50 to 60 years.

- Internal and external forces bring about business cycles. Internal forces occur within business activity and include such factors as production, income, demand, credit, interest rates, and inventories. External forces are outside the normal scope of business activity; they include population growth, wars, basic changes in the nation's currency, and natural catastrophes such as floods and droughts.

- During business cycles, inventories play various roles, depending on the phase of the cycles. During a trough, inventories drop as goods are supplied out of inventory and orders from producers are cut. Commercial loans decline, so banks can extend loans but businesses are reluctant to borrow. Because business loans are off, banks' reserves are rather high; high excess reserves and low demand force interest rates down. During expansion, inventory has to increase to meet demand. More goods are offered from producers, which may cause enough production to stimulate the economy to expand. During a peak, sales increase and thus inventories increase; production expands to meet consumer demand and to build up inventories. During contraction, demand slackens and prices stabilize, so producers, wholesalers, and retailers begin reducing their excess inventories. Overall, inventory accumulation and depletion is a major influence in the business cycle.

- When they increase some internal forces can lead the economy out of a trough. That is, if business starts to expand, increased production, employment, inventories, and financing can overcome the effects of a trough.

- Psychological forces affect the business cycle in that if investors think economic conditions in the immediate future are going to be good, they increase their investment in machinery, equipment, and buildings; consumers spend money more readily and sometimes seek additional credit. If investors and consumers think conditions will be bad, inventories are allowed to dwindle and more workers are not hired as readily, and consumers limit spending, hesitate to take on new debt, and perhaps save. The economy tends to slow down.

- During a trough, prices drop because demand is low. Cost too is lower because unemployed people, resources, and capacity are bidding against each other for jobs, sales, and rent. Because sales are off and prices are down, profits are low. During expansion, prices begin to rise sooner and faster than costs. The more favorable price–cost relationship tends to increase productivity and reduce costs. At the peak phase of the business cycle, some goods become relatively scarce, and marginal and higher-cost facilities are pressed into service, stimulating an increase in specific prices, which may trigger a general rise in price. During contraction, consumer demand may begin tapering off. Eventually, price increases halt or slow down, and the price level stabilizes. Costs continue to increase.

- Leading indicators generally precede the peaks of troughs of general business activity. Lagging indicators occur after the turning points for the general levels of business activity have been reached. The coincident indicators usually correspond to the peaks and troughs of general business activity.

- The major theories concerning the causes of the business cycle are the innovation theory, agricultural theory, psychological theory, rational expectations theory, monetary theories, underconsumption theories, and underinvestment theory.

New Terms and Concepts

Business cycle	Cyclical fluctuations	Agricultural theories
Peak	Internal forces	Psychological theory
Contraction	External forces	Rational expectations
Trough	Leading indicators	theory
Expansion	Roughly coincident indi-	Monetary theories
Trend	cators	Underconsumption
Seasonal variations	Lagging indicators	theories
Random fluctuations	Innovation theory	Underinvestment theory

Discussion Questions

1. What is the difference between a cyclical fluctuation and a trend?

2. What are the four phases of the business cycle? How can you determine the phase of the cycle that the economy is currently in?

3. What internal and external forces influence the level of business activity?

4. During an expansion and at a peak, what forces are building up that will eventually help bring about a contraction in the economy?

5. What role do inventories play in the business cycle?

6. How do interest rates affect the business cycle?

7. What evidence supporting the innovation theory of the business cycle have you observed in recent years?

8. Is the underconsumption theory of the business cycle valid? Why or why not?

9. What signals or indications are the various business indicators giving at the present time?

10. How is a recession defined according to the Bureau of Economic Analysis? How does this definition differ from that used by the National Bureau of Economic Research? What are the strengths and weaknesses of each approach?

Economic Applications

EconDebate

After learning about the business cycle, you can look at the concepts of productivity and growth. Find and click on the EconDebate link at http://econapps.swlearning.com. Then look under the Macroeconomics heading to find the "Productivity and Growth" link. You will see debates on many different topics regarding business growth.

15

CHAPTER REVIEW

16

Macroeconomic Policies

After studying Chapter 16, you should be able to:

1. List some of the automatic stabilizers of the economy.

2. Distinguish between monetary policy and fiscal policy in stabilizing the economy.

3. Explain the different ways in which the government can pay for its spending.

4. Demonstrate the effectiveness of using increased government spending versus a tax reduction to stimulate the economy.

5. Compare transfer payments and public works as objects of discretionary government spending.

6. Illustrate the differences between demand–pull and cost–push inflation.

7. List the methods by which the federal government can reduce spending as a contractionary policy.

8. Discuss the possible contractionary policies that are available in a wartime economy.

9. Analyze the Phillips curve in both the short run and long run.

Expansionary Policies
Monetary and fiscal policies that are used to try to increase the equilibrium level of income and output in the economy.

Contractionary Policies
Monetary and fiscal policies that are used to try to lower aggregate demand for output in the economy to a level that can be achieved with full employment of resources.

As we saw in Chapter 12, aggregate demand and aggregate supply can reach equilibrium at full-employment output or at less than full-employment output. Combined with an appropriate monetary policy, Keynesian analysis provides the basis for demand-management policies and measures designed to either expand or contract the economy. **Expansionary policies** are monetary and fiscal policies that are used to try to increase the equilibrium level of income and output in the economy. **Contractionary policies** are monetary and fiscal policies that are used to try to lower aggregate demand for output in the economy to a level that can be achieved with full employment of resources. This chapter will explain how both policies can be used to manage the economy, as well as give a historical overview of the success of such policies in meeting the desired policy objectives.

Expansionary Policies

Both economists and the general public are concerned with problems that result from recessions and unemployment. The cost of a severe depression can run to billions of dollars. The costs to society that accompany unemployment—bankruptcies, idle plants and equipment, and the waste of productive resources—are also important.

These losses are reflected in Figure 16–1, which shows the correlation among industrial production, unused capacity, and unemployment since 1987. When financial losses and serious social dislocations occur, fiscal and monetary policies and measures may be implemented to raise total output and income. Even in the absence of a recession, economic measures may be used to stimulate growth and provide higher levels of output, employment, and income.

AUTOMATIC STABILIZERS

Automatic Stabilizers
Forces within the economy that naturally tend to counteract recessions and inflation.

Over the past few decades we have developed a number of economic institutions or practices that serve as **automatic stabilizers** for the economy. An outstanding example is the Social Security system, devised to provide income to unemployed and elderly persons. Unemployment compensation and pension payments help maintain a steady level of consumption, even when recession occurs; they are shock absorbers that cushion the downward pressure of recession. Supplementary unemployment benefit plans and guaranteed annual income plans developed through labor–management negotiations are also helpful in this regard. In addition, economic stabilization is cited by defenders of federal farm price-support programs as a major reason for these programs. Other government welfare programs have a similar stabilizing effect. Corporate retained earnings and household savings can also serve as automatic stabilizers.

Fiscal Drag
The slowing effect on the economy that results from a budget surplus.

Fiscal Stimulus
The activating effect on the economy that results from a budget deficit.

A progressive tax structure is another automatic stabilizer. When national income increases, higher revenue from a given tax rate can result in a budget surplus and exert a **fiscal drag** on the economy to help ward off increases in the price level. On the other hand, if national income falls during a recession, the smaller revenue from taxes causes a deficit and leads to government borrowing, creating a **fiscal stimulus** for the economy.

MONETARY POLICY

Recall from Chapter 11 that the Federal Reserve can and does influence the amount of money and credit in the economy. An increase in the money supply and lower interest rates can raise the level of aggregate expenditure during periods of unemployment.

The Fed can help increase the money supply by purchasing government bonds in the open market with checks drawn against its own account. This, in turn,

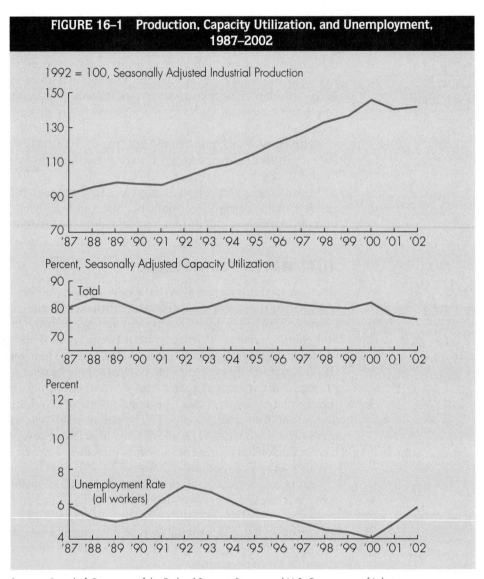

FIGURE 16–1   Production, Capacity Utilization, and Unemployment, 1987–2002

Sources: Board of Governors of the Federal Reserve System and U.S. Department of Labor.

increases banks' excess reserves and encourages them to make loans. A reduction in the reserve requirement produces the same result, since in either case banks are better able to make loans. Increasing the money supply lowers interest rates, and at lower interest rates some investment projects that were not attractive become more appealing. This practice tends to encourage private investment. Increased investment raises aggregate expenditure, which causes aggregate demand to shift to the right. The increase in aggregate demand increases the equilibrium level of total income, output, employment, and prices.

Translating monetary policy into changes in output often runs into some problems. Banks may choose to hold excess reserves and not increase lending. And even if loans are made easier to obtain, there is no certainty that business firms will increase their borrowing. If a recession has become serious and the prospect for improvement in business conditions is slight, firms may hesitate to borrow freely, even if credit is readily available at a low interest rate.

Economic growth and price stability are primary objectives of monetary policy. Because of its limitations, however, regulation of the money supply is only a partial corrective to instability. The fiscal powers of the government are probably more effective when used to increase aggregate demand, total income, and total output, especially during a period of serious unemployment.

DISCRETIONARY FISCAL POLICY

Four general fiscal policies can be developed to promote maximum income with full employment in a closed economy:

1. Consumption may be stimulated by increasing the marginal propensity to consume.
2. Conditions favorable to investment may be encouraged.
3. Government spending may be used in an effort to increase aggregate expenditures.
4. Taxes may be reduced to increase disposable income.

The federal government has a powerful tool for stabilization in its fiscal policies and measures. Government revenues and spending may be adjusted in a manner that will bolster the economy during a recession, combat inflation when the economy is overheating, and promote economic growth in the long run. Let's begin our study of fiscal policy by looking at the government's sources of revenue and the direction of its spending. Three ways to finance government spending are available: tax financing, debt financing, and financing by creating money.

Tax Financing

If taxation is used to finance increased government spending, the government must exercise caution to not tax funds that would otherwise be used for consumption or investment. There is little advantage in having the government spend more at the expense of consumption and private investment. In such a case, aggregate expenditure remains constant, and no increase in total output and employment results. On the other hand, if idle funds (those not used for consumption or investment) are taxed, government spending leads to an increase in aggregate expenditure through the multiplier effect. In fact, if the government could design a tax to absorb all idle funds, aggregate expenditure could always be made equal to total output through government spending. However, the prospect of designing and enforcing such a tax is rather remote. Furthermore, the fairness of such a tax is questionable. Generally, any tax structure absorbs consumer and investment funds to a significant degree.

Debt Financing

Crowding Out
Occurs when deficit spending by the government forces private investment spending to contract.

Borrowing is a more desirable method of raising funds for government spending than taxation when the purpose is to increase aggregate expenditure and total output. The source of borrowing, however, has a direct bearing on the effect of this policy. The government may borrow from consumers, firms, or banks. In any case, the resulting change in aggregate expenditure depends on whether or not idle funds are borrowed. If the government borrows funds by selling bonds to people and firms who otherwise would have used the funds for consumption and investment, the positive effect of government spending on the economy will be offset by the reduction in private spending. This phenomenon is known as **crowding out**. Aggregate expenditure will show no net increase and interest rates will rise. On the other hand, if people and firms use idle funds to purchase the government bonds, a net increase in aggregate expenditure will result when the government spends these funds, bringing about the desired effect of increasing total income and employment.

In fact, people and firms typically use otherwise spendable funds to buy government bonds. Therefore, borrowing from banks is generally recognized as the most useful method of causing an increase in aggregate expenditure. Of course, banks may use depositors' money to buy the government bonds, and to this extent there is merely a transfer of funds from the depositors to the government. However, because many depositors do not intend to use their deposits for immediate consumption or investment, government borrowing from banks does tend to increase the level of total income and employment.

Ricardian Equivalence Theorem
The proposition that it makes no difference whether government spending is financed by taxes or by a deficit.

A controversial view of the effects of deficit financing is the **Ricardian equivalence theorem**. Named after the eighteenth-century economist David Ricardo, this view contends that it makes no difference whether the deficit is financed by increased taxes or by deficit spending. In either case, the theorem holds there is transfer of resources from the private sector to the government and there is no net effect on the aggregate economy. Based on rational expectations, Ricardo held that individuals realize that deficits must be paid off in the future and therefore taxes will rise to pay off the debt. Given this knowledge, they will reduce spending just as they would if taxes were raised today.

Financing by Creating Money

Finally, we look at the case in which the government finances its purchases by creating money. In many countries this is a straightforward operation because the treasury has the legal right to issue currency to pay for government spending. In the United States the process is a little more complicated because the U.S. Treasury does not have the legal right to issue currency to pay for goods and services; it can only issue government securities. Thus, the Treasury must sell bonds to the Federal Reserve to finance government spending. When the Treasury sells bonds to the Fed, the latter pays for them by crediting the Treasury account. The Treasury then issues checks to pay for the purchases. These checks become deposits when recipients deposit them in their banks. In this case, the result is an increase in the money supply and increased aggregate expenditure.

An alternative way to reach the same conclusion is for the Treasury to sell bonds to the public. Then the Fed buys the bonds from the public through an open-market purchase, which (as you saw in Chapter 11) increases the money supply. This is the way financing through money creation most often works because the Fed usually purchases bonds through the open market rather than directly from the Treasury.

This method of financing government spending is frequently called *printing money* because it increases the money supply. It is also referred to as *monetizing the debt* because government debt issued to finance government spending has been removed from the hands of the public and has been replaced by deposits that will increase the money supply.

Some economists, though, suggest that the government should simply use printed money. Because the government has the right to coin money and to regulate its value, they think it would be wise to bypass the banks and print the money directly as needed for federal government spending to generate economic activity. These economists argue that banks should not be paid an interest rate for providing a service that is fundamentally a function of the government. If the government printed the money instead of relying on selling bonds, it could avoid the cost of paying interest. As an alternative, they suggest using interest-free financing. With this method, the Treasury would sell non-interest-bearing notes to the Federal Reserve Banks, which in turn would create deposits for the government.

NET*Link*

Take a virtual field trip to the United States Department of the Treasury.

http://www.ustreas.gov

METHODS OF INCREASING GOVERNMENT SPENDING

Once government spending has been chosen as a means of raising aggregate expenditure in order to increase the level of total income and employment, the question remains of exactly how to accomplish the objective. Three methods are generally suggested: increase spending and hold taxes, hold spending and decrease taxes, and increase both spending and taxes proportionately.

Increase Government Spending and Hold Taxes

This method involves an increase in the amount of money spent by the government. For example, if the government previously spent $1,000 billion annually and taxed the same amount, it had a balanced budget. Now suppose that the government increases spending to $1,050 billion annually. If taxes remain constant, the government must borrow $50 billion for its additional spending. If the government borrows from the banks, then consumers and firms do not have to give up spendable funds in the form of higher taxes. As a result, total spending should increase for the economy as a whole. Again, total income increases not just by $50 billion, but by some multiple thereof, depending on the size of the multiplier. Under this method, the government can easily maintain close control over the direction of additional government spending.

Hold Government Spending and Decrease Taxes

This method is often referred to as the *tax rebate plan*. It also results in a deficit budget. For example, suppose that the government previously ran a balanced budget of $1,000 billion annually, as in our first case. If the government decreases taxes by $50 billion annually, its revenues fall $50 billion short of the needed amount. As a result, the government borrows $50 billion. Although the government is not spending any more, those who receive the $50 billion tax rebate are expected to spend the money for either consumption or investment. Thus, total income and output increase by $50 billion times the multiplier. To the extent that recipients of the rebate may save a portion of the $50 billion, the impact of this method on total income and employment is lessened. The direction of private spending may also be less effective than that of government spending. This method is politically popular, however, because most consumers and firms are happy about reduced taxes. It is also possible to combine elements of the preceding two methods by simultaneously increasing government spending and decreasing taxes.

Increase Government Spending and Increase Taxes Proportionately

This method maintains a balanced budget, but its effectiveness is limited by the fact that, in raising taxes, the government may absorb private funds that otherwise would have been spent for consumption and investment. Because most tax measures force consumers and investors to give up spendable income, a larger amount of government spending is needed to raise the level of total income and employment a given amount by this method than by the first two methods mentioned. By using either of the previous methods, the government can raise total income by $50 billion times the multiplier.

Any attempt to raise aggregate expenditure through government spending that is financed strictly by taxation eliminates the multiplier effect because the effect of the multiplier on the increased government spending is offset by the reverse multiplier effect of the decrease in consumer and business spending. The balanced-budget multiplier is always equal to 1. Thus, if government spending is increased by $50 billion and taxes by $50 billion, total income will be increased by $50 billion $\times$ 1 = $50 billion.

DISCRETIONARY GOVERNMENT SPENDING

If a decision is made to use deficit spending to raise the level of total income and employment, a question naturally arises about the direction of such discretionary government spending. Should the government increase its everyday services? Should it provide new services? Should the spending be for consumption or investment purposes? Should it be used to create public-sector jobs? Should it be concentrated or diversified? How much should it be, and how long should it last? Obviously, the decision to use deficit financing is only the beginning of the issue. It is possible, for example, to alleviate the effects of unemployment or poverty by using direct monetary transfer payments to the unemployed and the poor or by spending funds for public works or public-sector job programs.

Transfer Payments

Although using transfer payments ensures that those suffering most from unemployment will receive direct aid, it may be less effective overall than government spending in the form of public works. If an unemployed person receives a transfer payment, the bulk of the payment is spent for consumption, which increases the level of economic activity to only a limited degree. And even if the person is employed on a project such as the removal of trash along an interstate highway, the total effect is not much greater. The capital needed to put workers on such a job is limited to rakes, shovels, wheelbarrows, and perhaps a few trucks. Furthermore, spending a direct income payment primarily for consumer goods may have no greater effect than to decrease unintended excess inventories of consumer goods.

Public Works

On the other hand, a large public works project—for example, a bridge, a dam, a highway, or an office building—requires using a large amount of capital goods and producing a large amount of supplies, such as iron, cement, lumber, electric wiring, and glass. Furthermore, transportation is stimulated by the movement of these goods. Payments are made to contractors, who in turn pay subcontractors, suppliers, and transportation companies, in addition to the workers directly on the job. These workers then spend on consumption. Consequently, other workers are employed in the production of consumer goods that these workers purchase. All this tends to heighten the multiplier effect. Thus, more secondary and tertiary employment is generated through public works than by a leaf-raking project or by simple transfer payments.

As a way to reduce unemployment, public works appear to serve the purpose better than other means. Moreover, afterward there is something to show for the spending and production efforts involved. In addition, workers have jobs and are able to purchase the consumer items they require.

Problems with Discretionary Government Spending

To its credit, discretionary government spending can be used to fill the gap between output and aggregate expenditure when consumption and investment are insufficient to maintain a high level of employment. Government spending can even be used to provide useful public goods such as parks and highways.

However, discretionary government spending has some problems. Among the most serious problem is that it is very difficult to end a government spending program, because every program has a political constituency. As a result, spending continues beyond when it is needed, and the government deficit continues to grow. Another problem relates to when the government spending is needed and how long it takes to get started. In the case of large public works, the agency involved may take years to acquire the land, permits, plans, and so on to begin the project. By the time the project is underway, discretionary spending may no longer be needed, and the expansionary fiscal policy designed to combat recession may simply fuel subsequent inflation.

Not only is government spending considered less efficient than private investment spending but if the private sector sees government spending as a form of temporary fiscal fine-tuning, the response is less likely to be robust. People don't fully or predictably respond to one-shot expansionary policies.

Expanding the Economy

The economic, social, and political woes of unemployment underscore the need for problem solving. In serious depressions, unemployment imposes a hardship not only on individual employees and their families but also on the economy as a whole. Widespread and prolonged unemployment results in a loss of individual income and frequently a deterioration of working skills. Furthermore, the loss to the economy in goods and services can be tremendous. Labor time lost today is gone forever. It is true that workers could work double time tomorrow to make up time lost today, but they could also work double time without having lost the original time.

Under the laissez-faire policy and self-adjusting mechanisms of classical economic doctrine, little could be done during a depression except to wait for full employment to return. But when millions of workers are unemployed, people go hungry, mortgages are foreclosed, property values drop, factories close down, and members of Congress are flooded with complaints. Under these conditions, it is difficult to stand by and wait for the economy to adjust to a high level of employment. Furthermore, many people (especially voters) tend to blame adverse economic conditions on the political party in power. Therefore, in addition to the humanitarian motive (promoting the public welfare) and economic justifications, political considerations usually enter the picture when a decision is made about the use of expansionary measures.

THE GREAT DEPRESSION

At the time of the presidential elections in 1932, nearly 12 million persons (25 percent of the labor force) were unemployed in the United States; millions more were only partially employed. In short, one out of every four workers was idle, and many of the others were working only part-time.

Upon taking office, President Roosevelt pinpointed the primary objective of his administration: to halt the downward spiral of output, employment, income, and prices by bringing about an upward expansion of the economy through activist monetary and fiscal policies. Like Keynes, Roosevelt thought that it was the government's responsibility to take action to bolster the economy. The money supply was eventually increased, even to the extent of devaluing the dollar, and fiscal policy became a tool to increase the level of total income and employment. Public works and deficit spending were the order of the day. In fact, budget deficits averaged in excess of $3 billion annually during the 1929–1940 period.

Although the Roosevelt administration and Congress may not have been influenced by Keynes, they certainly adopted policies that paralleled those of the Keynesian analysis. Experience between 1933 and 1945 with the New Deal's public-spending program indicated the following:

1. Early attempts to alleviate unemployment repudiated the pump-priming theory. (This was the notion that it would just take a one-time dose of government spending to put the economy on the road to recovery—like pump-priming a water well.)

2. Developments verified the multiplier theory.

3. Although it was large, spending during the 1930s was insufficient and indicated the need for a huge outlay of government spending during a severe period of depression.

4. The war proved that a sufficiently large outlay of government spending can restore an economy suffering from high unemployment to full employment within a relatively short time.

5. Better results are obtained through spending on public works than could be obtained through transfer payments.

President Roosevelt's New Deal policies closely resembled those advocated by the Keynesian analysis, especially the idea of deficit spending and public works. Further evidence that we have accepted much of Keynesian theory can be found by analyzing the Employment Act of 1946 and the Full Employment and Balanced Growth Act of 1978.

Expansionary Policies of the 1960s

Fiscal actions consistent with Keynesian analysis were also taken by the Kennedy and Johnson administrations in the 1960s. President Kennedy was concerned that the conditions of maximum employment, maximum production, and maximum income, as called for by the Employment Act of 1946, were not being met. In 1963 the economy was growing at 3 percent annually, compared with a potential growth rate of 4.5 percent. To stimulate economic growth, personal and corporate income tax cuts of $11.5 billion and excise tax cuts of some $6 billion were enacted by Congress during 1964 and 1965. These cuts were financed by deficit spending for the purpose of increasing aggregate demand for goods and services and for improving total income and employment.

By early 1966, the economy was experiencing a real economic growth rate of over 5 percent and was approaching full employment. The expansionary policies of the 1960s were implemented not because of a recession or depression, but to stimulate economic growth. But with the war in Vietnam escalating in 1966, concern shifted to possible contractionary measures to control inflation. The recession beginning in 1974, however, drew attention once again to the need for expansionary measures.

Expansionary Policies of the 1970s, 1980s, and 1990s

Five recessions occurred in the U.S. economy between the years 1970 and 2003. Not only was the recession of 1974–1975 the most severe since the Great Depression but it was also characterized by stagflation–stagnation or sluggishness in the production sector of the economy and inflation in the price sector. The 1980s experienced two recessions in a very short interval of time. The economy slid into recession in 1980 and again in 1982. Unemployment peaked at 10.7 percent during this recession, the highest rate in over 40 years. The recession of 1990–1991 was preceded by federal legislation containing a deficit reduction package of $496 billion. Rather than stimulate the economy, increased income taxes served as strong contractionary measures.

THE RECESSION OF 1974–1975

With the advent of the 1974–1975 recession, unemployment rose above 5 percent by mid-1974. Inflation, however, was running at an annual rate of 12 to 13 percent, which put the economy back in a position of stagflation. By November, 1974, unemployment had risen to 6.5 percent. By April, 1975, unemployment was at 8.9 percent and still rising. Faced with a decline in real output over five consecutive quarters, a reluctant Ford administration had to admit that the economy was in a state of recession and that conditions were likely to get worse before they got better. Faced with simultaneous recession and inflation, President Ford met with his economic advisers in December, 1974 to determine the feasibility of shifting the focus of government economic policy from one of fighting inflation to one of economic expansion and fighting unemployment.

In January, 1975, President Ford submitted to Congress a comprehensive economic program that included a tax reduction and a proposed federal budget deficit of $51 billion. In the spring and early summer, income tax rebates of $23 billion were distributed to taxpayers. In addition, several other measures, including expanded public employment programs and financial aid for home purchases, were discussed in Congress. On the monetary side, the Fed agreed to expand the money supply at a faster pace, and the prime rate fell to 7 percent by midyear.

THE RECESSIONS OF 1980 AND 1982

When the economy slid into a modest recession in 1980, limited measures were used to offset the downswing. Unemployment rose from 5.8 percent in 1979 to 7.1 percent in 1980 and reached a high of 7.6 percent in the latter part of the year. When President Reagan assumed office, the unemployment rate stood at 7.4 percent, but the inflation rate was near the double-digit level. It appeared that the country had weathered the short 1980 recession. The prime rate of interest, however, was slightly over 20 percent, a record high level. Productivity per labor hour was at a low ebb.

President Reagan directed his main economic policy efforts toward reducing the rate of inflation. Accordingly, his administration implemented policies to increase aggregate supply. The goals of Reagan's supply-side measures were to encourage savings, stimulate investment, and motivate work effort. The administration supported the Fed's tight monetary policy as a means of combating inflation. But in spite of a tax reduction and other measures calculated to expand production, recession reemerged in 1982.

The rate of unemployment exceeded 10 percent in the second half of 1982 and the first half of 1983. Severe production cutbacks occurred in basic industries such as housing, auto, steel, and machine tools. In response to sluggish investment, large-scale layoffs, wage reductions, piling up of inventories, and a record number of bankruptcies, President Reagan extended unemployment benefits and provided funds for increased public works employment. The Fed increased the supply of money, and the discount rate was cut from 14 percent in late 1981 to 8.5 percent by December, 1982. The prime rate tumbled from 16.5 percent to 11 percent in the same time period, and the rate of inflation fell below 5 percent.

With the unemployment rate at 10.7 percent, Congress and the administration tolerated a federal deficit of $128 billion in fiscal 1982 and a deficit of $208 billion—at that time, the largest ever—in fiscal 1983. Although economic recovery began in early 1983, unemployment still averaged 9.5 percent for that year. It fell to 7.4 percent in 1984 and was still at 7.1 percent during 1985, when both the discount and prime rates were cut again. With some sluggishness apparent in the economy in late 1985 and early 1986, the discount rate was lowered and the prime rate fell accordingly. By September, 1986, the discount rate had been reduced to 5.5 percent and the prime rate was at 7.5 percent. They were still at those levels in the spring of 1987.

THE 1990–1991 RECESSION

Economic expansion continued for the next two years, with unemployment dropping to 5.2 percent in early 1990. At the same time, real GDP grew at a 3.9 percent rate in 1988 and at a 2.5 percent rate in 1989, while the price level rose by 4.4 percent and 4.6 percent in those two years and by 6.1 percent in 1990.

There was some softness in the economy in the last quarter of 1989 and the first two quarters of 1990, when the real GDP growth rate declined to 0.3 percent, 1.7, and 0.4 percent, respectively. By October 1, 1990, the federal deficit for fiscal year 1990 had reached $220 billion, which was $120 billion over the target established by the amended Balanced Budget and Deficit Control Act of 1985. Finally, early in November, 1990, after months of haggling between President Bush and Congress, a new deficit budget reduction package was agreed upon and signed by the president. Starting with the 1990 fiscal year, it called for a $492 billion reduction in the projected deficit over a five-year period.

The package increased income taxes, eliminated some deductions, raised user fees, and imposed higher excise taxes. On the other hand, it proposed numerous cuts in federal spending. Although such a package, including higher taxes and lower government spending, would do little if anything to stimulate the economy, it would serve as a strong contractionary measure.

The economy continued contracting in 1990, with the real GDP falling by 1.6 percent in the fourth quarter. The downswing continued into 1991 as the first-quarter real GDP declined another 3.3 percent. Based on the two consecutive quarterly declines in the real GDP, the National Bureau of Economic Research declared that the U.S. economy was officially in a recession that had started in July, 1990.

During the recession, the Fed increased the money supply and, in a series of moves, lowered the discount rate from 7.0 to 5.5 percent by May, 1990. During that time, the prime interest rate at commercial banks declined from 11.0 percent to 8.5 percent. Unemployment had risen to 6.8 percent by March, 1990, and the inflation rate moderated.

THE 2001 RECESSION

The 2001 recession was previously described in some detail in Chapter 15 as part of our analysis of business cycles. This recession was unique insofar as it brought about an unprecedented number of interest rate cuts in one year by the Federal Reserve. On the fiscal side, Congress passed the Economic Growth and Tax Relief Act of 2001. The most immediate stimulus resulting from the act was the rebate checks that were sent to taxpayers around midyear. Married taxpayers received lump-sum checks of $600, while single individuals received $300. In addition to tax rebates, marginal income tax rates were cut, as well as federal estate taxes. However, these tax cuts were enacted to promote long-term economic growth and reduce the federal tax burden in the private sector. They were not enacted as countercyclical measures. On the spending side, the federal government extended unemployment benefits and sharply increased funding for defense spending and homeland security after the events of September 11.

Despite these efforts to stimulate economic growth, recessionary forces proved to be stubborn. Although the 2001 recession in the United States officially ended in the fourth quarter, unemployment and personal and corporate bankruptcies both increased in 2002. Private investment spending and commercial real estate fell sharply, but consumer spending held up during the period, as did residential construction.

Recession and Deflation

Disinflation
A slowdown in the rate of inflation.

Deflation
A persistent decline in the level of prices.

During the last half of the previous century, the monetary and fiscal policies of industrialized countries focused on keeping inflation in check. However, a number of countries in recent years are experiencing disinflation, as their rate of inflation declines. Although disinflation is generally a good thing, a general concern is that disinflation may lead to deflation, as has occurred in Japan. **Disinflation** refers to a slowdown in the rate of inflation. **Deflation** is the opposite of inflation: a persistent decline in the price level.

Recessions generally respond to monetary and fiscal tools as well as to internal cyclical forces that stimulate economic recovery. Falling prices are normally viewed as a positive thing because we can buy more goods with our money. Computer prices, for example, have been declining for years as a result of technological and productivity advances. But as long as the decline in the price of computers and other goods and services is generally counterbalanced by rising prices in other goods and services, overall price stability prevails. But with deflation, declining prices outweigh rising prices.

Episodes of chronic deflation, like inflation, create instability and inflict hardships. As an economy slips from disinflation to deflation, prices and wages fall. With prices falling faster than gains in productivity, many companies are unable to service their debt and are faced with bankruptcy. Much of this debt was incurred to support expected expansion. Assets such as real estate and stocks are also vulnerable to the pressure of declining prices. Debtors must pay back debt in dollars more valuable than the ones they originally borrowed. Retirees and others who live off of their savings suffer from deflation because interest rates are so low that savings can be exhausted.

The process is difficult to reverse. As prices fall, consumers postpone many purchases, believing that prices will be lower in the weeks and months ahead. The value of money increases with future consumption rather than with present consumption. As people hold their money, the velocity of money declines and the economy remains stagnant. Monetary authorities can eventually become frustrated in attempts to expand the economy. As interest rates fall, nominal interest rates can approach zero percent. Although seemingly free, the cost of money is expensive in real economic terms. For example, if the nominal interest rate is 1 percent and prices are falling by 2 percent, the real interest rate is 3 percent and central banks have little leeway left to lower rates. Combined with a contraction in the supply of credit, the result can be prolonged economic stagnation.

Japan is the first major industrialized country to experience serious deflation since the 1930s. Japan has suffered through a long and painful stagnation that began in 1991 and continued into 2003. The Japanese stock market index peaked in 1989 at approximately 39,000 yen before falling to almost 9,000 yen in 2001, a 75 percent loss. The collapse in stock prices accompanied by sharp drops in real estate prices triggered falling demand and rising unemployment. A large number of nonperforming loans accumulated in the Japanese financial system. In response, banks contracted the supply of credit to potential borrowers and called in loans collateralized by stocks and real estate that were worth a small fraction of their former value. These financial actions created a serious credit crunch in the economy. In 2000, the recession was accompanied by deflation, as retail and wholesale prices declined. The Bank of Japan had lowered short-term interest rates from a peak of 8.3 percent in 1991 to less than 1 percent by 2000. Despite numerous attempts to restore growth on the part of the government, the economy proved resistant to monetary and fiscal attempts to promote economic recovery.

Japan is not alone in dealing with deflation. Argentina experienced falling prices in 1999, 2000, and 2002, and Hong Kong experienced a decline in the general price level each and every month between late 1998 and late 2002.

Most economists don't believe short-term deflation is a serious matter, but chronic deflation as has occurred in Japan causes painful personal hardships and a misallocation of a nation's resources.

Contractionary Policies

Inflation
A persistent increase in the level of prices.

Before proceeding to the policy steps that can be implemented to contract the economy in inflationary periods, it is important to develop an understanding of the meaning of the term *inflation*. **Inflation** is defined as a persistent increase in the general price level. Inflation can occur in a fully employed economy or in an economy operating at less than full employment.

TYPES OF INFLATION

There are two broad types of inflation, each brought about by the interaction of numerous forces. Because inflation can originate from either the demand side or the supply side, the contractionary policies employed to combat inflation differ depending on the underlying cause of rising prices.

Demand–Pull Inflation

Demand–Pull Inflation
Inflation that occurs when the total demand for goods and services exceeds the available supply of goods and services in the short run.

Demand–pull inflation occurs when the aggregate demand for goods and services exceeds the aggregate supply of goods and services in the short run. This is much more likely to occur in a fully employed economy because of the difficulty such an economy has producing additional goods and services to satisfy the demand. Competitive bidding for relatively scarce goods and services forces prices upward. Excess spending may come from several sources: Consumers may decide to spend past savings, the government may operate at a deficit, consumer credit may be liberalized, commercial and bank credit may be extended, or the money supply may otherwise be increased. Generally, when purchasing power increases faster than the productivity of our economy, demand–pull inflation results.

Cost–Push Inflation

Cost–Push Inflation
Inflation characterized by a spiral of wage and benefit cost increases and price increases.

The second type of inflation is known as **cost–push inflation,** characterized by a spiral of wage and benefit cost increases and price increases. It is a backward shift in the aggregate supply curve. This may occur in either a fully employed or an underemployed economy. It is difficult to say whether it starts with increased wages, higher material costs, or increased prices of consumer goods. If wages or material costs do increase for some reason, however, producers are likely to increase the prices of their finished goods and services to protect their profit margins. Rising prices, in effect, decrease the purchasing power of wages. As a result, wage earners, especially through their unions, may apply pressure for further wage increases. This then leads to further increases in the price of materials and finished products, which in turn triggers further wage increases. Eventually, the cycle develops into the *wage–price spiral.* Cost–push inflation is also aggravated by the rising costs to private enterprise of providing greater fringe benefits, such as vacations, paid holidays, pensions, and hospital and health insurance coverage for employees.

Stagflation
Higher unemployment and inflation occurring at the same time.

Cost–push inflation originates on the supply side of the economy. When cost–push pressures result in both inflation and a higher unemployment rate, this is known as **stagflation.** Stagflation occurred during the 1970s as the economy slowed down and demand decreased but the price level continued to rise.

Measures to Reduce Total Spending

Keynesian analysis offers an explanation of the causes and cures for unemployment and demand–pull inflation at full employment. Unfortunately, the Keynesian approach did not provide an adequate framework for dealing with cost–push inflation and stagflation.

During periods of demand–pull inflation, aggregate demand is greater than aggregate supply. Two alternatives exist for combating inflationary pressures in this situation. The better of the two is to increase the total output of goods and services to satisfy excess demand. But because this is not easily done in a full-employment economy in the short run, we must rely on the second alternative: reduce total spending.

A number of methods of reducing total spending in the economy exist. The reduction can be made in government spending, in investment, and/or in consumption. In any case, both the economic and the political effects of such actions must be considered. The method selected frequently depends on particular circumstances in the economy. Wartime inflation, for example, requires special measures.

AUTOMATIC STABILIZERS

Automatic stabilizers may not be strong enough to restrain inflation during an upswing in the economy. Nevertheless, they are still there. When employment is at a high level, income taxes are maximized and disbursements for unemployment compensation and some welfare spending are minimized, which helps rake off excess spendable funds from the economy. Similarly, the flow into and out of private supplementary unemployment funds has a contractionary effect. Our personal and corporate income tax structure may yield a full-employment surplus, which likewise has a contractionary effect and may even cause a fiscal drag on the economy. With rising incomes, personal and corporate savings may increase and act as a deterrent to inflation.

MONETARY POLICY

The Federal Reserve System may use monetary policy to combat inflation. Measures designed to decrease the money supply and increase the rate of interest tend to discourage investment, lowering aggregate expenditure and tending to bring investment into line with savings. In the ideal situation, investment is reduced to a point where it just fills the gap between consumption plus government spending and total output at full employment. Here there is an advantage in having a central monetary authority that can easily influence interest rates in order to raise or lower aggregate expenditure. The contractionary effects of a rise in the interest rate, however, can be offset. Businesses will not hesitate to borrow and invest even at higher interest rates if profits are rising, as frequently occurs when prices and, consequently, profits rise quickly during an inflationary period. According to the Keynesian analysis, little can be done to control the demand for capital in the absence of direct regulations. For this reason the government must rely on the Fed to tighten the money supply and manipulate interest rates to combat inflation.

OTHER MEASURES

The government may discourage investment and consumption by other means, such as by imposing credit restraints on both commercial and consumer loans. For example, it may limit borrowing for stock market purchases, it may tighten up restrictions on housing credit, and it may restrain consumer credit. The government may also try to encourage individuals and firms to save instead of spend and, if absolutely necessary, it may impose voluntary or mandatory price and wage controls.

GOVERNMENT SURPLUS

Aggregate expenditure may be reduced during an inflationary period by using policies that are the opposite of those used to increase aggregate expenditure during a recession. First, the government can limit its spending to essentials. Furthermore, it can operate with a surplus budget to reduce consumption and investment. If the government taxes more than it spends, aggregate expenditure tends to be reduced. In this case, unlike with expansionary policies, the government should try to tax spendable funds (those that are going to be spent on consumption and investment) rather than idle funds. The government can combat inflation by building up a surplus in three ways: hold taxes and decrease spending, increase taxes and hold or decrease spending, or decrease taxes and decrease spending.

Hold Taxes and Decrease Spending

If taxes are held constant and government spending is decreased to combat inflation, the most effective method is to decrease spending in areas that tend to have the greatest multiplier effect. This method is also more palatable to the public than an increase in taxes. On the other hand, a reduction in government services necessitated by a decrease in spending may meet with some public resistance.

Increase Taxes and Hold or Decrease Spending

If higher taxes are to be used to combat inflation, taxes should be increased so that they absorb funds that otherwise would be spent on consumption or investment. Here again public sentiment may have to be weighed. If taxes are already high—as they are likely to be during an inflationary period—consumers and investors may not be receptive to the idea of even higher taxes. If this method is used to combat inflation, accompanying the higher taxes with a decrease in spending produces a double effect.

Decrease Taxes and Decrease Spending

The combination of lower taxes and lower government spending can be contractionary if taxes are decreased in areas where the money would otherwise be held idle. This practice reduces total spending by the amount of the decrease in government spending, provided that those who receive the tax reduction do not spend it. A major problem with this method involves designing a tax rebate that will not release spendable funds. Even if such a plan could be designed, it would be difficult politically to justify a tax rebate that primarily benefits higher-income groups.

Regardless of the method used, the essential thing is to reduce aggregate demand. Thus, it is beneficial for government to build up a budget surplus, because in this way it can absorb excess spendable funds in the economy. Through taxation, the government can reduce aggregate demand to a point where it equals aggregate supply, thereby removing or lessening demand–pull inflationary pressure. A reduction in government spending can be used to bring total investment plus government spending into equality with savings. It can reduce government spending to a point where investment just equals the gap between consumption plus government spending and total output at full employment. On the other hand, an increase in taxes can be used to reduce consumption and investment to such a degree that government spending just fills the gap between private aggregate expenditure and total output, thereby eliminating the inflationary pressure.

If the government does use a surplus budget to combat inflation, the government must keep rather than spend the surplus. If it chooses to spend the surplus during the inflationary period, the desired contractionary effects will be wiped out. Government spending merely replaces the private-sector spending on consumption and investment, and the inflationary pressures remain. The desired contractionary effect of a surplus is also negated if the government uses the surplus to reduce the national debt because the recipients of debt repayments may spend the funds rather than save them.

BORROWING

Another way to reduce the amount of spendable funds in the economy is to sell government bonds. This can be an effective method of reducing aggregate expenditure, because payments made to the Federal Reserve for the bonds use money that would otherwise have been spent. Bond sales can be used alongside or in place of an increase in taxes. Frequently, it is easier to get firms and individuals to give up spendable funds through bond purchases than through taxation.

Wartime Inflation

Some of our strongest inflationary pressures occur during wartime periods because of the government's large demand for military goods and services. A wartime economy can entail a significant reallocation of productive resources. The causes of wartime inflation are basically the same as the causes of demand–pull inflation in peacetime. In either case, aggregate demand exceeds the productive capacity of the economy at full employment. Demand–pull inflation in wartime conditions can be augmented by cost–push, structural, or social inflation. The measures used to tackle wartime inflationary pressures are different from those used to combat peacetime inflation. It should be noted that the measures presented are more likely to be employed if the war effort is prolonged, costly, and seriously inflationary.

NEED FOR REDUCING CONSUMPTION AND INVESTMENT

In effect, it is necessary to reduce the effective demand for consumption and investment by an amount sufficient to permit government expenditure to fit into the gap between total output and the effective demand for consumption plus investment. Because much of private investment may be converted into wartime production, the primary task is to reduce the demand for consumption, and strong governmental measures may be required.

Taxation

The ideal measure to combat wartime inflation is heavy taxation. Through taxation, purchasing power can be transferred from individuals and firms to the government. This reduces the effective demand of the private sector of the economy and makes room for the necessary government spending on military goods and services. At the same time, it gives the government the means to make its purchases without going into debt. The most effective taxes are those that primarily reduce consumption because a considerable amount of private investment will still be essential. For example, very stiff income and sales taxes are beneficial. However, there may be considerable political and social opposition to such taxes.

Voluntary Savings

A second method of combating wartime inflation is a program of voluntary savings, especially on the part of the consumer. The best method of accomplishing this is to encourage consumers to buy government bonds. In this way they not only will give up the purchase of consumer goods but also will transfer purchasing power to the government, which it can use to buy war materials. Available evidence does not indicate that voluntary savings ever have been sufficient to arrest wartime inflation.

Compulsory Savings

Because taxation plus voluntary savings are generally inadequate to finance a war, some advocate that more positive measures be exercised by the government. One of these is a program of compulsory savings. Compulsory savings may be justified on the basis of need and the common good. A compulsory savings plan would require that a deduction in addition to income taxes be made from each individual's paycheck. This money would be credited to a special savings account that would remain blocked, except for emergencies, for the duration of the war or longer. Interest on these savings would be paid by the government.

If compulsory savings are to be used, it is only equitable to hold the price level constant. It would be unfair to force individuals to save in order to reduce consumer demand and then let the value of their savings deteriorate by permitting prices to rise. Thus, if necessary, price and wage controls could be used to hold the price level.

Other Measures

Other devices are sometimes used to reduce or to limit consumption and investment during a wartime period. For example, the rationing of goods and services may be used, especially when civilian products are in short supply compared with demand. Usually rationing via the allocation of coupons is used as a supplement or substitute for pricing as a rationing mechanism. Credit controls that increase the down payment and raise the size of installment payments by shortening the loan maturity on big-ticket items can be instrumental in limiting the demand for goods and services. Credit restraints can also be used to restrict the purchase of homes. Higher interest rates and tighter money, of course, can limit private investment. Wage, price, material, and workforce personnel controls may likewise be utilized during a wartime period.

During World War II and the Korean War, many of these measures were employed. However, during the Vietnam War severe contractionary measures were avoided. Defense and private domestic expenditures both increased, as did government deficits, inflation, and interest rates. Subsequent military engagements in the Caribbean, Middle East, Africa, and Europe did not entail hard economic choices. They were short in duration and/or relatively small in terms of their impact on the domestic economy.

But what about the future? If a prolonged war should break out, it is not inconceivable that some, if not all, of these measures may be employed. Current increases in expenditures are being financed on a Vietnam-like model, with neither shared economic sacrifice nor war-focused priorities. So far the increases are manageable. But the cost of fighting global terrorism in coming years, plus the possibility of a war in the Middle East followed by a long military presence could change all that. So, too, could sharply rising oil prices.

The Trade-Off Between Unemployment and Inflation

Once the economy is at full employment, it is difficult to ride the crest of the economy at the point where unemployment is minimized and the price level stabilized. The debate in recent years about the trade-off between increased unemployment and an increase in prices has renewed interest in a concept known as the **Phillips curve.** This curve was developed by the British economist A. W. Phillips, who studied the relationship between the level of unemployment and nominal wage increases in the United Kingdom from 1861 to 1913. When unemployment was high, nominal wage increases were smaller, and when a low level of unemployment existed, wage increases were larger. Based on his historical data, Phillips concluded that the nominal wage level would stabilize with a 5 percent unemployment rate.

Phillips Curve
A curve showing the relationship between unemployment and inflation.

In the 1960s, U.S. economists began to apply the Phillips curve to portray the relationship between the inflation rate and unemployment. Figure 16–2 shows the relationship between inflation rates and the unemployment rate in the United

FIGURE 16–2   Unemployment–Inflation Experience, 1960–2002

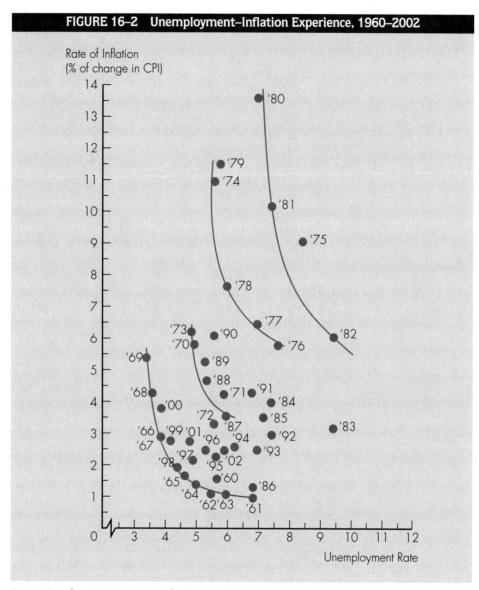

Source: Data from U.S. Department of Labor, *Monthly Labor Review.*

States for the period 1960 through 2002. During the 1961–1969 period, the inverse relationship between the inflation rate and unemployment was quite evident, as shown by the downward-sloping Phillips curve. Thus, it would appear that lowering unemployment could only occur at the expense of higher inflation and vice versa.

However, during the 1970s the Phillips curve shifted to the right. This may have resulted from structural changes in the economy. During the 1970s the labor force experienced major changes in its composition, as labor force participation rates for women and teenagers increased significantly. Both groups at that time had higher rates of unemployment at any given rate of inflation. During the late 1970s and early 1980s, the Phillips curve continued to shift to the right. Rather than demand–pull inflation, this was a period in which cost–push inflation prevailed, accompanied by severe stagflation. Cost–push inflation in the economy resulted primarily from sharp spikes in energy prices accompanied by increases in the cost of other productive resources. Consequently, the nation experienced both higher inflation rates and higher rates of unemployment. However, in the late 1980s and 1990s the Phillips curve shifted downwards to the left but the trade-off became less pronounced.

The Phillips curve played a large role in determining macroeconomic policy issues in the 1960s. But the shifting Phillips curve created policy problems, because policymakers could no longer determine what inflation rate would be needed to achieve a given rate of unemployment. It is now generally held by economists that the Phillips curve more accurately describes the short-run rather than the long-run relationship between inflation rates and unemployment rates. According to the theory of rational expectations, in the long run the Phillips trade-off disappears altogether.

The reason the Phillips curve is thought not to work in the long run is based on the the belief that over time the economy tends to operate at the *natural rate of unemployment*. Figure 16–3 assumes the natural rate of unemployment is 6 percent and that the existing inflation rate is 0 percent. Let us now assume that an election year is approaching and Congress wishes to lower the unemployment rate by pursuing expansionary policies that will lead to an increase in aggregate demand. Increasing aggregate demand increases profit, output, and employment as long as the wage rate is stable. Further assume that policymakers are willing to accept a 3 percent inflation rate in order to reduce the unemployment rate to 5 percent. In the short run, the economy moves from point a to point b in Figure 16–3. As indicated by the movement along PC_1, success has been achieved. The unemployment rate is now 5 percent, and the inflation rate has risen to 3 percent. This is consistent with the Phillips trade-off of unemployment and inflation. However, this only succeeds if wage rates remain stable. But because workers see that their real wage is less, they not only seek to get the 3 percent back in purchasing power, they anticipate a future inflation rate of 3 percent and bargain for an additional 3 percent wage hike for the following year. Now, higher wage payouts reduce profits, causing production to fall and unemployment to rise back to its natural rate of 6 percent. But the inflation rate has not fallen, for it remains at 3 percent. This can be seen at point c on PC_2. Repetition of this process causes the inflation rate to accelerate and the short-run Phillips curve to shift upwards as workers' expected inflation rate rises in recognition of the increases in the actual rate of inflation. This results in a long-run Phillips curve that is vertical. Therefore, the conclusion to be drawn is that persis-

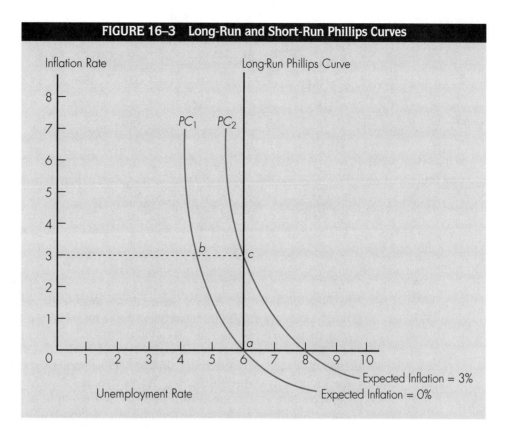

FIGURE 16–3   Long-Run and Short-Run Phillips Curves

tent attempts by policymakers to stimulate aggregate demand to reduce the unemployment rate below the natural rate will fail and cause an ever-increasing rate of inflation. This can be seen by upward shifts in the short-run Phillips curves from PC_1 to PC_2. As long as workers correctly anticipate future inflation rates, policymakers will be frustrated as the inflation rate continues to rise and the unemployment rate reverts back to the natural rate. This is consistent with the new classical school's theory of rational expectations as described in Chapter 12.

But even if the Phillips curve does not hold up in the long run, it is still true that policymakers must generally choose between which of the problems is more important, inflation or unemployment.

HYPERINFLATION IN LATIN AMERICA

Hyperinflation
Inflation that feeds on itself to go out of control, creating severe distortions in the economy and rendering currency almost worthless.

Inflation problems are not unique to the United States. Most countries have had serious bouts with inflation at one time or another. In recent years, some of the most dramatic cases of inflation have occurred in Central and South America. Because of their severity, they constitute examples of hyperinflation. **Hyperinflation,**

TABLE 16–1 Latin American Inflation Rates 1985–2001 (Selected Countries and Years)									
	1985	1989	1990	1992	1993	1994	1995	1998	2001
Argentina	672%	3,030%	2,314%	25%	11%	4%	3%	1%	4%
Bolivia	11,750	15	17	11	9	9	9	4	2
Brazil	226	1,287	2,938	1,009	2,148	2,669	84	2	8
Chile	31	17	26	15	13	11	8	5	4
Guatamala	19	11	41	10	12	12	12	6	8
Mexico	58	20	27	16	10	7	35	19	7
Peru	163	3,399	7,482	74	49	24	11	7	2
Venezuela	11	84	41	31	38	61	60	30	12

Sources: *Statistical Abstract of the United States,* 1991–2001 and *World Fact Book,* various years.

NETLink

Examine some facts about the economies of various Latin American countries at

http://www.cia.gov/cia/publications/factbook/index.html

or runaway inflation, creates severe distortions in the economy and renders currency almost worthless. Left unchecked, the impact upon national output and employment can be devastating. It can also produce social and political upheaval.

Table 16–1 presents inflation rates for selected countries in Latin America since 1985. Bolivia, Peru, Argentina, and Brazil experienced the most severe inflation of the group of countries presented. Prices changed daily in these countries as printing presses ran off money much faster than the output of goods and services could grow. Fearing hyperinflation reminiscent of post-World War I Germany (prices changed hourly, workers were paid daily, and some people used near-worthless money for wallpaper), each of these nations took drastic steps to get inflationary pressures under control.

Contractionary tools included enacting wage and price freezes, sharply reducing government spending, implementing tight money policies, issuing new currencies, devaluing currencies, reducing tariffs, and eliminating the policy of indexing wages and prices to the inflation rate.

Bolivia is an example of a country that took corrective action against inflation. Between 1984 and 1985, consumer prices increased by over 11,000 percent—an obvious case of hyperinflation. Unable to collect sufficient taxes to keep up with the rapid growth of government spending, Bolivia was printing 1-million-, 5-million-, and 10-million-peso notes daily. Contractionary efforts included the devaluation of its currency by 93 percent, cuts in government spending, and wage and price freezes. As a result of these actions, the inflation rate in Bolivia has fallen below 5 percent.

Although inflation rates have diminished markedly in many Latin American countries, inflation remains a problem. Even double-digit inflation rates for extended periods can cause havoc in an economy. Success in combating inflation must be measured over longer periods of time because the possibility always exists that painful and contractionary policies cannot be sustained for political and social reasons, as well as economic ones.

Contracting the Economy

The federal government used many strong and broad measures to control inflation during World War II and during the Korean War. However, for our purposes, the past few decades provide a suitable period for study, analysis, and evaluation of our attempts to use contractionary measures. During this span of time we experienced varying degrees of price stability, moderately rising prices, and strong inflationary pressures. Higher taxes, voluntary savings, budget surpluses, tight money, higher interest rates, wage and price controls, and credit controls have been used to combat inflation. Table 16–2 provides background data for our discussion.

THE 1960s

After several years of relative price stability during the 1950s, some price increases became apparent in the economy in the latter half of 1961. President Kennedy

TABLE 16–2 Employment, Unemployment, and Inflation 1960–2002 (Selected Years)					
Year	Employment (Thousands)	Unemployment (Thousands)	Rate of Unemployment*	CPI (1982–1984 × 100)	Rate of Inflation
1960	65,778	3,852	5.5%	29.6	1.7%
1970	78,678	4,093	4.9	38.8	5.7
1980	99,303	7,637	7.1	72.6	13.5
1990	117,914	6,874	5.5	130.7	5.4
1991	116,877	8,426	6.7	136.2	4.2
1992	117,598	9,384	7.4	140.3	3.0
1993	119,306	8,734	6.8	144.5	3.0
1994	123,060	7,996	6.1	148.2	2.6
1995	124,900	7,404	5.6	152.4	2.8
1996	126,704	7,236	5.4	156.9	3.0
1997	129,558	6,739	4.9	160.5	2.3
1998	131,463	6,210	4.5	163.0	1.6
1999	134,420	5,685	4.1	166.6	2.2
2000	135,208	5,655	4.0	172.2	3.4
2001	135,073	6,742	4.8	177.1	2.8
2002	130,793**	8,266**	5.8	181.5	2.4

*Civilian workers.
**Preliminary.
Sources: *Economic Report of the President* (Washington, D.C.: U.S. Government Printing Office, 2003) and Bureau of Labor Statistics.

established a set of voluntary wage and price guideposts. As a guide for noninflationary wage behavior, the rate of increase in wage rates (including fringe benefits)
in each industry was to be equated with the national trend in overall productivity
increase. At that time the average productivity per worker in our economy was increasing about 3 percent annually, so the guideposts initially recommended that
wage increases be held to about 3 percent per year. This would allow the increase
in wage costs to be absorbed out of rising productivity, without requiring a price
increase.

With inflation still an issue, President Johnson called for the imposition of a
temporary 10 percent surcharge on personal and corporate income taxes as a means
of decreasing aggregate expenditure. Congress passed legislation to this effect
in 1968.

The impact of the surtax fell more heavily on savings than expected. Consumption did not lessen, but the rate of savings fell sharply. Capital spending accelerated because investors thought that the 7 percent investment credit might again
be suspended as a contractionary measure.

By mid-1968, a number of hefty national wage increases occurred within the
economy, adding to the cost–push inflationary element. The shortage of skilled and
even unskilled labor was evident in the economy. Average hourly wage gains of
7 percent in manufacturing industries during the year, plus a reduction in savings,
offset the impact of the income tax surcharge.

All this caused prices to continue their upward movement through 1968. By
the end of the year, the CPI had risen 4.7 percent. Thus, despite adoption of a
strong fiscal measure to accompany somewhat restrictive monetary measures, little
success was achieved in arresting the upward movement of prices in 1968.

THE 1970s

Continued economic pressures involving prices, wages, and the balance of payments forced President Nixon in August 1971 to make drastic and sweeping
changes in his administration's domestic and international economic policies.
Among other measures, he declared a 90-day freeze on all prices, wages, and rents;
temporarily suspended the convertibility of dollars into gold; imposed a 10 percent
surcharge on imports; froze a scheduled pay increase for government employees;
sought to reinstitute tax credits as a means of stimulating investment and jobs; and
asked Congress to reduce personal income taxes and to repeal the 7 percent excise
tax on automobiles. The 90-day freeze was followed by a Phase II control period
that allowed noninflationary wage and price increases.

The immediate effectiveness of Nixon's New Economic Policy in combating inflation can be gauged somewhat by the fact that during the six months before the
freeze prices increased at an annual rate of 4.5 percent, but in the five months subsequent to the freeze they increased at an annual rate of 2.2 percent. The price
level for 1972, during which price controls existed for the entire year, increased by
3.2 percent.

In January, 1973, President Nixon announced Phase III of his New Economic Policy, which in effect reestablished voluntary guideposts for price and wage increases. The initial guidepost figures were 2.5 percent and 5.5 percent annually for prices and wages, respectively.

The removal of compulsory Phase II controls proved premature, however, so on June 13, 1973, President Nixon declared a 60-day freeze on prices. Wages were not affected by this freeze. Instead of ending the freeze on all goods at the end of the 60-day period, the government unfroze prices selectively, and Phase IV controls were imposed on various categories of goods and services at different times before and after the 60-day period.

In spite of an economic slowdown, prices soared in 1974. Unemployment moved above 5 percent and reached 6.5 percent by the end of the year, its highest level in more than a decade. President Ford then presented his contractionary program, which advocated a tax surcharge, a decrease in federal spending, a balanced budget, several energy-saving and fuel conservation measures, tougher antitrust enforcement, a number of measures to encourage savings, exhortations to consumers to shop for bargains, and establishment of a consumer committee and an organization of inflation fighters.

But as the economy deteriorated over the next few months, it became evident that there was a problem of both high unemployment and high inflation. Clearly, the state of the economy had slipped into stagflation. Real GDP had dropped for a third consecutive quarter, unemployment had reached 6.5 percent, and double-digit inflation still prevailed. This period of stagflation was brought about by several supply shocks to the economy, including the oil embargo, the crisis in agricultural foodstuffs, and the phasing out of wage and price controls. The Carter administration was caught in the dilemma of trying to attack high inflation and high unemployment at the same time. In 1978, Carter announced a set of voluntary wage–price standards. These standards suggested that wage increases over the next 12 months be held to 7 percent. The new wage–price standards elicited a mixed reaction and were also largely unsuccessful.

Overall, the contractionary economic policies pursued by the Nixon, Ford, and Carter administrations met with little success. The decade of the 1970s saw inflation average 8 percent, unemployment never below 4.9 percent, and negligible real income gains.

THE 1980s

When President Reagan took office in 1981, unemployment was running at a rate of 7.4 percent annually, the inflation rate was near the double-digit level, the discount rate was 14 percent, and the prime interest rate was a record 21.5 percent. It is not surprising that policymakers were anxious for new solutions.

Rather than resort to Keynesian measures, Reagan sought to implement a number of supply-side measures to encourage savings, stimulate investment, and motivate work effort for the purpose of expanding the economy and reducing inflation. Many of these measures were incorporated into the Economic Recovery Tax Act of 1981. The Tax Act included a 25 percent reduction in personal income taxes to be spread over a three-year period, a reduction in the top marginal tax rate, reductions in corporate tax rates, tax credits on new investment, tax exemptions for interest earned on special all-savers accounts, and indexation of income tax rates starting in 1984. A year later the president and Congress found it necessary to rescind some of the tax reductions, impose some tax increases for fiscal 1983, and enact some new tax measures to keep the federal deficit for fiscal 1983 from becoming too large.

Disinflation—a slowdown of the rate of inflation—continued during the economic recovery. The inflation rate hovered around 3 percent through mid-1986. It moved above 4 percent in 1987 and remained near that level until 1990, when it averaged 6.1 percent. A steep decline in oil prices, continued importation of large amounts of low-priced products, lower interest rates, moderation in wage increases, and declining food prices contributed to the lowering of the inflation rate. But one of the biggest products of the decade was a huge increase in the national debt caused by historically large budget deficits.

THE 1990s

The annual rate of inflation remained below 4 percent through 1986. It moved above 4 percent in 1987 and remained at that level until 1990, when it averaged 6.1 percent. In early 1990, the annualized change in the CPI was 5.3 percent, the discount rate was 7.0 percent, and the prime interest rate stood at 10.0 percent.

President Bush and his policymakers wanted lower interest rates as economic growth slowed in the fourth quarter of 1989 and the first quarter of 1990. The Fed, however, was concerned about a possible resurgence of inflation and steadfastly maintained the 7.0 percent discount rate. Once again an administration faced with stagflation had the dilemma of choosing between expansionary measures and contractionary measures.

Although President Bush could have suggested (as some members of Congress did) that taxes be increased to narrow the federal deficit and help combat inflation, he was reluctant to do so because of his presidential campaign pledge of "no new taxes." In November, 1990, economic growth was still sluggish and unemployment was rising. The Kuwaiti oil crisis preceding the Gulf War added to the stagflation. At that time Bush signed the 1991 federal budget agreement calling for tax increases, spending cuts, and other measures projected to result in a $492 billion reduction in the anticipated deficit over the next five years.

While the budget agreement offered little to stimulate the economy, the increased taxes and reduction in government spending would serve as a strong contractionary measure. Still, government spending was not actually being reduced; rather, the previously projected increases were being lowered. In July, 1990, the economy entered a recession, evidenced by the negative real GDP growth rates for the last quarter of 1990 and the first quarter of 1991. The Fed increased the money supply and lowered the discount rate in a series of moves from 7.0 percent in December, 1990 to 5.5 percent by May, 1991. During that time, the prime rate fell and inflation moderated, with deflation occurring in some months.

The prime interest rate at commercial banks declined from 11.0 percent to 8.5 percent. Unemployment had risen to 6.8 percent by March, 1990, and the inflation rate moderated. After bottoming out in the first quarter of 1991, the economy entered into the expansionary phase of the business cycle.

When President Clinton took office in 1993, economic recovery was still weak and job growth appeared slow. Clinton sought to expand the economy while bringing the budget deficit under control. This approach was based on the idea that reducing the federal budget deficit would bring down interest rates and stimulate private investment. The results were highly favorable, for the expansion became the longest on record. What makes this expansion somewhat unique is that fiscal policy was contractionary over the period, while monetary policy was largely expansionary. Inflation averaged 2.6 percent from 1993 to 2000, while the unemployment rate dropped to near 4 percent in 1999. Success against inflation was aided by sharp declines in computer prices, a drop in oil prices, rapid growth of industrial capacity, and downward pressure on the prices of imported goods. Most importantly, fiscal actions to reduce the deficit were accompanied by an accommodating monetary policy.

Summary

- Monetary policy has as its objectives economic stability, economic growth, and price stability. Monetary policy involves regulation of the money supply by the Fed. Increasing the money supply can raise the level of aggregate expenditure during periods of unemployment. The goal of fiscal policy is to promote maximum income with full employment in a closed economy.

- Among the automatic stabilizers of the economy are the Social Security system, pension payments, unemployment compensation, farm price-support programs, and the federal personal income tax.

- A fiscal stimulus *activates* the economy as a result of a budget deficit. A fiscal drag *slows* the economy as a result of a budget surplus.

- The government can pay for its spending via tax financing, debt financing (borrowing), and creating money by selling bonds.

- If the government increases its spending, but does not increase taxes, total spending for the economy as a whole should increase because the government is borrowing from the banks and not individuals. If the government decreases taxes, it results in a deficit budget. If government spending is held but taxes are decreased, there is less revenue for the government, which then has to borrow.

- Transfer payments and public works are two forms of discretionary government spending that can be used to raise the level of total income and employment. Transfer payments are less effective overall than public spending in the form of public works because much of the payment received is spent for consumption, thus increasing the level of economic activity somewhat.

- *Deflation* is a persistent decline in the level of prices. Disinflation is a slowdown in the rate of inflation. Disinflation is usually considered a good thing. Deflation becomes a problem only when it is chronic and severe as in the case of Japan.

- *Inflation* is a persistent increase in the level of prices. *Stagflation* is inflation and higher unemployment at the same time. *Demand–pull inflation* occurs when aggregate demand exceeds aggregate supply. *Cost–push inflation* results from a spiral of wage and benefit cost increases and price increases. It is a backward shift of the aggregate supply curve. *Hyperinflation* is inflation that goes out of control and makes currency almost worthless.

- Measures to contract the economy include automatic stabilizers, a tight monetary policy, and running a surplus in the government budget. A government surplus can result from holding taxes constant and decreasing spending, increasing taxes and holding constant or decreasing spending, and decreasing both taxes and spending.

- Wartime inflation involves different measures to contract the economy. These include taxation, voluntary savings, forced savings, wage and price controls, credit controls, and a number of other tools.

- The Phillips curve shows the short-run trade-off between inflation and unemployment. In the long run, the Phillips curve breaks down largely because of rational expectations on the part of labor.

- Historically, many nations have experienced bouts of hyperinflation. In some Latin American countries, inflation has increased at an annual rate of over 2000 percent. In 1985, Bolivia experienced an inflation rate of over 11,000 percent.

New Terms and Concepts

Expansionary policies
Contractionary policies
Automatic stabilizers
Fiscal drag
Fiscal stimulus
Crowding out

Ricardian equivalence
  theorem
Disinflation
Deflation
Inflation
Demand–pull inflation

Cost–push inflation
Stagflation
Phillips curve
Hyperinflation

Discussion Questions

1. How does unemployment compensation act as an automatic stabilizer for the economy? What do you think of the proposals adopted in past recessions that extended unemployment compensation?

2. What are the three ways by which the government can finance its spending?

3. What are the merits of increased government spending versus a tax reduction, provided that either involves a deficit?

4. What are the advantages of government spending on public works, as compared with transfer payments, as a means of alleviating a trough? What are the disadvantages of this approach?

5. How does a progressive income tax rate serve as an automatic stabilizer to offset inflation?

6. To combat inflation, is it better to decrease government spending and hold taxes constant, or to hold government spending constant and increase taxes? Explain.

7. Why is it that measures that diminish or eliminate demand–pull inflation may not work successfully against cost–push inflation?

8. What do you believe causes hyperinflation in Latin American countries?

9. Why is inflation difficult to combat if it occurs during a recession, as it did in 1974 and 1980?

10. Are voluntary wage and price standards, such as those President Carter suggested, likely ever to work in our economy? Why or why not?

Economic Applications

EconNews

Learn more about inflation and how it occurs in the real world by going to http://econapps.swlearning. com and clicking on the EconNews icon. Then, click on the "Employment, Unemployment, and Inflation" link under the Macroeconomics heading to find current news stories about inflation.

16

CHAPTER REVIEW

17

Taxation, Budgetary Policy, and the National Debt

After studying Chapter 17, you should be able to:

1. Identify the major characteristics of a good tax.

2. Distinguish between the benefits-received and ability-to-pay theories of taxation and give an example of each.

3. Define and give examples of proportional, progressive, and regressive tax rate structures.

4. Illustrate why the burden of a tax does not always fall on the taxpayer.

5. Identify the major sources of federal tax funds and describe the various taxes recently proposed.

6. Explain the three major purposes of taxation.

7. Demonstrate how the federal budget can be used to stabilize total output and moderate business cycles.

8. Critically analyze some of the problems resulting from the national debt.

9. Compare the relative size of the U.S. national debt to that of several other countries.

As residents, we expect to obtain certain goods and services from our various levels of government. The institutional arrangement for financing government spending for these goods and services is taxation. For decades, the primary purpose of taxation was to raise sufficient revenue to cover the cost of services that the various levels of government provided—federal, state, and local. Therefore, a balanced budget was a perennial target.

Over the years, certain services have become associated with a particular level of government. For instance, national defense and Social Security are associated with the federal government, and education and highway construction are associated with state and local governments. In fact, however, all three levels of government now participate in providing some services, such as education and public welfare.

Taxation

Certain sources of taxes are traditionally connected with specific levels of government. For many years, personal and corporate income taxes were levied by the federal government only. The federal government also levied tariffs (taxes on imported goods) and excise taxes (sales taxes on specific goods and services). The general property tax and sales tax were used by state and local governments. Now, however, many sources of revenue are being taxed by more than one level of government. Income, for example, is commonly taxed by federal, state, and local governments.

CHARACTERISTICS OF A GOOD TAX

These canons of taxation go back to the days of Adam Smith and other classical economists. To merit the mark of good taxation, a tax must possess the following characteristics:

1. There must be a *justifiable* reason for the tax.
2. The tax must be *equitably* applied to taxpayers.
3. There must be *certitude* regarding the amount of the tax and the taxpayer's obligation.
4. The tax must be *convenient* to levy and collect.
5. The tax must be *economical* insofar as the cost of collection is small compared with the revenue generated by the tax.

EQUITY OR FAIRNESS IN TAXATION

What is a fair or equitable tax? Various attempts have been made to establish principles for distributing the tax burden fairly.

Cost of Service

Cost-of-Service Theory
The theory that consumers should contribute toward the cost of general government in proportion to the cost of the governmental services they receive.

The **cost-of-service theory** suggests that consumers should contribute toward the cost of general government in proportion to the cost of the governmental services they receive. The services implied here include those for health, sanitation, fire and police protection, and all others performed specifically for the individual. Other kinds of services, including the construction and maintenance of highways and schools, should, according to this theory, be paid directly through user fees.

Except as a means of financing a few minor government services, the cost-of-service approach is untenable. First, it is impossible to calculate the costs of the services to each individual. How, for example, can the costs of fire and police protection be fairly allocated among consumers? Second, adopting such a principle would mean denying any responsibility on the part of the state for those not able to pay for public services.

Benefit Received

Benefit-Received Theory
The theory that consumers should contribute taxes in proportion to the benefits received from the services of government.

The **benefit-received theory** of taxation holds that consumers should contribute in proportion to the benefits received from the services of government. It is closely related to the cost-of-service theory; in fact, the two theories may simply be different aspects of the same general idea. For example, a person with $100,000 worth of real estate should pay 10 times as much in taxes as a person with only $10,000 worth. This principle is the one followed in levying taxes on real estate. It implies that a person who owns more property or wealth receives more protection from government and it costs government more to render these protective services.

Although the benefit-received theory possesses some validity, applying it to all taxes would be difficult. First, how could the value of a service be calculated? How should the costs of public education be allocated? Certainly, the value of a public education may be different for the children of the poor than for those of the rich, who may prefer private education. Although the benefit-received theory is not practicable as a guide for the formulation of taxes in general, it does operate in certain cases. Gasoline and liquor taxes and marriage and automobile license fees are all based on the benefit-received theory to a certain extent. User fees are also based on this theory.

Ability to Pay

Ability-to-Pay Theory
The theory that consumers should contribute taxes consistent with their ability to pay.

The **ability-to-pay theory** of taxation holds that consumers should contribute taxes consistent with their ability to pay. It is usually supported with minimal argument. But how should the ability to pay taxes be determined? Should proportional standards be used, with the tax based on something such as real estate or income? Or should the tax be designed to produce an equality of sacrifice on the part of those who are taxed?

Proportional Standard

One belief is that all taxes should be proportional. For example, if the tax base is real estate, then the total amount of the taxes that property owners pay should vary with the value of their property; or if the tax base is income, the amount of the tax should be proportional to the income received. Unfortunately, the proportional-standard concept does not reflect serious consideration of the relative sacrifices involved in the payment of taxes by consumers with varying amounts of income or wealth. However, the proportional idea is widely accepted, and this makes it important. In recent years, various proposals have been submitted in Congress to change the U.S. progressive income tax to a proportional or flat-rate tax.

Equality-of-Sacrifice Doctrine

Equality-of-Sacrifice Doctrine
The idea that consumers should contribute taxes on the basis of their marginal utility of income.

The **equality-of-sacrifice doctrine** of taxation is based on the diminishing marginal utility of income. As a general rule, the law of diminishing marginal utility tells us that the more dollars we have, each additional dollar provides decreasing amounts of satisfaction. Thus, when income is low, the marginal utility of a dollar is greater than when income is high. If a family with an income of $30,000 is required to pay $3,000 in taxes, the sacrifice of paying out valuable dollars needed for essentials is much greater than the sacrifice entailed by a family with an income of $200,000 paying $20,000 in taxes. Proportional income taxes, according to the equality-of-sacrifice doctrine, require a greater sacrifice for lower-income families.

The Tax-Rate Structure

Tax Rate
The percentage by which the tax base is multiplied in calculating the total tax that must be paid.

Tax Base
The value of the object upon which the tax is levied.

The tax-rate structure determines the amounts that individual taxpayers are called on to pay in taxes. The amount of a tax is determined by multiplying the tax rate times the tax base. The **tax rate** is a percentage; the **tax base** is the value of the object upon which the tax is levied. For example, if the rate is 20 percent of a person's gross income, the percentage indicated is the rate and the gross income stated in terms of dollars is the base. In the case of taxes on real estate, the rate is usually given as so many mills (thousandths) or cents per dollar or as a percentage of the assessed valuation. Thus, the rate might be stated as 5 cents per dollar or 5 percent of the assessed value of the property. The relationship of rates to changes in the base is indicated by the terms *proportional, progressive,* and *regressive.*

PROPORTIONAL RATES

Proportional Tax Rate
A tax rate that remains the same regardless of the size of the base.

A **proportional tax rate** is one that remains the same regardless of the size of the base. For example, a 5 percent proportional tax on an income of $10,000 would amount to $500 and that on $100,000 would amount to $5,000. A strong argument in favor of a proportional rate is that, after payment, taxpayers are left in the same relative position that they were in before the tax. Many who advocate proportional taxes admit that the rate structure may not impose an equal sacrifice on taxpayers, but they argue that no satisfactory criterion for sacrifice has yet been demonstrated. Moreover, they argue that proportional (or flat-rate) taxes are simple to administer.

PROGRESSIVE RATES

Progressive Tax Rate
A tax rate that increases as the size of the base increases.

General acceptance of the view that ability to pay should be used as a criterion for taxation has led some taxes to be applied at a progressive rate. A **progressive tax rate** increases as the size of the base increases. Thus, a tax rate of 1 percent on the first $1,000 of taxable income, 2 percent on the second $1,000, and so on is progressive.

Of course, if this rate of progression were continued, the tax would absorb all income beyond $100,000.

Opponents argue that progressive rates are unfair because they penalize the possession of wealth, the earning of income, and the exercise of hard work. But many of the great fortunes in any generation in the United States are gained through inheritance, a special skill or talent, or good fortune, rather than through industriousness. As a result—and perhaps because there are relatively few persons with exceptionally high incomes—lawmakers in the United States tend to sanction progressive income taxes. What constitutes a reasonable progressive rate, however, is debatable.

Under a progressive tax rate system, the marginal tax rate usually differs from the average tax rate. The marginal tax rate—normally, the highest rate—applies only to income above a certain level. Consequently, an income earner's average tax rate is less than his or her marginal rate.

REGRESSIVE RATES

Regressive Tax Rate
A tax rate that decreases as the size of the base increases.

A **regressive tax rate** decreases as the size of the base increases. For example, a tax rate of 5 percent on an income of $1,000, 4 percent on an income of $2,000, 3 percent on $3,000, 2 percent on $4,000, and 1 percent on $5,000 is regressive.

Although a sales tax is a proportional tax based on the amount of purchases, its opponents argue that the share of smaller incomes spent for taxable goods is higher than that of larger incomes. With a 4 percent sales tax, for example, a family with a $24,000 annual income may purchase $20,000 worth of taxable goods and services and pay sales taxes of $800. On the other hand, a family with a $100,000 income may purchase $60,000 worth of taxable goods and pay sales taxes of $2,400. Consequently, the lower-income family pays at a rate of 3.3 percent ($800/$24,000) of its income, whereas the higher-income family pays at a rate of only 2.4 percent ($2,400/$100,000) of its income. However, it is incorrect to call the sales tax regressive because the base of the tax is purchases, not income. Both families are paying a proportional tax rate, 4 percent, when the tax is compared with its proper base. Those who describe the sales tax as regressive should be careful to emphasize that it is regressive in relation to income, not in relation to its true base, purchases.

To recapitulate, a proportional tax is one in which the rate remains the same as the base increases, a progressive tax is one in which the rate increase keeps pace with or exceeds the rate of increase in the base, and a regressive tax is one in which the rate decreases as the base increases. Some taxes have elements of one or more different rates in their structure.

The Tax Burden

The burden of a tax does not always fall on the person or the firm paying the tax. Where it does fall depends on the slopes of the supply and demand curves for the product being taxed. For example, the burden of taxes on cigarettes, liquor, and other consumer goods with very inelastic demands is usually shifted to the final consumer. The tax is paid by the manufacturer or distributor, who, because of the inelastic demand for the product, then adds the amount of the tax to the selling price of the good and passes the burden of the tax on to the consumer.

The burden of many taxes can be shifted, but not the burden of a tax on personal income. The fact that the burden of some taxes can be shifted more easily than that of others is one reason for the continuing debate over what taxes should be levied. By definition, a **direct tax,** such as an income tax, cannot be shifted; an **indirect tax,** such as an excise tax on liquor, can be shifted. The distinction between the two terms is clear, but in individual instances it is not always evident whether a tax is direct or indirect.

Three aspects of **tax shifting**—passing the burden from one taxpayer to another—are recognizable. The **impact of a tax** is the financial burden entailed in paying the tax. For example, when an importer of Scottish tartan cloth pays the import duty, the impact of the tax is on the importer, but the importer then adds the amount of the tax to the price of the material. A tailor who subsequently buys the cloth in effect reimburses the importer for the amount of the duty paid; the tailor in turn adds that amount to the overall price of garments made from the cloth for customers. Therefore, the burden of the duty is on the final customers. The same thing is true of sales taxes when the amount of the tax is added to the selling price of the good or service and is thus passed on to the final purchaser.

The **incidence of a tax** is the point at which the burden of the tax ultimately rests. For example, the incidence of a cigarette tax is on the consumer. The **effect of a tax** is the economic consequence of paying the tax. For example, the increase in the price of a good resulting from paying a tax on it is an effect. If the increase in price results in a decrease in the quantity of the good purchased, this result is another effect of the tax.

The burden of many taxes, particularly excise taxes, tends to be shifted forward to the ultimate purchaser. Occasionally, however, the effect is shifted backward. This occurs when an increase in price due to the tax results in lower sales and consequently a decrease in the demand for resources to produce the good. In such a case, part of the effect of the tax shifts backward to the suppliers of the materials and labor involved. How much of a tax can be shifted forward or backward depends on the price elasticities of demand and supply.

Direct Tax
A tax that cannot be shifted, such as an income tax.

Indirect Tax
A tax that can be shifted, such as an excise tax on liquor.

Tax Shifting
Passing the tax burden from one taxpayer to another.

Impact of a Tax
The financial burden entailed in paying a tax.

Incidence of a Tax
The point at which the burden of a tax ultimately rests.

Effect of a Tax
An economic consequence of paying a tax.

Federal Taxes

Certain sources of taxes are traditionally connected with specific levels of governments. For many years, personal and corporate income taxes were levied by the federal government only. The federal government also levied tariffs (taxes on imported goods) and excise taxes (sales taxes on specific goods and services). The general property tax and sales tax were used by state and local governments. Now, however, many sources are being taxed by more than one level of government. Income, for example, is commonly taxed by federal, state, and local governments. Figure 17–1 shows the sources and uses of federal funds for fiscal 2003. A quick look at the chart tells us that individual income taxes and social insurance receipts account for 82 percent of the federal government dollar. Notice also that corporate income taxes account for 10 percent, and excise taxes account for 3 percent of the federal dollar.

The *personal income tax* provides the largest share of federal tax dollars. It is basically a progressive tax, but, with numerous deductions and exemptions, it is less progressive than it appears. The top tax rate in 2002 was 35 percent for couples with taxable incomes over $171,950 and for individuals with taxable incomes in excess of $141,250. Married couples and individuals earning in excess of $307,050 of taxable income are subject to a surcharge tax of 3.6 percent, bringing the highest tax rate to 38.6 percent. Because the tax is graduated, the marginal tax rates are higher than the average tax rates that individuals actually pay.

Social insurance taxes account for 35 percent of the federal budget dollar. These taxes are known as *employment* or *payroll taxes* and are comprised of Social Security taxes for old age, survivors, and disability insurance and the Medicare tax for hospital insurance. The Social Security tax is proportional insofar as all individuals

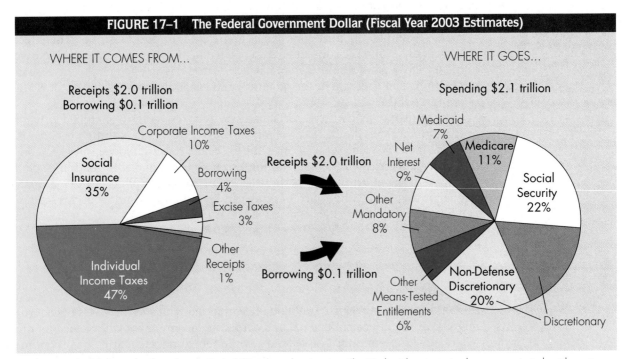

FIGURE 17–1   The Federal Government Dollar (Fiscal Year 2003 Estimates)

WHERE IT COMES FROM...

Receipts $2.0 trillion
Borrowing $0.1 trillion

Corporate Income Taxes 10%
Social Insurance 35%
Borrowing 4%
Excise Taxes 3%
Other Receipts 1%
Individual Income Taxes 47%

Receipts $2.0 trillion

Borrowing $0.1 trillion

WHERE IT GOES...

Spending $2.1 trillion

Medicaid 7%
Net Interest 9%
Medicare 11%
Other Mandatory 8%
Social Security 22%
Other Means-Tested Entitlements 6%
Non-Defense Discretionary 20%
Discretionary

*Means-tested entitlements are those for which eligibility is based on income. The Medicaid program is also a means-tested entitlement.
Source: Budget of the United States Government, Fiscal Year 2003.

pay the same tax rate on wage income. In 2002, employers and employees each contributed 6.2 percent for Social Security and 1.45 percent of a wage earner's income for Medicare. The base amount or earnings cap in 2002 for Social Security was $84,900. There is no limit on the base amount for the Medicare tax. Because of the income cap on the Social Security tax and the fact that it applies only to wage income, the tax becomes regressive. Higher-income earners pay a lower percentage of their total incomes than do lower-income earners. The regressive nature of the tax is lessened, however, because the payout formula provides low-income earners more dollars of benefit, per dollar paid in, than high-income earners.

The *corporate income tax* rate has been as high as 52 percent between 1952 and 1962 and as low as 1 percent in 1913. In 2002, the rate for corporate income was 35 percent for corporations with net income in excess of $18.3 million. The corporate income tax supplies 10 percent of federal funds. It is an indirect tax that is largely progressive in its effects. *Federal excise taxes* account for 3 percent of the federal budget dollar and until recently had declined steadily in relative importance. However, in recent years Congress has increased the excise tax on such items as tobacco products, telephone usage, and air travel passenger tickets. The excise tax on luxury automobiles was eliminated in 2003. The excise tax is an indirect tax that is considered to be very regressive. In examining the use of the excise tax, it becomes apparent that the tax is placed on goods and services for which there is a relatively inelastic demand. It also has been suggested that the excise tax is also used to influence social behavior.

MAJOR TAX PROPOSALS

Growing dissatisfaction with the complexity of the current personal income tax, as well as the cost of compliance, has resulted in several tax proposals that would entail a complete overhaul of the federal tax system. The following four tax proposals have generated support in recent years.

The Flat Tax

Flat Tax
A single tax rate on incomes.

The **flat tax** would replace the progressive income tax with a single tax rate of somewhere between 15 percent and 20 percent. Various versions of the flat tax have been proposed in Congress and in recent presidential campaigns. In its pure form, the flat tax is imposed at a single rate for businesses and individuals, with no deductions or credits. Large personal exemptions would allow low- and some middle-income taxpayers to pay no tax whatsoever. This feature incorporates a degree of progressivity in the tax system. Other versions of the flat tax retain certain deductions, such as the interest deduction on home mortgages and charitable donations, and do not exclude all investment income from taxation.

The flat tax does satisfy most of Adam Smith's maxims. Only the question of fairness remains because many critics believe that most such tax proposals favor the wealthy. The flat tax not only sharply reduces taxes on high salaries, but it also eliminates taxes on savings and investments, including dividends, interest on savings, capital gains, inheritances, and Social Security benefits. What appears to be a proportionate tax can be regressive to middle-income taxpayers. There is no denying, however, that the major advantage of the tax is its simplicity and the fact that most Americans favor the principle if not the details of a flat tax.

Consumption Tax

Consumption Tax
A tax on incomes excluding savings.

A **consumption tax** exempts savings from taxation. Proponents of the consumption tax contend that the tax is both fair and equitable because consumption reflects a household's own judgment as to what it can afford to spend and provides a good indication of the ability to pay. For this to be true, however, a consumption tax would have to provide generous exemptions to the poor and near poor. Administratively, the consumption-based tax would be levied in much the same way as the personal income tax. A taxpayer would take annual income, add gifts and bequests as well as net borrowings, and subtract all savings. The remainder would equal consumption, and the resulting amount minus exemptions would be taxed.

All sources of income would be treated equally. Wages would not be differentiated from interest or dividends or capital gains. None of these sources of income would be taxed, and the income itself would be taxed only if consumed, rather than saved.

Value-Added Tax

Value-Added Tax (VAT)
A tax on the increase in value as goods pass along through the production process to the market place.

The **value-added tax (VAT)** is an integral part of the tax systems of many industrial countries, including members of the European Union. The value-added tax collects taxes at each stage of production. Under the VAT, a business would pay the tax on all the materials and services required to manufacture the product. In effect, the VAT taxes the increment in value as goods pass through production and manufacturing stages to the marketplace. The value-added tax is paid by the producer and is passed along to the consumer in the selling price of the good. Thus, the consumer pays for the VAT in the form of higher retail prices. Table 17–1 presents the current value-added tax rates for selected European countries. VAT rates range from a high of 25 percent in Denmark to a low of 7.5 percent in Switzerland.

National Sales Tax

National Sales Tax
A tax collected on the final sale of goods and services.

A **national sales tax** is a form of consumption tax similar to state and local sales taxes. Like these taxes, the national sales tax is considered highly regressive; it imposes a heavier burden on low-income taxpayers because they spend a larger share of their incomes on essential purchases. Unlike the value-added tax, the national sales tax is collected on the final sale of goods and services. Consequently, it is collected from the consumer and not from the business firm that adds value to the product. In addition to being much simpler than the current federal income tax, the national sales tax would collect billions of dollars in unreported income from

TABLE 17–1 Value-Added Tax Rates of European Countries			
Country	VAT Rate	Country	VAT Rate
Denmark	25.0%	Netherlands	17.5
Iceland	24.5	United Kingdom	17.5
Norway	23.0	Portugal	17.0
Finland	22.0	Spain	16.0
Austria	21.0	Germany	15.0
Ireland	21.0	Luxembourg	15.0
Italy	19.6	Turkey	15.0
Sweden	20.0	Cypress	8.0
France	20.0	Switzerland	7.5
Greece	18.0		

Source: World Trade Organization, 2002.

those people who make a living by engaging in illegal activities and from those who do not pay income taxes.

Purposes of Taxation

Taxation is used for a variety of purposes. Three major purposes or objectives are discussed in the following paragraphs.

COVERING THE COSTS OF GOVERNMENT

For decades, the primary purpose of taxes was to raise sufficient revenue to cover the cost of the services provided by various levels of government. Accordingly, a balanced budget was an ongoing target. In seeking a balanced budget, the government could take certain measures to ensure achieving its objective. If economic expansion promised to yield a surplus of tax revenues, the government could reduce taxes, expand its services, or repay some of the government debt. On the other hand, during a period of economic contraction, when falling tax revenues threatened to produce a deficit, the government could tighten its economic belt and reduce spending.

REDISTRIBUTION OF INCOME AND WEALTH

Since the Great Depression, more use has been made of taxation as a means of redistributing income and wealth in the U.S. economy. Relying on the ability-to-pay concept, lawmakers have taxed consumers and businesses in higher income levels at higher rates to provide revenues for services that are shared in greater proportion by those in lower income levels. Higher corporate and personal federal income tax revenues (which go into the general fund), for example, may be used to provide public service employment for the unemployed, the elderly, or food stamps for the poor. In other instances, tax credits or rebates may be given in larger proportion to lower-income taxpayers. The use of taxation as a means of redistributing income has become a very controversial issue in recent years.

ECONOMIC STABILIZATION

Over the past 70 years, the U.S. government has used fiscal policy, that is, taxation and government spending, to try to stabilize total income and output. During that time, it has developed a set of fiscal measures to combat recessions and inflation and to stimulate the rate of economic growth. The use of these fiscal measures involves the federal budget and has an effect on total output and the price level.

Budgetary Policy

The federal budget's size, growth, and nature, that is, whether it is balanced or unbalanced, affect the U.S. national debt. Interrelated are monetary measures involved in financing any deficit. These measures may influence the structure and maturity of the national debt. Management of the national debt can have a stabilizing or destabilizing effect.

TYPES OF BUDGETS

The type of budget affects the level of total output to some degree. There are three possible types: a balanced budget, a deficit budget, and a surplus budget.

Balanced Budget

In general, a balanced budget has a neutral effect on the economy. Because government spending equals taxes in a balanced budget, total spending in the economy remains unchanged. Therefore, what consumers and business firms give up in spendable funds to pay their taxes is counterbalanced by government spending of the tax receipts. At times, however, it is possible for a balanced budget to have an expansionary effect in the economy, which occurs if the government taxes idle funds that consumers and businesses otherwise would not have spent. Aggregate expenditure then increases.

The expansion of aggregate expenditure through the multiplier effect depends on the propensity of citizens to consume or save. Assume that the marginal propensity to consume is 100 percent. In such a situation there would be no multiplier effect because the adverse effect of taxes on the private sector would be offset by government spending of the tax receipts through the public sector.

However, if the people saved one-fifth of their income and the federal budget were balanced at $1,000 billion, then theoretically the government would be taxing $200 billion of funds that were otherwise going to be saved. When the government spent these funds, it would have an expansionary or inflationary effect, depending on the employment in the economy. This effect would be lessened, of course, to whatever extent the savings would have been used for private investment.

Deficit Budget

A deficit budget generally increases total income and output or increases the price level, depending on the status of employment in the economy. With a deficit budget, the government spends more than it taxes and, to take care of the excess spending, the government must borrow funds. If it borrows idle funds, aggregate expenditure will increase because the government's total spending will exceed the amount of spending given up by firms and consumers through taxation. Therefore, the level of total output will increase if the economy is at less than full employment, or prices will increase if the economy is at full employment. A deficit budget is frequently referred to as a *fiscal stimulus*. The fiscal stimulus, however, is offset to some extent if the government borrows funds that consumers and businesses might otherwise have spent on consumption and investment.

Surplus Budget

A surplus budget occurs when government spends less than it receives in tax revenues. Government spending is insufficient to offset the decline in spending given up by consumers and businesses in the form of taxes. The result is a net decrease in aggregate expenditure. Consequently, a surplus budget is sometimes called a *fiscal drag* on the economy. This drag effect, of course, is lessened to the extent that the government taxes idle funds that would not have been spent otherwise. It can also be offset if the government uses the surplus to retire its national debt. At times a surplus budget may be used as a contractionary measure to slow down the rate of inflation.

THE BUDGET AS A STABILIZER

If used properly, a budgetary policy can help stabilize the economy and moderate business cycles. A surplus budget helps prevent inflation during a peak period, and a deficit budget helps offset unemployment during a trough. The use of budgetary policy as an anticyclical device is shown in Figure 17–2.

When the budget is used as a tool for economic stabilization, the goal is to balance the budget over the entire business cycle, instead of trying to do it annually. To accomplish this, the surplus of the peak would have to equal the deficit of the trough—a difficult task. For instance, a question might arise about whether policymakers should begin by building a surplus during the peak and then spending it during the next trough or whether policymakers should incur the deficit during

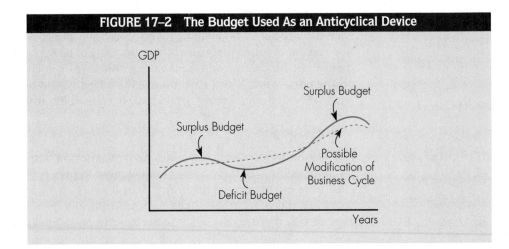

FIGURE 17–2   The Budget Used As an Anticyclical Device

the trough and then repay the debt with the surplus obtained during the subsequent peak.

Assuming that the first method is used, a second problem arises. How much surplus needs to be accumulated during the peak? This depends not only on the inflationary pressures of expansion but also on the estimated deficit during the subsequent contraction in the economy. It is practically impossible, however, to determine what the duration and the intensity of the peak will be, let alone the duration and the severity of the subsequent trough. Therefore, it is usually more feasible to run the deficit first. This approach also has its weaknesses. How can policymakers be assured that the subsequent expansion will be long enough or strong enough to permit accumulation of a surplus sufficient to pay off the deficit incurred in the previous contractionary period?

Another weakness of the deficit-first method is that, although most legislators are willing to use deficit spending during a recessionary period to help alleviate unemployment, many are reluctant to take the measures necessary to build up the needed surplus during prosperous times. In short, deficit spending to increase total output can be very popular with the public during a recession, but increased taxes or reduced government spending to combat inflation are seldom popular.

Any surplus acquired during a peak period should be held in reserve for best results. It should not be used to pay off the national debt until the level of economic output begins to stabilize or decline. If the surplus is used immediately to pay off the debt incurred during the trough, it will inject an amount equivalent to the surplus into the circular flow. If the recipients of debt repayments spend or invest the money received from the government, these funds will offset the reduced consumption due to higher taxes, and aggregate expenditure in the economy will remain the same. Consequently, the surplus budget will have a neutral effect instead of being contractionary. For purposes of stabilization, it is better to hold the surplus funds until total output begins to decline. Repayment of the debt at that time will increase aggregate expenditure when the recipients of debt repayments spend or invest these funds.

The process of using the budget as a stabilizer is further complicated when stagflation occurs, that is, when inflation exists during a recession or general slowdown in total output. A surplus budget at such a time would aggravate unemployment and be extremely unpopular politically.

THE FULL-EMPLOYMENT BALANCED BUDGET

Full-Employment Balanced Budget
A measure of the potential revenue and spending that would result if full employment existed.

In the 1960s, the idea of a **full-employment balanced budget** combined the goal of balancing the budget, the need for fiscal policy, and awareness of the effects of automatic stabilizers into one concept. According to this concept, the actual budget need not be balanced, but tax rates and government spending should be set so as to balance the budget at the full-employment level of income and output. The theorists who developed this idea said that policymakers should not look at the actual deficit or surplus, but at what the surplus or deficit would be at the full-employment level of output.

The actual deficit is a poor measure of fiscal policy because it reflects not only decisions about taxing and spending but also the state of the economy. If total income falls far below the full-employment level, automatic stabilizers will create a deficit as tax revenues fall and transfer payments rise. This deficit is entirely appropriate, because it helps stabilize the level of income and output. Indeed, if the economy were at full employment, there might not be a deficit at all.

When a deficit exists, it does not necessarily signal that the government is pursuing an expansionary fiscal policy; the president and Congress may even be pursuing a contractionary policy. The deficit may instead be the result of automatic stabilizers and recessionary conditions. When economists want to measure the direction of fiscal policy, they look at changes in the full-employment budget surplus or deficit, rather than at changes in the actual deficit.

Of course, if the federal budget is used as a fiscal tool to stabilize total output and if deficits develop over an extended period of time, the national debt will grow. The growth of a national debt creates other problems. Moreover, the actual management of the national debt can have a stabilizing or destabilizing effect on the level of total output.

Problems of the National Debt

Our experience with budgetary policy as a means of stabilizing total income and output is rather limited. It is difficult, therefore, to determine whether deficits and surpluses can be timed accurately and planned to be of the proper size to stabilize the economy. Furthermore, policymakers do not have sufficient experience to determine whether, in the absence of emergencies, the deficits and the surpluses will

NET_Link_

For an up-to-date examination of our national debt, check out the U.S. National Debt Clock.

http://www.brillig.com/debt_clock

offset each other sufficiently to prevent a growing debt. The United States incurred a sizable debt during the depression of the 1930s as a result of deficit-spending fiscal policies. Without having the chance to lower this debt, it entered World War II, which pushed the debt up to about $285 billion. The opportunity to reduce the debt was frustrated again by the outbreak of the Korean conflict in 1950. The onset of the Vietnam War in the mid-1960s interfered with experiments in using the budget for economic stabilization. In subsequent years, although the United States has not faced economic and military crises of the same magnitude, it has made very little headway in reducing the debt. In fact, the total national debt, now over $6.2 trillion, has grown to such proportions that it presents several major problems.

BANKRUPTCY

Many people mistakenly think that the debt may become so large that it will bankrupt the nation. They believe that the federal government may get into a situation where it will be unable to pay off the debt. This misunderstanding arises from a failure to distinguish clearly the true nature of government financing and the power of the federal government to raise tax revenues.

When the federal government borrows money, it borrows primarily from consumers, businesses, and banks within the economy. When it makes repayments on the debt, the money stays within the economy. There is no reduction in the nation's total assets when the government makes a repayment on the debt. Furthermore, the government's ability to repay is governed only by the total assets of the economy or, more immediately, by the total income of the economy and the government's ability to tax. For example, the total national debt in fiscal 2002 was approximately $6.2 trillion. Since the GDP was about $10 trillion and the total national income was over $8 trillion, the total income of the nation was obviously sufficient to take care of debt repayment if the government had been willing to raise taxes sufficiently to obtain the funds required to pay it off.

Theoretically, but unrealistically, the government could tax a sufficient amount to pay off the debt in a single year. If policymakers were to do this, it would not reduce the total income or assets of the nation as a whole. The taxation and repayment of the debt would merely redistribute income or cash assets inside the economy. The income given up by consumers and firms in the form of taxes would be offset by payment to those holding the debt. Thus the total income or assets of the economy would be the same after payment of the debt as before. The major difference is that the income and assets held by particular consumers and firms would change. On the other hand, foreign and international institutions held over 17 percent of the total national debt in 2002. A decrease in total income would result if they took their repayment out of the country.

Although a tax rate sufficient to pay off the debt in a single year would be prohibitive, over a long period the government could operate at a surplus sufficient to pay off the debt. Surpluses obtained during expansionary periods could be used to pay the debt during periods of contraction in the economy.

REDISTRIBUTION OF INCOME

Why doesn't the government take more positive steps to pay off the debt? There is reluctance to reduce the debt by sizable amounts both because the large tax necessary to do so would be politically unpopular and because doing so would be economically disruptive. One important problem involved would be the redistribution of income brought about by repayment of the debt.

If the debt were to be paid off rapidly, heavy taxes would reduce aggregate expenditure, especially among lower- and middle-income groups. Whether the reduction in aggregate expenditure would be offset when the government used tax money to pay off the debt would depend on what the recipients of debt repayments did with the money they received. As Table 17–2 shows, the national debt is held primarily by banks, businesses, government agencies, consumers in the higher-income groups, and foreigners. Because it is very likely that the debt holders' marginal propensity to consume or to invest would be less than that of the taxpayers in total, aggregate expenditure in the economy would probably be reduced.

Of course, if the debt holders spent the income they received at the time the debts were repaid, aggregate expenditure would not fall. It would therefore be best to pay off the debt during periods of less than full employment, with money obtained through taxes during an inflationary period. In this way, the debt could be used as a tool for economic stabilization.

TABLE 17–2 Percentage Ownership of the U.S. National Debt, March 2002

Owners of the Debt	Percentage Held
Federal Reserve banks and government accounts	52.5
Private investors	
Insurance companies	1.5
State and local governments	3.5
Depository institutions[1]	3.2
Foreign and international institutions	17.5
U.S. Savings Bonds	3.3
Mutual funds[2]	4.5
Individual investors[3]	9.4
Pension funds	4.6
TOTAL	100.0

[1]Includes commercial banks, savings institutions, and credit unions.
[2]Includes money market mutual funds, mutual funds, and closed-end investment companies.
[3]Includes individuals, brokers, dealers, trusts, estates, and others.
Source: Federal Reserve Board of Governors and U.S. Treasury.

BURDEN OF THE DEBT

Many people believe that the burden of paying the debt is passed on to future generations. The extent to which this is true depends on whether we consider the debt's effect on the total economy or on consumers and firms.

Effect on the Total Economy

In terms of the total economy, it is impossible to pass on the real cost of the debt to future generations. The real cost of the debt to the total economy can be measured only by calculating the loss of goods and services that consumers and firms forgo when they give up their purchasing power to buy government bonds. When consumers and investors purchase such bonds, they buy fewer goods and services for themselves, and they give the government revenue to purchase the goods and services it needs. World War II was a prime example of this action. The decrease in consumer goods output was the real cost of the debt. The people in the economy at the time the debt was incurred shouldered the real burden of the debt through the loss they experienced of goods and services.

For the economy as a whole, debt repayment, whether immediate or postponed until future generations, will not cost anything in terms of goods and services. As a result of the redistribution of income when the debt is repaid, some consumers and firms will suffer a loss of purchasing power; but this loss will be offset by the gains of others, and no net decrease in purchasing power in the economy will take place. For example, if the debt were to be repaid in a single year, the total tax necessary would be about $6.2 trillion. The tax would decrease aggregate expenditure and result in decreased output. When the government paid out the $6.2 trillion to debt holders, however, it would tend to offset the adverse effect of the tax, so total income in the economy would remain the same. Aggregate expenditures, and therefore output, would remain the same, provided the marginal propensity of the debt holders to consume and invest was the same as that of the general taxpayers. There would be no loss of total goods and services at the time the debt was repaid. For this reason, viewing the economy as a whole, it is impossible to pass the cost of the debt on to future generations.

Effect on Consumers

On the other hand, the burden of the debt with respect to consumers and firms can be passed on to future generations. If the government were to pay off the debt in a relatively short period—say, within the generation in which the debt was incurred—the particular consumers taxed to pay the debt would have to give up purchasing power. Thus, each would be personally burdened with a share of the cost of the debt to the extent that each was taxed. If payment of the debt were postponed for a generation or two, however, the tax would instead fall to a large extent on the descendants of the consumers and businesses that were in the economy at the time the debt was incurred. Thus, even though the net cost or burden of the debt cannot be passed on to future generations, the individual burden can.

THE MONEY SUPPLY AND THE DEBT

Another problem involved in repaying the debt is the effect of the repayment on the money supply. When an individual or a business loans the government money, the money supply does not increase. For example, if Allan Sanchez buys a government bond for $1,000, he generally pays cash for it. The result is merely a transfer of cash from the individual to the government, with no change in the total money supply. If the Federal Reserve lends the government money, however, it can pay for the bonds in cash or by creating a checkable deposit against which the government can write checks. In Chapter 11, we saw that the creation of demand deposits increased the money supply. Therefore, if the Fed were to buy $5 million worth of bonds and pay for them with a checkable deposit, it would increase the money supply accordingly. As noted in Chapter 16, this process is referred to as *monetizing the debt.*

The debt is also monetized when the Fed buys government bonds from the public. The money bond holders receive is normally deposited in banks, adding to bank reserves, which are the basis for expanding checkable deposits.

When the government goes into debt by borrowing from the Fed, it increases the money supply and thus either increases the level of total output or adds inflationary pressures to the economy. In 2002, the money supply as measured by M_2 was approximately $5.6 trillion. A portion of the money supply in the form of demand deposits came into existence as a result of the sale of government bonds to the Federal Reserve banks. Therefore, the national debt directly supported a portion of the total money supply.

A decrease in the money supply tends to decrease the level of total output and/or decrease the price level, unless it is offset by some other force, such as an increase in the velocity of money. Just as the debt is monetized when the government borrows from the Fed, the money supply is decreased when the debt is paid off. Thus, if the government were to reduce the national debt substantially over a relatively short period of time, it could reduce the money supply so abruptly and significantly that the level of total output would be adversely affected. On the other hand, payment of the debt would be beneficial during a period of full employment, insofar as it could reduce inflationary pressures. But during periods of less than full employment, such debt repayment could be harmful to the economy as a whole.

SIZE OF THE DEBT

The mammoth size of the U.S. national debt has discouraged serious attempts at repayment. Figure 17–3 portrays the rise in total national debt for selected fiscal years from 1970 to 2002. Of the $6.2 trillion national debt figure for 2002, approximately

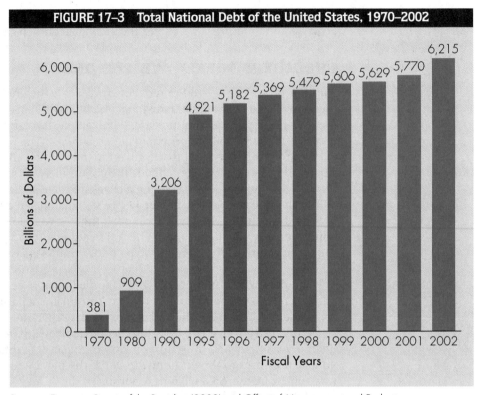

FIGURE 17–3   Total National Debt of the United States, 1970–2002

Billions of Dollars

Fiscal Years

Values shown on bars: 381 (1970), 909 (1980), 3,206 (1990), 4,921 (1995), 5,182 (1996), 5,369 (1997), 5,479 (1998), 5,606 (1999), 5,629 (2000), 5,770 (2001), 6,215 (2002)

Sources: *Economic Report of the President* (2002) and Office of Management and Budget.

$2.7 trillion was held by the federal government in trust funds. Thus, the amount of national debt held by the public amounted to approximately $3.5 trillion.

Although the United States has not reduced the size of the debt in absolute terms, increased productivity and higher national income have reduced its size relative to gross domestic product since 1950. In fact, GDP increased more than twice as fast as the national debt during the period 1950 to 1974. During the 1980s, however, debt rose faster than GDP. Figure 17–4 traces the debt–GDP ratio from 1950 to 2002 for that portion of the national debt held by the public. As shown in the exhibit, national debt has climbed back to 34 percent of GDP from a low of 25 percent in 1974. If debt figures include the $2.6 trillion held in government trust funds, the ratio of national debt to GDP in 2002 would increase to 60 percent. Because government-owned debt is owed to the government itself, the amount of debt held by the public is usually used as a measure of national debt.

Analysts occasionally suggest postponing payment on the debt because it will become less burdensome as the years go on. To the extent that the nation's total income increases through increased productivity, this suggestion has some merit.

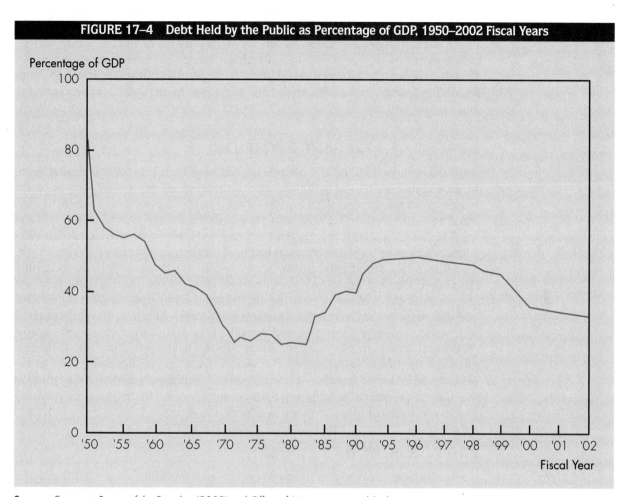

FIGURE 17–4   Debt Held by the Public as Percentage of GDP, 1950–2002 Fiscal Years

Percentage of GDP

Fiscal Year

Sources: *Economic Report of the President* (2002) and Office of Management and Budget.

But if the increase in total income is brought about primarily by higher prices, the suggestion is a poor one, because worse problems than that of debt retirement will result from rising prices. Furthermore, if inflation causes the purchasing power of a bond at maturity to be less than the purchase price of the bond, the public may not be willing to purchase bonds when the government needs money in the future.

REFUNDING THE DEBT

Because government debt obligations may reach maturity at times when the U.S. Treasury does not have the money to pay them, the problem of refunding the debt arises. At such times, the federal government generally issues and sells new bonds to raise money to pay off the matured obligations. This, however, may not be easy to accomplish, especially when billions of dollars' worth of securities may be maturing over a short period of time. Furthermore, the government is sometimes forced to pay a higher interest rate when it borrows funds for this purpose. Refunding can be a problem, because over $500 billion of the national debt becomes due and payable annually.

BURDEN OF INTEREST PAYMENTS

Included each year in the U.S. federal government budget is $200 billion or more for paying interest on the national debt. Although taxation for the payment of this interest does not impose a net burden or cost on the economy as a whole, it does cause an annual redistribution of income and therefore a burden to consumers and firms in the economy. If the government had originally increased taxes instead of going into debt or if the government had paid off the debt shortly after incurring it, a smaller total burden would have been imposed on consumers in the economy than when the debt repayment is postponed. The redistribution of income necessary to retire the debt is not only the amount of the principal but also the billions of dollars required to cover annual interest on the debt. This interest is offset in part by interest earned by various government trust funds, but the net interest payable on the federal debt in 2002 was an estimated $189 billion. Furthermore, as interest rates rise, the cost of carrying the debt rises. It is a matter of judgment whether society would be better served by undergoing the hardship of paying off the debt in a relatively short period or, by giving up more total income but making the hardship less severe, by spreading it over a longer period of time.

PRODUCTIVITY OF THE DEBT

If a business firm borrows money to erect a new building, buy machinery and material, or hire additional labor to produce goods, it expects to increase its total output. The loan it receives is said to be productive because it increases the total output of the company and improves its profits. In fact, firms borrow billions of dollars annually for this very purpose.

Similarly, consumers may borrow to increase their purchasing power, especially if purchasing certain goods has greater utility now than it would have in the future. Evidently, many of us are swayed by the appeal of present utility because consumers borrow billions of dollars each year to buy homes, cars, furniture, and the like.

Government borrowing and debt may be productive, or it may increase the total utility of the economy in much the same manner as do business and consumer loans. Financing dams, reforestation projects, highways and roads, educational facilities, labor retraining, medical research, space exploration, pollution control, and urban renewal through debt can be very productive. In some cases, total utility may be increased by improved roads, recreation facilities, new drugs, and the like. Like private consumers and firms, policymakers must decide whether the increased productivity and utility that result from their use of borrowed funds outweigh the disutility of paying off the debt.

The Road to Budget Surplus

The government incurred its first deficit in 1792, and it generated 70 annual deficits between 1900 and 1997. But deficits realized prior to 1981 pale in comparison to those that followed. In the early 1980s, the federal government cut taxes and greatly increased military spending. Also, the recession of 1981–1982 reduced revenues and increased federal outlays for unemployment insurance and similar programs that are closely tied to economic conditions. Resulting budget deficits caused the government to pay interest on more national debt at a time when interest rates were at historically high levels. As a result, the deficit soared. With mounting pressure to move the federal budget into balance and reduce debt accumulation, Congress enacted several laws to bring the federal budget into balance by constraining spending and raising taxes.

DEBT REDUCTION

The first of these laws was the Balanced Budget and Emergency Deficit Control Act of 1985. Also known as the Gramn–Rudman–Hollings Act, it called on Congress to reduce the deficit each year and to produce a balanced budget by 1991. Faced with the prospect of huge spending cuts in 1987, however, the president and Congress amended the law, postponing a balanced budget until 1993. Despite these legislative efforts, the fiscal year deficit in 1991 was recorded at $220 billion, just shy of the record $221 billion deficit of 1986.

Concern over the failure to reduce budget deficits led Congress to pass the Budget Reduction Act of 1990. This act called for reducing federal deficits by about $500 billion over a five-year period starting in 1991. This was to be accomplished by increased taxes and spending cuts. The key provision of this law was that annual limits were set for discretionary spending, and proponents of new spending plans or lower taxes were forced to offset additional costs by cutting other entitlements or raising other taxes. But, again, deficits continued to rise, climbing to $269 billion in 1991 and $290 billion in 1992. Additional legislation was passed in 1993 and again in 1997. The Revenue Reconciliation Act of 1993 was another attempt to cut the deficit by raising taxes and cutting expenditures over a five-year period. In 1997, the Balanced Budget Act called for $247 billion in savings in five years.

YEARS OF SURPLUS

Budget deficits began declining in 1993 and continued declining until 1998. In fiscal 1998, the federal budget recorded a surplus of $69 billion, its first surplus in three decades. For three consecutive fiscal years following the 1998 surplus, the federal budget recorded annual budget surpluses totaling more than $488 billion. These surpluses were the result of reduced federal government spending, particularly discretionary spending, and soaring tax revenues. The dramatic increase in tax revenues was tied to overall economic prosperity and a robust stock market. Investors in the stock market generated high capital gains tax revenues for the federal government from the sale of individual stocks or stocks sold within mutual funds.

Based on the surpluses of the 1998–2001 fiscal years, the Congressional Budget Office at one time projected that by 2011 total surpluses would reach $3 trillion. This sum included money generated by off-budget programs, such as Social Security. In fact, without off-budget surpluses of $99 billion in 1998 and $160 billion in 2001, the federal budget would have been in a deficit in both years. Sizable surpluses such as those seen in the 1998–2001 years triggered a number of debates as to how these surpluses could most effectively be used in the future. However, these debates became moot in fiscal 2002, as the budget slipped back into a deficit.

RETURN TO DEFICITS

The reoccurrence of deficits was the product of the recession of 2001, the sharp decline in capital gains tax revenues, tax cuts, the attacks of September 11, the increased expenditures for national security, the war against terrorism, and increased discretionary spending by the federal government. Although the 2002 deficit was but 1.5 percent of GDP, it caused concern because of the budget's quick drop from a surplus of 2.4 percent of GDP in 2000. Unfortunately, a new era of sustained deficits is now likely. Although the Congressional Budget Office still projects a return to surplus in 2006, the likelihood of this happening is questionable because of the CBO's underlying assumptions. In order to generate a surplus in 2006, the projections exclude many possible costly initiatives that would increase the probability of a deficit. Possible costly initiatives might include the extension of several expiring tax cuts, relief from the alternate minimum tax on individuals, an expanded war on terrorism, higher homeland security costs, and increased Medicare and prescription drug expenses, to name a few. As of August 2002, the budget surplus projected by the year 2011 was $336 billion, appreciably lower than the $3 trillion amount previously forecast.

INTERNATIONAL COMPARISON OF DEBT

The inability of the United States to balance its budget over time is not unique among developed nations. However, chronic budget deficits in the United States and elsewhere result in large amounts of public debt. Although the United States has the world's largest debt in absolute terms, it does not have the largest debt relative to gross domestic product.

Figure 17–5 compares the gross public debt of the United States in 2002 with the gross public debts of 11 other countries. As this figure shows, Italy, Japan,

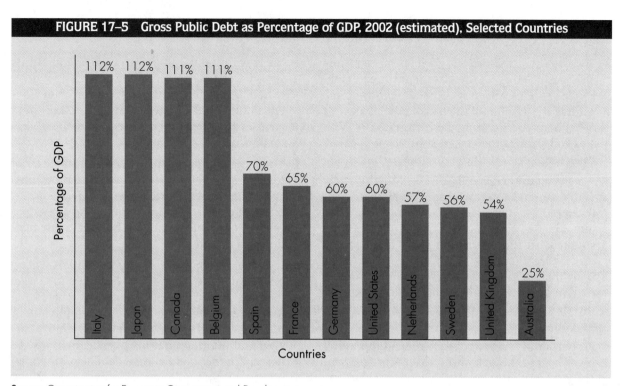

FIGURE 17–5   Gross Public Debt as Percentage of GDP, 2002 (estimated), Selected Countries

Source: Organization for Economic Cooperation and Development.

Canada, and Belgium have outstanding public debt greater than their gross domestic products. The United States falls near the lower end of the countries presented.

In the past, many nations reduced their public debt by inflating their economies and devaluating their currencies. With a global economy, however, these options are less attractive. On the other hand, deflationary measures impose heavy costs in terms of lost output and employment.

Summary

- The five characteristics of a good tax are: a justifiable reason exists for the tax; the tax is equitably applied to all taxpayers; there is a certitude regarding the amount of the tax and the taxpayer's obligation; the tax must be convenient to levy and collect; and the tax must be economical to collect compared with the revenue it generates.

- According to the benefits-received theory, individuals should pay taxes based on benefits they receive. The ability-to-pay theory holds that individuals should pay an amount of taxes consistent with their ability to pay. The equality-of-sacrifice theory is based on the belief that individuals should pay taxes according to their marginal utility of income. The cost-of-service theory contends that taxes should be paid in proportion to the cost of service received

- Proportional tax rates always remain the same, regardless of the size of the base. A progressive tax rate increases as the size of the base increases. A regressive tax rate decreases as the size of the base increases.

- The largest sources of federal tax revenues are the personal income tax and social insurance taxes. Increasing dissatisfaction with the personal income tax has brought forth proposals to replace the personal income tax with a flat tax, consumption tax, value added tax, or national sales tax.

- The three major purposes of taxation are: covering the costs of government, redistributing income and wealth, and stabilizing the economy. If there is a surplus of tax revenues, theoretically the government can reduce taxes, expand its services, or repay some of the government debt. When falling tax revenues prevail, the government could reduce spending. Taxes and government spending are used to try to stabilize total income and output.

- The federal budget can be used as a stabilizer of total output because it can moderate business cycles and help stabilize the economy. A surplus budget helps prevent inflation during a peak period; a deficit budget helps offset unemployment during a trough.

- It is not true that eventually the nation will be bankrupt if the federal debt becomes too large, because most of the debt is domestic. That is, the federal government borrows from individuals, businesses, and banks within the economy. Foreign and international institutions own but 17 percent of the total national debt. Also, the government's ability to repay is governed only by the economy's total assets and the government's ability to tax.

- Various laws have been enacted—including the Gramm–Rudman–Hollings Act of 1985, the Revenue Reconciliation Act of 1993, and the Balanced Budget Act of 1997—for the purpose of bringing the budget into balance by restricting spending and raising taxes.

- Budget deficits began to decline in 1993. Budget surpluses were recorded in fiscal years 1998–2001. A deficit occurred once again in the 2002 budget.

New Terms and Concepts

Cost-of-service theory
Benefit-received theory
Ability-to-pay theory
Equality-of-sacrifice
 doctrine
Tax rate
Tax base
Proportional tax rate

Progressive tax rate
Regressive tax rate
Direct tax
Indirect tax
Tax shifting
Impact of a tax
Incidence of a tax
Effect of a tax

Flat tax
Consumption tax
Value-added tax
National sales tax
Full-employment
 balanced budget

Discussion Questions

1. Should ability to pay be the primary basis of taxation? Why or why not?

2. Is the current progressive federal income tax used in the United States equitable? Why or why not?

3. How is the U.S. taxing system used to redistribute income and wealth? Should it be used for this purpose?

4. Is it feasible to balance the federal budget over the period of a cycle? Give reasons.

5. If you owned a $5,000 government bond, would you be willing to relieve the government of its obligation to pay you in the interest of eliminating the national debt? Why or why not?

6. How would the concept of interest-free financing for federal borrowing alleviate the interest burden of the national debt?

7. Should the U.S. government be required to balance the budget annually? Why or why not?

8. Distinguish between total national debt and the amount of national debt held by the public. What is the significance of classifying debt into the two categories?

9. What are the dangers (if any) of foreigners holding a large percentage of the U.S. national debt?

10. Do you think the budget surpluses recorded in the 1998–2001 period are likely to be repeated in the foreseeable future? Why or why not?

Economic Applications

EconDebate

Find debates on taxes and budgets by clicking on the EconDebate icon at http://econapps.swlearning.com. Find the Macroeconomics heading and click on "Taxes, Spending, and Deficits." This link provides debates about topics of taxes and U.S. spending.

17

CHAPTER REVIEW

18

International Trade and Aid

After studying Chapter 18, you should be able to:

1. Discuss the benefits of international trade in terms of the principle of comparative advantage.

2. Describe the various arguments in favor of tariffs and identify why some tariffs may be justified. Analyze the impact of tariff barriers on domestic prices, output, and employment.

3. Recognize the various nontariff barriers to free trade and describe why each might be used.

4. Discuss how and why U.S. policies toward international trade have changed over time.

5. Describe the important features of the U.S.–Canada Free Trade Agreement and NAFTA and discuss the possible impact of North American economic integration on the U.S. economy.

6. Understand the nature of the economic integration in Western Europe and compare and contrast the European Union with the United States.

7. Discuss the role of the World Bank in providing foreign aid.

An Overview of International Trade

Just as trade between different sections of a nation can improve the welfare of all people involved, so too can trade between nations benefit both the exporter and the importer. Different languages, habits, and customs are no more valid reasons for refusing to carry on trade than are imaginary boundary lines between states or regions a valid reason for stifling trade within a nation.

In some nations, the amount of international trade is minimal, but in others it is an important portion of the nation's total output and trade. In many countries, including Canada, Denmark, Great Britain, Norway, and Switzerland, the value of either exports or imports amounts to more than 20 percent of their gross domestic products. Although the United States has a much larger total value of foreign trade than any other nation in the world—indeed, the value of its merchandise exports alone exceeds the total output of many nations—the value of its exports is 7 percent of its GDP, while the value of its merchandise imports is approximately 12 percent of GDP. Figure 18–1 shows U.S. merchandise exports by region in 2002. As can be seen from the figure, Canada and Mexico constitute the largest markets for U.S. exports. Table 18–1 presents some of the leading exports and imports in broad categories. Capital goods, excluding automobiles, accounted for the largest dollar volume of both U.S. merchandise exports and imports in 2002. The amount of merchandise trade activity fluctuates with changing economic conditions throughout the world.

THE IMPORTANCE OF OIL

The United States' dependence on foreign oil is a case in point. In 1973, petroleum imports amounted to $8.4 billion and constituted 12 percent of the total value of U.S. merchandise imports. Following the oil embargo in 1973–1974, however, oil prices quadrupled, and petroleum imports rose to $27 billion, or 26 percent of the value of U.S. imports. But by 1989, oil-exporting nations were faced with excess supply and

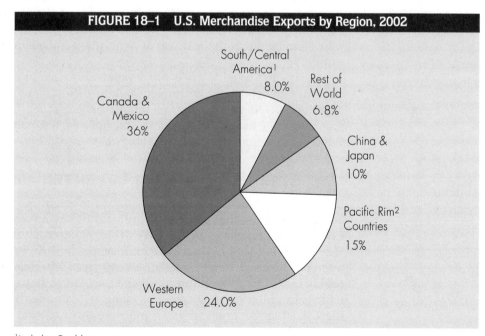

FIGURE 18–1   U.S. Merchandise Exports by Region, 2002

South/Central America[1]
8.0%

Rest of World
6.8%

Canada & Mexico
36%

China & Japan
10%

Pacific Rim[2] Countries
15%

Western Europe   24.0%

[1]Includes Caribbean nations.
[2]Excludes China and Japan.
Source: Department of Commerce.

TABLE 18–1   Major U.S. Merchandise Exports and Imports, 2002 ($ Billions)

Exports	Value	Imports	Value
Capital goods, except automobiles	$291	Consumer goods	$284
Industrial supplies and materials*	157	Capital goods, except automobiles	308
Consumer goods	84	Industrial supplies and materials*	269
Automobile vehicles, engines, and parts	78	Automobile vehicles, engines, and parts	204
Food, feeds, and beverages	50	Food, feeds, and beverages	50

*Includes petroleum and petroleum products.
Source: Department of Commerce.

falling prices, benefiting nations dependent on foreign oil. Oil imports to the United States, for example, had diminished to 10 percent of the total value of all imports.

In 1990, the world marketplace for oil was once again disrupted by events in the Middle East. With Iraq's invasion and occupation of Kuwait, the world price of oil quickly soared to nearly $40 per barrel as fears of shortages spread throughout industrialized nations. With the end of the Persian Gulf war in early 1991, the price of oil declined to prewar levels. Throughout most of the 1990s, oil prices fluctuated moderately. In the days immediately following September 11, prices quickly shot upwards once again. With the threat of war, the price of oil increased to $35 a barrel in early 2003.

Today the United States is still dependent on oil as its primary energy source, and it is still dependent on foreign nations to supply most of its oil. The United States imports 51 percent of its oil requirements and relies on OPEC for about half that amount. Canada, Mexico, and Venezuela each supply the United States with about the same amount of oil as Saudi Arabia.

COMPARATIVE ADVANTAGE REVISITED

International trade takes place as nations seek to improve their economic well-being by applying the principle of comparative advantage in production. As was explained in Chapter 2, the principle of comparative advantage holds that nations (like individuals) should specialize in the goods or services that they have the ability to produce at a lower opportunity cost than other nations face. By allocating resources to their most efficient use and specializing in particular forms of output, nations can increase their total output and then trade the gains they make from specialization for products from other countries. Total world output is larger through the application of the principle of comparative advantage than it would be if each nation sought to become self-sufficient.

A variety of factors may result in nations developing a comparative advantage in particular goods. Japan, for example, has a large, well-educated, and highly skilled labor force that can efficiently produce such goods as cameras, automobiles, and televisions. Australia, with large amounts of land and a relatively small population, specializes in producing wheat, wool, and meat products. Because of its favorable climate and large, unskilled labor force, Brazil is a world leader in the production of coffee. The United States, with its highly skilled labor force, has a comparative advantage in industries that require intensive investment in research and development: aircraft, machinery, and technology.

In addition to increased output as a result of comparative advantage, international trade brings other important benefits. Consumers benefit because markets become more competitive and consumers have more options to choose. Auto buyers in the United States enjoy a wide variety of choices because of the availability of imports from Japan, Korea, and Western Europe in addition to domestically produced automobiles. By providing more choices, foreign trade also serves to restrain price increases, particularly if the domestic industry consists of only a few large firms.

International trade also enables capital-intensive firms to expand in size and lower their production costs through economies of scale. Boeing, for example, because it can produce for the world market, is a more efficient airplane manufacturer than it would be if sales were restricted to the United States.

For centuries, economists have supported the argument for free trade based on the principle of comparative advantage. Nevertheless, most nations of the world are reluctant to adopt a free-trade policy, and numerous restrictions continue to be invoked in the area of international trade.

Barriers to Free Trade

Although economic arguments strongly favor free trade, most decisions affecting international trade are made in the political arena. Unfortunately, the pressures of politics and seeming short-run economic advantages usually overshadow the less obvious long-run advantages of free trade. Consequently, many restrictions still prevail in trade markets throughout the world today. One of the most common forms of restriction is the tariff.

Tariff
A duty or tax levied on foreign imports.

Specific Tariff
A tariff expressed in absolute terms, such as 25 cents per pound or per unit of a good.

Ad Valorem Tariff
A tariff expressed in relative or percentage terms, such as 15 percent of the value of the imported good.

THE TARIFF

A **tariff** is a duty or tax levied on foreign imports. It may be a **specific tariff,** expressed in absolute terms, such as 25 cents per pound or per unit of a good. Or it may be an **ad valorem tariff,** expressed in relative or percentage terms, such as 15 percent of the value of the imported good.

Purpose of a Tariff

A tariff may be levied for either revenue or protective purposes. In the early days of the United States, the primary purpose of import duties was to raise revenue to help defray the expenses of operating the new federal government. Later, however, the U.S. government adopted a largely protectionist tariff policy to protect new industries.

To be effective, a tariff must serve one purpose or the other. The two objectives are to a large extent opposite. If a tariff is designed to obtain revenue, it must be high enough to yield a revenue, but not so high that it discourages the importation of goods and services. Otherwise, very little revenue will flow from the tariff. On the other hand, if protection is desired, the tariff must be high enough to keep out foreign products, even though the tariff will yield very little for revenue purposes. Although an optimal tariff might serve both purposes to some extent, it cannot serve either purpose as well as a tariff tailored to a single objective.

Arguments for Free Trade

There are many other sources of government revenue, and at present a relatively small amount of income is derived from import duties. Therefore, it is difficult to support any argument asserting that a tariff is essential to raise revenue.

The gain or advantage of trade between regions or nations is obvious. The fundamental argument for free trade, and against protective tariffs, is that tariffs deny individuals and nations the benefits of greater productivity and a higher standard of living that result from absolute and comparative advantage. Tariffs disturb and restrict the free movement of goods and services, eliminate the advantages of specialization and exchange, and prevent the optimal use of scarce resources. From an economic point of view, the argument for free trade is so basic that most arguments against free trade and for tariffs are easy to refute. As a result, people who favor trade restrictions must use several lines of attack to make a dent in the free-trade defense. Even at that, they must move outside the area of economics to find their most effective arguments against free trade.

Regardless of what type of argument is put forth, the consumer ultimately pays the tariff. Although the customs duty itself is levied on the importer, the higher cost of doing business is generally passed on to the consumer in the form of higher prices. The main beneficiaries of the tariff are relatively inefficient producers and (in the short run) their employees, whose jobs are more secure because of the tariff.

Arguments for Tariffs

Numerous arguments in favor of tariffs have been offered. They touch on the military, social, and political aspects of international trade, as well as on economic issues. Although a few of the arguments have merit, most are seriously flawed. By and large, tariffs are difficult to justify from a long-run economic point of view.

Protecting infant industries. The goal of protecting infant industries is one of the oldest and most valid grounds for supporting a tariff. It was instrumental in promoting the shift in U.S. tariff policy from one based on generating revenue to one based on protectionism in the early part of the nineteenth century. In its simplest form, this argument asserts that new or infant industries, especially in developing nations, are frequently at a cost disadvantage compared with mature firms in the same industry in more developed nations. It follows that if this cost disadvantage is removed by applying a tariff to industry imports from foreign countries, the infant industry will be given an opportunity to grow and develop so that it can eventually compete with foreign producers on an equal footing. True infant-industry protectionists maintain that the tariff should be continued only until the firms in the domestic industry have reached a state of maturity. At that point the tariff should be removed, and the domestic industry should then compete unaided with the foreign imports.

Leveling the playing field. A similar argument is made for the so-called scientific tariff designed to equalize the cost of production between domestic and foreign producers. Advocates of this tariff argue that it would remove any advantage foreign producers might enjoy as a result of the availability of raw materials, differences in efficiency, lower wages, government subsidies, and the like. It would equalize the cost (including the tariff) or the price of foreign and domestic products. Consequently, it would remove the fundamental benefits and rationale—increased productivity, lower costs, and a higher standard of living—for international trade.

Protecting U.S. jobs. It is often suggested that using tariffs creates or protects domestic jobs. Arguments of this type tend to be shortsighted, taking into account only one side of international trade and focusing exclusively on the industry in question. They propose that if tariffs are imposed, foreign products will be kept out of the United States. As a result, consumers will purchase domestically produced goods and services, which in turn will result in increased domestic output and employment.

Proponents of this argument forget, however, that international trade is a two-way street. In addition to importing goods and services, we also export them. Foreigners cannot continue to buy from us unless they have U.S. dollars, and the primary way they obtain these dollars is by selling goods to the United States. If we impose tariffs and cut down imports, foreigners will have fewer U.S. dollars with which to buy U.S. goods. Therefore, any immediate increase in employment generated by tariffs will be offset by a decrease in output and employment in U.S. export-producing industries. A tariff also brings about a transfer of income from the purchasers of the protected domestic product to the domestic producers (and employees) of that product.

Protecting high U.S. wages. Protectionists frequently argue that tariffs are necessary to protect high U.S. wage rates. They point out that most foreign workers receive lower wages than do U.S. workers, and they conclude that foreign exporters have an unfair advantage over domestic producers. They also contend that if lower-priced foreign goods are admitted into the United States, competition will force U.S. producers to cut costs (particularly wages) in an effort to stay in business.

In assessing this argument, we should first recognize that the wage cost per unit of a good produced is more important in determining cost than is the wage rate itself. Productivity per worker varies among different countries. Nations with high wage rates often have lower unit labor costs than nations with low wage rates because of higher levels of productivity per work hour. Where this is true, there should be no need for tariffs to protect the high wage rates.

On the other hand, in situations where the wage cost per unit is lower in some foreign industries than domestically, it is economically unwise in the long run to subsidize the less efficient domestic producer with a tariff. A better solution is to force the domestic producer to improve efficiency and lower costs or to go out of business. As a result, labor, capital, and other resources will be channeled into more productive uses.

Protecting against dumping. Selling surplus products in a foreign market at a price below cost or at a price below the price at which they are sold in the domestic market is referred to as **dumping.** The argument for using tariffs to protect against dumping is based on the idea that dumping constitutes a form of unfair competition that harms domestic producers and leads to monopoly power on the part of foreign exporters.

Dumping
Selling surplus products in a foreign market at a price below cost or at a price below the price at which they are sold in the domestic market.

The dumping of surplus products in a foreign country may occur in order to penetrate the market or to increase profits through discriminatory pricing techniques. By selling products abroad at prices below cost, foreign producers could be trying to drive out domestic producers in order to monopolize the market. After eliminating competition, the foreign producer could then raise prices and reap monopoly profits. Dumping also constitutes an effective use of discriminatory pricing, whereby different prices are charged for the same product in different markets. By charging higher prices at home and lower prices abroad, where there is greater competition, companies can maximize their profits through cost savings attributed to large-scale production.

Most countries, including the United States, have antidumping laws. If dumping occurs and resulting competitive damage can be shown, the federal government may impose an antidumping tariff on the imported product.

Dumping benefits consumers, at least in the short run, by providing competitive products at lower prices than those charged by domestic producers. The use of tariffs to protect domestic producers from dumping is economically justified if its purpose is to prevent a foreign producer from gaining such a large market share as to monopolize the domestic market. However, documented cases of dumping are relatively few and do not justify widespread and permanent tariffs. Charges of dumping made by U.S. producers are often seen abroad as an attempt by these producers to restrict imports while maintaining high prices. In 1999, the U.S. Department of Commerce determined that 12 countries, including Brazil, Japan, Venezuela, and South Africa, were guilty of dumping over $800 million worth of steel into the United States. Because damage resulted to the domestic steel industry and its workers, the U.S. imposed penalties and countervailing tariffs.

Retaining money at home. One of the weakest arguments for tariffs is the assertion that they keep money at home instead of sending it abroad. Thus, it is often stated that if we buy a car from Japan, we have the car but Japan has the money; but if we buy an American car, we have both the car and the money. Proponents of this argument lose sight of the fact that the Japanese eventually use most of the dollars they receive from the sale of their automobiles to purchase other U.S. goods and services, and the dollars thus return to the United States.

Developing and protecting defense industries. One of the strongest and most valid protectionist arguments for tariffs is that they are needed to help develop and protect defense industries. Protectionists argue that the United States should establish and maintain tariffs for industries producing strategic defense materials. Such protective measures would help ensure a steady domestic source of materials for military goods. Moreover, placing restraints on imported strategic goods would allow the government to stockpile large reserves in the event of war. Without tariff protection, inefficient strategic industries might have to close down as a result of foreign competition. Subsequently, the economic resources used in these industries would be dispersed elsewhere, and if war should break out, the nation might find itself militarily vulnerable. Currently, many producers of strategic military goods and services are protected by tariffs, subsidies, or other measures.

Diversifying industry. A similar argument is put forth regarding the use of tariffs to support diversification of the industrial structure of a nation. When a country specializes in the production of one or a few goods, its economy is exposed to potentially wide fluctuations in the demand for its product(s). A number of developing countries derive more than 80 percent of their total export earnings from a single commodity. Examples of such countries include Greenland (seafood), Uganda (coffee), Equatorial Guinea (lumber), as well as most OPEC nations. Under these circumstances, a softening of world demand and prices can bring sharp contractions in the economy. Therefore, tariffs can be used to keep out imports and to encourage the development of certain industries in the domestic economy. With a broader industrial structure, the economy will be more stable and less vulnerable to fluctuations in world demand for certain products. Although this argument has merit, it has relatively little application to developed economies, which are known for their widely varied industries.

Recent U.S. Tariff Activity

The United States is far from being a free-trade nation. Like other nations, it continues to use trade barriers when it deems them to be in its best economic and political interests. The most highly publicized case in which the United States recently erected trade barriers occurred in 2002 when it slapped tariffs on steel imports. The United States has long complained that foreign countries were routinely dumping steel products into the country, costing thousands of jobs and resulting in numerous plant closings. To support its actions, the United States claimed that over 30 steel firms were forced to close since 1998 as a result of steel imports.

The United States imposed 30 percent tariffs on most steel products entering the country. The tariffs drop to 24 percent in the second year and 18 percent in the third year, and then expire. The stated purpose of the imposing of tariffs was to al-low large steel firms enough time and protection to bring production costs down and upgrade equipment. It was seen as an attempt to maintain a viable domestic integrated steel industry in the future, while at the same time securing political support in states in which the steel industry has suffered most. In response to strong complaints from the European Union, the United States excluded a number of steel products. This action reduced the effect of the steel tariff.

Examples of other common products recently involved in trade wars include lumber and tomato exports from Canada into the United States. In the case of lum-ber, the United States charged in 2001 that Canada had unfairly subsidized soft-wood lumber producers, allowing Canadian lumber mills to sell lumber in the United States below market prices. The United States imposed a tariff of 19.3 per-cent on Canadian softwood lumber for the alleged subsidy and imposed another 9.7 percent for dumping lumber into the United States. Tomatoes joined the list of products in trade disputes when the United States announced that it was going to impose antidumping duties of approximately 32 percent on tomatoes grown in Canadian greenhouses and exported to the United States. Canadian greenhouse tomato sales in the United States had increased from $4 million in 1990 to over $155 million in 2002, resulting in the bankruptcies of several large U.S. green-houses. Canada disputed U.S. claims that it competes unfairly in lumber and tomato products.

Effect of Tariffs on Trade

The impact of tariffs on trade can be illustrated through the use of supply and de-mand curves. Assume that in the absence of foreign trade the equilibrium price and quantity of television sets in the United States are P_e and Q_e, as depicted in Fig-ure 18–2a. In this case, domestic demand is totally satisfied by domestic supply.

Now assume that the United States becomes an open market for television sets, with no tariffs applied on foreign imports. In Figure 18–2b, the domestic supply and demand for television sets are again represented by D and S. However, if foreign producers can produce and ship television sets to the United States for a delivered price of P_1, then the new supply curve becomes S_1. This supply curve is perfectly elastic and indicates that with free trade, an unlimited quantity of imports is available at that price. The market share for domestic producers at the price of P_1 has shrunk to $0Q_1$, while the market share now held by foreign producers is Q_1Q_2. The total number of television sets supplied by both domestic and foreign produc-ers amounts to $0Q_2$, and the new equilibrium position occurs at point B.

If a tariff is applied to imported television sets to protect American producers, the perfectly elastic supply curve shifts upward to S_2, reflecting the higher price brought about by the tariff. The new equilibrium is at point C in Figure 18–2b. With tariff protection, domestic producers can increase their market share from $0Q_1$ to $0Q_3$; at the same time the foreign producers' market share declines from Q_1Q_2 to Q_3Q_4. At the consumers' end, the results of the tariff are a higher price per set and fewer units purchased. At the producers' end, domestic producers are better off

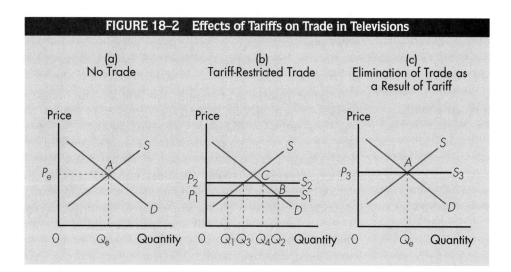

FIGURE 18–2   Effects of Tariffs on Trade in Televisions

(a) No Trade

(b) Tariff-Restricted Trade

(c) Elimination of Trade as a Result of Tariff

and foreign producers are worse off. As the tariff increases, these effects become more pronounced. For example, if the tariff is raised so that the new market price becomes P_3 (as in Figure 18–2c), domestic demand is once again satisfied entirely by domestic supply, and the tariff effectively acts as an embargo on foreign imports. As can be seen from the equilibrium position at point A, zero units are supplied by foreign producers at that price.

The tariff in our example results in a misallocation of resources—not only in the television industry but throughout the economies of the United States and the exporting nations. Resources are misallocated because output, employment, and income have been directed away from the more efficient foreign producers and toward the less efficient domestic producers. Consumers are forced to pay higher prices for less total output. In effect, the tariff constitutes a subsidy to domestic producers that is financed by higher prices paid by consumers.

The economy would be better served if free trade were permitted. In cutting back on their output of television sets, domestic firms would be releasing scarce resources for more efficient use in other sectors of the economy. Free trade would also yield increased output, employment, and income in the more efficient foreign industry. Because tariffs encourage overproduction by inefficient firms and under-production by efficient ones, total world output declines as a result of the misallocation of resources.

NONTARIFF BARRIERS TO TRADE

Nontariff Barriers
Devices other than tariffs
that grant an advantage
to domestic producers.

In addition to tariffs, **nontariff barriers** are often used to grant an advantage to domestic producers. Each has effects similar to those of a tariff: restricting imports, granting aid to domestic producers in competition with foreign imports, and encouraging the export of goods. The most frequently used nontariff barriers are import quotas, embargoes, export subsidies, voluntary restraint agreements, and exchange controls.

Import Quotas

Import Quota
A maximum absolute amount of a particular good that may be imported.

An **import quota** is a maximum absolute amount of a particular good that may be imported. Setting definite limits on the amount that may be imported protects the domestic producer and industry against the full effect of foreign competition. Consequently, it is similar in effect to (but more restrictive than) a tariff. Sometimes both a tariff and a quota are used, in which case the limited amount that can be imported is subject to a customs duty.

Tariff Quota
A device that places a financial penalty on imports above a certain quantity.

Another form of quota is the **tariff quota,** which does not set absolute limits on imports but places a financial penalty on imports that exceed a certain quantity. Thus, the tariff quota permits a certain amount of an imported good to come in at one tariff rate but then charges a higher tariff rate for imports over and above this so-called optimum amount.

In 1999, the World Trade Organization supported U.S. claims that the European Union had used quotas and tariff quotas over a six-year period to discriminate against banana imports from Latin America, including those exported and distributed by U.S. companies. The WTO allowed the United States to retaliate by enacting $191 million in tariffs against a number of European products entering the United States. Because the increased tariffs on targeted products were so high, the U.S. tariff eliminated importation of those products. In effect, the tariff became an import quota of zero. In 2001, the United States and the European Union reached an agreement that calls for the European Union to continually increase quotas of bananas from Latin America countries until 2006. At that time, the European Union will shift to a tariff-only system. Satisfied with this resolution, the United States dropped trade sanctions it had previously imposed against EU imports.

Embargoes

Embargo
Complete cessation of trade with another nation or in certain products.

An **embargo** involves the complete cessation of trade with a particular nation or a cessation of trade in certain products. It is usually implemented for noneconomic reasons. An embargo may be applied to imports, exports, or both. When applied, the embargo has the same effect as an export or import quota of zero.

The United States has had an embargo in trade with Cuba since 1960 (about a year after Fidel Castro's rise to power). In 1973, an embargo was placed on oil exports from Arab oil-producing states to the United States because of the latter's support for Israel. In 1975, fearing a possible domestic shortage, the United States placed an embargo on grain exports to the former Soviet Union; it did so again in 1980 as a punitive measure in response to the Soviet Union's invasion of Afghanistan.

Over the years, the United States has also placed embargoes on the export of specific military hardware to several Middle Eastern countries and on the importation of illegal drugs. In 1986, the United States government placed an embargo on trade with South Africa to express opposition to that nation's apartheid policies.

And in 1990, the United States (and the United Nations as a whole) placed an embargo on trade with Iraq in retaliation for its attempt to annex Kuwait. As of 2002, the United States had sanctions in place against Sudan, the Taliban in Afghanistan, Iraq, Cuba, Iran, Syria, Libya, North Korea, Liberia, and Sierra Leone. It also had explicit sanctions against various factions and terrorist groups throughout the world.

Export Subsidies

Export Subsidy
A government payment to private firms to encourage the exportation of certain goods or to prevent foreign discrimination against exporters who must sell at a world price that is below the domestic price.

An **export subsidy** is a government payment to private firms to encourage the exportation of certain goods or to prevent discrimination against exporters who may have to sell their product at a world price that is below the domestic price. In some cases, direct cash payments are made for the exportation of some goods. In others, the large-scale sale of surplus farm products is promoted through the use of subsidies. In the United States, for example, the government may purchase surplus crops, such as wheat and cotton, from U.S. farmers at government-supported prices (which have often been above the domestic market price) and then sell these crops to foreign nations at world prices below the U.S. domestic price. The government thus pays a subsidy to have goods exported. European countries typically grant direct export subsidies on a wide range of agricultural products. Payments are based on the difference between the European Union's internal price and the world price.

Voluntary Restraint Agreements

Voluntary Restraint Agreement
An agreement between two governments to limit the exporting country's exports to the importing country.

A **voluntary restraint agreement** is an agreement between two governments by which the government of the exporting country agrees to limit the amount of a product it sends to the importing country. Exporting nations agree to voluntary restraint agreements in order to avoid more stringent trade barriers.

Although voluntary restraint agreements constitute a relatively new trade barrier, the United States has made extensive use of them, particularly in such industries as textiles and automobiles. In 1981, for example, the Japanese government agreed to limit exports of Japanese automobiles to the United States in response to pressure from the latter. The United States was motivated by a desire to protect its domestic automobile industry. The agreement resulted in significantly higher prices being charged for Japanese automobiles in the United States, due to their scarcity. Faced with reduced competition and the higher prices for Japanese automobiles, U.S. producers raised their prices as well. Thus, once again, consumers paid the price for restructured trade.

Exchange Controls

Exchange Controls
Devices that ration a country's scarce foreign exchange or set up multiple exchange rates.

The flow of international trade can be affected greatly by the use of **exchange controls.** Such controls may take the form of rationing a nation's scarce foreign exchange, thereby limiting overall imports into the nation. More specific regulation of imports is possible through the use of multiple exchange rates, through which different exchange rates are set for various goods. This practice allows a country to encourage the importation of some goods while discouraging the importation of others. Because exchange rates can be set directly by the government, they can be applied readily to restrict the free flow of goods and services, much as tariffs and quotas can.

Latin American countries have used exchange controls extensively whenever a financial crisis erupts. In 2002, Argentina resumed the use of exchange controls as the country staggered under a heavy debt burden and a multiple-year recession. The Central Bank banned exchange traders and banks from buying dollars at the market price. Controls limited the sale of dollars to $1,000 for each individual or $10,000 for each company in order to stem the loss of reserve currency.

U.S. Trade Policy

In its early history, the United States enthusiastically promoted world trade, but its attitude has changed from time to time. Initially, the new nation used tariffs primarily to generate revenue. As a result, tariffs were low to encourage the importation of goods so that more tariff revenues could be collected. In fact, in the first few decades of the nation's existence, 90 percent or more of the revenue the federal government obtained came from tariffs.

Although protection became more important in United States tariff policy thereafter, tariffs continued to be a major source of federal revenue until the Civil War. As protection became predominant with the growth of U.S. industry, tariff rates continued to climb. After World War I, tariff rates reached a new high, but they were pushed still higher by the Hawley–Smoot Tariff Act of 1930. Shortly thereafter, hardly any imported good could avoid a tariff, and some rates exceeded 100 percent of the original value of the good. The average tariff, as a percentage of the value of all imports, was about 33 percent.

RECIPROCAL TRADE AGREEMENTS

The Great Depression of the 1930s ushered in a new policy of lower tariffs. Under the Reciprocal Trade Agreements Act of 1934, the president was given authority to lower tariffs by as much as 50 percent without further congressional approval, provided that other nations would make reciprocal concessions. As a result of this act, more than 30 separate agreements were made with foreign nations.

Most-Favored-Nation Clause
A provision of the Reciprocal Trade Agreements Act that generalized concessions made in bilateral agreements to all nations.

Included in the Reciprocal Trade Agreements Act was the famous **most-favored-nation clause** by which concessions made in bilateral agreements were generalized to all nations. When the United States lowered its tariff on wool imports from Australia, for example, this lower rate automatically applied to imported wool from any other nation that did not discriminate against the United States. In short, all nations received the same tariff benefits that were extended to most-favored nations. On the other hand, the United States did not enter into any trade agreements with a foreign nation unless the latter extended the same tariff concessions on various goods to the United States that it gave to its most-favored nation(s).

Although tariffs were reduced substantially under the Reciprocal Trade Agreements Act during the next two decades, the reductions and coverage permitted by the act were weakened by various amendments and revisions. In 1951, an **escape clause** became a part of the act. This clause permitted tariff rates to be raised if the Tariff Commission found that the insufficiency of existing tariffs was causing harm or seriously threatening domestic producers. A 1954 amendment prohibited any tariff reduction that might threaten national security. These reservations were carried through in both the Trade Expansion Act of 1962 and the Trade Act of 1974.

Escape Clause
A provision in the amended Reciprocal Trade Agreements Act that permitted tariffs to be raised if domestic producers were suffering under the existing tariff.

THE EXPORT–IMPORT BANK

The United States has tried to promote freer trade by direct internal legislation and by cooperation through international organizations and agreements. It has also given foreign countries substantial financial assistance in an effort to promote world trade. In addition to holding membership in the World Bank, the International Monetary Fund, and other financial organizations, the United States has its own bank for financing world trade.

Created in 1934, the Export–Import Bank was chartered primarily for the purpose of financing exports from the United States. It was anticipated that the Export–Import Bank would help finance anticipated increases in trade with the former Soviet Union (officially recognized by the United States in 1933) and various Latin American countries. Today, the Bank is a source of aid in trade with numerous countries throughout the world, particularly developing countries. Under certain conditions, the Bank guarantees U.S. exporters that they will be paid for the sale of their goods to foreign nations. Sometimes the Bank makes loans to foreign importers to enable them to buy U.S. goods. Mainly, the Bank finances private exports and imports between the United States and other nations that cannot be financed at reasonable rates through regular international financial channels. The Bank's transactions largely benefit small businesses.

As a result of growing financial resources, the Bank has begun making loans for private and government development projects in developing nations. However, the Export–Import Bank is not an aid or development agency, but a government-held corporation managed by a board of directors selected by the president of the United States.

TRADE EXPANSION ACT OF 1962

The policy favoring lower tariffs was reinforced in the United States by passage of the Trade Expansion Act of 1962. This act had three purposes: (1) to stimulate U.S. economic growth and enlarge foreign markets for its products, (2) to strengthen economic relations with foreign countries through the development of open and nondiscriminatory trading in the free world, and (3) to prevent communist economic penetration of the free world. The act contained special provisions for dealings and agreements with the European Common Market.

To ease any hardship that might result from liberalizing trade restrictions, the act provided relief for import-injured industries. For example, individual firms were eligible for adjustment assistance under certain conditions. Workers laid off or displaced because of increased foreign imports were also eligible for assistance. Assistance has been periodically extended to some autoworkers, steelworkers, and other manufacturing workers as conditions warranted.

Under the authority given to the president by the Trade Expansion Act of 1962, the United States entered into negotiations with other nations to bring about substantial reductions in world tariffs. After three years of difficult negotiations in the Kennedy Round, the 53 nations participating in the talks, under the sponsorship of the General Agreement on Tariffs and Trade, agreed on a massive reduction in tariffs.

TRADE ACT OF 1974

In 1974, Congress passed the Trade Act of 1974 to succeed the Trade Expansion Act of 1962. Provisions of this act cleared the way for the United States to play a major role when 105 nations met in Geneva to draw up new rules of international trade and commerce in the spring of 1975. The act gives the president a wide range of options for opening trade doors around the world, including (1) reducing or raising U.S. tariffs during negotiations; (2) imposing an import surcharge of up to 15 percent; (3) reducing or eliminating nontariff barriers such as export subsidies, import quotas, investment restrictions, health and safety codes, and pollution standards, subject to congressional approval; and (4) retaliating against unreasonable foreign restrictions on U.S. trade. The act also permitted the president to extend most-favored-nation treatment to communist nations. Like its predecessor act, the Trade Act of 1974 provides various types of assistance to import-injured firms and workers.

GATT and Multinational Trade Negotiations

General Agreement on Tariffs and Trade (GATT)
An agreement calling for equal treatment of all nations in international trade, the reduction of tariffs, and the easing or elimination of import quotas.

After World War II, several of the Allied nations (not including the Soviet Union) met for the purpose of promoting free trade among nations of the world. The outcome was the **General Agreement on Tariffs and Trade (GATT),** which was drawn up at Geneva in 1947 and signed by 23 nations, including the United States. GATT called for equal and nondiscriminatory treatment of all nations in international trade, for the reduction of tariffs through reciprocal trade agreements, and for the easing or elimination of import quotas. One major provision of the act extended the most-favored-nation status to all signers.

Because of a series of successful GATT negotiating rounds between 1947 and 1961, substantial progress was made in liberalizing trade agreements among major trading partners. As a result of the combined achievements of the Geneva, Annecy,

Torquay, and Dillon rounds of trade negotiations, tariffs were cut by 73 percent. The Kennedy Round, which was completed in 1967, produced additional tariff cuts of 62 percent and included antidumping agreements. In 1979, the Tokyo Round led to an agreement on a trade package to relax tariff and nontariff barriers. This package included tariff cuts by the United States that averaged 30 percent, with reciprocal reductions by its trading partners. GATT's promotion of international trade was instrumental in the overall economic growth and improved standard of living in the world's three major industrial sectors: North America, Europe, and Japan.

THE URUGUAY ROUND (1986–1993)

During the 1980s, some members of GATT expressed a strong concern over a new wave of protectionism. At the United States' urging, another round of GATT negotiations was launched in Punta del Este, Uruguay, in 1986 to respond to this concern. The Uruguay Round of negotiations was intended to improve the existing GATT articles and procedures, to negotiate reductions in tariff and nontariff barriers, and to address a list of major specific issues.

The United States sought measures to liberalize trade in agricultural products, protect individual property rights, reduce barriers to direct international investments, and extend the rules of GATT to cover services such as telecommunications, insurance, and computer and data processing.

The Uruguay Round was completed on December 15, 1993, three years later than originally scheduled. The Uruguay Round produced agreement among GATT members to lower tariffs on merchandise trade in such key areas as construction, medical and agricultural equipment, pharmaceuticals, toys, and furniture. Agreement was reached to cut tariffs from 50 to 100 percent on important electronic items, including semiconductors and computer parts. Significant reductions also occurred in textiles and apparel.

The United States was able to win greater protection for patents, copyrights, and trademarks, and negotiators were able to agree on comprehensive rules governing trade and investment in services, including telecommunications, professional, and financial services. In the international investment area, the Uruguay Round prohibits local content requirements that force foreign firms to use a set amount of locally produced inputs, and it also prohibits *trade balancing*. Trade balancing is a requirement that a foreign affiliate must export as much of its production as it imports for use as inputs.

Throughout the Uruguay Round, the most difficult and contentious issue was agriculture, for virtually every developed country in the world subsidizes agricultural products. Some success was achieved in obtaining commitments among members to reduce export subsidies and domestic subsidies and to increase market access.

With the passage of the Uruguay Round, the 47-year-old GATT went out of business on January 1, 1995. In its place, the World Trade Organization (WTO) was formed. Table 18-2 summarizes GATT negotiating rounds since 1947.

TABLE 18–2 GATT Negotiating Rounds			
Negotiating Round	Dates	Number of Participants	Tariff Cut Achieved (percent)
Geneva	1947	23	
Annecy	1949	13	
Torquay	1951	38	73
Geneva	1956	26	
Dillon Round	1960–1961	26	
Kennedy Round	1964–1967	62	35
Tokyo Round	1973–1979	99	30
Uruguay Round	1986–1993	125	40

Note: Tariff cuts achieved are those agreed to by the major industrial countries on industrial products. The tariff cut achieved in the first five negotiations is an estimate. Tariffs fell from an average of about 40 percent at the time of GATT's founding to 7 percent by the beginning of the Tokyo Round.
Source: General Agreement on Tariffs and Trade.

World Trade Organization

World Trade Organization (WTO)
A multinational organization that replaced GATT for the purpose of overseeing trade agreements and resolving trade conflicts.

NET*Link*

Learn more about the World Trade Organization at:

http://www.wto.org/

The World Trade Organization (WTO) is a multinational organization of 144 nations that oversees international trade agreements and resolves trade conflicts. The WTO has four main objectives: (1) to ensure equal trading rights among members, (2) to support free trade and the reduction and elimination of tariffs, (3) to eliminate trade subsidies, and (4) to establish binding rules to ensure fairness and consistency in trade.

In enforcing trade rules, the WTO functions as a judicial court that makes binding rulings when members are in dispute. Member nations gave the WTO such powers in order to ensure fast and fair resolution of trade disputes. It was the WTO that ruled in favor of the United States in its claim that the European Union was unfairly restricting the importation of bananas from U.S. multinational companies, and again it was the WTO that overruled the European Union when it tried to embargo hormone-treated beef from the United States on health grounds.

Free-trade advocates support the WTO as a way to ensure fairness in trade and to enhance global prosperity. On the other hand, strong opposition is voiced by activists who claim that the WTO fails to address a number of important and contentious issues. Usually, these issues center on labor practices and on health and the environment. Critics call for the WTO to enforce minimum labor standards in developing countries, arguing that manufacturers are exploiting workers in sweatshop conditions. Health concerns lead to pressure exerted on the WTO to overrule domestic measures intended to protect public health, as was the case in the export of U.S. hormone-treated beef into Europe. Environmental objections are similar in nature. For example, detractors point to the WTO ruling whereby U.S. laws seeking to protect endangered sea turtles were deemed a violation of fair trade. U.S. law prohibited imports of shrimp from countries that allow shrimpers to use nets unless they are equipped with trap doors that allow turtles to escape.

There is also discontent within the member ranks of the WTO. Agriculture remains a contentious issue. Many nations, particularly Japan and those in the European Union, seek to maintain farm subsidies and slow the advance of agricultural imports. Europe and Japan also want to include limits on the use of antidumping legislation favored by the United States. Developing nations are now demanding a louder voice in the governance of the WTO and are seeking greater openness and access to the organization's decision-making process.

Since its creation in 1995, the WTO has been the forum for successful negotiations to open markets in a number of areas. It has also been involved in settling nearly 200 trade disputes among members. The United States has filed more trade disputes than any other nation, followed by countries comprising the European Union. In the past, trade agreements tended to focus almost exclusively on barriers to imports that countries erected at their borders; disputes therefore had a similar focus. But the WTO applied international trade law to telecommunications and other services, where the issues now involve domestic regulations. The clash between trade rules and domestic rules governing such things as food safety or environmental protection is likely to cause increasing tension among members in the years ahead.

North American Economic Integration

Although the United States strongly advocates free trade, foreign countries often claim that the United States sends mixed signals on protectionism. In the United States, as in most nations, protectionism tends to become a strong political force whenever economic conditions are unfavorable. Pressure for trade protection comes mainly from U.S. industries that are vulnerable to foreign competition, such as the textile, automobile, steel, and machine tool industries, and from organized labor, which fears the loss of jobs for U.S. workers. Hundreds of bills have been introduced in Congress to protect U.S. industries, but despite such pressures the United States entered into trade agreements that in the long run will have a major impact on the U.S. economy.

U.S.–Canada Free Trade Agreement

The U.S.–Canada Free Trade Agreement was implemented in 1989 and called for the reduction of several major nontariff barriers and the removal of many restrictions on cross-border investments. All tariffs between the United States and Canada are scheduled to be eliminated. The growth in trade between the United States and Canada for the 1990–2002 period is shown in Figure 18–3. In 2002 the value of U.S. exports to Canada totaled $161 billion, while imports from Canada were $211 billion.

Products must be U.S. or Canadian or both to qualify for duty-free treatment under the agreement. Tariffs will remain on imports from third countries according to the rule of origin established by the agreement. **Rule of origin** is a trade term that defines the minimum percentage of a country's exported products that must be produced or substantially changed within the border of the exporting country. Products containing imported components from a third country must be changed in ways that are physically and commercially significant prior to being exported to satisfy the rule-of-origin requirement.

Rule of Origin
A trade term that defines the minimum percentage of a country's exported products that must be produced or substantially changed within the border of the exporting country.

The U.S.–Canada Free Trade Agreement constituted a logical and important breakthrough in the expansion of free trade in the hemisphere, and it served as the foundation for creating an even larger free trade area involving the United States, Canada, and Mexico.

NORTH AMERICAN FREE TRADE AGREEMENT

On January 1, 1994, a historic trade agreement by the United States, Canada, and Mexico went into force. This agreement, known as the North American Free Trade Agreement (NAFTA), is having far-reaching consequences for all three countries. The North American Free Trade Agreement has produced the largest trading bloc in the world, with a combined gross domestic product of nearly $12 trillion.

NETLink

For a searchable index of the NAFTA agreement visit

http://www.ciesin.org/TG/PI/ TRADE/nafta.html

Because Mexico is the United States' third-largest trading partner, after Canada and Japan, and the United States is the largest trading partner of Mexico, the economies of the two countries are strongly interdependent. Figure 18–3 indicates that in 2002 U.S. exports to Mexico were valued at $98 billion and imports from Mexico totaled $135 billion.

The benefits of NAFTA to the United States stem from expanded free trade with a large and growing market, increased competition, and more business investment opportunities for U.S. firms in Mexico. Benefits to Mexico accrue from more open access to the United States, greater capital investment in Mexico, and a more stable economic environment. Through NAFTA, Canada protects its status in international trade and gains equal access to Mexico's market.

Numerous U.S. industries, including automobile, agriculture, energy and petrochemicals, electronics and communications, and financial services are major beneficiaries of NAFTA. Many firms in these industries are located in Mexico through the maquiladora program. **Maquiladoras** are export-oriented plants, most often, but not exclusively, located near the U.S.–Mexico border, that are exempt from paying import duties on raw materials and parts that are used in making final products. The textile industry was the first industry to avail itself of the maquiladora program, but over time other manufacturing and labor-intensive industries also opened factories across the border. Maquiladoras account for approximately 45 percent of U.S. merchandise imports from Mexico, and over 600,000 Mexican workers are employed at these sites.

Maquiladoras
Export-oriented plants, most often but not exclusively located near the U.S.–Mexico border.

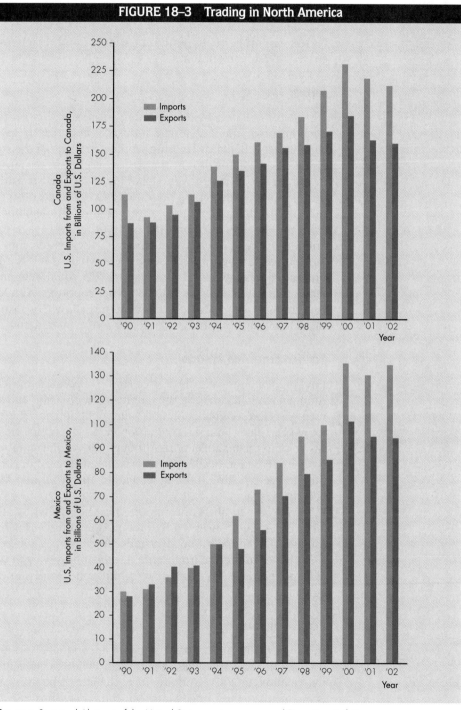

FIGURE 18–3 Trading in North America

Sources: *Statistical Abstract of the United States,* various years, and Department of Commerce.

The North America Free Trade Agreement remains a highly controversial issue in the United States and also in Mexico and Canada. In addition to rule-of-origin issues, two other issues pertaining to labor and the environment are critical to its successful implementation.

Labor Issues

Although NAFTA is being phased in over many years, it is having a negative impact on employment in certain industries and local areas. Thus, it is not surprising to find that U.S. manufacturing workers are among the strongest critics of NAFTA. Labor organizations protest that U.S. companies are transferring production facilities to Mexico to take advantage of lower labor costs. Although wages are not the only factor in determining plant location, labor costs do represent a large share of manufacturing costs. These fears are not unfounded, but the loss of jobs resulting from the movement of production to other low-wage countries, such as Taiwan and Singapore, is already occurring. In other words, jobs transferred to U.S. affiliate companies might be transferred elsewhere if not to Mexico. Maquiladoras are often used to support the view that NAFTA could help preserve jobs in the United States that would have been lost to other countries. Although some production has been transferred to Mexico, maquiladoras allow U.S. firms to maintain their share of such production, rather than losing entire operations.

Environmental Issues

Environmentalists have also voiced strong opposition to NAFTA. Without tough environmental regulations and the enforcement of health and safety standards, environmentalists foresee greater air and water pollution and substandard health conditions for workers along both sides of the border. As support for their position, environmentalists point to the maquiladoras. Although the maquiladoras created jobs for Mexicans, workers settled in border towns lacking adequate infrastructures to accommodate them. Severe pollution of the water, air, and ground in Mexican border towns has been the result.

Environmentalists are supported in their views by labor organizations. Many labor groups are concerned that many U.S. industries will head to Mexico to avoid tougher U.S. antipollution laws and thus cause U.S. job losses. Environmental concerns have led the Environmental Protection Agency to work with Mexican agencies to ensure the enactment of safety and health standards as part of the final agreement.

Future Issues

In 1994, NAFTA provided a number of tax and tariff incentives to companies setting up maquiladoras. However, in accordance with the agreement, many of these incentives expired in 2001. Not only have the imposed tariffs raised the cost of imported components to the United States but companies must now also pay taxes on income and assets in Mexico. Costs are also rising due to higher wages and a stronger Mexican currency. These shifting economic trends have diminished the value of maquiladoras to many companies. As a result, a number of companies have closed plants in Mexico and are relocating operations in other low-cost countries, such as China, Vietnam, or Indonesia. Unless tax and tariff adjustments are enacted, the exodus is likely to continue. Mexico, on the other hand, would like to make the transition from a border economy based on unskilled, cheap labor to one based on technology and greater labor skills, much in the same way as Singapore and Malaysia.

At some point in the future, it is expected that Chile will be invited to join NAFTA. Chile's eventual entrance into NAFTA would enlarge the trade area by some 15 million people and add a GDP of $160 billion. Although NAFTA membership may not be imminent, Chile's candidacy is enhanced by its progress toward a stable economy, a free market, and successful privatization of 90 percent of its state-owned corporations. As a first step, Chile entered into a separate free-trade agreement with Canada in 1996.

As the United States continues to work with Chile in seeking NAFTA membership, it has proposed a far more ambitious trade plan encompassing all of the Americas. The proposed Free Trade Area of the Americas stretches from the Bering Strait in Alaska to Cape Horn at the tip of South America and includes 34 countries with a population of 800 million. Talks are underway and are scheduled to conclude by 2005. If the trade area becomes a reality, the plan calls for the complete elimination of tariffs and import quotas among countries.

European Economic Integration

Since the end of World War II, many dramatic developments have occurred in international economics. One such development has been the voluntary efforts by a number of nations to integrate some of their economic activities for their mutual benefit. Another development has been the effort of various affluent nations to extend economic and technical assistance to developing nations. Both these movements are significantly influencing economic, social, political, and military relations in nations throughout the world.

The most significant economic integration effort is the one being made in Europe. It is projected as a series of steps involving coordination, cooperation, and eventually full economic integration.

EUROPEAN COMMON MARKET

The Common Market traces its origins back to 1952 with the formation of the European Coal and Steel Community. This organization was formed for the purpose of pooling the coal and steel resources of six nations and eliminating their trade barriers on coal, iron ore, iron, and steel. The six nations joining in the agreement were France, West Germany, Italy, Belgium, the Netherlands, and Luxembourg.

The success of the European Coal and Steel Community led to the formation of the *European Economic Community (EEC)* or *Common Market* (promoted in part by the United States) by the same six nations in 1958. The Common Market established four goals: (1) to abolish tariff and import quotas among the six nations within 10 to 12 years, (2) to establish within a similar period a common tariff applicable to all imports from outside the Common Market area, (3) to attain eventually the free movement of capital and labor within the Common Market nations, and (4) to adopt a common policy regarding monopolies and agriculture.

By 1968, all tariff barriers among the six nations had been removed, two years ahead of schedule. The common external tariff was achieved a few years later. Progress was also made toward common internal policies regarding monopoly control, transportation, and social security systems. By 1982, the member nations had formed the *European Monetary System (EMS),* which established the *European Currency Unit (ECU)* as a common monetary unit of account. The existence of the Common Market contributed to the economic growth and prosperity of Western Europe during this period.

Great Britain did not join the Common Market when it was formed because it was reluctant to abandon its special treatment of other members of the British Commonwealth. Later, during the 1960s, Great Britain attempted to join the Common Market. But its requests for admission were denied on two occasions because of conditions Britain attached to entry. By 1973, however, these differences were reconciled and, along with Denmark and Ireland, Britain became a member of the Common Market. In 1981, the second enlargement of the Common Market occurred with the addition of Greece. Then, in 1986, the membership of the Common Market expanded again when Spain and Portugal joined.

In 1987, the official name of the Common Market was changed from the European Economic Community (EEC) to the European Community (EC). Also at that time the group of 12 nations undertook the most ambitious and significant action since the creation of the Common Market. The membership agreed that by the end of 1992 member nations would constitute a single European market. Although it was not fully implemented by the target date, the 1992 plan will eventually fuse member nations into a true common market far more powerful than that envisaged by the original six Common Market nations.

The 1992 initiative was based on the belief that after 30 years, the original thrust of the Common Market had weakened. As European industries became less competitive, they lost market share in major industrial sectors to Japanese and U.S. competitors. The continued existence of nontariff barriers led to fragmented industries, protected national markets, and less influence in world markets. Over time, country-specific tax rates, customs procedures, national standards, and technical regulations encouraged European and foreign exporters to treat each country as a separate market.

The 1992 plan called for the free movement of people, capital, goods, and services across EC borders. Thus, any good or service that is acceptable to proper authorities of one country will be acceptable to those of any other. In fact, the plan called for a market almost as economically integrated as the U.S. market, except that it lacked a common currency, a central banking structure, and a federal tax system.

EUROPEAN UNION

Maastricht Agreement
The Maastricht Agreement on European Economic and Monetary Union, the first move in transforming the European Community, an economic community, into the European Union, a political union with a common currency.

European Union
An organization seeking full political and economic integration among member countries.

Economic and Monetary Union (EMU)
Countries within the European Union that share a single currency and central bank.

Euro
Common currency of countries within the Economic Monetary Union.

In 1991, another step was taken with the Maastricht Agreement toward full integration of member nations. Named after the Netherlands city in which talks were held, the **Maastricht Agreement** on European Economic and Monetary Union was the first move in transferring the European Community from an economic community into a political community with a common currency. With the implementation of the Maastricht Agreement in 1993, the European Community became officially known as the **European Union.** In 1995, the European Union expanded its membership to include Austria, Finland, and Sweden, for a total of 15 nations.

In 1999, the **Economic and Monetary Union (EMU)** was formed as an outgrowth of the European Union. Of the 15 member EU nations, 12 countries joined the Economic and Monetary Union. The EMU established a single currency and a single central bank among its members. A single currency and a single central bank eliminate the need to exchange currency and reduce business uncertainties due to exchange-rate variability and differing monetary and fiscal policies. To participate in the EMU, countries had to meet monetary and fiscal targets dealing with inflation rates, interest rates, budget deficits, government debt, and exchange rates. The United Kingdom, Sweden, and Denmark opted not to join at that time. As of January 1, 2002, these 12 nations no longer print their own money. The **euro** is now circulating and has replaced national currencies such as the franc, mark, and lira.

The European Union now claims a population of 376 million and a gross domestic product of about $9 trillion. Most likely candidates for EU membership in the near future include the Czech Republic, Poland, Hungary, Estonia, Slovenia, Romania, Lithuania, Latvia, Slovakia, and Bulgaria.

The European Union is an important trading partner for nations throughout the world. It accounts for approximately 40 percent of all trade worldwide, and after Canada, it constitutes the largest export market for the United States. Figure 18–4 indicates that in 2002 the United States exported over $144 billion in goods to the European Union. U.S. exporters will continue to benefit from the 1992 plan and the European Monetary Union as long as European integration proceeds in an orderly and open manner.

TRADING BLOCS AND THE WTO

In addition to the European and North American trade blocs, other regional trading groups are in various stages of development throughout the world. Examples include the Caribbean Common Market (CARICOM), the Australia–New Zealand Economic Relations Trade Agreement, the Economic Community of West African States, and the Asia–Pacific Economic Cooperation (APEC), as well as others. Trade

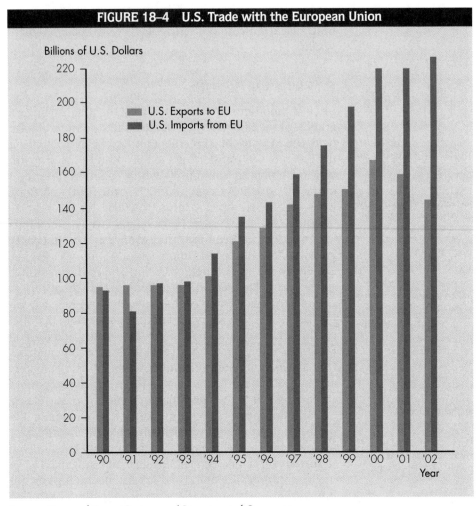

FIGURE 18–4   U.S. Trade with the European Union

Billions of U.S. Dollars

- U.S. Exports to EU
- U.S. Imports from EU

Sources: *Survey of Current Business* and Department of Commerce.

blocs are seen as steppingstones toward multilateralism because once the commitment to market forces is made at the regional level it will be easier to expand in scope. Blocs can be viewed as a way to reduce barriers to international trade and investment more efficiently than multinational negotiations. Markets that previously remained closed to individual countries may now be opened by the force and leverage of the bloc.

The fact that trade blocs discriminate against outsiders is not in itself a violation of WTO rules, but new rules have to be agreed upon as to what is and what is not permissible in managing bloc trade. If the Uruguay Round of negotiations is a future indication of the length of time it takes to agree on multilateral trade, the political will of many countries may be directed at forming blocs rather than preserving the

WTO. If future WTO talks collapse, the multilateral system would be weakened, and the blocs could resort to protectionist policies involving bilateral arrangements. Such protectionist action could be based on political expediency, rather than concern for world welfare. Trading blocs may then increase protectionist policies by promoting their own industries at the expense of foreign competition.

Aid Through the World Bank

Since World War II the United States has been a large contributor to foreign aid through various international institutions. The World Bank is one such institution. Established in 1945, the World Bank consists of the International Bank for Reconstruction and Development (IBRD) and the International Development Association (IDA).

INTERNATIONAL BANK FOR RECONSTRUCTION AND DEVELOPMENT

The IBRD was created in 1945 and is now owned by the governments of 184 countries. It makes and guarantees loans for productive reconstruction and development projects, both from its own capital (which is provided by its member governments) and by mobilizing private capital. The bank's capital is structured in such a way that risks are shared by all member governments roughly in proportion to their economic strength.

The present capital holdings provided by member nations exceed $183 billion, with the United States accounting for approximately 17 percent of this amount. Loans generally have a grace period of 5 years and are repayable over 20 years. From its inception in 1945 through fiscal 2001, the IBRD had approved loans of $360 billion to borrowers in 128 countries.

The IBRD has traditionally financed all kinds of capital infrastructure projects, such as roads, railways, ports, power facilities, and telecommunications systems. However, its development strategy also emphasizes investments that make poor people in developing countries more productive and integrate them into the development process as active partners.

In response to the debt crisis of developing nations, the IBRD began a program of structural-adjustment lending in 1980. Loans are granted to support programs of specific policy changes and institutional reforms designed to use resources more efficiently. It is anticipated that structural-adjustment lending will ease balance-of-payment problems for developing countries and also will provide the foundation and incentive for future growth.

INTERNATIONAL DEVELOPMENT ASSOCIATION

This IDA was established as an affiliate of the World Bank in 1960, largely at the insistence of the United States. The IDA seeks to provide assistance for the same purposes as the IBRD, but primarily to very poor countries and on financial terms that impose a lighter burden on their balance of payments than do other World Bank loans. The IDA lends to countries that have a per capita income of $885 or less.

Membership in IDA is open to all members of the IBRD, and 160 nations were members in 2001. The funds used by IDA, called *credits* to distinguish them from IBRD loans, come mostly in the form of subscriptions, general renewals from industrialized and developed nations, and transfers from the net earnings of the IBRD. IDA credits are made only to governments, and they have 50-year maturities at no interest. After a 10-year grace period, 1 percent of the credit is to be repaid annually for 10 years; then, in the remaining 30 years, 30 percent is to be repaid annually.

In fiscal 2001, the IDA disbursed the equivalent of $6.8 billion in credits to less-developed nations. Sub-Saharan Africa and South Asia were the most important regions for IDA projects.

Summary

- International trade is important to the United States because the absolute dollar value of its annual exports and imports exceeds that of any other nation in the world; the United States is the world's leading international merchandise trader.

- The law of comparative advantage holds that nations should specialize in the activities in which they have the greatest advantage or the least disadvantage compared to other nations. The benefits of international trade in terms of the law of comparative advantage are increased production (nations can increase their total output and then trade the gains they make from specialization for products from other countries); more competitive markets thus giving consumers more options from which to choose; ability to provide more choices, thus restraining price increases, and enabling capital-intensive firms to expand in size and lower their production costs through economies of scale.

- Tariffs are duties or taxes levied on foreign imports. The various arguments in favor of tariffs are protecting infant industries, equalizing costs, protecting U.S. jobs, protecting high U.S. wages, protecting against dumping, retaining money at home, developing and protecting defense industries, and diversifying industry. Tariffs that can be justified economically for specific industries and/or under specific circumstances are those used to help a domestic industry until it reaches a state of maturity, those used to prevent dumping, and those used to protect and help develop defense industries.

- In addition to tariffs, other nontariff barriers are used. Import quotas restrict the amount of a commodity that may be imported; they protect the domestic producer and industry against the full effect of foreign competition, and thus are similar to but more restrictive than tariffs. Tariff quotas are financial penalties on imports that exceed a certain amount. Embargoes forbid trade with another nation or in certain products. They

have the same effect as an export or import quota of zero. Export subsidies are government payments to private firms to encourage export of certain goods or to prevent discrimination against exporters who may have to sell at a world price below the domestic price. Voluntary restraint agreements are made between two governments and limit the one country's exports to the other. Such agreements are entered into to avoid more stringent trade barriers. Exchange controls are used to ration a country's scarce foreign exchange. With this practice, countries can encourage the importing of some commodities while discouraging the importing of others.

- The World Trade Organization replaced GATT as the multinational organization that oversees international trade agreements and resolves trade conflicts. It seeks to promote a free as possible flow of trade.

- The North American Free Trade Agreement was signed into law by the United States, Canada, and Mexico and became effective in 1994. NAFTA creates the largest trading bloc in the world, with a combined gross domestic product of nearly $12 trillion.

- The European Union continues to progress toward the goal of merging into a single market, with greater freedom in the movement of people, capital, goods, and services across borders. The Maastricht Agreement resulted in a single currency and a common central bank for 12 of the 15 members who joined the Economic and Monetary Union.

- The World Bank provides foreign aid through the International Bank for Reconstruction and Development (IBRD) and the International Development Association (IDA). The IBRD makes and guarantees loans for productive reconstruction and development projects. The IDA provides aid to very poor countries and at better financial terms than those of the IBRD.

CHAPTER REVIEW

New Terms and Concepts

Tariff

Specific tariff

Ad valorem tariff

Dumping

Nontariff barriers

Import quota

Tariff quota

Embargo

Export subsidy

Voluntary restraint
  agreement

Exchange controls

Most-favored-nation
  clause

Escape clause

General Agreement on
  Tariffs and Trade
  (GATT)

World Trade Organiza-
  tion (WTO)

Rule of origin

Maquiladoras

Maastricht Agreement

European Union

Economic and Monetary
  Union (EMU)

Euro

Discussion Questions

1. How does the principle of comparative advantage discussed in Chapter 2 promote world trade?

2. What is the relative importance of international trade to the United States and to foreign nations?

3. Why are a revenue tariff and a protective tariff considered incompatible?

4. How can international trade raise the standard of living of the two countries involved?

5. Is the argument that a tariff is needed to protect infant industries valid? Why or why not?

6. What form of protectionism is most effective in limiting competition from foreign producers?

7. How does international free trade affect the prices of domestic products?

8. What is the current membership of the European Monetary Union? How successful has the transition to a single currency been?

9. What effects do you believe NAFTA will have on future jobs, income, and economic growth in the United States, Mexico, and Canada?

10. Should U.S. aid to developing nations be given directly or through international organizations? Explain.

Economic Applications

EconData

Check out the EconData link at http://econapps.swlearning.com to find information on International Trade. Look under the World Economy heading and click on the "International Trade" link to find data about the International Economy.

19

The Balance of International Payments

After studying Chapter 19, you should be able to:

1. Describe why a nation's balance of trade may change as economic development progresses.

2. Explain the importance of a nation's balance of payments and describe each of the major components.

3. Demonstrate the use of debits and credits to record transactions contained in balance-of-payments accounts.

4. Explain how a gold standard is a basis for establishing exchange rates and for eliminating balance-of-payments deficits and surpluses.

5. Understand the workings of the Bretton Woods system and how fixed exchange rates were maintained.

6. Determine how flexible exchange rates can correct a disequilibrium in the balance of payments.

7. Describe the origin and purpose of the International Monetary Fund.

8. Briefly trace the changes that have occurred in the international financial system since World War II and describe their impact on the United States.

It should be apparent by now that the economic actions of the United States (and other individual nations) frequently have international repercussions. There are over 6 billion people in the world, living in more than 190 countries. Differences in the productivity, natural resources, population, and types of goods produced in these countries help encourage trade among them. In addition, successful businesses seek to expand trade beyond domestic boundaries. All this, plus a general lack of domestic self-sufficiency, naturally promotes world trade among various nations. Of course, payment must be made for goods and services exchanged, and this raises the complex issue of providing payment.

Balance of Trade

As nations engage in world trade, some tend to export more than they import from other specific nations, and vice versa. In many cases of multilateral trade, however, a surplus in trade with one nation may be offset by a deficit in trade with another nation. Country A, for example, may export $100 million in goods to country B, but it may import $100 million from countries C and D combined. At the same time, country B may export $100 million in goods to countries C and D. In such a case, not only would world exports be equal to world imports—as they necessarily must be—but all nations would have an even balance of exports and imports.

Balance of Trade
The relative levels of exports and imports a country experiences over a period of one year.

This does not happen often, however. Usually, some nations end up with a favorable balance of trade, in which exports exceed imports, and others have an unfavorable balance of trade, in which imports exceed exports. **Balance of trade** refers to the relative levels of exports and imports a country experiences over a period of one year. The term *favorable balance* is something of a misnomer, however. It was popularized in the eighteenth and nineteenth centuries, when economists stressed that a nation with an excess of exports over imports could force its debtor nations to pay the difference in gold and silver. We shall see later, however, that a nation with a continuous favorable balance is eventually placed at a disadvantage when foreigners experience a shortage of the favored nation's currency and are

TABLE 19–1	Exports and Imports of Merchandise for the United States (Millions of Dollars)*		
	Exports	Imports	Excess of Exports (+) or Imports (−)
1970	$ 42,649	$ 39,866	+$2,603
1975	107,088	98,041	+9,047
1980	224,237	249,574	−25,388
1985	213,990	338,279	−124,289
1990	388,705	497,558	−108,853
1995	574,879	749,348	−174,469
1997	679,715	876,366	−196,651
1998	670,246	917,178	−246,932
1999	683,021	1,030,152	−347,131
2000	771,994	1,224,417	−452,207
2001	718,762	1,145,927	−427,165
2002**	682,586	1,166,939	−484,353

*Merchandise trade statistics are presented according to balance of payments data.
**Preliminary.

Sources: *Economic Report of the President* (Washington DC: U.S. Government Printing Office, 2002) and Bureau of Economic Analysis.

unable to continue to purchase from it. Economists today recognize that a nation that sells abroad must also buy from foreign nations in order to give them its currency to use in purchasing its goods.

History also reveals a correlation between the economic development of a nation and the status of its balance of trade. Emerging or developing nations are generally heavy importers, especially of machinery, equipment, and various types of finished goods. Exports in a nation's early stages of economic growth generally consist largely of raw materials from the nation's natural resources. A developing nation, lacking aid and investment capital, must finance imports by diverting sufficient quantities of natural resources and agricultural goods from domestic to foreign (export) uses. As a country develops and is able to produce more of its own capital and finished goods, it will have less need for imports and an even balance of trade may come about. Finally, with its debts liquidated, a fully developed industrial nation tends to be a large exporter of capital. Consequently, a nation may shift from being a longtime debtor to being a creditor as its balance of trade shifts from one side to another. For nearly a century prior to 1971, the United States usually had an annual excess of exports over imports of merchandise. More recently, however, the opposite trend has taken place, as reflected in Table 19–1.

Balance of Payments

More important than the balance of trade in international economics is the balance of payments. Although the flow of merchandise constitutes a major category of international transactions, it constitutes only part of a nation's balance of payments. Whether a nation experiences a deficit or a surplus in its balance of payments depends on many other financial transactions. Therefore, even if a nation has a favorable balance of merchandise trade, it cannot be assured of having a favorable balance of payments. During the 1960s, for example, the United States consistently experienced favorable balances of trade while recording sizable deficits in its balance of payments.

The **balance of payments** is a statistical account of the financial transactions between nations over a period of one year. Despite what the term implies, the balance of payments more closely resembles an income statement showing the flow of goods, services, and assets than it does a balance sheet portraying the value of assets, liabilities, and stockholders' equity. Because the balance of payments is a scorecard of international payments, it is important to understand how transactions are recorded.

Any international transaction that provides a claim for payment from another country to the United States is entered as a **credit** in the U.S. balance of payments and recorded with a plus (+) sign. Conversely, a **debit** is recorded whenever a transaction gives rise to a claim by foreign countries for payment from the United States. Debit transactions are designated by a minus (−) sign.

Balance of Payments
A statistical account of the financial transactions between nations over a period of one year.

Credit
An international transaction that provides a claim for payment from another country.

Debit
An international transaction that creates an obligation of payment to another country.

The balance of payments can be divided into four major categories: current account, capital account, statistical discrepancy, and settlement account. Because the sum of the debit items (−) must equal the sum of the credit items (+), the end result must be a net balance in the overall international account. Keeping this information in mind, we can begin examining the 2002 balance of payments statement for the United States.

CURRENT ACCOUNT

Current Account
A portion of the balance of payments concerned with the purchase and sale of goods and services.

Most transactions in the **current account** involve the purchase and sale of goods and services. When the United States exports such items as grain to Russia, Coca-Cola to Japan, or Dell computers to Canada, these transactions are recorded as credits in the U.S. balance of payments. In each case, the sale of these products gives rise to claims for payment to the United States. Conversely, when Americans purchase Japanese watches, Italian shoes, and French wines, an outflow of currency from the United States results. All such claims for payment from the United States by foreign nations are recorded as debit entries in the U.S. balance of payments. As Table 19–2 indicates, U.S. exporters sold $683 billion worth of merchandise to foreign buyers in 2002, while U.S. importers purchased over $1.16 trillion worth of foreign merchandise in the same year. Combined U.S. merchandise trade showed a net debit of $484 billion for the year.

In addition to income from merchandise trade, income generated from services performed by one country for another is also included in the current account. Table 19–2 presents several major categories of service transactions. One category is expenditures for net travel and transportation. This category includes travel charges and tourist expenditures on goods and services in foreign nations. Thus, when an American tourist flies Air France to Europe, the airfare is recorded as a debit transaction because it creates a demand on the United States for payment. If the tourist later buys a bottle of perfume in Paris, this too counts as a debit entry. Purchasing perfume in Paris has the same effect on the balance of payments as importing French perfume to the United States for consumption. Similarly, expenditures by foreign tourists for air travel on United Airlines are credits in the U.S. balance of payments, as are the sums of money foreigners spend at Disney World in Orlando, Florida. Table 19–2 shows that during 2002, the United States had a debit balance in travel and transportation of almost $3 billion.

The current account also includes investment income. Interest, dividends, and corporate profits that U.S. individuals and institutions receive from investments throughout the world constitute a flow of funds into the United States. Thus, when IBM in Italy and H.J. Heinz in England return profits to the United States or when U.S. citizens receive dividends from an international mutual stock fund, these are recorded as credit entries. But when German investors receive interest payments on U.S. government securities or when Sony sends its profits in the United States back to Japan, debit transactions are entered in the U.S. balance of payments. In

Table 19–2 United States Balance of Payments, 2002 (Billions of Dollars)			
Current Account			
Merchandise trade		−484.4	
Exports	+682.5		
Imports	−1,166.9		
Travel and transportation, net		−2.7	
Investment income, net		−11.8	
Military transaction, net		−7.3	
Other services, net		+58.9	
Balance on goods, services and incomes			−447.3
Unilateral transfers		−56.0	
Balance on current account			−503.3
Capital Account			
Changes in foreign private assets in the U.S.		+534.4	
Changes in U.S. private assets abroad, net		−152.8	
Changes in government assets other than reserves, net		+.4	
Balance on capital account			+382.0
Settlement Account			
Change in U.S. official reserve assets		−3.8	
Change in official assets in the U.S.		+96.7	
Balance in settlement account			+92.9
Statistical Discrepancy			+28.4
Overall Balance			0

Source: Department of Commerce, Bureau of Economic Analysis (March 2003).

2002, the United States had a debit balance of $11 billion in the current account because of investment income transactions.

Military transactions are also contained in the current account. The sale of military hardware by the United States to countries such as Israel is part of its total exports and is a credit entry. Conversely, overseas military expenditures associated with maintaining U.S. military bases around the world constitute an outflow of dollars with much the same monetary effect as tourist spending abroad. In addition to paying for U.S. military forces abroad, we spend billions more in the form of military grants to foreign countries. Table 19–2 indicates that military transactions produced a debit balance of $7 billion in 2002.

The current account also consists of unilateral transfers. Whenever the United States sends money abroad for foreign aid, emergency relief, or other similar purposes, a debit entry results in the current account of the U.S. balance of payments. Likewise, when residents of the United States send money to residents of other countries or when Americans retire to foreign countries and receive American pension and Social Security payments, these transactions are recorded as debit entries. From this total must be subtracted the amount of money American nonresidents send back to the United States from abroad. In 2002, unilateral transfers produced a debit balance of $56 billion.

The total of all entries in the current account yields a balance on the current account. In 2002, a debit balance existed of about $503 billion, as shown in Figure 19–1 and Table 19–2. When debits exceed credits in the current account, a deficit results that must be offset by surpluses elsewhere.

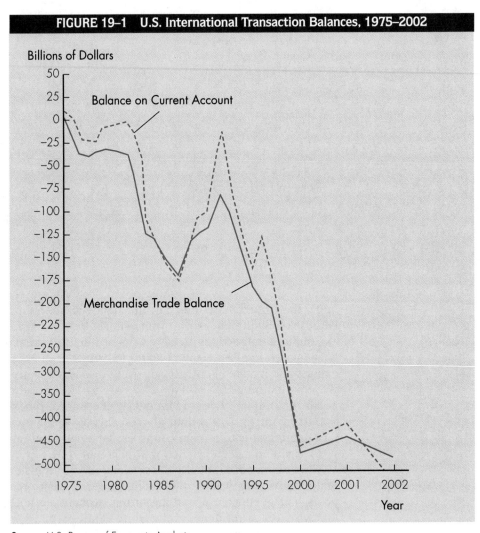

FIGURE 19–1   U.S. International Transaction Balances, 1975–2002

Billions of Dollars

Balance on Current Account

Merchandise Trade Balance

Source: U.S. Bureau of Economic Analysis.

CAPITAL ACCOUNT

The **capital account** is the financial account in the balance of payments. It measures the difference between sales of assets to foreigners by the United States, and U.S. purchases of assets located abroad. The capital account does not include income received from investments, for investment income is included in the current account. Although the capital account includes changes in government nonreserve assets abroad, these transactions are relatively small compared to private capital flows.

Whenever private citizens and businesses in the United States buy assets abroad, these transactions are capital outflows and they are recorded as debits in the capital account. For example, when General Motors acquires or constructs an automobile plant in Europe or when U.S. citizens purchase securities in Swiss-owned Nestlé or make deposits in the Bank of Montreal, the resulting outflow results in a debit entry. Capital is acquired, but there is an outflow of money in exchange. Conversely, credit entries are produced whenever foreigners acquire U.S. companies, purchase U.S. securities, corporate securities, and U.S. currency, or make deposits in U.S. banks.

In 2002, foreigners invested more capital in the United States than the United States invested abroad. Capital flows into the United States increased by $534 billion, while capital outflows totaled $153 billion. The current account plus the capital account should have been in balance, but because the deficit in the current account exceeded the surplus in the capital account, there was a net deficit in the U.S. balance of payments of $121 billion. How is this imbalance resolved? It is resolved by means of the official settlement account.

SETTLEMENT ACCOUNT

The **settlement account** shows how the deficit or surplus was financed. In 2002, the United States provided more dollars to the rest of the world than it earned back through exports. These excess dollars represented claims against the United States and were satisfied by government actions taken in the settlement account. The settlement account helps maintain stability in financial markets by adjusting official reserve holdings. Faced with a net deficit, the United States reduced the number of dollars in the world by pursuing several settlement actions. The U.S. government sold official reserve assets, such as foreign currency, in exchange for dollars. This action increased the supply of foreign currency and decreased the number of dollars outstanding and reduced claims for payment. The United States also swapped *special drawing rights* from the International Monetary Fund for foreign currency and transferred special drawing rights to other countries to hold as a future claim against the United States. Another deficit-reducing action was the continued holding by foreign countries of some of the excess dollars comprising the deficit. If foreign countries decide to hold dollars, this amounts to a form of credit or loan, but dollars held abroad represent future claims against the United States. It should be remembered that other countries are exercising somewhat similar options as the

United States, so it is the net effect that is important. Relative to the total size of the balance of payments, the usual size of official settlement transactions is not terribly large, but nevertheless is extremely important. In 2002 the figure amounted to a net credit of $93 million.

STATISTICAL DISCREPANCY

Statistical Discrepancy
Balance of payments account that adjusts for inaccurate and incomplete data.

Given the highly complex methods used to compute a nation's balance of payments statement, all entries in both the current and capital account are subject to misreporting because of inaccurate or incomplete data. In recognition of this fact, the balance of payments includes an adjustment item termed **statistical discrepancy.** The **statistical discrepancy** account ensures that the balance of payments is in balance. In any given year, the size of the statistical discrepancy figure may be affected by such transactions as smuggling, unrecorded bank deposits, or incomplete estimates of tourist spending. However, the largest factor usually accounting for the discrepancy is found in the capital account. By adding a credit of $28 billion in 2001, the overall U.S. account is balanced.

BALANCE-OF-PAYMENTS DEFICITS AND SURPLUSES

Because balance-of-payments deficits, such as the one the United States experienced in 2001, are settled by changes in official reserve assets and by changes in the dollar holdings of foreign governments, some international trade analysts object to the use of deficits and surpluses to describe the balance of payments. They contend that both sides of the balance-of-payments account must be equal, just as any other balance sheet based on the double-entry method of accounting must. Although this is technically correct, the terms *deficit* and *surplus* are commonly used today by economists, financiers, and government officials when referring to the balance of payments.

A more precise treatment of balance-of-payments deficits and surpluses deals with the balance of payments by excluding government settlement account transactions. This way of approaching the balance of payments emphasizes that the surplus or deficit itself is not nearly as important as the means of settlement. Whether the means is a temporary stopgap or a more nearly permanent measure has a significant impact on how well it corrects a balance-of-payments problem.

Foreign Exchange Rates

As trade takes place among different countries, goods and services are exchanged, international investments are made, and money and asset flows settle differences between debtor and creditor nations. Most of the international exchange of goods

NET*Link*

For a calculation of foreign currency exchange, check out Olsen & Associates Currency Converter.

http://www.oanda.com/convert/ classic

and services is carried on by individual persons and business firms, so the question naturally arises as to how payment should be made for the purchase of foreign goods and services.

International sales are similar to domestic sales, except that international sellers usually want to be paid in their own domestic currency for the goods they sell, rather than in the domestic currency of the buyers. Consequently, a conversion must be made from the buyer's currency to the seller's currency to complete the transaction.

Suppose that a U.S. sporting goods store desires to purchase six bicycles at a total cost of £1,000. If the rate of exchange between British pounds and U.S. dollars is £1 = $1.50, the U.S. retailer will go to a bank such as the Chase Manhattan and purchase a British bank draft for £1,000 by paying the U.S. bank $1,500, plus a small service charge. The sporting goods store will then mail this draft on a British bank to the British bicycle manufacturer, who will present it to a bank in London—let us say Barclays Bank—for payment of the £1,000 or for deposit to an account. The Chase Manhattan and other U.S. banks dealing in foreign exchange maintain deposits in foreign banks such as Barclays Bank of London, so Barclays Bank will honor the draft and reduce by £1,000 the deposit account that the Chase Manhattan Bank holds with it.

On the other hand, if a British manufacturer wants to purchase $1,500 worth of tools and equipment from a U.S. machine tool shop, the British manufacturer will go to a bank—again let us say to Barclays Bank in London—and purchase a U.S. bank draft for $1,500, paying £1,000 for it, plus a service charge. In this case, when the British manufacturer sends the bank draft to the U.S. tool company, the tool company will present the draft for payment at the Chase Manhattan Bank. After paying the U.S. exporter $1,500, the bank will debit the London bank's dollar deposit account by this amount on its record.

In this way, the $1,500 paid to the Chase Manhattan Bank by the U.S. importer for the £1,000 foreign exchange draft can be used to pay the U.S. machine toolmaker who presents the $1,500 draft sent to it by the British importer. In London, the £1,000 paid by the British importer for the $1,500 bank draft can be used to pay the £1,000 draft presented by the British bicycle manufacturer. In this simplified case, as depicted in Figure 19–2, the foreign deposits of the respective banks remain the same. Clearly, many foreign trade transactions can be paid by offsetting charges without requiring any actual currency flow among nations. Imbalances in trade often exist between nations, however, and these imbalances must somehow be settled in one way or another.

Currency exchange rates between countries play an important role in international economics. An **exchange rate** is the price of one currency in terms of another currency. A particular exchange rate may make buying foreign goods and services more expensive or less expensive. A U.S. importer who can purchase a British pound for $1.50, for example, may find it profitable to obtain a £10 British camera that would not be profitable at an exchange rate of $2.00 to the pound. Because a change in the exchange rate can actually reverse the flow of goods and currencies between

Exchange Rate
The price of one currency in terms of another currency.

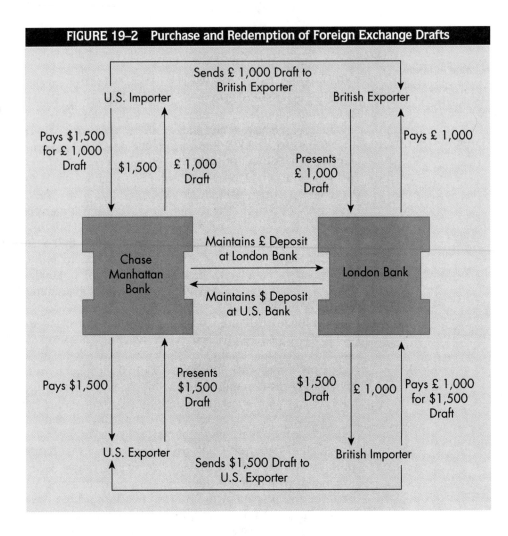

FIGURE 19–2   Purchase and Redemption of Foreign Exchange Drafts

different countries, it is essential to understand how exchange rates are determined. Exchange rates may be fixed or flexible, depending on what system is in force.

Fixed Exchange Rates

During the twentieth century, there were two major fixed exchange rate systems used by developed nations as a means of conducting international payments. Prior to the 1930s, the gold standard was used to establish exchange rates. From 1944 to 1973, a different fixed rate system stemming from the Bretton Woods agreement was used. Although essentially a fixed exchange rate system, the Bretton Woods system allowed for a degree of exchange rate flexibility.

GOLD STANDARD

Gold Standard
Use of gold as the basis for defining the value of various currencies.

A common basis for establishing exchange rates in the earlier part of the last century was the gold standard. Under the **gold standard,** nations defined their currency in terms of gold. The purchase and sale of gold were unrestricted, and countries were free to import and export gold to settle international balances of payment. A nation on the gold standard stood ready to convert its currency into gold on demand. Hence, the amount of gold each nation held affected its money supply and its level of domestic economic activity.

The value of the U.S. dollar was at one time defined as approximately 1/20 an ounce of gold, and the value of the British pound was defined as 1/4 an ounce of gold. At these approximate values, the British pound exchanged for five times as much as a dollar; thus, the exchange rate between dollars and pounds was set at £1 = $5. The gold standard required fixed exchange rates. **Fixed exchange rates** are exchange rates that are controlled by the government and maintained at a prescribed level.

Fixed Exchange Rates
Exchange rates that are controlled by the government and maintained at a prescribed level.

Whenever these fixed exchange rates differed from their predetermined values, they would automatically be restored. Suppose, for example, that the price of a pound rose in terms of a dollar to £1 = $6. At this exchange rate, U.S. importers would find it cheaper to purchase gold with dollars than to exchange their dollars directly for pounds. Similarly, when the price of £1 fell below $5, British importers would find it less costly to convert their pounds into gold and ship gold as payment for U.S. imports. Consequently, the dollar price of £1 remained at $5 because U.S. traders would refuse to pay more than $5 for £1, and British traders would refuse to accept less.

Under this system, adjustments in the balance of trade or in the flow of gold appeared as changes in the price level in individual countries. If the United States experienced a trade deficit with Great Britain, the dollar price of the pound would rise above $5 and gold would flow from the United States to Great Britain as a means of settling the deficit. But because the United States had tied its money supply to its gold holdings, the outflow of gold would automatically diminish the U.S. money supply and depress domestic prices. Great Britain, on the other hand, would receive an increased inflow of gold. Under conditions of full employment, the result would be higher prices brought about by an increased money supply. The combination of higher prices in Great Britain and lower prices in the United States would discourage U.S. imports from Great Britain, while encouraging British imports from the United States. Consequently, the initial trade deficit would be corrected, and the decreased demand for British pounds and the increased demand for U.S. dollars would restore the exchange rate to its fixed level.

Because the gold standard produced balance-of-payments adjustments through changes in interest rates, output, employment, and price levels in each nation, domestic goals were at the mercy of balance-of-payments adjustments. Deficit nations had to experience high rates of unemployment and recession, while surplus nations experienced the effects of inflation.

One of the main problems associated with the gold standard was the supply of gold itself. For long periods of time the world gold supply changed very little because of the lack of gold discoveries. This had a deflationary effect on prices and production, as the demand for money outstripped the supply. Conversely, when major gold strikes occurred, there would be a worldwide inflation. Overall, the supply of gold simply could not keep pace with the growth in world trade, and as the supply of gold shrank it became useless as a reserve against balance-of-payments debts.

The Great Depression brought an end to the gold standard. After many nations failed to stimulate their exports by repeated currency devaluations, individual countries began to abandon the system. Faced with the conflict of operating in accordance with the rules of the gold standard and meeting its domestic goals and responsibilities in the midst of the Great Depression, the United States went off the gold standard in 1933. It then became illegal for U.S. citizens to hold gold except for certain medical and industrial purposes. All gold held by private citizens had to be turned in to the U.S. Treasury. From that point on, the gold standard was dead, and no organized system for setting international exchange rates existed until the end of World War II.

THE BRETTON WOODS SYSTEM

With the demise of the gold standard and the outbreak of World War II, an unstable exchange rate situation developed as more and more nations adopted some form of exchange control. Nations throughout the world recognized that more stability in exchange rates was desirable, but by some method less rigid than the gold standard. In 1944, an international conference was held in Bretton Woods, New Hampshire, to create a new exchange rate system.

The Bretton Woods agreement produced an exchange system that combined the features of the gold standard and floating exchange rates. Each country had to fix the value of its currency in terms of gold, but the U.S. dollar, rather than gold, served as the primary basis for international payments. The U.S. dollar became the reserve currency of the system and was used to settle international debts. Although each country defined a par value for its currency, there was no connection between a country's gold and its money supply.

International Monetary Fund (IMF)
An international body originally created to provide temporary loan assistance to nations with deficit balances of payments but now deeply involved in long-term developmental lending.

Unlike the gold standard, there was no automatic correction for deficits and surpluses in a country's balance of payments. To stabilize exchange rates and provide temporary loan assistance to nations with balance-of-payments deficits, Bretton Woods created the **International Monetary Fund (IMF).** To meet its objectives, the IMF created a pool of currencies from which countries could borrow to meet balance-of-payments deficits. Because this pool of funds eventually proved to be

Special Drawing Rights (SDRs)
A collectively managed asset of the IMF that constitutes the principle source of international reserves.

insufficient for international liquidity, the IMF created special drawing rights in 1970. **Special drawing rights (SDRs)** are a collectively managed asset of the IMF, sometimes referred to as *paper gold*. Special drawing rights are IOUs of the IMF. Along with the U.S. dollar, gold, convertible currencies, and ordinary borrowing rights at the IMF, SDRs constituted another form of international reserve money.

Under the Bretton Woods system, a country could use international monetary reserves to maintain its par rates of exchange between its currency and the currencies of other countries. This fixed exchange rate system required that exchange rates be maintained within a narrow band, so as to provide exchange rate stability. A country's exchange rate could increase or decrease by 1 percent before corrective action was deemed necessary. For example, from 1949 to 1961 the British pound was pegged at an official price or par value of £1 = $2.80. If the value of the British pound decreased to £1 = $2.70, this decline of over 3 percent was outside the agreed-upon 1 percent band. Consequently, Great Britain would either purchase pounds in the international market with dollars or other major currencies it had on reserve or borrow funds for this purpose from the IMF. Likewise, if the pound increased in value to £1 = $2.90, Great Britain would buy dollars with pounds to bring about exchange rate stability. This system of stabilizing exchange rates could succeed if swings in the value of the country's currency were relatively small and temporary.

In 1962, the Canadian government agreed to establish an official exchange rate at which $1 Canadian was equal to 92.5 cents U.S. With the use of supply and demand curves, Figure 19–3 depicts how Canada might restore exchange rates in

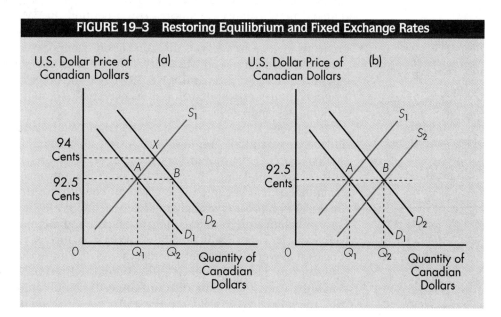

FIGURE 19–3 Restoring Equilibrium and Fixed Exchange Rates

accordance with the Bretton Woods system of fixed exchange rates. In Figure 19–3a, the demand curve for Canadian dollars by Americans is represented by D_1 and the supply of Canadian dollars available to Americans is represented by S_1. The vertical axis represents the U.S. dollar price of Canadian dollars, or the amount of U.S. money that it would take to buy a Canadian dollar. The horizontal axis measures the quantity of Canadian dollars. Assume the official fixed exchange rate is $1 Canadian = $0.925 U.S. and that there is an exchange rate equilibrium at point A. Now assume an increase in demand for Canadian dollars by Americans either because of an increase in imports to the United States or because more Americans are traveling to Canada. This results in a shift in the demand curve to the right (to D_2). Market forces would tend to drive the price of Canadian dollars upward to 94 cents U.S., as indicated by point X. However, because the official exchange rate is fixed, the market exchange rate is short-lived. The Canadian government would then intervene by buying up U.S. dollars with Canadian dollars in order to maintain the official exchange rate. As a result, the supply curve of Canadian dollars shifts to the right in Figure 19–3b, and a new equilibrium is reached at 92.5 cents and Q_2 Canadian dollars. In supporting its exchange rate, the Canadian government pumped $Q_1 - Q_2$ additional Canadian dollars into the marketplace.

Under the Bretton Woods system, a country that faced a chronic surplus or shortage position in the market for its currency was expected to implement expansionary or contractionary domestic policies that would correct balance-of-payments surpluses and deficits. Such actions could bring about a better balance between the supply and demand for a currency. However, if domestic economic policies did not remedy the imbalance, a country could petition the IMF to change the official exchange rate by either a devaluation or revaluation of its currency. **Devaluation** occurs when a country lowers the value or official price of its currency. For example, because the British pound was overvalued, Great Britain devalued the pound from a par of £1 = $2.80 to a par of £1 = $2.40. On the other hand, **revaluation** occurs when a country raises the value of its currency. Germany revalued the deutsche mark in 1961 and 1969.

The fixed exchange rates established after World War II became increasingly difficult to maintain for many countries, including the United States. The economies of Japan and Europe were a far cry from their war-torn status in 1944. By the end of the 1960s, these countries had not only recovered from wartime destruction but had become more competitive with the United States. As a result, the dollar became increasingly overvalued, and the United States began running chronic balance-of-payments deficits. Japan and Germany, on the other hand, were experiencing chronic surpluses in their balance of payments, as well as currencies that were substantially undervalued. With the United States depleting its gold stock to finance its deficits, the end of the Bretton Woods system was near. When the United States in 1971 announced that it would no longer buy and sell gold, the link between gold and the dollar was broken and the era of the Bretton Woods system was over.

Devaluation
The result of a country's lowering the value or official price of its currency.

Revaluation
The result of a country's raising the value or official price of its currency.

Floating Exchange Rates

Late in 1971, the United States devalued the dollar, and the pegged exchange rate bands were widened to +2.25 and −2.25 percent. But actions such as these failed to achieve exchange rate stability, and a general system of floating exchange rates resulted. **Floating exchange rates** are exchange rates that are allowed to change with changes in the supply and demand for currencies. By 1973, the floating exchange rate system was adopted by most nations, although at times major trading countries do intervene by buying and selling currency in order to maintain their exchange rates within acceptable ranges. In this sense, the present system is one of partially floating exchange rates. Because of the extent of intervention by industrial nations, the floating exchange rate system is often referred to as a **dirty float.** Many smaller nations, however, continue to maintain fixed exchange rates.

One of the major advantages of a floating exchange rate is that countries are free to pursue their own domestic economic policies without being tied to international exchange rate commitments. There are disadvantages as well. Wide swings in exchange rates can disrupt international trade and investment as currencies depreciate and appreciate in currency markets. **Depreciation** refers to a decline in a currency's value brought about by a change in the supply and demand for that currency. **Appreciation** of a currency refers to a rise in value of a currency because of market forces. Another disadvantage is that an important discipline over monetary and fiscal policy is lost.

Figure 19–4 shows the effect of floating exchange rates on the U.S. and Canadian dollars. Assume that the exchange rate is $1 Canadian to $1 U.S. The U.S.

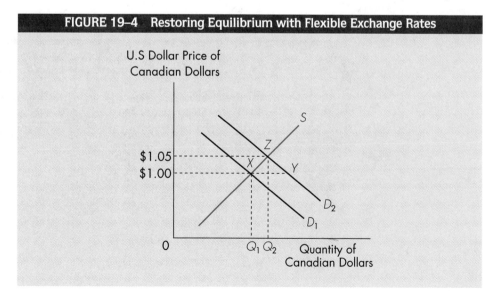

FIGURE 19–4   Restoring Equilibrium with Flexible Exchange Rates

demand curve for Canadian dollars (D_1) slopes downward to the right, indicating that as Canadian dollars become less expensive, Canadian goods become cheaper to Americans. The supply curve of Canadian dollars (S) slopes upward to the right, indicating that as the Canadian dollar becomes more expensive or valuable compared to the U.S. dollar, American goods will become cheaper to Canadians and they will increase their purchases. The intersection of the supply and demand curves determines the equilibrium U.S. dollar price of a Canadian dollar (shown as point X in Figure 19–4).

If Americans increase their purchases of Canadian goods and spend more as tourists while visiting Canada, the demand for Canadian dollars will increase. The increase in demand for Canadian dollars by Americans is shown by the shift in the demand curve from D_1 to D_2, creating a shortage of Canadian dollars equal to the amount of XY at the exchange rate of $1 Canadian to $1 U.S. But increased demand for the Canadian dollar causes the Canadian dollar to appreciate in value. The new equilibrium exchange rate is at point Z. The price of the Canadian dollar has risen to $1.05 in U.S. currency, and the U.S. dollar has in effect been discounted to 95 cents. Now an item that formerly cost U.S. importers or tourists $10 U.S. will cost $10.50. Floating exchange rates have produced currency valuations reflecting the impersonal operations of supply and demand in the marketplace.

Table 19–3 lists the exchange rates of five trading partners of the United States for selected years from 1990 to 2002. Also included is the exchange rate for the European Monetary Union. These exchange rates are presented in terms of currency units per U.S. dollar. Comparing values for 1990 and 2002, the Japanese yen is now stronger, the euro is roughly the same, and the British pound, Swiss franc, Swedish krona, and Canadian dollar are weaker in terms of the U.S. dollar.

Table 19–3 Exchange Rates of Selected Countries (Currency Units per U.S. Dollar)*						
Year	British Pound	Swiss Franc	Japanese Yen	Swedish Krona	Canadian Dollar	EMU Euro
1990	0.52	1.39	145.0	5.92	1.16	—
1995	0.65	1.18	93.9	7.14	1.37	—
1999	0.61	1.5	113.7	8.27	1.48	—
2000	0.62	1.69	107.8	9.17	1.48	1.06
2001	0.66	1.69	121.5	10.34	1.55	0.92
2002	0.64	1.47	118.1	9.35	1.56	1.01

*Yearly averages.
Source: Board of Governors of Federal Reserve System

International Monetary Fund

Today, with the existence of the IMF, any particular nation that has a deficit balance of payments or a shortage of foreign exchange is not required to alter its domestic prices (as was the case under the gold standard) or to change its exchange rates to obtain relief. Furthermore, the mechanism of the IMF was originally designed to prevent large fluctuations in exchange rates. Any member nation that has a shortage of a particular type of foreign exchange can obtain temporary relief by borrowing exchange or special drawing rights (SDRs) from the IMF.

A country with a balance-of-payments deficit can use the IMF's special drawing rights to settle its indebtedness to others, rather than transferring ownership of its own currencies. In effect, the debtor nation buys the needed exchange from the IMF with its own currency. Nations that continuously experience a deficit balance of payments or shortage of exchange and whose difficulty cannot be corrected by temporary borrowing from the IMF may have to seek other remedies. All member nations have agreed that they will consult the IMF on all such major international problems before undertaking devaluation of their currencies.

The International Monetary Fund was established under the Bretton Woods agreement for the purpose of managing a system of fixed exchange rates. In the early 1970s, that system collapsed, and since that time the IMF is an institution in search of a mission. In the 1990s, the IMF assumed the role of bailing out developing countries experiencing financial crises. In this capacity, the IMF has provided bailout loans to such countries as Mexico, Thailand, Indonesia, South Korea, and Russia. More recently, Turkey, Argentina, Uruguay, and Brazil required financial assistance. In 2002, Brazil's relief package totaled $34 billion.

Because of its changing mission, the IMF has come under increasing criticism. Critics point out that bailing out countries with emergency loans to avoid financial calamity in international markets is a far cry from providing financial support to countries with short-term balance-of-payments problems. They point out that the IMF has failed in many cases to promote financial stability within countries receiving funds and to achieve rapid economic recoveries. Russia and Indonesia are pointed to as examples. Its lending policies and its remedies for countries receiving emergency funds have also been criticized vigorously. Many contend that the IMF has wasted enormous sums of money in its new role, and they call for the complete abolishment of the IMF, claiming that it has outlived its purpose.

With the IMF changing its mission to long-term lending to developing countries, the distinction between the roles of the World Bank and the IMF is not clearly defined. Both institutions tie their lending to developing countries, to structural economic reforms, and to programs designed to achieve short-term financial stabilization. A growing consensus in the world economic community holds that the functions of both the IMF and the World Bank need to be reappraised in light of the dramatic changes unfolding throughout the world.

U.S. Balance of Payments

The history of the United States' balance of international payments reflects world events: the depression of the 1930s, the flight of capital from Europe before World War II, the postwar dollar shortage, the rebuilding of the European and Japanese economies, the gold outflow, the worldwide energy and resource crises, the collapse of the Soviet Union, and the development of powerful regional trading blocs.

DOLLAR SHORTAGE

The United States was the only major nation in the world whose industrial structure was unscathed by World War II. Consequently, many war-torn countries, especially in Europe, turned to the United States to purchase essential goods and services. Because these nations had little in the way of imports to offer in exchange for exports during World War II, the United States developed large surpluses in its balance of payments. The result was an extreme dollar shortage in international exchange markets throughout the world from the late 1940s to the mid-1950s, as foreigners clamored for U.S. dollars.

In the late 1950s, a dramatic shift in demand for U.S. dollars occurred. By this time, many countries had rebuilt their economies with new and modern industrial structures that increased their productive capacity considerably. They no longer depended as much on the United States for goods and services. In fact, many of them had begun competing successfully with the United States in world markets. Although the United States retained a favorable balance of trade, the size of the export–import gap dwindled. The United States continued to increase outlays for military operations overseas, to extend large grants and loans to foreign nations, to increase direct investments abroad, and to purchase short- and long-term foreign securities. As a result, many nations began accumulating dollar reserves. As foreign nations became less inclined to hold dollars, the situation was reversed, and instead of a dollar shortage, foreign nations began building up large claims against U.S. dollars.

GOLD OUTFLOW

Because these dollar claims were now not needed to buy additional U.S. goods and services, some nations used them to purchase short-term U.S. government securities on which they received interest income. Many nations, however, requested gold payment in exchange for their dollar claims. As a result, a continuous drain or outflow of gold from the United States occurred. Some authorities viewed the gold drain with alarm and took numerous steps to arrest the outflow of gold. Measures included reducing overseas military spending, decreasing foreign aid, reducing U.S. tourism, adopting more tying clauses with foreign aid, accelerating export promotion, and taxing U.S. investments abroad.

To reduce the gold drain from the United States and to ease the shortage of international liquidity, major financial nations of the world (through the IMF) agreed to create $9.5 billion in Special Drawing Rights in 1970. Because SDRs can be used to settle international obligations, this move took some of the pressure off the demand for dollars and gold.

The stable price of gold was temporary, however. A near crisis of the French franc resulted in a devaluation of the franc and a revaluation of the German (deutsche) mark. Later in the same year, the Swiss franc and the Austrian schilling were revalued, and the deutsche mark and the Netherlands guilder were allowed to float. Floating currencies allowed the market to determine exchange rates instead of basing such rates on pegged values. Within a short time, the average appreciation of the major world currencies against the dollar was approximately 11 percent. In 1971, the United States experienced a substantial deterioration in its trade position and faced a deficit balance of trade for the first time in nearly a century. Consequently, the price of gold began to rise substantially. It was under these circumstances that President Nixon, on August 15, 1971, established a 10 percent surcharge on imports and suspended the convertibility of dollars for gold.

DEVALUATION OF THE DOLLAR

It was evident that the U.S. dollar was overvalued in world markets and that the currencies of several other nations—especially those with substantial surplus balances of payments, such as Japan and West Germany—were undervalued. It was also evident that the United States could not continue forever as a major supplier of international liquidity for the entire world. In spite of this, the action of President Nixon startled the international financial world and brought about serious repercussions.

The United States subsequently used the 10 percent surcharge as a club to encourage various nations to adjust their currencies and to take other steps to improve world trade. In December; 1971, after numerous meetings, the Group of Ten (Belgium, Canada, France, Great Britain, Italy, Japan, the Netherlands, Sweden, West Germany, and the United States), in cooperation with the IMF, agreed to the Smithsonian Accord, by which they pledged to work for an effective realignment of important world currencies. In early 1972, the U.S. import surcharge was modified; concurrently, the dollar was devalued by 8.57 percent when Congress officially raised the price of gold to $38 per ounce. As a part of the international accord, the Japanese agreed to revalue the yen, and the deutsche mark and the guilder were allowed to continue floating before new exchange values were set for them. In addition, to provide greater flexibility in official exchange rates, the official band within which exchange rates were permitted to fluctuate was widened from 1 to 2.25 percent.

The United States' balance of payments failed to improve substantially in 1972. At the same time, international monetary authorities failed to come up with any further solutions to world monetary problems, and the relationship of the U.S. dollar vis-à-vis foreign currency (especially the deutsche mark and the yen) continued to deteriorate. Consequently, in February, 1973, the United States again devalued the dollar. This time the value of the dollar was decreased by 10 percent and the price of gold was raised to $42.22 per ounce. Increased reliance on high-priced oil imports and surging inflation aggravated the U.S. balance of trade deficit, which reached then-record deficits of more than $30 billion in 1977 and 1978. This further weakened the U.S. dollar in foreign exchange markets.

MORE RECENT EXPERIENCES

The dollar improved markedly (about 65 percent) from 1980 to 1984 in relation to other major currencies. By the beginning of 1985, it was at its highest level since flexible exchange rates were adopted in 1973. As the dollar's value appreciated in financial markets, however, U.S. current account deficits continued to worsen. Deficits in the current account increased to $40 billion in 1983, to $107 billion in 1984, and to $117 billion in 1985. During this period, the United States experienced an economic growth rate that exceeded that of most of its trading partners. With increased national income, demand for foreign imports also increased. A relatively rapid growth rate, combined with low inflation rates, increased after-tax business profits, and higher real interest rates stimulated unprecedented foreign demand for dollar-denominated assets. As a result, despite huge trade deficits, the dollar continued to strengthen.

After four consecutive years of strong appreciation, however, the U.S. dollar began to depreciate in March, 1985. By March, 1986, the dollar had depreciated approximately 30 percent against major currencies. Several factors prompted this. As real interest rates in the United States fell, foreign demand for dollar-denominated assets declined. In addition, the decline in world oil prices decreased foreign demand for dollars (oil payments are denominated in U.S. dollars). Another important factor was the continued increase in the supply of dollars resulting from the growing deficit in the U.S. current account. Thus, the supply of dollars increased as the demand for dollars decreased.

A further impetus to dollar depreciation resulted from the September, 1985, meeting of finance ministers and central bank governors of the Group of Five countries in New York. These countries (Japan, France, West Germany, Great Britain, and the United States) agreed that further appreciation of nondollar currencies was desirable. To this end, they resolved to adopt coordinated policies promoting real economic growth and intervene whenever necessary in foreign exchange markets to stabilize the dollar. In 1986, with the addition of Italy and Canada, the Group of Five became the Group of Seven. In 2000, the Group of Seven voted to include Russia as a member but retained the Group of Seven name for the committee. Meetings of these countries are an important forum for directing the course of international monetary policy.

The dollar weathered numerous global financial storms throughout the 1990s. It retained its strength through a war in the Middle East, economic turmoil in Russia, financial crisis in Mexico, a regional currency and economic crisis in Southeast Asia, several economic emergencies in South America, most notably those in Argentina and Brazil in 2001 and 2002, and short-term swings in the value of the currency throughout the period. Through all of these crises, the strength of the U.S. economy and consequently the dollar as a reserve currency enabled the world economy to quickly restore confidence in the international financial system. The U.S. dollar retains its status as the most important currency in the world.

For the first time since Bretton Woods, another currency has aspirations of becoming an international reserve currency that will rival the U.S. dollar. The long-term effect of the European Monetary Union's euro currency is not clear. As a strong regional currency, the euro has the potential of creating numerous changes in the international monetary system. Should the European Union expand its membership as planned, and if a majority of its members join the EMU, particularly the United Kingdom, then the European Union would become an even greater force in international monetary affairs. To counteract this, it is suggested that the United States work with countries throughout the Americas to create an American Monetary Union or a dollarization of currencies.

It is more evident than ever before that the United States cannot unilaterally control its destiny, as it seemed able to do in the twentieth century. Participating in a full-fledged, international global economy requires continuing adjustments.

Summary

- Since 1970, the United States has consistently bought more merchandise from the rest of the world than it has sold to its world trading partners. For nearly a century prior to 1970, the United States had a favorable balance in its merchandise trade account.

- The balance of payments is a statistical account of the financial transactions between nations over a period of one year. Its major components are the current account (the purchase and sale of goods and services), the capital account (the flow of capital investments excluding investment income between nations), the settlement account (an account that finances remaining outstanding claims), and statistical discrepancy (adjustment for inaccurate or incomplete data).

- In balance-of-payment accounts, a credit, recorded with a plus sign, is entered to denote any international transaction that provides a claim for payment from another country to the country maintaining the account. A debit, designated by a minus sign, indicates a transaction in which the country maintaining the account is paying a claim from another country.

- A fixed or controlled exchange rate allows a nation to avoid the severe effects on domestic employment, income, and prices that sometimes occur because of exchange rate corrections in a freely fluctuating exchange rate system. The gold standard incorporated fixed exchange rates by defining currency in terms of gold. The amount of gold a country held determined its money supply and the level of domestic economic activity.

- The Bretton Woods agreement established another form of fixed exchange rates. This system combined the features of the gold standard and floating exchange rates. The dollar became the international reserve currency, and there no longer was a connection between a country's gold supply and its money supply.

- Flexible (floating) exchange rates can correct a disequilibrium in the balance of payments because they change with market conditions of supply and demand. Flexible rates can eliminate balance-of-payments deficits and surpluses by changing the relative cost of international goods and services.

- The International Monetary Fund (IMF) was established in 1944 as a result of an international conference held in Bretton Woods, New Hampshire. Its purpose was to provide temporary loans to nations with deficit balances of payments. Recently, the IMF has become deeply involved in long-term developmental lending.

- The period following World War II was characterized by a dollar shortage. In the late 1950s, the supply and demand shifted and there was a glut of dollars in the world market. Today, the dollar remains as the international reserve currency, appreciating and depreciating as economic and financial conditions change. As the European Union continues to expand, the euro may challenge the dollar's supremacy in international finance.

New Terms and Concepts

Balance of trade
Balance of payments
Credit
Debit
Current account
Capital account
Settlement account
Statistical discrepancy

Exchange rate
Gold standard
Fixed exchange rates
International Monetary
  Fund (IMF)
Special Drawing Rights
  (SDRs)
Devaluation

Revaluation
Floating exchange rates
Dirty float
Depreciation
Appreciation

Discussion Questions

1. How can a nation have a favorable balance of trade but still have a deficit balance of payments?

2. How does direct private investment by Americans abroad affect the U.S. balance of payments?

3. If interest rates in foreign nations rise substantially compared with interest rates in the United States, what effect will this have on the U.S. balance of payments?

4. If a U.S. merchant were to purchase a dozen Viking sewing machines from Sweden, what process would be involved in making payment for the machines?

5. What is the difference between a floating exchange rate and a fixed exchange rate?

6. When exchange rates were pegged to the gold standard, how did the flow of gold from a debtor nation to a creditor nation eventually tend to reverse the balance of payments?

7. Should the United States devalue the dollar further in an effort to improve its balance of payments? Explain.

8. If a speculator purchases $1 million worth of Swiss francs, and the United States subsequently devalues the dollar by 20 percent, how much in dollars will the speculator gain or lose by converting the francs back into dollars after the devaluation?

9. Given the recent experience of the International Monetary Fund, what is now the primary function of this organization?

10. What factors are responsible for the United States' large merchandise trade deficits?

Economic Applications

EconNews
The EconNews link, found at http://econapps.swlearning.com, provides a wide range of stories about international money. Look under the World Economy heading and click on "International Finance." This link takes you to many news articles, study questions, and sources for further research and information.

19

CHAPTER REVIEW

Glossary

A

Ability-to-Pay Theory The theory that consumers should contribute taxes consistent with their ability to pay.

Absolute Advantage The ability to produce a good or service using fewer resources than other producers use.

Absolute Measure of Poverty A definition of poverty based on a specific level of annual income for a given-sized household.

Ad Valorem Tariff A tariff expressed in relative or percentage terms, such as 15 percent of the value of the imported good.

Administered Price A predetermined price set by the seller, rather than a price determined solely by demand and supply in the marketplace.

Aggregate Demand (AD) Curve The total amount of real output that buyers in an economy will purchase at various alternative price levels.

Aggregate Expenditure (AE) Total planned spending for goods and services by consumers, businesses, government, and foreign buyers.

Aggregate Supply (AS) Curve A plot of various quantities of total real output that producers will offer for sale at various price levels.

Agricultural Theories Theories of the business cycle that relate the general level of business activity to the weather.

Allocative Efficiency Occurs when consumers pay a price equal to marginal cost.

Appreciation A rise in a currency's value brought about by a change in the supply and demand for that currency.

Automatic Stabilizers Forces within the economy that naturally tend to counteract recessions and inflation.

Average Fixed Cost (AFC) The total fixed cost divided by the number of units produced.

Average Product (AP) The total output divided by the number of units of an input used.

Average Revenue (AR) The revenue per unit of output sold.

Average Total Cost (ATC) The total cost divided by the number of units produced; also, the average fixed cost plus the average variable cost.

Average Variable Cost (AVC) Total variable cost divided by the number of units produced.

B

Balance of Payments A statistical account of the financial transactions between nations over a period of one year.

Balance of Trade The relative levels of exports and imports a country experiences over a period of one year.

Benefit-Received Theory The theory that consumers should contribute taxes in proportion to the benefits received from the services of government.

Bilateral Monopoly A situation in which only a single buyer exists on one side of a market and only one seller (the monopolist) exists on the other side.

Branch Banking The practice of operating multiple outlets of a single depository institution throughout a state, a region, or the nation.

Break-Even Point The output level at which total revenue equals total cost.

Business Cycle The rise and fall of economic activity relative to the economy's long-term growth trend.

C

Capital Goods used to produce other goods and services.

Capital Account   A portion of the balance of payments depicting the flow of capital investments between nations (excluding investment income).

Capital Consumption Allowance   The amount of depreciation and obsolescence in the GNP.

Capital Goods   Economic goods used to produce other capital goods or consumer goods.

Cartel   An organization of independent firms that agree to operate as a shared monopoly by limiting production and charging the monopoly price.

Change in Demand   A change in the amounts of the product that would be purchased at the same given prices; a shift of the entire demand curve.

Change in Supply   A change in the amount of the product that would be offered for sale at the same given price; a shift of the entire supply curve.

Change in the Quantity Demanded   Movement along the demand curve that occurs because the price of the product has changed.

Change in the Quantity Supplied   Movement along the supply curve that occurs because the price of the product has changed.

Checkable Deposits   Checking deposits at banks and other depository institutions, including demand deposits (checking accounts), NOW accounts, ATS accounts, and share draft accounts.

Circular Flow of Income   The cyclical operation of demand, output, income, and new demand.

Civilian Labor Force   All persons in the total labor force except members of the resident armed forces.

Clayton Act   A federal law passed in 1914 that outlaws certain business activities not specifically covered by the Sherman Act.

Command Economy   An economy in which a central authority makes most of the economic decisions regarding production, distribution, and consumption.

Comparative Advantage   The ability to produce a good or service at a lower opportunity cost than other producers face.

Competition   Rivalry among individuals and firms for sales to consumers; the natural regulator that makes the free market system work.

Concentration Ratio   A measure of market power calculated by determining the percentage of industry output accounted for by the largest firms.

Constant Returns to Scale   A change in total inputs brings about a proportionate change in total output.

Consumer Goods   Economic goods that are directly utilized by the consuming public.

Consumer Price Index (CPI)   An index that compares the price of a group of basic goods and services as purchased by urban residents.

Consumer Surplus   The difference between what consumers would have been willing to pay and what they actually pay for the product.

Consumption   The use of a good or service.

Consumption Function   Any equation, table, or graph that shows the relationship between the income that consumers receive (disposable income) and the amount they plan to spend on currently produced final output.

Consumption Tax   A tax on incomes excluding savings.

Contraction   A noticeable drop in the level of business activity.

Contractionary Policies   Monetary and fiscal policies that are used to try to lower aggregate demand for output in the economy to a level that can be achieved with full employment of resources.

Cooperative   A business owned by the people who use it or buy from it.

Corporation   A separate legal entity, apart from its owners or shareholders, that functions as a business.

Cost-of-Service Theory   The theory that consumers should contribute toward the cost of general government in proportion to the cost of the governmental services they receive.

Cost–Push Inflation   Inflation characterized by a spiral of wage and benefit cost increases and price increases.

Credit   An international transaction that provides a claim for payment from another country.

Cross Elasticity of Demand   A measure of the responsiveness of the quantity demanded of one product as a result of a change in the price of another product.

Crowding Out   Occurs when deficit spending by the government forces private investment spending to contract.

Currency   Paper money and coins.

Current Account   A portion of the balance of payments concerned with the purchase and sale of goods and services.

Cyclical Fluctuations   Changes in the level of business activity that come about regardless of the trend, seasonal variations, or random forces.

Cyclical Unemployment   Unemployment that arises from less than full use of productive capacity in an economy due to a recession or depression.

D

Debit   An international transaction that creates an obligation of payment to another country.

Decreasing Returns to Scale   A change in total inputs brings about a less than proportionate change in total output.

Deflation   A persistent decline in the level of prices.

Demand   A schedule of the total quantities of a good or service that purchasers will buy at different prices at a given time.

Demand Curve   A line that indicates the number of units of a good or service that consumers will buy at various prices at a given time.

Demand Schedule   A table showing the various quantities of a good or service that will be demanded at various prices.

Demand–Pull Inflation   Inflation that occurs when the total demand for goods and services exceeds the available supply of goods and services in the short run.

Depreciation   A decline in a currency's value brought about by a change in the supply and demand for that currency.

Devaluation   The result of a country's lowering the value or official price of its currency.

Direct Tax   A tax that cannot be shifted, such as an income tax.

Dirty Float   A term used to describe a floating exchange rate system with government intervention to stabilize currencies.

Discount Rate   The interest rate at which depository institutions borrow funds from the reserve banks.

Diseconomies of Scale   Forces that cause long-run average cost to increase as plant size increases.

Disinflation   A slowdown in the rate of inflation.

Disposable Personal Income (DPI)   Personal income minus personal taxes.

Distribution   The allocation of the total product among the productive resources.

Double Coincidence of Wants   In a barter economy, the need to find a match between what each of two traders wants to obtain and what each wants to offer in exchange.

Dumping   Selling surplus products in a foreign market at a price below cost or at a price below the price at which they are sold in the domestic market.

E

Economic Efficiency   Occurs when firms produce at the minimum point on their long-run average cost curves.

Economic Good   An object or service that has utility, is scarce, and is transferable.

Economic Growth   An increase in an economy's total output of goods and services.

Economic Liberalism   An economic philosophy that promoted freedom of action for the individual and the firm through the doctrines of free trade, self-interest, private property, laissez-faire, and competition.

Economic Monetary Union (EMU)   Countries within the European Union that share a single currency and central bank.

Economic Policy   What is actually done under a given set of circumstances.

Economic Profit   Any revenue in excess of all costs (including a normal profit).

Economic Theory   Develops rules and principles of economics and is a guide for action under a given set of circumstances.

Economics   A social science that studies how people and institutions within a society make choices and how these choices determine the use of society's scarce resources.

Economies of Scale   Forces that cause long-run average cost to fall as plant size increases.

Effect of a Tax   An economic consequence of paying a tax.

Elastic Demand   Demand that exists when a percentage change in price causes a greater percentage change in quantity demanded; an elasticity coefficient greater than 1.0.

Elasticity of Supply   A measure of responsiveness of quantity supplied to a change in price.

Electronic Banking   Financial transactions that entail the electronic transfer of funds.

Embargo Complete cessation of trade with another nation or in certain products.

Employed Labor Force All employed workers, including persons who did not work at all during the census week because of illness, bad weather, vacation, or labor disputes.

Enterprise The act of organizing and assuming the risk of a business venture.

Entrepreneur A person who organizes and assumes the risk of a business venture.

Equal Distribution of Income An income distribution in which all households receive the same income.

Equality-of-Sacrifice Doctrine The idea that consumers should contribute taxes on the basis of their marginal utility of income.

Equation of Exchange A relationship between the supply of money and the price level.

Equilibrium A stable flow of total output and income.

Equilibrium Price The price at which the quantity demanded equals the quantity supplied.

Equitable Distribution of Income An income distribution based on the application of some objective standard.

Escape Clause A provision in the amended Reciprocal Trade Agreements Act that permitted tariffs to be raised if domestic producers were suffering under the existing tariff.

Euro Common Currency of countries within the Economic Monetary Union.

Eurodollars U.S. dollars deposited in foreign banks and consequently outside the jurisdiction of the United States.

European Union An organization seeking full political and economic integration among member countries.

Excess Reserves Any reserves that a bank may have over and above the legally established required reserves.

Exchange The process of trading surplus quantities of specialized products to others for other goods or services.

Exchange Controls Devices that ration a country's scarce foreign exchange or set up multiple exchange rates.

Exchange Rate The price of one currency in terms of another currency.

Exclusive Dealing Requiring buyers of goods to agree not to purchase from competing sellers.

Expansion A rising level of business activity.

Expansionary Policies Monetary and fiscal policies that are used to try to increase the equilibrium level of income and output in the economy.

Explicit Costs Expenditures for production that result from agreements or contracts.

Export Subsidy A government payment to private firms to encourage the exportation of certain goods or to prevent foreign discrimination against exporters who must sell at a world price that is below the domestic price.

External Forces Elements outside the normal scope of business activity.

F

Family A group of two or more persons who live in the same dwelling and are related by birth, marriage, or adoption.

Federal Funds Market A fairly well organized market where interbank borrowing takes place.

Federal Reserve System A system composed of various bodies, organizations, and committees for regulating the U.S. money supply.

Federal Trade Commission Act A federal law passed in 1914 creating the FTC to police unfair business practices.

Fiat Money Money that is not redeemable for a commodity and is accepted on faith.

Financial Capital Money that can be used to purchase capital goods.

Fiscal Drag The slowing effect on the economy that results from a budget surplus.

Fiscal Stimulus The activating effect on the economy that results from a budget deficit.

Fixed Costs Costs that remain constant as output varies.

Fixed Exchange Rates Exchange rates that are controlled by the government and maintained at a prescribed level.

Flat Tax A single tax rate on incomes.

Floating Exchange Rates Exchange rates that are allowed to change with changes in the supply and demand for currencies.

Free Good   A good that lacks the element of scarcity and therefore has no price.

Frictional Unemployment   Unemployment that arises from normal operation of the labor market—job terminations by employees, discharges, or relocation.

Full-Employment Balanced Budget   A measure of the potential revenue and spending that would result if full employment existed.

Full-Employment Unemployment Rate   The rate of unemployment that can be expected from normal frictional unemployment in an otherwise fully employed labor force.

G

GDP Implicit Price Deflators   An index that converts GDP and related data from current-dollar figures to constant-dollar figures, taking into account some changes in the quality of various products.

General Agreement on Tariffs and Trade (GATT)   An agreement that called for equal treatment of all nations in international trade, the reduction of tariffs, and the easing or elimination of import quotas.

Gini Coefficient   An index that summarizes the inequality revealed by the Lorenz curve in a single number.

Gold Standard   Use of gold as the basis for defining the value of various currencies.

Gross Domestic Product (GDP)   The current market value of the total final goods and services produced within the United States.

Gross National Product (GNP)   GDP plus the value of goods and services produced by U.S. resources abroad less the value of goods and services produced by foreign resources in the United States.

H

Herfindahl Index   A measure of market power calculated by summing the squares of the market shares of each firm in the industry.

Household   Includes all persons, related or unrelated, who occupy a housing unit, including individuals living alone.

Household Wealth   The value of a household's total assets minus its liabilities. Also known as net worth.

Human Capital   The stock of labor talents and skills used to increase productivity.

Hyperinflation   Inflation that feeds on itself to go out of control, creating severe distortions in the economy and rendering currency almost worthless.

I

Impact of a Tax   The financial burden entailed in paying a tax.

Implicit Costs   A firm's opportunity cost of using its own resources or those provided by its owners without a corresponding cash payment.

Import Quota   A maximum absolute amount of a particular good that may be imported.

Incidence of a Tax   The point at which the burden of a tax ultimately rests.

Incidence of Poverty   The percentage of persons in a particular group who are officially classified as having income below the poverty threshold line.

Income Elasticity of Demand   A measure of the responsiveness of quantity demanded to a change in income.

Increasing Returns to Scale   A change in total inputs brings about a greater than proportionate change in total output.

Indirect Tax   A tax that can be shifted, such as an excise tax on liquor.

Individual Demand   The quantity of a good or service that an individual or firm stands ready to buy at various prices at a given time.

Individual Supply   Quantities offered for sale at various prices at a given time by an individual seller.

Inelastic Demand   Demand that exists when a percentage change in price causes a smaller percentage change in quantity demanded; an elasticity coefficient less than 1.0.

Inflation   A persistent increase in the level of prices.

Injections   Added spending in the circular flow that are not paid for out of current resource income.

Innovation Theory   The theory that business cycles are caused by breakthroughs in the form of new products, new methods, new machines, or new techniques.

Interlocking Directorates   Boards of directors of competing firms with one or more members in common.

Internal Forces Elements within the very sphere of business activity itself.

International Monetary Fund (IMF) An international body originally created to provide temporary loan assistance to nations with deficit balances of payments but now deeply involved in long-term developmental lending.

Interstate Banking The practice of conducting banking operations across state lines.

Investment Spending to purchase capital goods.

L

Labor The time and effort expended by human beings involved in the production process.

Labor Force Participation Rate The civilian labor force expressed as a percentage of the civilian noninstitutional population.

Labor Market Discrimination Discrimination that occurs if the employment and earnings practices are based on factors unrelated to worker productivity, such as race, sex, age, or national origin of the worker.

Lagging Indicators A group of 7 indexes whose turning points occur after the turning points for the general level of business activity have been reached.

Laissez-Faire A policy of no government intervention in the economic activities of individuals and businesses.

Land All the resources of the land, sea, and air.

Law of Demand The quantity of a good or service purchased is inversely related to the price, all other things being equal.

Law of Supply The quantity offered by sellers of a good or service is directly related to price, all things being equal.

Leading Indicators A group of 11 indexes whose upward and downward turning points generally precede the peaks and troughs of general business activity.

Leakages Flows out of the circular flow that occur when resource income is received and not spent directly on purchases from domestic firms.

Liquidity The ease with which an asset can be converted into the medium of exchange.

Long Run A period of time in which all productive resources—including machinery, buildings, and other capital items—are variable.

Lorenz Curve A graph that traces the percentage relationship between the portion of total income received and the portion of all households or families in the economy.

M

M1 Money Stock Most liquid definition of money; includes currency, travelers checks, and checkable deposits.

M2 Money Stock The total of M1 and savings deposits, small time deposits, and money market funds.

M3 Money Stock The total of M2, large negotiable certificates of deposit, and Eurodollars.

Maastricht Agreement The Maastricht Agreement on European Economic and Monetary Union, the first move in transforming the European Community, an economic community, into the European Union, a political union with a common currency.

Macroeconomics Deals with the aggregates of economics, including total production, total employment, and general price level.

Maquiladoras Export-oriented plants, most often but not exclusively located near the U.S.–Mexico border.

Marginal Cost (MC) The change in the total cost resulting from production of one more unit of output.

Marginal Product (MP) The change in total output resulting from an additional unit of input.

Marginal Propensity to Consume (MPC) The ratio of the change in consumption spending to the change in disposable or after-tax income; the slope of the consumption function.

Marginal Propensity to Save (MPS) The ratio of the change in planned saving to the change in disposable income; the slope of the saving function.

Marginal Revenue (MR) The change in total revenue that results from the sale of one more unit of output.

Market Demand The sum of the individual demands in the marketplace.

Market Economy An economy in which the decisions about what to produce, how much to produce, and how to allocate goods and services are made primarily by individuals and firms in the economy.

Market Supply Sum of the individual supply schedules in the marketplace.

Member Banks Commercial banks that belong to the Federal Reserve System.

Microeconomics Deals with the economic problems of the individual, the firm, and the industry.

Mixed Economy An economy that contains a mixture of perfect and imperfect competition and of regulated and unregulated industries.

Monetary Theories Theories that the business cycle is caused by the free and easy expansion of the money supply.

Money Anything generally accepted in exchange for other goods and services.

Money Market Funds Deposits held in accounts that are invested in a broad range of short-term financial assets, such as government and corporate bonds.

Money Multiplier The reciprocal of the reserve ratio.

Money Stock Quantity of money in existence at any given time.

Monopolistic Competition A market structure in which relatively many firms supply a similar but differentiated product, with each firm having a limited degree of control over price.

Monopoly A market structure in which only one producer or seller exists for a product that has no close substitutes.

Monopsonistic Competition A market structure in which there are many buyers offering differentiated conditions to sellers.

Monopsony A market structure in which there is a single buyer.

Moral Suasion A number of different measures that the Federal Reserve Board uses to influence the activities of banks.

Most-Favored-Nation Clause A provision of the Reciprocal Trade Agreements Act that generalized concessions made in bilateral agreements to all nations.

Multiplier The relationship between a change in aggregate expenditure and the resulting larger change in national output or income.

N

National Income (NI) The total productive resource costs of the goods and services produced by our nation's economy. Also, the income earned by the owners of productive resources in producing GDP.

National Sales Tax A tax collected on the final sale of goods and services.

Natural Rate of Unemployment The rate of unemployment that would occur if the economy were producing at its full potential.

Net National Product (NNP) GNP minus capital consumption allowances.

Nonpersonal Time Accounts Negotiable CDs and large CDs that require notice before withdrawal is made.

Nontariff Barriers Devices other than tariffs that grant an advantage to domestic producers.

Normal Profit The amount of profit necessary to induce an entrepreneur to stay in business.

Normative Economics The area of economics dealing with what ought to be.

O

Occupational Segregation Channeling people into occupations according to sex or race.

Oligopoly A market structure in which relatively few firms produce identical or similar products.

Oligopsony A market structure in which there are only a few buyers.

Open-Market Operations The Fed's continuous purchase and sale of government securities on the open market.

Opportunity Cost The value of the next best alternative that must be sacrificed when a choice is made.

Opportunity Cost of Productive Resources The amount of payment necessary to attract productive resources away from their next-best opportunities for employment.

Optimal Scale of Operation The level of output at which the long-run average cost is at a minimum.

P

Partnership A business owned by two or more persons.

Peak The highest level of economic activity in a particular cycle.

Perfect Competition A market structure that assumes four characteristics: numerous sellers are present in the market, all selling identical products; all buyers and sellers are informed about the market and prices; there is free entry into and exit from the market; and no individual seller or buyer can influence price—instead, price is determined by market supply and demand.

Personal Income (PI)   The current income received by persons from all sources.

Phillips Curve   A curve showing the relationship between unemployment and inflation.

Positive Economics   The area of economics dealing with what is.

Poverty Threshold Line   The established annual income level that separates the poor from the nonpoor.

Predatory Pricing   Selling at unreasonably low prices to destroy competitors.

Price Ceiling   A government-mandated maximum price that can be changed for a good or service.

Price Discrimination   Charging different customers different prices for the same good.

Price Elasticity of Demand   A measure of the sensitivity or responsiveness of quantity demanded to a change in price.

Price Floor   A government-mandated minimum price that can be changed for a good or service.

Price Index   A measuring system for comparing the average price of a group of goods and services in one period of time with the average price of the same group of goods and services in another period.

Prime Rate   The rate at which individuals and firms with the best collateral can borrow.

Principle of Diminishing Marginal Returns   The fact that, as more and more units of a variable resource are added to a set of fixed resources, the resulting additions to output eventually become smaller.

Privatization   The shifting or returning of government economic functions or services to the private sector of the economy.

Producer Price Index (PPI)   A measure of the average prices received by producers and wholesalers.

Producer Surplus   The difference between what firms would have been willing to accept as a price for the product and the price they actually receive.

Product Differentiation   Establishment of real or imagined characteristics that identify a firm's product as unique.

Production   The creation or addition of utility.

Production Function   The physical relationship between resource inputs and product output.

Production Possibilities Curve   A graphical view of the alternative combinations of different goods and services a society can produce given its available resources and technology.

Productive Resources   Inputs or resources necessary before a person or business can engage in the production of goods or services; specifically, labor, land, capital, and enterprise.

Profit   The incentive for obtaining and using resources to produce goods and services that consumers will buy; also, the excess of revenue over all costs of production.

Progressive Tax Rate   A tax rate that increases as the size of the base increases.

Proportional Tax Rate   A tax rate that remains the same regardless of the size of the base.

Psychological Theory   The theory that when investors and consumers react according to some belief about future conditions, their actions tend to transform their outlook into reality.

Public Good   An economic good to the supplier but a free good to the user.

Purchasing Power Parity   The number of units of currency needed in one country to buy the same amount of goods and services that 1 unit of currency will buy in another country.

Q

Quantity Theory of Money   A classical view of the nature of money as being passive, so that the quantity of money and the price level are proportional when other conditions are stable.

R

Random Fluctuations   Changes in economic activity from unexpected or unusual events.

Rational Expectations Theory   An economic theory suggesting that individuals and businesses act or react according to what they think is going to happen in the future after considering all available information.

Real GDP The gross domestic product as expressed in constant dollars.

Real Income The constant-dollar value of goods and services produced; also, the purchasing power of money income.

Real Output Output adjusted for changes in the price level.

Real Per Capita Disposable Income Per capita disposable income adjusted for changes in the price level.

Regressive Tax Rate A tax rate that decreases as the size of the base increases.

Relative Measure of Poverty A definition of poverty based on the average annual incomes earned by other households.

Representative Money Money that is redeemable for a commodity, such as gold or silver.

Required Reserves The amount of reserves that member banks must hold against checkable deposits.

Revaluation The result of a country's raising the value or official price of its currency.

Ricardian Equivalence Theorem The proposition that it makes no difference whether government spending is financed by taxes or by a deficit.

Roughly Coincident Indicators A group of 4 indexes whose turning points usually correspond to the peaks and troughs of general business activity.

Rule of Origin A trade term that defines the minimum percentage of a country's exported products

S

that must be produced or substantially changed within the border of the exporting country.

Saving Function The relationship between the amount of disposable income consumers receive and the amount they save.

Savings Deposits Interest-bearing funds held in accounts that do not allow for automatic transfer services.

Say's Law The classical view that if supply creates its own demand, then all goods offered for sale must be purchased.

Science An organized body of knowledge coordinated, arranged, and systematized according to general laws or principles.

Seasonal Variations Recurring fluctuations in business activity over a given period, usually one year.

Settlement Account A portion of the balance of payments in which remaining outstanding claims are financed.

Sherman Antitrust Act A federal law passed in 1890 that outlaws restraint of trade and any attempt to monopolize.

Short Run A period of time in which some productive resources are fixed.

Sole Proprietorship A business owned and run by a single person.

Special Drawing Rights (SDRs) A collectively managed asset of the IMF that constitutes a principle source of international reserves.

Specialization The process of limiting the scope of an economic unit's productive efforts instead of trying to produce everything it needs.

Specific Tariff A tariff expressed in absolute terms, such as 25 cents per pound or per unit of a good.

Stagflation Higher unemployment and inflation occurring at the same time.

Statistical Discrepancy Balance of payments account that adjusts for inaccurate and incomplete data.

Structural Unemployment Unemployment caused by an imbalance between the skills possessed by workers and the skills demanded in the labor markets.

Substitution Effect Increased sales at the expense of other firms.

Supply The total quantities of a good or service that sellers stand ready to sell at different prices at a given time.

Supply Curve A line showing the number of units of a good or service that will be offered for sale at different prices at a given time.

Supply Schedule A table showing the various quantities of a good or service that sellers will offer at various prices at a given time.

T

Tariff A duty or tax levied on foreign imports.

Tariff Quota A device that places a financial penalty on imports above a certain quantity.

Tax Base The value of the object upon which the tax is levied.

Tax Rate   The percentage by which the tax base is multiplied in calculating the total tax that must be paid.

Tax Shifting   Passing the tax burden from one tax-payer to another.

Time Deposits   Funds that earn a fixed rate of interest and must be held for a stipulated period of time.

Total Cost (TC)   The sum of total fixed cost and total variable cost at a particular level of output.

Total Income   The total value of the goods and services produced over a period of time (usually a year).

Total Labor Force   All persons in the noninstitutional population who are either working or seeking work.

Total Product   The sum of all the goods and services produced by an economy over a given period of time.

Total Revenue (TR)   The amount of revenue or income received from the sale of a given quantity of goods or services.

Traditional Economy   An economy based on self-sufficiency, with barter as the form of trade.

Transaction Accounts   The various forms of checkable deposits, including regular checking accounts, NOW accounts, ATS accounts, and share draft accounts.

Transactions Approach   An analysis of the equation of exchange that assumes that any money received is spent directly or indirectly to buy goods and services.

Transfer Payment   A payment of money in return for which no current goods or services are produced.

Trend   The directional movement of the economy over an extended period of time, such as 20 to 30 years.

Trough   The lowest level of business activity in a particular cycle.

Tying Contracts   Contracts requiring the buyer of one good to purchase another good as well.

U

Underconsumption Theories   Theories that the business cycle is caused by the failure to spend all national income, resulting in unsold goods, reduced total production, and consequent reductions in employment and income.

Underemployment   A condition in which a worker in the labor force is employed but not working to full capacity.

Underground Economy   The unregulated portion of the economy involving goods and services that are produced and exchanged without the use of monetary transactions.

Underinvestment Theory   The theory that recessions occur because of inadequate investment in the economy.

Unemployed Labor Force   All persons in the labor force who are not currently working but are actively seeking work.

Unemployment   A condition in which workers in the labor force are not currently working at all.

Unit Elastic Demand   Demand that exists when a percentage change in price causes an equal percentage change in quantity demanded; an elasticity coefficient equal to 1.0.

V

Utility   The ability of a good or service to satisfy a want.

Value Added   The change in value of an intermediate or end product attributable to completion of a productive stage.

Value-Added Tax (VAT)   A tax on the increase in value as goods pass along through the production process to the market place.

Variable Costs   Costs of production that vary as output changes, such as the costs of labor and materials.

Voluntary Restraint Agreement   An agreement between two governments to limit the exporting country's exports to the importing country.

W

Wealth   All goods and resources having economic value, such as machinery, equipment, buildings, and land.

World Trade Organization (WTO)   A multinational organization that replaced GATT for the purpose of overseeing trade agreements and resolving trade conflicts.

Index

Note: The letter *f* following a page number denotes figure; the letter *t* denotes table.